THE SAS COMBAT HANDBOOK

THE
SAS COMBAT
HANDBOOK

JOHN E. LEWIS

THE LYONS PRESS

GUILFORD, CONNECTICUT

AN IMPRINT OF THE GLOBE PEQUOT PRESS

Acknowledgments:

"Project Delta" is an extract from *Green Berets at War* by Shelby L. Stanton.
Copyright © 1985 by Shelby L. Stanton. Originally published in Great Britain by
Arms and Armour Press Ltd.

"Son Tay" by Leroy Thompson originally appeared in *Elite*. Copyright © 1987 by
Marshall Cavendish Partworks Ltd.

2 4 6 8 10 9 7 5 3

ISBN 1-58574-440-9

The Library of Congress Cataloging-in-Publication Data is available on file.

CONTENTS

ELITE UNITS

THE SAS: PROTOTYPE OF THE SPECIAL FORCE

The British Army Special Air Service

The SAS began life in the desert. It was founded by David Stirling, a lieutenant in the Scots Guards, who had fought with No.8 Commando in the Mediterranean. Injured during parachute training, he drew up plans for a new type of long-range commando organisation while hospitalized in Cairo. He presented them through General Neil Ritchie to the perceptive commander of British Forces in the Middle East, General Auckinleck, and was rewarded with promotion and command of the 'L' detachment, Special Air Service Brigade. The unit designation was a fiction intended to deceive but the SAS had been born.

Stirling planned the SAS as a strategic force, attacking targets deep in the enemy heartland where they thought they were safe. From air bases in North Africa to the valleys of southern France, the SAS inflicted constant damage and tied down thousands of enemy soldiers guarding installation and sweeping the countryside for these elusive raiders.

The SAS was disbanded after the war, but resurrected within two years. A territorial regiment, 21 SAS, was created and some members volunteered for a new organisation, the Malaya Scouts (SAS). The latter were formed for counter-guerrilla operations against the communist rebels in Malaya. In 1952, this unit was redesignated 22 SAS and spearheaded the jungle war. Stirling's original belief that a small elite force could achieve results out of all proportion to its size was proved correct a second time.

As the British Empire disintegrated, the SAS were involved in guerrilla wars from Asian jungles to the Middle East. From 1969 the regiment was committed to action much closer to home, as handfuls of men were detached to Northern Ireland. SAS involvement was on a small scale until Prime Minister Harold Wilson publicly announced in January 1976 that he was sending in the SAS. This was without reference to the regiment, which had very few men available when this politically inspired statement was issued.

The SAS's counter-terrorist role was developed in response to the massacre of the Israeli athletes in Munich during 1972. In 1980 the world saw for the first time the sinister black combat suits and gas masks of the SAS's CRW (Counter Revolutionary Warfare) team. An SAS team stormed the Iranian Embassy in London releasing the hostages and killing all but one of the terrorists – a stunning success.

HECKLER & KOCH MP5

The Heckler & Koch MP5 machine pistol has become one of the most widely used weapons of its type. When the SAS stormed the Iranian Embassy in London in 1981, TV viewers in the UK saw it in action for the first time. British airport police were also issued with the MP5 in 1986 following the terrorist attacks at Rome and Vienna. Firing from a closed bolt, the MP5 is probably the most accurate sub-machine gun in production today. It is manufactured in a number of variants, including silenced or cut-down weapons for clandestine operations and is available with telescoping or fixed stocks. Although the MP5 is more complex and considerably more expensive than most other SMGs, its accuracy means that it is the favoured weapon of special operations and hostage rescue units around the world.

Specification
Cartridge: 9-mm parabellum; Weight:3kg; Length: (stock folded) 49 cm; Cyclic rate of fire: 800 rounds per minter; Magazine: 15 or 30 round box; Effective range: 200m.

Assessment
Reliability *****; Accuracy *****; Age ***; Worldwide users ***.

In 1982 the Argentine invasion of the Falklands gave the SAS the opportunity to demonstrate their more traditional skills. SAS patrols ranged behind enemy lines to scout their positions and raid vital targets.

SAS patrols were landed on the Falklands well before the main landings at San Carlos.

Although the Task Force received intelligence on the Argentine positions from American satellites and RAF reconnaissance aircraft, these could not give the whole picture. The Falklands are under cloud cover for much of the time, an only foot patrols could discover the information needed.

Four-man patrols abseiled down from Royal Navy helicopters at dead-of-night. They had no hope of support if anything went wrong. 'Special Forces' may have a glamorous image in the public mind, but there was little glamour being stuck in a cramped observation post in the Falklands. It was bitterly cold and wet. Rations had to be eaten cold for much of the time as nearby Argentinians could have detected the smell of cooking.

Just before the British forces landed at San Carlos, the SAS went over to the offensive. An SAS patrol paddled over to Pebble Island where the Argentinians had based a small force of aircraft on the grass airstrip there. They took cover overlooking the enemy position and guided in the main attack force: 45 men of 'D' Squadron, SAS, who landed from two Sea King helicopters during the early hours of 15 May.

They planted demolition charges on six Pucará ground attack aircraft, four T-34C Turbo Mentors belonging to the Argentinian navy, and a Short Skyvan transport. The Argentinians did not realize they were being attacked until the aircraft – and about a ton of stacked ordnance which the SAS also blew up – began to explode. Covered by 80 rounds of 4.5-in gunfire from HMS *Glamorgan* the raiders escaped with only two men wounded.

After the landings at San Carlos, SAS patrols continued to probe the enemy defences, paving the way for the successful ground assaults that overwhelmed the Argentinian garrison.

The campaign in the South Atlantic was followed by more successful counter terrorist work in Northern Ireland and

THE SAS IN THE GULF WAR

The Gulf War was widely presented as a showcase for the latest guided weapons technology. In fact few of the 'smart' weapons could have been quite so clever without the skill and bravery of the world's most secretive military units. Soldiers of the SAS and US Army Special Forces infiltrated Kuwait and Iraq months before the ground assault began.

These daring recce patrols helped the Allied forces build an intelligence picture of the enemy forces. But the SAS's job did not end when the full scale war began. SAS men crept into positions overlooking vital targets to illuminate them with laser designators; guided bombs could then home in and destroy them with pinpoint accuracy. SAS patrols took part in the great 'Scud' hunt that began when Saddam Hussein's mobile missile launchers began firing on Israel and Saudi Arabia.

The launchers were hidden during the day and only moved into their firing positions under cover of darkness. Allied Special Forces roved the deserts of western Iraq in search of them. The extent of these operations was never made public, and precise details will remain top secret for many, many years. Prime Minister John Major would only hint at the regiment's role when he praised its contribution to Operation Granby (see p. 206).

Gibraltar. The SAS is now world famous, and the subject of continued and unwelcome media interest. As the anonymity of its soldiers is vital to their safety, the regiment's very success now poses an added danger to its future operations.

Birth of a legend

Most of the North African campaign of 1940-43 was fought out in the narrow coastal strip which runs the long arc from Tunis to Cairo. South of the coastal strip lies the Sahara, an immense secret place of shifting sands and cauldron-like heat. Few paid much attention to this wilderness, but in its unguarded vastness a young British second-lieutenant saw the possibility for a new type of unit to operate. A unit which would strike swift and hard, and then disappear like a phantom into the desert from which it had emerged. Jon E Lewis tells of the early days of the SAS.

The Special Air Service was conceived in a hospital bed in Egypt. Injured during some unofficial parachute training David Stirling, a subaltern with No 8 (Guards) Commando, decided to use his enforced stay in the Alexandria Scottish Military Hospital to develop a scheme for special operations in the desert.

On his release from hospital in July 1941, Stirling determined to bring his plan to the attention of the Commander in Chief. As C-in-Cs are not, by and large, in the habit of granting interviews to junior officers Stirling decided to ignore the usual channels. Instead he hobbled on his crutches to British Army Middle East HQ and tricked his way past the sentry. Inside, Stirling found his way into the office of the Deputy Commander Middle East, one General Neil Ritchie. Stirling apologized to the somewhat surprised Ritchie for the unconventional call, but insisted that he had something of 'great operational importance' to tell him. Ritchie offered him a seat, and Stirling pulled out the pencilled memo on a desert raiding force he had prepared in hospital.

Ritchie spent several minutes reading it. It was then Stirling's turn to be surprised. Ritchie looked up and said brusquely, "I think this may be the sort of plan we are looking for. I will discuss it with the Commander in Chief and let you know our decision in the next day or so". The C-in-C was General Auckinleck, new to his command and under pressure from Churchill to mount an offensive. Stirling's plan was indeed what Auckinleck was looking for. It required few resources, and it was original. The unit Stirling proposed was to operate behind enemy lines in order to attack vulnerable targets like extended supply lines and airfields. What is more the raids were to be carried out by very small groups of men, between five and ten, rather than the standard commando force of hundreds.

Meanwhile, Ritchie looked into Stirling's background. He was pleased with what he found. David Stirling, born in 1915 was the youngest son of the aristocratic Brigadier Archibald Stirling of Keir. After three years at Cambridge David Stirling had joined the Scots Guards, before transferring to No 8 Commando. As part of the 'Layforce' brigade, No 8 had been dispatched to North Africa where its seaborne raids had all been proved to be wash outs. The unit, along with the rest of Layforce, had been marked for disbandment. Stirling however, had remained so keen on the commando idea that he had jumped – literally – at the chance of doing some parachuting with chutes that another officer in No 8, Jock Lewes, had scrounged. The jumping trials had taken place near Mersa Matruh. The aircraft used, a lumbering Valentia bi-plane, was not equipped for parachuting and the men had secured the static lines which open the parachutes to seat legs. Stirling's parachute had caught on the door and snagged. He had descended far too rapidly and damaged his back badly on landing. Which is how he had come to be in Alexandria Hospital.

Three days after his meeting with Ritchie, Stirling was back at Middle East HQ, this time with a pass. Auckinleck saw him in person. Stirling was given permission to recruit a force of six other officers and sixty men. The unit was to be called 'L Detachment, SAS Brigade'. The SAS stood for Special Air Service which did not exist. The name was dreamed up by Brigadier Dudley Clarke, a staff Intelligence Officer, as a means of convincing the enemy that the British possessed a large airborne force in North Africa. To mark his new appointment, Stirling was promoted to captain.

The recruiting took less than a week. There were two particular officers Stirling wanted. The first was Jock Lewes who was in Tobruck, where he had been carrying out small raids against enemy outposts. A scholar and Oxford rowing 'blue', Lewes was also a daring soldier. He agreed to join. So did the Northern Irishman, Paddy Mayne, then under close arrest for striking his commanding officer. Before the war, Mayne had been a rugby player of international rank. Most of the rest of the unit were recruited from the Guards Commando then at a camp at Genefa. Selection was based on Stirling's impression of the men at brief interviews. He also told them that if they failed to make the grade in training they would have to return to their units.

By August 1941, Stirling had established his force at Kabrit, 100 miles south of Cairo. Equipment was conspicuous by its absence. The camp consisted of two small tents for personnel, one large supply tent and a wooden sign saying 'L Detachment – SAS'. Being in his own words, a 'cheekie laddie', Stirling decided that the equipment L Detachment needed in view of the parsimony of the Quartermasters, would have to be 'borrowed' from a New Zealand camp down the road. Thus the first – and highly unofficial – mission of L Detachment was a night raid on the New Zealand camp, filling L Detachment's one and only 3 ton truck with anything useful that could be found.

The next day, L Detachment boasted the smartest – and most luxuriously furnished – British camp in the Canal Zone. Training then began in earnest. From the start, Stirling insisted on a high standard of discipline – equal to that of the Brigade of Guards – and the pursuit of excellence. To achieve such standards demanded a combination of the right character and sheer physical fitness. One early recruit to Stirling's L Detachment, Fitzroy Maclean, recalled that: "for days and nights on end, we trudged interminably over the alternating soft sand and jagged rocks of the desert, weighed down by heavy loads of explosive, eating and drinking only what we could carry with us. In the intervals we did weapon training, physical training and training in demolitions and navigation."

Additionally, everyone joining the SAS had to be a parachutist, since Stirling envisaged airborne insertions for his force. No RAF instructors – or indeed aircraft – were available, so the SAS developed its own parachute training techniques. These involved jumping from ever higher platforms or from the back of trucks moving at 30 mph. The unit then moved on to make its first live jump from a Bombay aircraft. Two men died when their 'chutes failed to open. "That night", recalled SAS 'Original' Bob Bennett, "we went to bed with as many cigarettes as possible and smoked until morning. Next day every man (led by Stirling himself) jumped; no-one backed out. It was then that I realized that I was with a great bunch of chaps." Thereafter parachute training progressed smoothly.

There were other problems though. Prime among them was the type of bomb which would be carried by the SAS raiding parties; it had to be small enough to be easily transportable, but big enough to do the job. The requisite device was invented by Jock Lewes, a small incendiary bomb made of oil, plastic and thermite. Appropriately enough it became known as the Lewes bomb.

Stirling sharpened his men for action with a training raid on the large RAF base at Heliopolis outside Cairo. An RAF Group-Captain had been unwise enough to tell L Detachment that their planned enterprise of attacking enemy aircraft on the ground was unrealistic. Although the airfield guards had been warned of their coming, and daily reconnaissance planes sent up, the SAS could not be kept out. After marching 90 miles across the desert by night and hiding up by day, they placed stickers representing bombs on the RAF aircraft before slipping away into the desert darkness.

To celebrate their success, L Detachment were given a few days leave in Cairo. Before they had lacked an identity, but training had made them into a cohesive unit. They took pride too, in their new unit insignia. The design of the cap badge was the result of a competition won by Sergeant Bob Tait who came up with a flaming sword of Damocles emblem. David Stirling added the motto 'Who Dares Wins'. The one problem was the unit's headgear: a white beret. After this drew unceremonious wolf whistles in Cairo, it was hurriedly replaced, first by a khaki forage cap, then by the famous sand-coloured beret.

After their leave, the men of L Detachment assembled to hear the details of their first real attack, scheduled for the night of 17 November 1941, when five SAS groups would parachute into the desert near Gazala and attack the five forward German fighter airfields. It was to be the opening prelude to Auckinleck's attempt to relieve Tobruk. Stirling assembled his men. "With luck", he told them, "we'll polish off Rommel's entire fighter force." There were whistles and cheers.

Alas, L Detachment's luck was out.

The weather forecast on the morning of 16 November looked ominous. The wind was strong and it looked as though it might rain – far from ideal conditions for parachuting. Even so, Stirling decided to press ahead with the mission, partly because Auckinleck expected it, mostly because many of the men who had joined the SAS had done so out of disgust for the continual cancellation of their commando operations. To call off the drop, Stirling concluded, would have been catastrophic for morale. At 19.30 the five Bombays containing L Detachment left the runway, flying first out to sea, then turning inland to cross the coast well behind German lines. The aircraft tossed around wildly in the wind, and the ground below was totally obscured by the darkness and the sandstorm. The drop was more than a failure, it was a disaster. Of his group, Stirling was the first to jump. It was so black and murky that he could not see the ground. He waited and waited for the impact. He recorded later that it was like being suspended in space. Then there was a smashing blow. For some seconds he was unconscious but luckily nothing was broken. It took him nearly an hour to assemble the rest of his stick who had been dragged all over the desert by the wind. One man could not be found, others were injured, and vital supplies were missing. They had some Lewes bombs, but no detonators and so could not carry out their mission. Stirling resolved on the spot that never again would detonators and bombs be packed separately. There was nothing to do but call off the planned attack and attempt to walk the forty miles into the desert for the planned rendezvous with a motor patrol for the Long Range Desert Group (LRDG).

It took several days for the SAS parties to reach the LRDG rendezvous. Some never made it. Of the fifty-one officers and men who had jumped into the storm three days before, only five officers (including Stirling himself) and eighteen men were left. Any other man would have given up the idea of a special desert force.

Stirling, however, decided to press ahead. Fortunately for him the Eighth Army Command had more to think about than the fortunes of a small band of irregulars; the counter-offensive against Rommel had become bogged down by tough German resistance. So Stirling withdrew with the remnants of his unit to a remote oasis at Gialo, where he began preparing for another mission. He had already abandoned the idea of parachuting into the desert. At the rendezvous with the LRDG, David Lloyd-Owen of the latter unit had proposed that his patrols could get Stirling and his men to and from their targets. Although essentially a reconnaissance group such a task was easily within the LRDG's capability. Stirling accepted with alacrity. Now at Gialo, Stirling and his men pored over maps. A quick success was obviously necessary to wipe out the failure of the first raid, if hostile elements at GQ were not to succeed in burying the fledgling SAS.

In only a matter of days Stirling's idea was vindicated. In early December an SAS group under Paddy Mayne destroyed 24 enemy aircraft at Tamet airfield, while Bill Fraser's party destroyed 37 at Agedabia. Two weeks later, Paddy Mayne led a six-man group back to Tamet and accounted for a further 27 aircraft. A group led by Stirling himself reached the airfield at Bagush but were unable to plant their bombs. Their improvized response to this situation was to prove so successful that it was used often in future: a motorized charge down the airstrip, blazing away at the aircraft with machine guns and grenades from the back of the LRDG jeeps.

Fitzroy Maclean later wrote of the huge success of these raids: "Working on these lines, David achieved a series of successes which surpassed the wildest expectations of those who had originally supported his venture. No sooner had the enemy become aware of his presence in one part of the desert than he was attacking them somewhere else. Never has the element of surprise, the key to success in all irregular warfare, been more brilliantly exploited. Soon the number of aircraft destroyed was well into three figures."

It was not only aircraft which received the attention of the SAS. Stirling was quick to see the vulnerability of Rommel's supply lines. Convoys were attacked, harbours raided. Recruits flocked to join L Detachment. Stirling himself was promoted to Major in January 1942. Seven months later, Stirling's force had grown to Regimental size (750 men) and was renamed 1 SAS.

Perhaps the real proof of the SAS concept was that it survived without the presence of its founder, it wasn't dependent on the charisma and drive of only one man. David Stirling led from the front and in January 1943 he paid the price. He was captured in Tunisia by the Germans. The SAS went on without him, not only in North Africa, but into Italy, France, Holland and eventually Germany. By 1945, the idea David Stirling had conceived in his hospital bed had become more than a war-winning unit. It had become a legend.

◉ EYEWITNESS

SAS in South East Asia

A former member of the SAS Regiment describes his experiences in Malaysia with a small team of troops sent to win the 'hearts and minds' of the villagers along the border with Borneo and Indonesia. Many of the tribesmen had never seen a white man before, and winning them over presented novel problems to the British soldiers.

"When the confrontation between Indonesia and the fledgling Malaysia ended in 1968, the British presence was reduced to a mere token force, as the terrorist problem officially no longer existed. In practice however, there was still a problem, and the best military solution lay in wholesale search-and-destroy missions. But the British could not overtly engage in such operations and so they were disguised as 'hearts and minds' operations.

"There were, and still are, many primitive tribes living in the highlands. They were officially designated as being Aboriginal Peoples; government policy was to try to educate them slowly into the ways of civilization, restricting contact to essential medical services.

"So it was that various elements of Far East Land Forces found themselves ostensibly visiting Aboriginal villagers (when they could find them) in order to dispense medical supplies and basic medical aid. Weapons and ammunition could be carried because these were always taken into the jungle, even on exercise.

"I was attached to a 'hearts and minds' team as a specialist in combat intelligence. It was my job to talk – usually via an interpreter – to the headman of any village we came to and find out if there was any activity in the area. Gradually, I'd hope to build up some sort of picture of any terrorist organisation, figuring out who they were, where they were based, what weapons they had and so on. As well as myself, we had a signaller, a medic, four minders who could act independently if they had to, an interpreter/tracker who spoke some of the local dialects, and the boss, a young captain, who came from the same regiment as the minders.

"All in all, it was one of the best jobs I ever had – we were on our own and I got to see the kinds of people who you only ever read about; the Aborigines. Lovely, gentle people they were, but a little confused by some of the medical practices they were being taught.

"I remember one village we came to, the headman came out to meet us and the old boy had a very well developed chest – a sort of geriatric Page Three. It worried our medic quite a bit until finally we found out what had happened. Apparently a government team had been there about a year before, preaching the virtues of birth control. Then, when they left, they gave the village a year's supply of birth control pills. Well there was no way that the headman was going to let valuable medicine be used by mere women, so he scoffed the lot himself. As a result he developed breasts as well as beginning to talk in a high pitched voice. Our medic explained that an enemy had cursed the medicine and with great ceremony the remaining pills were burned.

"We used to travel initially by Land Rover or canoe, though sometimes we were choppered in. We'd choose one village as a base and then try to cover a 1- to 20-mile radius around it. For weapons we had Armalites, SLRs, shotguns, grenades, some Claymore mines and a GPMG. Usually, the boss and a couple of minders would disappear off on their own for two or three days, particularly if we got what looked like hard info on a terrorist group somewhere in the area.

"In theory, if we found that there was a terrorist group

nearby we were supposed to contact HQ Farelf, who would contact the Malaysian authorities, who would send in their own boys. In practice, if the boss thought that we couldn't handle it ourselves he'd get in touch with another 'hearts and minds' team who would whistle over to give a hand. I'm not sure, but I think that prisoners were regarded as being an embarrassment, so if there was any action terrorists who weren't killed were allowed to get away – after all the more stories they told their mates in Thailand or Burma about how unfriendly Malaya had suddenly become the better for all of us.

"The first time I saw action, I was driving the Land Rover back from the nearest town some 30 Klicks away. The track was an old logging road, so it was quite brutal. There was tall primary jungle on one side and burnt-out lallang (secondary jungle) on the other.

"Anyway, suddenly I heard that sharp 'pop-pop-pop' that means some joker's using an SMG and the front offside tyre was blown out. This was at the very start of the 'hearts and minds' campaign, so I don't think the terrorists had realized that the Brits posed an actual threat. But in a mad moment I got out of the vehicle - which anyway had slewed across the track – and shouted out: 'You effing idiot, I'm British!' Funny what goes through your mind at the time . . . all I can remember now is being furious because I'd have to spend time repairing the bloody tyre!

"There was a moment of silence during which I suddenly realized that I was not in a good position and that maybe I should try to sneak off into the lallang behind me. Then I hear a voice from the primary jungle shouting 'Sorry Johnny!' Then nothing. After about half an hour I finished shaking, changed the tyre – have you ever tried changing a tyre from underneath a vehicle? – and got back to camp. The boss and the minders were still laughing about it weeks later and for a time it looked as if 'British Johnny' was going to be my permanent nickname!"

The Australian SAS in Vietnam

Andrew Freemantle left the British Army in 1969 and served for three years with the Royal Australian Regiment and Australian Special Air Service. He served for 11 months in Vietnam

"On 22 May 1971, I was commanding the standby patrol in the Australian SAS squadron base on the hill at Nui Dat, South Vietnam. The task of my five man team on that day was to be prepared at short notice to deploy, by a variety of methods, either to reinforce or assist one of our patrols already in there.

"One such patrol (call sign 23, a five man recce patrol) had been operating for five days some 50 miles to the north of Nui Dat, in an American area usually patrolled by the 1st Air Cavalry and notorious for its high level of enemy activity.

On 21 May, patrol 23 had reported seeing and hearing some main force Viet Cong constructing bunkers in an area of thick secondary jungle. The patrol had attempted a close recce, but it had great difficulty getting very close to the enemy because large numbers of dried leaves on the ground made quiet movement almost impossible. But it was clear from the number of enemy seen and the amount of general enemy movement in the area, that a significant position, possibly a battalion base, was being constructed.

"The commander of patrol 23 had decided to withdraw to a safer area and call for the assistance of a standby patrol. This would give him a better chance of being able to fight his way out if he got into trouble, or of being able to create a diversion should either patrol be compromised.

"So on the morning of 22 May, my patrol, patrol 15, abseiled through the trees to reinforce patrol 23, in an area far enough away from the enemy sighting to make it impossible for them to hear us. Various diversionary tactics were used to disguise the whereabouts of our helicopters, but because of the frequent chopper movements in much of South Vietnam (unlike previous jungle campaigns such as Malaya or Borneo) the use of helicopters to insert a covert patrol was not as risky as it might seem.

"Once on the ground we received an update of the situation. Then we patrolled carefully towards where patrol 23 had seen the enemy. This took several hours, but by 14.30 we were in the vicinity of the enemy camp. By this stage our rate of movement had slowed to about 100 metres in an hour, and we were all acutely aware of an enemy presence, even though we'd not yet seen anyone.

"Without warning a Viet Cong soldier, dressed in green and carrying an AK-46, appeared from behind a tree about five metres away and opened fire. By this time in the tour we were quite quick on the draw, so he flew back in a hail of fire from our automatic SLRs and M16s.

"Then all hell broke loose. Obviously we'd walked right into the middle of what appeared to be a major VC bunker complex. Within a few seconds we were under fire from six occupied bunkers, dug in an L shaped configuration We were forced to go to ground in a shallow depression about seven metres from the nearest bunker.

"My patrol seemed to be under fire from three bunkers along the bottom of the L, and the patrol we'd been sent to reinforce was about 20 metres away, under fire from bunkers along the side of the L. The enemy, of course, were firing through slits in the front and sides of each bunker, so when we started to throw grenades at them they exploded harmlessly either on the trench parapet or on top of the metre or so of overhead protection that formed the roof of each bunker.

"But when the enemy threw grenades at us we had no such protection, and things became quite lively. Mick, my medic, was soon wounded in the shoulder and leg. I felt a great whoosh behind me and a stinging sensation in my backside. An enemy grenade had gone over our heads and exploded just behind us.

"The ensuing fire fight lasted for about 20 minutes and was conducted at ranges of no more than 20 metres. I remember admiring the coolness of trooper Hans, already the holder of the DCM, firing deliberately and steadily at the muzzle flashes from the nearest bunker, while branches leaves and wood chips thrown up by enemy fire flew all around him.

"Meanwhile, I took stock of a rapidly deteriorating situation. The options were simple: either storm what was largely an unknown but well protected objective, or get the hell out of it and live to fight another day. I decided on the latter course, and I must say it's a decision I have never regretted.

"By this stage we'd all fired at least 200 rounds apiece, and thrown or fired most of our grenades. At that moment some bright spark fired a 4-mm CS gas cartridge at a bunker and missed. But the resulting cloud of gas, together with white phosphorous smoke, created enough confusion to allow us to break contact, using individual fire and movement, crawling on our bellies and pulling our wounded.

"In spite of the noise and confusion my 2IC, Clive, an ex-Royal Marine, had remembered to make ready a time delay smoke container to mark the camp so that bombers could attack it later from the air. I watched with alarm as the hand on the watch of the timing device fell off as he put the smoke container down behind a tree. With great presence of mind he pulled out a knife, smashed the watch glass with the handle and carefully repositioned the hand. By this time everyone else had withdrawn, and I was rather keen to join them.

"Twenty minutes later we reached a small clearing, and we were all extracted by winch, under cover of fire from helicopter gunships that suppressed the enemy throughout.

"Only one of us needed hospital treatment, and the rest of us needed a beer on our return to base."

◉ *EYEWITNESS*

With BATT in Oman

In 1970 the Sultan of Oman was overthrown by his son with a little help from the SAS. The new regime received immediate British assistance against the communist backed Adoo guerillas who were based over the border in Yemen. The SAS and its attached units were known as BATT (British Army Training Team) and was to train the loyal Arab army and the Firquat tribesmen. I was part of a four-man despatch team working as ATLOs (Air Transport Liaison Operators). In fact we flew operational despatch sorties and any underslung equipment sorties.

"One day, Dave, myself and an SAS psyops (psychological operations) trooper were briefed on a sortie for early the following day. We were to fly along the coast until we came to the border, and then fly parallel until we reached a certain grid reference which was a known *Adoo* area. We were to shower it with leaflets, calling on the enemy to surrender, telling them they would be well treated and, more importantly, that they would be well paid for the brand new AK-47 rifles the Russians had given them. This 'hearts and minds' campaign was proving highly successful.

"We took off from Salalha at 06.00 in a battered Britten-Norman Defender which had its machine guns and rocket pods removed to give more room for fuel and the payload – four men and a lot of leaflets in cardboard boxes. We had no weapons other than those we carried with us: two SLRs, an M16 and the pilot's pistol.

"At 13,000 ft we levelled off. The drone of the engines made talking impossible and we each sat in our own silence. Occasionally through the haze I caught sight of an Arab dhow. Was it a friendly fishing boat or a Communist gun-runner? The only way to find out would be to overfly it at a couple of hundred feet and without our usual machine guns and rockets, this would have been decidedly unhealthy. We droned on.

"We had no parachutes. I had been told by one pilot that if we received a direct hit from a rocket we would be instantly incinerated. We performed a slow turn to the right, and through the window I saw the forbidding peaks of the mountains and the Omani coastline getting closer. Then we were crossing the moonscape wastes of the desert towards the foothills. The ground was covered in huge boulders. Not a good place for a crash-landing.

"'Running in,' the pilot shouted over the nose of the engine. We got busy on the boxes, splitting bundles of leaflets and preparing them for the drop. One or two that got loose fluttered around in front of the cabin like demented flies. 'OK start dropping now,' came the command. We grabbed handfuls of leaflets and threw them out and back into the slipstream ensuring that they were well separated by the time they met the ground. Within two minutes we had emptied the aircraft, and for good measure, we tossed the empty boxes out as well. The pilot turned the plane around and headed for the coast and relative safety.

"We had just sat down and strapped in when Dave, who had been admiring the view, turned and shouted, 'I think I just saw a smoke trail below us.' We all looked at each other. The pilot did not need to be told twice: he banked violently to starboard and started a series of banks and turns that we hoped would confuse the missile below us, homing in on the heat of our engine exhausts. Unlike other aircraft in the war zone we carried no heat deflectors, magnesium flares or any other jamming devices. If we were to survive it would mostly be by luck.

"After a few rapid turns my bacon and eggs from breakfast were making a comeback and at that moment if I'd had a chute I would have jumped. My knuckles were white from gripping the seat strap. A look at the others confirmed that they were in the same state. I gulped in cold air from the open door. Suddenly we were levelling off. I looked at the pilot who was going about his business as if nothing had happened.

'What's going on?' I yelled.

'No sweat!' he shouted.

'What about the SAM?' we all wanted to know.

'Must have been a short-range job; never got anywhere near us.'

"We breathed a sigh of relief. The pilot didn't intend giving the *Adoo* another chance and our plane went into a rapid dive, the engine noise changing to a high-pitched whine. By the time we reached the sea we had gone from 13,000 ft to zero ft in about a minute and a half, and we were skimming the warm blue Arabian sea.

"Stripping off all my extra layers of clothing because of the heat, as we were now getting at low altitude, I noticed for the first time lots of large black shapes in the water below. I pointed at them. Our trooper nodded and mouthed the word SHARKS. The water didn't seem all that inviting any more. The flight back to Salalha was uneventful. On landing we waved farewell to our pilot and drove back to base to make our report."

The Battle of Mirbat

A little before dawn on 19 July 1972 an eight-man SAS BATT detachment stationed in Mirbat, Oman, was attacked by 250 Communist guerrillas or Adoo. *It was the beginning of a battle as extraordinary as that fought at Rorke's Drift or the Imjin River. The Sultanate of Oman – a British ally and strategically important Gulf nation – had been in a state of civil war in its southern province of Dhofar since the early 1960s. Originally Arab nationalists, the insurgent* Adoo *had become hardline Communists, aided and sponsored by South Yemen. The* Adoo *were a formidable enemy, well-trained and equipped with Soviet arms. However, their appeal had been weakened by the new Sultan, Qaboos, who had wooed over elements of the insurrectionists with promises of material progress. In order to reassert their influence, the* Adoo *needed victory against the Sultan's Armed Forces, the* firqat *(guerrillas who had changed sides) and the Sultan's British helpers, the Special Air Service. Hence the attack on Mirbat. Tom Verry gives this account.*

The nervousness of the men electrified the chill dank air. Silent, except for the slight chink-chink of a dislodged pebble or the hoarse whisper of a command, they lay in their assault positions, shamags pulled tight against the cold. Some sought relief from the tension by checking and rechecking their Kalisnikov AK-47s, others prayed to Allah, their lips wordlessly mouthing the Koran in the dark. Like soldiers everywhere they wanted the action to begin, the waiting over.

To the left of the *Adoo* the sky began to lighten. Before them, something over a thousand yards away, they could make out the low, flat roofs of Mirbat and the sea which surrounded it on two sides. Behind them lay the forbidding height of the Jabal, from which they had descended in the night in fast-moving parties of forty or more. Suddenly there was a single snap of a high velocity rifle, followed by the crackle of a 12.7 mm Shoagin machine-gun. Their presence had been spotted by a picket on the Jabal Ali, a small rise to the north of the town. Realizing that the element of surprise had been lost, *Adoo* mortarmen began to shower bombs on the town. The riflemen rose up and ran forward, raising their weapons to their shoulders as they did so. It was just before 5.30 a.m. on 19 July 1972.

Inside the town, the shells caused Captain M. J. A. Kealy of B Squadron, 22 SAS, to tumble out of his sleeping bag, seize his SLR and run up to the roof of 'BATThouse', as the training detachment's building was affectionately known. At 23 'Mike' Kealy had never been in action before; he was desperately worried, as he climbed upwards, about how he would behave under fire. And more, how he would command his seasoned NCOs and troopers who, technically at least, ranked below him.

Reaching the roof, Kealy was astounded by the sheer intensity of the assault. Previously the *Adoo* had satisfied themselves with desultory mortar and shell attacks, then hastily withdrawn. Now they were on the open ground just outside the perimeter wire which flanked the north and west of Mirbat. Through the half-light Kealy could see that the picket on the Jabal Ali had been overrun, and that a small stone fort held by twenty-five men of the Sultan's Dhofar Gendarmerie (DG) 700 yards away to the right was bearing the brunt of a pounding assault. Nearer, almost on the water's edge, was the Wali's Fort, occupied by pro-Sultan Askari tribesmen from northern Oman who were returning slow but accurate fire from the bolt-action .303 rifles. Shells were landing everywhere inside the town, throwing up plumes of dust. The noise was deafening. An artillery round whistled low overhead to explode behind the house.

Assessing the situation in a manner he found almost a reflex, Kealy ordered the team's sole mortar to lay down a white phosphorous smoke-screen. Meanwhile, Lance-Corporal Pete Wignall opened up with his .5 Browning, mounted on sandbags on the roof, and Corporal Roger Chapman unleashed a hail of GMPG rounds. Other SAS men calmly picked off the advancing *Adoo* with FN automatic rifles. Still they came forward, groups advancing under covering fire in textbook manner. Fire and movement. Fire and movement.

By now Kealy was apprehensive. The vigour of the enemy advance suggested that they knew the strength of those within Mirbat, a bare fifty fighting men. Grim-faced, he ordered Wignall to establish communications with base at Um Al Gwarif, and went downstairs to change his flip-flops for desert boots.

He returned within seconds to find the battle hotting up. Increasing daylight had not diminished the *Adoo*'s assault, only added to it. Explosions pummelled the BATThouse, some of the enemy rounds coming from the foreshore to the south: the town was surrounded. From a corner of the roof, Corporal Bob Bradshaw purposefully identified targets for the SAS mortar and machine-guns.

Behind Bradshaw Trooper Savesaki, a Fijian with the SAS, talked urgently over the radio to a gun-pit in front of the DG Fort manned by an Omani, Walid Khamis, and another Fijian SAS trooper, Corporal Labalada. The gun-pit housed the 25 pounder of Second World War vintage. Labalada, Savesaki informed Kealy, had been hit in the chin. Kealy agreed to Savesaki's request to go to the aid of his countryman. For an agonizing minute the men on the roof watched Savesaki, a rugby player of renown, snake and sidestep bullets and explosions as he ran to the gun-pit – and disappeared safely over its sangar wall.

The 25 pounder began to belch shells at the *Adoo*, causing deaths and injuries by the score.

Yet the *Adoo* continued to move inexorably forward. From a position near the wire they opened fire on the DG Fort with RPG-7 rocket-launchers and a Carl Gustav, whose 84 mm rounds began to shred the ancient building. By now the *Adoo* were breaching the wire. All SAS fire was directed at the perimeter near the Carl Gustav. With the situation worsening, Kealy oprdered Trooper 'I' to request an airstrike and a casevac chopper from Um al Gwarif. The helicopter was dispatched immediately but the low cloud-cover ruled out an airstrike.

It was now 07.00 hours, and an eerie lull suddenly descended on the battlefield. The *Adoo*, having loosed off thousands of rounds, needed to bring up more ammunition. The SAS, not wishing to draw fire, responded with silence. Only the steady crump of the *Adoo* mortars broke the morning quiet.

Kealy took advantage of the temporary abatement of battle to try to raise the gun-pit on the walkie-talkie. There was no response. Worried, Kealy determined to make the dangerous run to the gun-pit, over 400 yards of open ground, himself. An argument broke out, the other SAS men at the BATThouse insisting they take the risk. Kealy refused to let anyone go in his stead, but agreed to take Trooper Tobin, his medical orderly. Cautiously, the two men slipped out of the BATThouse and began a crouched run to the fort. Almost in the same moment, Corporal Chapman left the BATThouse for the beach to guide in the casevac chopper, already making its approach.

For the *Adoo*, the appearance of the helicopter was a signal for battle to erupt afresh. A ferocious barrage of bullets and shells went up from the *Adoo* positions, causing Chapman to hurriedly warn off the helicopter with a red grenade.

The unwelcome restart of battle found Kealy and Tobin halfway to the gun-pit. A burst of heavy machine-gun fire zipped between them. The two men threw themselves flat, waited a moment, then began making their way rapidly forwards, one running, the other covering. Back at the BATThouse, the other SAS troopers tried to lay down suppressing fire. Eventually, Tobin reached the pit, a jump getting him over the wall. Kealy, close on his heels, vaulted into the pit's accompanying ammunition bay. To his disgust he landed on the body of a dead DG soldier. Glancing into the gun-pit, Kealy saw that Khamis, the Omani gunner, was dead, and the two SAS Fijians wounded. Savesaki, hin in the back, was propped against the sangar wall, his SLR somehow still emitting a steady fire. In the centre of the pit Trooper Labalaba, a bloody dressing on his face, was single-handedly loading and firing the 25 pounder. A hail of bullets ricocheted off its armoured shield, sparks flying. Then, as the Fijian reached down for another shell, he pitched forward silently, a bullet ending his life. Tobin sprang to take his place at the 25 pounder, but could only fire off one shell before an AK-47 bullet tore off his jaw, leaving him unconscious on the ground.

Only Kealy and Savesaki were left defending the gun-pit. The *Adoo* were now six or seven yards away and closing. A snap shot by Kealy felled a guerrilla who had Savesaki in his sights. The trooper, unaware, continued a steady crack-crack of shots at the enemy coming from the left. A torrent of LMG fire churned the ground just in front of the ammunition bay, one round passing so close to Kealy's head that he could feel the vibration from its spinning metal mass. Then came grenades, one landing on the lip of the bunker, its explosion almost bursting Kealy's eardrums. Desperate, he spoke into the radio and told the BATThouse to spray either side of the fort with machine-gun fire and mortars, as close in as they could get. To shorten the range, the SAS mortarman had to hug his charge vertical to his chest as someone else dropped the shells down the barrel.

Putting down the radio, Kealy watched in horror as a grenade hit the edge of the ammunition bunker and rolled down towards him, its black fuse burning. He steeled himself for the pain which was to come . . . but the grenade failed to explode. A damp squib. There was no time to wonder or give thanks. The gun-pit was being hammered by small-arms fire and blows from the Carl Gustav. Through the smoke and flying sand Kealy could see *Adoo* edging around the Fort wall. Now there were only feet away. Kealy put his rifle over the top and began desperately snapping off bullets.

At the moment when it seemed that Kealy and Savesaki could hold on no longer, when they would surely be overrun, a Strikemaster of the Sultan's air force miraculously appeared on the scene, its pilot steering the jet under the cloudbase of a mere 150 feet. Then another Strikemaster, cannons blazing, screamed over the battlefield. Seizing the ground-to-air radio in the BATThouse, Corporal Chapman began passing targets to the jets: a 500-kg bomb on the shallow wadi near the fort where the *Adoo* had ammassed for shelter; the Carl Gustav; the 7.62 mm machine-gun near the wire. Shells and rockets poured from the sky. To identify his friendly status to the jets, Kealy broke out a florescent marker panel and went to administer first aid to Savesaki. Although the airstrikes alleviated the situation at the gun-pit, the *Adoo* continued to ring the town, even setting up a fast counter-thrust from the east. Only land-based re-inforcements would save the battle for sure.

By fortunate coincidence, another SAS squadron was in Dhofar that day, waiting to take over from Kealy's B Squadron – due to end its tour of duty that very morning of 19 July. So it was that 23 men of G Squadron in SOAF helicopters arrived on the beach at Mirbat at 09.15, deploying themselves in two hit groups and wiping out an *Adoo* GPMG emplacement and several other enemy positions as they surged forward towards the town. A second wave of G Squadron reinforcements landed, engaging the guerrillas on the seaward side of Mirbat. Another relay of Strikemaster jets hammered *Adoo* positions on the Jabal Ali, almost obliterating them in a hail of red tracer and 20 mm cannon fire. From the BATThouse Chapman and Bradshaw watched the daredevil Omani pilots with something approaching awe.

Perceptibly, the tide of battle shifted. *Adoo* began to slink away through the shallow wadis towards their refuge in the mists of the Jabal. Even so, it was 10.30 before the helicopter evacuation of wounded from the LZ commenced. Troopers Savesaki and Tobin and the Omani gunner Khamis were first out. For a while it seemed as though Tobin's life might have been saved by some emergency first aid, but he died of his wounds shortly after arriving at Salalah Field Hospital.

Tobin and Corporal Labalaba were the sole SAS fatalities incurred during the Regiment's hardets test. For this loss the SAS took the lives of thirty *Adoo* and wounded scores more. More than this, they broke the guerrilla's morale. A proud warrior race, the *Adoo* of the Dhofar were beaten by warriors better than they. The *Adoo* never recovered from their defeat at Mirbat and ceased hostilities four years later. In retrospect, the SAS not only won the Battle of Mirbat but the Oman War.

Afterword

For his bravery and leadership at Mirbat, Captain Mike Kealy was awarded the DSO. Tragically, he died on an exercise in the Brecon Beacons in 1979. Trooper Tobin and Corporal Labalaba were posthumously awarded the DCM and a Mention in Dispatches respectively.

The Rescuers

The origins of SAS counter-terrorism in urban centres date back to the 'Keeni Meeni' (Swahili for moving unseen like a snake) period in Aden, during which the major commanding A Squadron SAS set up a Close Quarter Battle Course for a selected team of troopers. Thereafter, the evolution of SAS Counter Revolutionary Warfare (CRW) proceeded almost by accident; during a period in the early 1970s when the Regiment found itself without an active campaign it offered its service to the British government as trainers of bodyguards for VIPs. The government say this as a means of raising revenue, and hired out the Regiment to overseas heads of state. At the same time, at the Hereford HQ of 22 SAS, Bradbury Lines (later rechristened Stirling Lines in honour of the Regiment's founder), a special house was constructed to train marksmen in the skills of shooting gunmen in the close confines of a room without hitting VIPs or other hostages. Formally called the Close Quarter Battle House (CQB), it is more usually known as "the Killing House". (One exercise involves a trooper sitting amongst dummy terrorists, while other troopers burst in and riddle the dummies with live rounds). To maintain and improve the Regiment's new sill a permanent CRW Wing was set up. This remained a modest affair until the Munich massacre in September 1972, when seven Palestinians from "Black September" seized the dormitory occupied by Israeli Olympic athletes, killing two and taking nine as hostage. The West German government agreed to allow the gunmen and hostages safe passage out of the country, but as the party moved through Munich airport German security forces opened fire. In the wild gunbattle that followed all the hostages were killed. European governments became alarmed about their ability to deal with terrorism. The West Germans themselves responded by setting up Grenzschutzgruppe 9 (GSG9), an elite counter-terrorist unit. Britain, meanwhile, turned to the SAS who were given the resources needed to expand the CRW Wing to a cadre consisting of one officer and four instructors, who in turn would be responsible for teaching all aspects of counter-terrorist work to all troopers. In addition, a CRW team of about twenty troopers, drawn on rota from the four operational Sabre squadrons was to be available at immediate notice to deal with any hostage or terrorist situation.

In the aftermath of Munich, the SAS quickly established links with the CRW groups of other Western nations, including Germany's GSG9. These links would benefit both units at Mogadishu Airport, described here by Jon E Lewis, and London, in 1980.

Their tense faces blackened with camouflage paint, the commandos of the crack German anti-terrorist squad GSG9 edged slowly through the dark tropical night to the rear of the Boeing 737. Some held automatic pistols, others the Heckler & Koch MP5A2 sub-machine gun. One group of GSG9 edged to take up position under the Boeing's wings and nose, another crouched beneath its tail plane. Ladders were propped gently against the aircraft, and magnetic charges placed around the passenger doors. In readiness by the ladders waited two men from Britain's 22 SAS Regiment on temporary attachment to GSG9. The grim faced leader of GSG9, Ulrich Wegener, watched all these preparations with anticipation. Many questions racing through his mind. But one question looped and looped – could he get all the 79 hostages and crew off the hijacked airliner alive? Or would it turn into another massacre like Munich?

Wegener had commanded GSG9 from its creation in 1972, and had striven from the outset to made GSG9, recruited from the border police, an elite amongst CRW units. Rigorously selected (75 per cent of candidates fail entry) and trained, GSG9 men were also equipped with some of the most sophisticated weapons in the world, Model 19.357 Magnum handguns and Heckler & Koch MP5A2 sub-machine guns, the latter often in its MP5SD silenced version. After years of painstaking rehearsal for the real thing, GSG9 was now having the chance to prove its value – the storming of a hijacked jet on the runway of Mogadishu airport on 18 October 1977.

Five days before, at 13.00 hours on 13 October, Lufthansa Flight LH181 had lifted off the runway at Majorca's Palma airport and set course for southern France. It never reached its destination. Four Palestinian liberationists, two men and two women, had smuggled guns aboard in their baggage and had proceeded to hijack the plane in mid-flight. Their principal object was to force the West German authorities to release members of the armed revolutionary organization, Baader-Meinhof. The Palestinians also demanded a £9 million ransom.

A wild career across the skies of Europe, the Middle East and the Horn of Africa then followed as the Palestinians sought a safe haven. Meanwhile, a minister of the West German government together with a member of GSG9 had flown to London. The minister wanted Britain to use its influence in Dubai, where the hijacked aircraft was about to land, to ensure diplomatic clearance for GSG9; the representative from GSG9 considered that the SAS might have some useful equipment and knowledge. It quickly became obvious to all that an SAS team attached to GSG9 for the duration of the hijack would be a distinct advantage. The two SAS men selected were Major Alistair Morrison, MC then second in command of 22 SAS and Sergeant Barry Davies, BEM, who commanded the CT sniper group. With them went a collection of "flash-bangs", the SAS-invented magnesium-based concussion grenades which have the shock effect of stunning the enemy for valuable seconds.

Morrison and Davies flew out to Dubai, where they found Wegener and two of his men under virtual arrest. No sooner was this problem sorted out, than the hijacked aircraft flew on to the Republic of Yemen, where it for a time enjoyed sanctuary. Then the leader of the Palestinian gang, Mahmoud killed the captain of the airliner, Jürgen Schumann, for communicating with the security forces. Now flown by the co-pilot, the Boeing proceeded to Somalia on 17 October. Wegener and the two SAS men followed. Time, however, was running out for the hostages.

At Mogadishu, Mahmoud threatened to blow up the aircraft unless all his demands were met. To emphasize his seriousness he threw the body of Schumann onto the tarmac. From that moment on there was no possibility of a peaceful outcome. As a ruse to gain a few precious hours the negotiators told Mahmoud that 11 Baader-Meinhof members were being released. Even as Mahmoud was given this misinformation the main body of GSG9 arrived from Turkey and Wegener began putting the operation to storm the airliner, codenamed "Magic Fire" and based on a plan by Morrison and Davies, into motion.

At 01.00 hours on 18 October, GSG9 marksmen and troopers armed with grenade launchers moved out into the desert. Morrison and Davies began preparing their 'fireworks'. The operation began at 01.50. While two hijackers on the flight decks were kept talking by the control tower, the assault teams and the two SAS men moved into their positions. At 02.07, 23 minutes before Mahmoud's final deadline, a flaming oil drum was rolled onto the runway in front of the aircraft. Ladders were placed against the doors and magnetic charges carefully put into place. Morrison and Davies climbed silently on to the wing and along to the emergency passenger door. As the terrorists watched the fire, there was a massive explosion. The passenger doors at the rear and front of the aircraft were blow in. So was the emergency door above the port wing. Through this the SAS men threw in their flash-bangs which exploded with a deafening roar. The GSG9 assault teams waited a second or two and then kicked in the passenger doors and stormed into the aircraft. A fierce gun battle followed as GSG9 troopers neutralized the Palestinians at the front and rear of the plane. Mahmoud flung two grenades that exploded harmlessly under the seats before being cut down by a burst from a Heckler & Koch. One of the women Palestinians ran into a lavatory, where she was shot in the head by Wegener. As Wegener and the SAS men had guessed, the hostages strapped in their seats would be safe below the line of fire. No hostages were killed in the exchange. Of the Palestinians, three were killed, one was taken prisoner. One GSG9 trooper was slightly wounded. The storming of the aircraft had taken just five minutes.

On their return to the 22 SAS camp at Hereford, Morrison and Davies extolled the virtues of the Heckler & Koch MP5A2 that they had just witnessed in action. Tests confirmed its superiority over the American Ingram sub-machine gun used by the SAS CT teams, and it became the choice of the Regiment. In addition to firing at a rate of up to 650rpm, the 9 mm Heckler & Koch MP5A3 can, if need be fire single shots. It is light (2kg) and short (32.5cm). The first time the "Hockler" was used in action by the SAS was just three years later, during the Iranian Embassy siege.

The Falklands War

William Aymes recounts the remarkable story of the SAS in the Falklands conflict.

When the going gets tough the tough, as the adage has it, get going. On Friday 2 April 1982 Argentina invaded the Falklands Islands, two small British specks of land almost lost in the vastness of the South Atlantic sea. Immediately on hearing the news – via a BBC newsflash – Lieutenant-Colonel Mike Rose, the CO of 22 SAS, put the Regiment on stand-by and offered its services to Brigadier Julian Thompson of 3 Commando Brigade, Royal Marines. If there was to be a British counter-attack, Rose reasoned, it was a near certainty that the Commando Brigade, trained in amphibious warfare, would be in the van of the assault. It was Rose's intention that the Special Air Service would share the burden of combat – and, dare say it, the future limelight of military history – in what might be Britain's last colonial war.

The SAS appeal fell on favourably inclinded ears. On 4 April, after SAS soldiers had been frantically summoned back from leave, training courses, even patrols in the bandit country of Northern Ireland, an advance party from D Squadron flew south to Ascension Island. By the next day the rest of D Squadron, together with all their kit, was also airborne for Ascension, a telling tribute to the efficiency of the quartermasters at Stirling Lines, the SAS's headquarters.

The Squadron's landfall was the British-owned base in the middle of the Atlantic, just below the Equator. Although 3,885 miles from the Falklands it was the nearest British territory of serviceable use. Hot and cramped, Ascension had little to recommend it, so it was with small regret that the 90 troopers of D Squadron found their sojourn quickly curtailed. Injured British pride and morale required, the government of Margaret Thatcher felt, some form of immediate and dramatic military action. The chosen target was Grytviken, the former whaling station on the island of South Georgia, 870 miles south-east of the main Falkland Islands group.

The execution of Operation Paraquet – soon corrupted to Operation Paraquat, after the branded weedkiller – fell to D Squadron 22 SAS, alongside part of M Company, 423 Royal Marine Commando ('The Mighty Munch'), and 2 Section of the SBS, some 235 men in all. On 21 April the small assault force, carried in HMS *Endeavour*, HMS *Antrim* and HMS *Plymouth*, came in sight of South Georgia, an ice-bound mountainous wilderness which formed, before the Argentinian occupation, the base for the British Antarctic Survey. Since little was known about the deployment of Argentinian forces on the island, Major Guy Sheridan RM, the commander of the assault force, ordered covert recces. The Mountain Troop of D Squadron was inserted by helicopter in near white-out conditions of driving snow. Carrying 77lb of kit and hauling heavily loaded pulks (sledges), the Troop inched down the Fortuna Glacier. After a night of hurricane-force winds, the Troop commander, Captain John Hamilton, had no choice but to request extraction. Three A/SW Wessex helicopters landed on the glacier and embarked the men, but on take-off one of the helicopters suffered a white-out and crashed. All the troopers and crew escaped alive and were redistributed to the other helicopters. On take-off another Wessex crashed, again without loss of life, but leaving 13 men stranded on the glacier. Overloaded and running low on fuel, the pilot of the third 'helo', Lieutenant-Commander Ian Stanley, RN, had no choice but to fly back to *Antrim*. Yet later that day, in a virtuoso flying display, Stanley returned to the blizzard-swept glacier, located the survivors and embarked them. The machine, dangerously overloaded, barely made it back to the ship, crash-landing on the deck. For his valour and professionalism, Stanley was awarded the DSO.

With the Task Force's helicopter capability reduced by two-thirds, the planners decided to launch D Squadron's Boat Troop. Two of their five Gemini inflatables suffered engine failure, but three crews managed to get ashore and set up watch on Leith and Stromness on the night of 22 April. Three days later Commander Stanley successfully inserted an SBS patrol a few miles from Grytviken. Flying back to *Antrim* he spotted on the surface of the sea the Argentinian submarine *Santa Fe*, which he immediately attacked, straddling her with a pair of depth charges. These inflicted sufficient damage to prevent her diving, and she was shortly afterwards attacked by helicopters from *Endurance* and the frigate *Brilliant*. The *Santa Fe*, listing badly, limped into Grytviken, where her condition and the sight of British helicopters in hot pursuit caused near panic in the 130-strong enemy garrison. Although Sheridan and D Squadron's commanding officer, Major Cedric Delves, could only immediately muster 75 men they decided to exploit the Argentinian's set-back. To the roar of supporting gunfire from *Antrim* and *Plymouth*, directed by a Royal Artillery commando offier, previously infiltrated ashore, an SAS composite Troop landed about two miles from the settlement, to be followed by two composite RM/SBS Troops.

Screened from Grytviken by a small mountain, the SAS struck out and began to advance on the port. Some elephant seals, mistaken for Argentinian troops, were shot-up and a suspected enemy position – demolished promptly by a Milan missile – turned out to be an ancient piece of scrap iron. These hazards negotiated, the Troop ascended to the top of Brown Mountain to find the buildings of the port below festooned with white flags. The garrison surrendered without a shot, Sergeant-

Major Gallagher of D Squadron wasting little time in hauling down the Argentinian flag and replacing it with the Union flag. To their incredulity the SAS assault party discovered, from an enemy soldier who could speak English, that they had walked, blithely unaware, through a minefield ringing the Argentinian weapons pits. The next morning, 26 April, two troops from D Squadron, together with an SBS team, took the peaceful surrender of the Leith garrison. South Georgia was once again in British hands.

While D Squadron had South Georgia on its mind, another Squadron from 22 SAS, G Squadron, had been sailing towards the war zone on the RFA *Resource*. Since little in the way of aerial or satellite pictures of Argentinian positions on the Falklands was available, G Squadron was earmarked for old-style 'eye-ball' reconnaissance. Beginning on 1 May, eight four-man SAS patrols were inserted by Sea King helicopter, an earlier plan to parachute them in being cancelled at the last moment. (Also scrapped was a plan to crash-land two C130 aircraft, packed to the roof with SAS troopers, on the runway at Port Stanley, the SAS troopers rushing out – so the planners hoped – to bring the war to a swift conclusion.) As ever, the SAS troopers went into action heavily loaded with equipment and weapons. Their bergens bulged with waterproofs, rations, communications equipment and ammunition, while everyone carried an American-made 66 mm Light Anti-tank Weapon (LAW) which, together with the XM 203 (an Armalite rifle with a pump-action grenade-launcher attached to the underside), was the flavour of the campaign. The recce teams were dropped up to 20 miles from their lying-up positions (LOPs), on reaching which they established a forward observation post (OP). This was manned by two men during the day, while the other two manned the main 'hide', ofter a mere shallow depression scraped into the featureless, windswept terrain and covered with ponchos. Life in the hides was unrelentingly grim, with little or no chance to brew up hot food or drink, and cold, wet weather that seeped into the bones. The record for enduring a hide was 28 days, set by Sergeant Mather and his team above Bluff Cove.

As well as discomfort, danger was always present. On 10 June an SAS hide was discovered by the Argentinians. Captain John Hamilton of D Squadron – who by then had rejoined the main Task Force – and his signaller were surrounded. In the firefight which ensued, Hamilton was killed trying to cover his comrade's escape. For his bravery Hamilton was awarded a posthumous Military Cross. On several occasions, SAS and SBS patrols ran into each other, opening fire until both sides realized their mistake. One such 'blue-on-blue' incident ended tragically, with the death of SBS Sergeant 'Kiwi' Hunt.

The recce teams, however, achieved conspicuous results. One four-man patrol led by G Squadron's Captain Aldwin Wight was tasked with observing Argentinian movements around Port Stanley, and accordingly established a hide on Beaver Ridge overlooking the port, an area heavily patrolled by the enemy. The SAS team discovered a night dispersal area for Argentinian helicopters between Mount Kent and Mount Estancia. When this intelligence was relayed back to the fleet, two Harrier aircraft attacked the site, destroying three enemy helicopters.

Besides reconnaissance, the SAS was tasked to carry out its quintessential activity of offensive raiding. An early target was the Argentinian airstrip on Pebble Island where, just before dawn on 21 May, 11 1A-58 Pucara aircraft were destroyed on the ground by the Boat Troop and Mountain Troop of D Squadron. The attack commenced with a blitz of LAW rockets, mortars and small-arms fire from the SAS, which was complemented by the guns of HMS *Glamorgan*. With the Argentinians forced into cover, the SAS moved onto the airstrip and fixed explosive charges to the planes. Within 15 minutes all 11 aircraft had been destroyed, with only one SAS casualty, a trooper hit by shrapnel in the leg. The SAS men were then picked up by Navy helos, who arrived on the dot, perfectly ending a textbook operation.

On the night before the main Task Force landing at San Carlos, the SAS mounted a sequence of diversionary raids. These included the landing of 60 men of D Squadron, who 'yomped' for 20 hours to reach the hills north of Darwin to attack the garrison at Goose Green. Their intention was to simulate a battalion-sized (600 men) attack, and accordingly they rained down a torrent of LAWs, Milan missiles, GMPG rounds and tracer into the Argentinian positions. Such was the ferocity of the barrage that the enemy failed to probe the SAS positions and could only manage sporadic return fire. By mid-morning, the main landing accomplished, the SAS disengaged from Goose Green, marching north to meet 2 Para as they made their way inland. *En route*, the SAS were intercepted by a Pucara ground-attack aircraft. Fatalities seemed certain, but as the plane approached an SAS trooper launched an American Stinger missile. He scroed a direct hit, the aircraft exploding into flames.

Over the next fortnight SAS patrols continued their recces and probing missions. At the end of May D Squadron seized Mount Kent, 40 miles behind enemy lines, and held it for several days until reinforced by 42 Commando Marines. This despite aggressive – and brave – patrolling from Argentine special forces, which resulted in a series of sharp nocturnal firefights. After their relief, D Squadron was in action again, with five teams landed on West Falkland. But the considerable enemy garrisons at Fox Bay and Port Howard responded vigorously and enjoyed excellent radio-direction-finding equipment. It was on West Falkland that Captain John Hamilton lost his life.

The other SAS patrols were more fortunate and escaped detection to call down regular barrages of naval gunfire. To its disappointment a patrol from B Squadron – which had recently joined the Task Force by way of parachute drop into the Atlantic – was tasked to ambush a reinforcement of the garrison at Fox Bay, but the enemy failed to turn up. By now it was becoming clear to all that the war was in its last days.

There remained one major SAS raid, which was mounted in East Falkland on the night of 13-14 June. To take the pressure off 2 Para, who were assaulting Wireless Ridge a few miles west of Port Stanley, the SAS volunteered to put in a raid to the enemy rear – from the sea. Two troops from D Squadron, one from G Squadron and six men from 3 SBS rode into Port Stanley harbour on high-speed Rigid Raiders with the aim of setting fire to the oil-storage tanks there. As troopers from the Regiment later conceded, the raid was more audacious than wise. The Argentinians opened up with every available weapon, including triple-barrelled 20 mm Rheinmetall anti-aircraft cannon depressed to their lowest trajectory. These spewed out a constant stream of glowing red metal which obliged the raiders to withdraw if they were not to suffer heavy losses.

The next morning, 14 June, it was all over. Their morale gone and their position hopeless, the Argentinians surrendered. British victory owed no small part to the men of 22 SAS. Fittingly, therefore, the surrender was effectively taken by the Commanding Officer of 22 SAS Mike Rose.

The campaign to liberate the Falklands brought fresh glories to the pages of Regimental history, but they had their price. A few days after the attack on Pebble Island a helicopter cross-decking members of D Squadron from HMS *Hermes* to HMS *Intrepid* hit something, probably a giant petrel, which got sucked into its air intake. The Sea King plummetted into the icy water with the loss of 20 SAS troopers and attached specialists, plus one of the aircrew. It was the heaviest loss the Regiment had suffered in a single day since the Second World War.

With the end of the campaign, the SAS returned home to Stirling Lines. As ever, the Regiment was shy of publicity, the men slipping back into barracks without fanfare or applauding crowds. None returned more secretly than the SAS teams who had been sent to operate on the Argentinian mainland, primarily to provide early warning of enemy aircraft taking off, although a large-scale raid of the Rio Gallegos airfield was set in motion but aborted at the last minute. The only real evidence of these clandestine operations is a burnt-out Sea King helicopter from a squadron attached to the Task Force which was discovered on the shores of southern Chile. Some secrets may never be told.

AMERICAN ARMY SPECIAL FORCES

The Green Berets

The US Army's Special Forces originated in the early 1950s and established a base at Fort Bragg, South Carolina, site of the Army Special Warfare School. America has a rich history of operations by unconventional forces, dating back to the French and Indian wars in the days when the 13 colonies were still British and including Rogers' Rangers who were active during the War of Independence.

A vast conglomeration of special operations units grew like mushrooms during World War II, but they were quickly disbanded after the war. Interest was revived in the 1950s following the Korean War, and that led to the formation of the Special Forces.

At the time they were kept at low strengths. They were only grudgingly tolerated by the traditionalist in the army's high command, who did not like any unit with pretensions to elite status. Army administrators discouraged officers who wanted to spend more than one tour with the Special Forces, on the basis that they would lose experience in their basic branch, and thus be unfavourably looked on at promotion time.

With the inauguration of President John F Kennedy in 1961 the fate of the Special Forces changed. Kennedy strongly believed that such units were the best way to counter communist 'wars of liberation'. As it became chic in Washington to support the 'Green Berets', so named because of their distinctive headgear which had been approved by the President, their numbers increased by several orders of magnitude.

The original Special Forces mission was to organise guerilla warfare in enemy-held countries. That role changed as more and more Green Berets were sent to South East Asia, where they became increasingly involved in counter-insurgency operations.

The Special Forces were among the first Americans in action

in Vietnam: the 5th Special Forces Group took over the CIA's border surveillance programme, teaching the fundamentals of reconnaissance and local defence to remote tribes in Laos and the Vietnamese highlands. Operating in small teams with large numbers of native auxiliaries, often only marginally less hostile to the government in Saigon than to the communists, they ran patrols from border camps to uncover communist infiltration on the Ho Chi Minh Trail.

In more settled parts of Vietnam the Green Berets were assigned as advisors by the US military authorities, to provide anything from advice on personal health and drainage to teaching unarmed combat and demolitions to members of the Civilian Irregular Defence Groups.

Following the end of the war in South East Asia, the Green Berets suffered under the general malaise which afflicted the US armed forces but the low intensity conflict that now prevails worldwide ensured that they would not be disbanded. In 1987 Special Forces were made a separate branch of the army, and their orders now come via the US Special Operations Command, which incorporates all special operations units from all US services.

Today's Green Berets retain their training function: Special Forces teams can be found passing on their skills to special operations units around the world. Most recently, they have been organising South American and South East Asian units as part of the US governments's worldwide anti drugs campaign.

Training and guerilla warfare is not the whole story, of course. Delta Force, the US Army's hostage rescue unit, is part of the Special Forces. Special Forces also have major roles in conventional high-intensity conflict. During the Gulf War, Special Forces reconnaissance teams penetrated deep into Iraq, keeping watch on Iraqi troop movements, hunting 'Scud' launching sites, laser-designating targets for coalition air power, and scouting out routes for the coalition's ground offensive. Along with their counterparts in other services and from other armies, the Green Berets played a vital part in the eventual success of the anti-Saddam coalition.

With the Green Berets in Vietnam

George Perkins was an enlisted Combat Air Controller in the US Air Force who served with a Special Forces team during the early days of the Vietnam War.

"From the time 'advisers' first went to Vietnam in 1961 until the American withdrawal in 1973, a small band of US Air Force men had the difficult task of directing close air support. The airmen spent much of their time on the ground and faced as much danger as infantrymen.

"In those days, they didn't have time for fancy training to make you a Combat Air Controller. They just stuck you in the bushes, slung a radio over your back and told you to do the job. The job, of course, involved directing aircraft in attacks against ground targets. Prior to that time it had always been customary for the Air Force to have its own men on the ground – right there with the footslogging GIs – to direct close air support.

"In 1961, I was one of three dozen NCOs selected to become Air Commandos, our service's answer to the Green Berets - another 'elite' unit personally backed by President Kennedy. In the tidal marshlands at Eglin Air Force Base near Fort Walton Beach on the west Florida coast we were training for a war most Americans hadn't yet heard about.

"I stepped off a C-124 at Saigon's Tan Son Nhut Airport on 21 October 1962 along with a dozen other guys from the original Air Commando contingent. We wore ANZAC campaign headgear – Australian hats with turned up brims which were to become the Air Commando symbol. We were a close-knit group. On the day of my arrival, the guys were talking about how the Viet Cong had shot down one of our number. Major Al Saunders. Luckily he'd been rescued under heavy fire. Al had been piloting a T-28, the primitive fighter-bomber we were teaching the Vietnamese to fly.

"I was sent down to the Delta to a Special Forces 'B'

Camp run by 34-year-old Major Ernest Trevor from Columbus, Georgia. Trevor was a gung-ho Green Beret. He liked us Air Force guys but doubted we'd be much use to him. He was wrong.

"On 1 November 1962, South Vietnamese troopers under Trevor's tutelage were ambushed by a surprisingly heavy Viet Cong force. They were pinned down in a deserted hamlet by withering fire from a high, thickly-vegetated slope. Men were getting killed all around us. Mortar shells careened into our midst, coughing up clods of earth and spraying shrapnel. Bursts of automatic gunfire whipped over my head as I snake-crawled towards the spot where Major Trevor and Captain Andy Stockwell were assessing the situation.

"I got on the radio. A flight of T-28s was in the area, ready to help out.

"Do your stuff', Stockwell urged, a little sarcastically. 'Get those 28s in here and plaster the Cong.'

'That's what I'm here for, sir. But it isn't that simple.'

'Huh?'

'We have to pinpoint the VC. All I see is muzzle flashes.'

"I got on the radio and confirmed with the T-28 flight leader that he was carrying napalm and rockets. He was using the callsign 'Straight Flush', and I recognized the voice of Captain John R Watkins, the 'wild man' of our Air Commando outfit. Watkins was supposedly 'advising' the South Vietnamese who piloted the three other T-28s, but that was sheer fiction. He was in command.

"I learned that Watkins had sufficient fuel, and I instructed him to wait a mile south of the battle zone. I rounded up two of Trevor's Vietnamese troops and we began hacking our way uphill from the hamlet, slicing through the brush with machetes. It was sheer hell, lugging that PRC-10 radio and a Colt-Armalite rifle – the weapon developed by the Air Force which would later become the standard M16. Then we literally walked into three stray Cong. They were spindly little men in black garb, lugging carbines. Less than three metres apart, we exchanged gunfire. I killed two, one of my men got the third. My other man, Corporal Diem was hit in the shoulder and thigh and was bleeding profusely.

"Damn!" I though aloud. 'We've got to get closer.'

"I assured Diem we'd be back. With Sergeant Tranh, I kept going uphill through heavy brush. The Muzzle flashes from VC weapons were closer now.

"Suddenly the radio crackled. 'This is Straight Flush. How are you doing down there?' Captain Watkins' words carried to the VC above us. Suddenly, they were shooting at us. Traneh and I hit the deck as grenades began exploding in the heavy foliage nearby. But we'd seen enough: a row of men hunched over their guns behind a

ARMALITE AR-15 (M-16) RIFLE

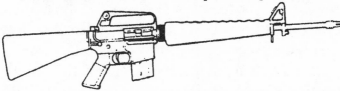

The AR-15 was one of the first of the modern 5.56-mm calibre rifles to enter service. Designed by Eugene Stoner in the late 1950s, the AR-15 made extensive use of pressed steel and plastic in its construction. Although it looked like a toy, it was a serious weapon. Firing high-velocity 5.56-mm ammunition, much smaller than the then standard 7.62-mm NATO round, it allowed soldiers to carry more ammunition into combat. It was designated M16 when issued to the US Air Force, and was to go on to achieve fame as the US Army's standard rifle in Vietnam. After initial reliability problems the M16 proved to be an effective battlefield weapon, and the current M16A2 variant is much improved.

Specification (M16A2)
Cartridge: 5.56-mm NATO; Weight: 4kg; Length: 1000mm; Cyclic rate of fire: 600 rounds per minute; Magazine: 20- or 30-round box; Effective range: 500m.

Assessment
Reliability ****; Accuracy ***; Age ****; Worldwide users ****.

straight barrier of sandbags on the ridge crest. There were at least 100 of them, far more than we'd thought.

"A grenade ripped off branches above my head. Shrapnel tore through my fatigues, slashing my arms, back buttocks. Tranh was cut up even worse. I clutched the radio desperately and cried out:

'Straight Flush, this is Amber Rose. Make a low firing pass from the south west over the village. Hit the slope three-quarters of the way up and give your bombs a 100 yard spread' Watkins couldn't believe it.

'Won't we be hitting you?'

'You'll be close. But if you don't do it quick we'll be cut to pieces.'

"I heard the whine of their engines as the T-28s dived and levelled off over the hamlet. Then the aircraft were roaring over our heads and silvery napalm bombs tumbled from their wings. The T-28s pulled away, leaving a fire storm sweeping over the ridge crest.

"Almost as an afterthought, one of the tiny fighter-bombers began spewing smoke. VC small arms fire had riddled its fuselage. The plane wobbled, fell and exploded against a hillside. Minutes later, it was all over. I came out, only mildly hurt, with Tranh and Diem. Trevor's men found 65 burnt corpses on the ridge crest – all Viet Cong. We had scored what the South Vietnamese would later call 'a great victory', but to me it was all a little sickening.

Son Tay

During the decade of direct US involvement in Vietnam, around 800 American military personnel were captured by the enemy, most of them USAAF aircrew shot down in raids over the North. The preferred tactic of the US Government was to negotiate the release of the captives (with occasional success), but in 1970 it decided to sanction more direct methods. This was the daring raid by Special Forces on Son Tay, the only attempt ever made to free prisoners held in the North, described here by Leroy Thompson.

It was only natural that such a task should fall to Special Forces. Formed in 1952 – although with a lineage dating back to the wartime Office of Strategic Services (OSS) – the Special Forces had been charged from the beginning with recovery operations, especially of downed pilots, in addition to their role as Unconventional Warfare (UW) experts. Initially, Special Forces – the 'Sneaky Petes' had been viewed with suspicion by the military establishment, but had grown in both size and stature after the inauguration of President J F Kennedy in 1961. In Vietnam, Special Forces were committed heavily – and often inappropriately – in the war, and the less than satisfactory outcome of that conflict for the US led the army subsequently to downgrade its commitment to unconventional warfare. After ill-starred roles in Iran, Grenada, El Salvador and at Paitilla airfield during the Panama invasion, Special Forces demonstrated their elite status in the Gulf, where their long range reconnaissance proved invaluable at identifying Scud missile sites.

When on 9 May 1970, an NCO of the USAF's 1127th Field Activities Group (1127th FAG), a special intelligence unit that correlated information about American POWs in North Vietnam, spotted what appeared to be a prison full of American POWs at Son Tay, some 37 km west of Hanoi from reconnaissance photographs, he started a chain of events that would eventually lead to one of the most daring Special Forces operations of the entire war. Once the Joint Chiefs of Staff had evaluated the information from the 1127th FAG and decided that a rescue was desirable, both for the well-being of the prisoners and for the morale of American fighting men and civilians, the go-ahead was given for SACSA (the Special Assistant for Counter-insurgency and Special Activities), Brigadier-General Donald Blackburn, to begin planning a rescue mission to free the POWs held at Son Tay.

Various photo-intelligence sources, including the Big Bird reconnaissance satellite, the SR-71 Blackbird and Buffalo Hunter reconnaissance drones, were also made available to gather the information necessary for the raid. By 5 June, a full briefing had been given to the Joint Chiefs, and Blackburn had received permission to continue planning the raid. A little over a month later, on 10 July, the Joint Chiefs gave Blackburn the

OK to begin implementing the plan. Blackburn, a real fire-eater who had commanded Philippine guerrillas during World War II and the Special Operations Group in Vietnam, wanted to lead the raid himself, but because of his knowledge of sensitive intelligence matters he was precluded. Instead the assignment went to Colonel 'Bull' Simons, a highly experienced Special Forces officer who had served under Blackburn and had a reputation for getting things done. The raiding force was known as the Joint Contingency Task Group (JCTG), and the mission itself was code named Ivory Coast. An area of Eglin Air Force Base in Florida was set aside for training the JCTG. Although Major-General Leroy Manor, the commander of USAF special operations at Eglin, was put in overall command, Simons was his deputy and in charge of leading the raiding force.

Since the optimum time for the raid appeared to be between 20-25 October, when the weather and moon would be most favourable, both men began selecting their teams: Manor, the air and planning elements, and Simons, the actual assault force. At Fort Bragg, hundreds of Special Forces troopers volunteered for the JCTG only knowing that it was hazardous and that the 'Bull' would be commanding. Some 15 officers and 82 NCOs, predominantly from the 6th and 7th Special Forces Groups, were chosen. As training progressed, the assault force, their backups and the support personnel would be selected from these 97 Green Berets.

To carry out realistic training, a mock up of the Son Tay compound was built at Eglin. So that Soviet spy satellites could not detect its presence, the mock up was designed to be dismantled during the day and quickly set up at night for training. Since the raid itself would be at night, training at night on the mock up was essential. As an additional training aid, a table top model of the camp, costing some $60,000, was also built.

Detailed training of the raiding force began on 9 September. Two problems involving the elimination of guards at the prison arose during this period. Simons was dismayed to find that even his best marksmen were having trouble getting more than 25 per cent of their shots on target at night. This difficulty was solved, however, by going outside the normal Army supply channels to acquire 'Singlepoint Nite Sites' for the sharpshooters' M16s. The other problem involved the need to saturate the guard towers around the Son Tay compound with fire. To solve this problem an HH-53 Super Jolly Green Giant equipped with 7.62mm miniguns was given the mission of chopping the towers down with a hail of fire.

The assault force was formed into three groups: the compound assault force of 14 men, who would actually be deposited inside the prison compound by crash landing an HH-3 helicopter; the command and security group of 20 men; and the support group of 22 men commanded by Simons himself. Five HH-53s, which could be refuelled in-flight and the HH-3 would carry the assault force.

REMINGTON 870

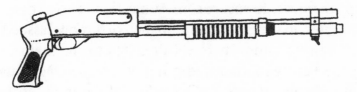

The Model 870 is one of the most widely manufactured shotguns of all time, being produced in sporting and hunting versions as well as in dedicated police and security variants. When the US Marine Corps conducted trials to find a combat shotgun in the mid-1960s, it was decided that the reliability of the 870's pump action gave it the edge over the semi-automatic weapons then available. The Model 870 has a seven-round tubular magazine and can fire a wide variety of ammunition ranging from light shot and riot rounds to heavy buckshot and flechettes. Its primary function in Marine hands is for use in boarding parties and as a security weapon aboard ship.

Specification
Cartridge: 12 gauge 2$\frac{1}{2}$-in; Weight: 3.6kg; Length: 1060mm; Cyclic rate of fire: pump action only; Magazine: 7 rounds in tubular magazine.

Assessment
Reliability *****: Accuracy **; Age ****; Worldwide users ****.

Beginning on 28 September, the assault force practised the actual assault with the air force crews who would fly the helicopters and other aircraft, which included three C-130s (two of which were Combat Talons equipped for command and control) and A-1 strike aircraft. The landing and assault were rehearsed again and again, with many simulations being 'live-fire' run-throughs. Alternative plans were also produced.

As the rehearsals progressed, Simons, a firearms enthusiast and expert ordered his supply people to come up with additional weapons and special equipment. Eventually, the teams were equipped with 12-gauge shotguns, 30-round M16 magazines, .45 automatic pistols, CAR-15s for the compound assault force, M-79 grenade launchers, LAWs, bolt cutters, cutting torches, chainsaws and special goggles. Some men carried cameras to record the prisoners' living conditions. Many items used in the raid had to be acquired outside of normal Army supply channels. To ensure communications during those critical minutes on the ground, the 56 men of Simons' assault force were given 92 radios: two AN-PRC-41s to maintain contact with the Pentagon via a radio link at Monkey Mountain in South Vietnam, 10 AN-PRC-77s for calling in air strikes, 24 AN-PRC-88s for communications between the various groups on the ground and finally, 56 AN-PRC-90 survival radios for escape and evasion.

Although the mission had not been approved by the target date of 20-25th October, Blackburn got the go ahead to begin moving personnel to Southeast Asia in preparation for the mission on 27 October. On 1 November, Blackburn and Simons, among others, left for Southeast Asia to lay the groundwork for the raid. By the 12th, both Blackburn and Simons were back in the States as the raiding force prepared to head for Thailand. Six days later, a few hours after the raiders had left for Takhli RTAFB (Royal Thai Air Force Base) in anticipation of receiving orders to carry out the raid, President Nixon gave the 'go' order. The weather and moon had to be right for the raid to take place and conditions were deemed acceptable on the night of 20/21 November.

On the evening of 20 November, the raiders were shuttled to

Udorn RTAFB from where the raid was launched at 2318 hours local time. Carrier aircraft from the *Oriskany, Ranger* and *Hancock* were also launched a couple of hours later, during the early morning of the 21st to create a diversion by staging a fake raid over Hanoi. At about 02.18 on the morning of 21 November, the raid itself began. As a C-130 flare ship illuminated the area with flares, the HH-53, code named Apple Three opened up on the guard towers of Son Tay Prison with its miniguns, bringing them crashing down.

Shortly thereafter, the HH-3 carrying the assault party commanded by Major 'Dick' Meadows, landed inside the prison compound: the whole group pressed against mattresses to cushion them against the crash. The HH-3, known as Banana One came to rest amid branches, leaves and other debris brought down by its whirling rotors during the crash descent. On landing, 'Dick' Meadows rushed out with his bullhorn shouting: "We're Americans. Keep your heads down. We're Americans. This is a rescue. We're here to get you out. Keep your heads down. Get on the floor. We'll be in your cells in a minute." The remainder of the assault party rushed into action, some men laying down suppressive fire, others streaking for the cellblocks to rescue the prisoners.

A few minutes later the command and security group landed just outside the prison's walls. The Support group led by Simons himself, however, had landed 400m off course at what was identified on the raiders' maps as a secondary school. Instead of a secondary school they found themselves outside a barracks housing Chinese or Soviet advisors to the NVA (North Vietnamese Army). School or not, though, Simons and his men proceeded to teach its denizens a lesson. Within minutes of touching down, many of the residents of the barracks had been killed, preventing them from reinforcing the prison compound and taking the other raiders by surprise. Within 10 minutes Simons had cleared the area and his men had been lifted back to the Son Tay compound, where they assisted the assault and security elements in eliminating several guards.

Despite the smoothness of the assault, however, the raiders discovered that there were no POWs in the prison. They had been moved elsewhere some weeks before the raid. This development had not been picked up by the US intelligence because no one had wanted to risk putting in any agents on the ground, and too much reliance had been placed on photographic intelligence.

Less than 30 minutes after the raid had started, the raiders were back on board their choppers and heading for Thailand. Casualties were light; only one raider had been wounded. The raid itself had gone almost perfectly. Even Simon's landing at the wrong complex was fortuitous as it allowed a surprise attack on an undetected enemy unit.

The raiders themselves had mixed reactions on the flight back to Thailand. They were disappointed that all of their training and effort had not resulted in the rescue of a single prisoner. However, they were also glad that they were all heading home, and justifiably proud of the precision with which the raid had been carried out.

The Son Tay raid was not a complete failure, despite the fact that no prisoners were rescued. It proved in very striking fashion that the North Vietnamese were vulnerable to attacks on installations close to home. As a result, the North Vietnamese had to tie down additional troops to guard sensitive areas, and they also lost some credibility with the Chinese and Russians, who feared that the US would continue to mount raids into North Vietnam. Indirectly the raid also led to some improvement in the treatment of American POWs.

It should not be forgotten, either, that Simon's party had killed dozens of the enemy, many of them foreign advisors, without taking any losses themselves. The Special Forces troopers, and the air force and navy pilots had carried out their jobs with great skill. It was a classic raid – get in quick, hit hard, get out fast, inflict maximum casualties – but the intelligence had been wrong, a failure which clearly illustrated the fact that intelligence is critical to special operations, especially raids into enemy territory. It is still not known why the North Vietnamese moved their prisoners from Son Tay, but it may be speculated that a rescue attempt was foreseen as the US were steadily building up pressure for their release.

The final point proven by the Son Tay raid was one that Donald Blackburn had been making ever since being appointed SACSA. He argued that North Vietnam was vulnerable to hit-and-run raids by highly-trained special operations forces. Other such raids might have secured the release of many of the American POWs held by the Hanoi government.

Delta Force

Surprisingly, the Unites States of America was slow to establish a specialist anti-terrorist and hostage rescue unit, although all too often it is Americans who are the victims of attacks. Perhaps the fact that terrorism is a phenomenon which is rarely encountered in the continental United States explains why the Department of Defense was three or four years behind European governments in setting up elite counter-revolutionary warfare units. It was not until November 1977 that Special Forces Operational Detachment Delta – Delta Force – came into being.

The driving spirit behind Delta Force was Colonel Charles Beckwith, a Special Forces officer who had been extremely impressed by Britain's SAS during an exchange tour in the early 1960s. For several years he badgered the Pentagon into setting up a similar unit in the US Army.

Selection for the new unit was very much SAS style, with hard physical, mental and psychological challenges weeding out nine out of 10 applicants. Once selected, the successful candidate is sent on a five month 'Operators' course, where he is introduced to the many and varied skills than an anti-terrorist commando is expected to master. These include assault tactics, hostage management, communications, observation using the latest high-tech gear, climbing, small boat work and parachuting. Since the majority of Delta Force candidates are from Special Forces or Ranger units they already possess many of these skills, but even so they learn a lot before moving to their operational troop.

Delta Force is organised into operational squadrons, each squadron is broken down further into troops. Marksmanship is a prime requirement in Delta Force and Force members train up to four hours a day, five days a week. Such intensive training leads to very high shooting standards: Delta snipers are expected to make nine first-round hits out of 10 at 1,000 yards, and score every time at 600 yards.

Like other elite counter-terrorist units, Delta Force has built its own 'House of Horrors' which simulates various kinds of combat situations, from hostage taking to aircraft hijacks. Hijacks are a favourite terrorist ploy, so Delta Force has practised assaults on airliners, and regularly runs training exercises at New York's Kennedy Airport and at other large international gateways.

Delta receives terrorist intelligence via US Government organisations such as the CIA, the Defense Intelligence Agency, the FBI, and from contacts with other anti-terrorist units around the world. Its members also make exchanges with the British SAS, Germany's GSG-9, the French GIGN and other similar units.

Delta was set up in less than a year, becoming operational in the middle of 1978. Just over a year later, the Force was alerted to a possible rescue mission as the US Embassy in Teheran was seized and the embassy staff held hostage. This was far from the mission they had trained for: penetrate hundreds of miles into hostile territory, making an assault in the middle of a major city and then getting clear with 100 or more freed hostages.

Months of intensive training went into 'Operation Eagle Claw', as the rescue mission was called. It was to involve Delta Force, Special Forces units from Germany, US Marine Corps helicopter pilots, US Navy helicopters and ships and US Air Force air support. It was all planned for the 25th April.

The mission was a disaster, although through no real fault of the men who took part. Command and control of the many disparate parts of the rescue operation were shambolic. The big MH-53 helicopters could not cope with the desert sand, and there were not enough of them. After three had broken down the mission had to be scrubbed. To add a final capper to the whole affair, a collision at the 'Desert One' airstrip deep inside Iran killed eight men and destroyed a C-130 and a helicopter.

Many lessons were learned from Operation Eagle Claw. The creation of the Joint Special Operations Command has given a single command body to clandestine operation units of all US services, and the formation of the Counter-Terrorist Joint Task Force (CTJTF) at Fort Bragg has significantly increased US capability in this specialised form of warfare. The CTJTF is a truly select formation, with elements from Delta Force, the US Navy's SEAL Team 6 and the US Army's highly secret Helicopter Task Force 160. The task force can also call on the aircraft of the USAF's 1st Special Operations Wing when necessary.

RUSSIAN ARMY SPECIAL FORCES

Spetsnaz

Special forces are by no means exclusive to the western powers. The Soviet Union had a number of elite units in the army, navy and marine branches of the military. These certainly survive in some form within the forces of the former Soviet countries, very possibly in virtually the same form. The account given below refers to the elite of the old Soviet elite, the Spetsalnaya Naznacheniya – the Spetsnaz.

Spetsnaz, the Soviets' special purpose troops came under the direction of the GRU and consisted of 16 Spetsnaz brigades, four Spetsnaz naval brigades, 41 independent Spetsnaz companies and the Spetsnaz regiments – the latter being available for senior commanders to use as the situation demanded. In peacetime, Spetsnaz numbered some 30,000 men; in the event of war or crisis those ranks could be expanded to 150,000.

The conscript collecting centres took in newcomers twice a year – in the winter period or the summer period. Your birthday dictated which one you attended as you were liable for service immediately after your 18th birthday. Women were not subject to compulsory military service, but were selected through KOMSOMOL and DOSAAF if they were interested in joining the Armed Forces.

At the centre, the conscript was interviewed and his documents scrutinised. Everything about a person was recorded. How did he do at school? Was he loyal to the communist system? Was he a party member? The all important KOMSOMOL and DOSAAF reports gave details of his fitness, military skills and determination.

At the top, the best were selected for the KGB, airborne, missile and intelligence units. A small number were selected for a unit they had never heard of – the Spetsnaz.

For the conscripts there were no weekends, and their day

LIFE AND DEATH TRAINING

Mobilised at short notice, to penetrate a defence base, troops are parachuted at night into a desolate region – such as Siberia – and are pursued by motorised infantry over vast distances. But the target is prepared for an attack and, during the raid, it is not unknown for young conscripts to be killed. The government of the Soviet Union was not answerable for deaths in realistic exercises, even in peacetime. This was the experience of troops on exercise as members of the Spetsnaz, the world's largest special forces organisation.

began at 06.00 hours with reveille, followed by strenuous exercises and an inspection before breakfast. Fit, strong, elite soldiers need food and they were well fed. Training then began in earnest, with the teaching and honing of military skills, including assault courses where the Soviet obsession with live firing tested the new soldier's mettle. From the very beginning live ammunition was used and accidents, even fatal ones were considered acceptable.

Those who fail to pass Spetsnaz training are sent to other units to complete their military service, knowing nothing of the elite unit they almost joined. At the end of the basic selection training course about 20 recruits were left from the original hundred in each group. The conscript was now a Spetsnaz soldier – but still with much to learn. He was constantly scrutinised by officers and senior NCOs.

The very best were selected for officer training, at a special Spetsnaz faculty at the higher airborne command school at Ryazan. They began four years gruelling training, which continuously tested them. Those who did not make the grade were re-assigned to airborne VDV units or the air assault troops.

Naval Spetsnaz consisted mostly of combat swimmers, supported by mini-submarines and specialist parachute troops. Based among Soviet naval infantry, each brigade had approximately 1,300 men (and an unknown number of women), which made the Soviet navy's Spetsnaz by far the largest amphibious special force in the world. Within the overall

Spetsnaz organisation the naval brigades were far more active than their army counterparts.

The Spetsnaz were well blooded in Afghanistan. From the numbers of them reported in action, it seems that they were often rotated to ensure that most special forces soldiers will have seen active service at some stage. It was difficult to distinguish Spetsnaz from Airborne troops in Afghanistan, but Mujahideen reports did identify Spetsnaz from their numbers and from the fact that they operate by local command decisions rather than waiting for higher authority to give orders.

In action, Spetsnaz proved themselves to be hard and well-trained troops, and were the only ones that the Mujahadeen

MIL MI-26 'HALO'

In Afghanistan Spetsnaz fought in large groups, exploiting the carrying capacity of the Halo. Marginally smaller than the 'Hook' but with a payload half as large again, the Mil Mi-26 'Halo' is the heaviest, most powerful helicopter in the world. Its clamshell rear loading doors open on to a cargo hold with the size and carrying capacity of the C-130 Hercules transport aircraft. It was the first helicopter in the world to be equipped with an eight blade main rotor, and it has been fitted with sophisticated avionics and navigation systems, allowing for auto-hover as well as day and night operations. The 'Halo' is currently in service with the Soviet armed forces and in India.

Specification
Length overall: 40.03m; Rotor diameter: 32.00m; Maximum cruising speed: 137 knots; Range: 800km; Load: 90 troops or 20,000kg underslung.

Assessment
Manoeuvrability **; Robustness *****; Versatility **; Worldwide users *

encountered who thought for themselves. They were even know to kill their own wounded rather than let them fall into the hands of the enemy. But this has been a common practice among opponents of the Pathans for many years – the fate of captured wounded was usually beyond description.

In both Czechoslovakia and Afghanistan the first Spetsnaz units on the ground were from the 'anti-VIP' companies, whose ruthless, systematic murder showed them to be a formidable force. Follow up units were from army Spetsnaz who took the war to the Mujahideen in the mountains.

Entry to the 'anti-VIP companies was for those soldiers who decided to remain in the Spetsnaz after their two years of conscription. They underwent additional training, with languages a priority. These units could be expected to make use of enemy uniforms and weapons and in many cases, especially in the preparatory phase before a formal declaration of war, they were intended to operate wearing civilian clothes.

TACTICS AND TECHNIQUES

ARCTIC ENVIRONMENTS

Basic Survival Requirements

Survival in Arctic and sub-Arctic conditions is survival against constant attack. Day and night, without respite, the cold lays siege to your body. There is no let-up; staying alive requires attention to detail for 24 hours a day. Clothes, shelter and food are your major weapons against the cold – plus a strong will to survive. Without the will, the battle is already lost.

Air temperatures of –40°C and wind velocities of 30 knots are common in Arctic and sub-Arctic terrains. In these conditions, without clothes, you would be dead in about 15 minutes.

CLOTHING

The most effective clothing provides a system of layers that trap warm air to form an effective insulation. If you are caught out in Arctic conditions due to vehicle failure, air-crash etc. improvise layered clothing and insulation.

Outer-shell garments should be windproof. Arctic conditions are usually dry, and waterproof outers (unless they are of 'breathing' material such as Gore-Tex) should be avoided, as they cause condensation to build up inside, soaking your inner garments.

Many fabrics lose their insulating efficiency when they are wet. Goose and duck down, very popular in dry-cold outer garments, clump disastrously when wet, losing the 'lofted' air spaces that give them their insulating qualities.

Cotton garments and kapok quilt fittings also become heavy and cold. Wool, on the other hand, functions well when wet, as do a range of modern synthetic materials such as polyester, which can be woven into single-layered clothing, used as quilting fillers, or processed into thick piles and fleeces which have the added advantage that they 'wick' moisture away from inside layers.

The effort expended in keeping warm should be regulated carefully to avoid overheating and sweating. Chopping a tree down to make a shelter could be a fatal expenditure of energy, burning up vital resources and soaking clothing with perspiration.

KEEP CLOTHING DRY

In cold temperatures, your inner layers of clothing can become wet from sweat and your outer layer, if not water-repellEnt, can become wet from snow and frost melted by body heat.

Wear water-repellent outer clothing, if available. It will shed most of the water collected from melting snow and frost. Before entering a heated shelter, brush off the snow and frost.

Despite the precautions you take, there will be times when you cannot avoid getting wet. At such times, drying your clothing may become a major problem. On the march hang your damp mittens and socks on your pack; sometimes the wind and sun will dry this clothing. Or you can put damp socks or mittens, unfolded, near your body so that your body heat can dry them.

In bivouac, hang damp clothing inside the tent near the top, using drying lines or improvised racks. You may even be able to dry each item by holding it before an open fire. Dry leather items slowly. If no other means are available for drying your boots put them between the sleeping bag shell and liner. Your body heat will help to dry the leather.

10 Key Clothing Tips

1 Underclothing:

This should be a polypropylene shirt and pants: the material allows ventilation, the zip is shielded from the skin, the cuffs can be extended over your wrists, and a broad tail on the shirt prevents a gap when you bend over.

2 Thermal clothing:

This is your second layer and is ideally a 'duvet' jacket with hood and salopettes. This type of clothing should not be worn when on the move unless it is extremely cold.

3 Combat shell clothing:

The third layer is usually a windproofed camouflaged smock

and trousers, loose and baggy and so trapping a layer of 'dead' air that is warmed by your body. The trouser legs open on the outside from ankle to knee to permit them to be removed without taking your boots off.

4   **Waterproof clothing:**

This fourth layer should ideally be made of Gore-Tex which is waterproof but allows body heat condensation to escape. It should not be the top layer when the temperature is at or below freezing point because escaping condensation will form an ice shell that will lower your body temperature.

5   **Over-whites:**

The fifth and top layer is a set of lightweight oversmock and trousers. When the weather is not too bad, this can be the top layer omitting the camouflage smock and water-proofs.

6   **Cap comforter:**

Elite units prefer a dark coloured wool watch cap but on issue are cold weather caps with protective flaps. Balaclavas and ski masks are also used, but remember that when your ears are covered your hearing – the first line of defence against the enemy – will be impaired.

7   **Eye protection:**

Wear polarized sunglasses on bright days. As extra protection in wind and snow you will need goggles.

8   **Mitts:**

Must be worn to prevent frostbite and especially when you have to touch anything metal. Mitts have a special trigger finger so that you can fire your weapon. Link one mitt to the other by a cord through the sleeves of your smock so that you can take them off without losing them.

9   **Socks:**

Feet must be kept dry. Wet socks should be changed as soon as possible and dried.

10 **Boots:**

These should be well insulated and should preferably be

sealed with Gore-Tex gaiters. Wash the boots inside and out once a month.

FROSTBITE

The prime dangers of cold-weather conditions are frostbite and hypothermia, as the cold strikes at both the outer and inner body. Your extremities – hands, feet, ears and nose – are particularly susceptible to frostbite, but any exposed skin is at risk, and the risk is multiplied by wind speed.

The wind-chill factor transforms modestly-cold temperatures into deadly, tissue-destroying assaults on the body. An 18 mph wind in a 9.5°C temperature results in a –23.3°C wind-chill temperature. At wind chill temperatures below –6°C exposed flesh freezes in 60 seconds or less. An ambient temperature (measured by thermometer) of –28.8°C is converted by a 35 mph wind into a deadly –59.4°C wind chill temperature. At this level, flesh freezes in 30 seconds.

Removing a mitten long enough to undo clothing and urinate can result in frostbitten fingers. Deep frostbite which can result in lost fingers, toes or even limbs, kills by incapacitating the victim. But gangrene can also easily set in, and that will indeed see you off unless you get medical help.

The first sign of frostbite may be a waxy whiteness on the skin. Keep a close eye on your companions for these patches. If

---

TEMPERATURE CONVERSION

Most of the world's military use the Celcius scale, but some readers may be more familiar with Fahrenheit. Here are some approximate conversions.

50°C	120°F
30°C	90°F
20°C	70°F
10°C	50°F
0°C	32°F
–10°C	15°F
–20°C	–5°F
–30°C	–20°F

PREVENTING FROSTBITE

It is easier to prevent frostbite or to stop it in its early stages than to thaw out and take care of badly-frozen flesh.

1 Wear enough clothing for protection against cold and wind.

2 Clothing and equipment must not restrict the circulation.

3 Do not touch cold metal or oils at extreme low temperatures.

4 Avoid unnecessary exposure to strong winds.

5 Exercise the face, fingers and toes to keep them warm and to detect any signs of numbness.

6 Watch your mate/buddy for any signs of frostbite, he should do the same for you.

7 Thaw any frozen spots immediately.

you are on your own periodically feel your face and ears for the typical numbness.

If you encounter frostbite, rub snow onto the area until the whiteness or numbness disappears. Alternatively, gently compress the affected area with a warm hand. Do not rub the frostbitten area directly; you are likely to break the skin, leading to an open wound and infection.

Hypothermia

Hypothermia occurs when the temperature of the inner body-core, which houses the vital organs, falls below 35°C. The normal inner body temperature is 36.8°C.

As hypothermia sets in, movements slow up, thought processes are dulled, and you begin to lose co-ordination. You're dying on your feet, though you probably won't know it. Your speech becomes slurred. When your body temperature falls to 25°C and below, death is almost inevitable.

One of the best ways of dealing with hypothermia is to put the victim naked inside a sleeping bag with another person, also naked. A second person can also administer the warm sweet drinks (such as honey, dextrose, sugar or cocoa) and food necessary for recovery. DO NOT FORCE AN UNCONSCIOUS PERSON TO DRINK

If you manage to get back to civilisation, the hypothermia victim can be immersed in a warm bath. But start with the trunk area first, otherwise there's a risk of cardiac arrest and shock.

A victim will also need some time to recover, because the attack will have profoundly affected the circulatory system.

TRENCH FOOT

Trench foot and immersion foot result from many hours or days of exposure to wet or damp conditions at a temperature just above freezing. The feet become cold and swollen and have a waxy appearance. Walking becomes difficult and the feet feel heavy and numb. The nerve and muscles suffer the most damage but gangrene can also occur in extreme cases and it may become necessary to have the foot or leg amputated.

The best preventative is to keep the feet dry. Carry extra socks with you in a waterproof packet. Wet socks can be dried against the body. Wash your feet daily and put on dry socks.

DEHYDRATION

In cold weather bundled up in many layers of clothing, you may be unaware that you are losing body moisture. Your heavy clothing absorbs the moisture, which evaporates in the air. You must drink water to replace this loss of fluid. Your need for water is as great when it's cold as when it's hot.

One way to tell if you are becoming dehydrated is to check the colour of your urine in the snow. If it makes the snow dark yellow, you are becoming dehydrated and need to replace body fluids; if the snow turns light yellow or remains normal, you're OK.

There's a condition called 'cold diuresis' which is an increased output of urine caused by exposure to cold. It decreases body fluids, which must be replaced.

SUNBURN

Exposed skin can become sunburned even when the air tem-

AVOID OVERHEATING

When you get too hot, you sweat and your clothing absorbs the moisture. This affects your warmth in two ways; dampness decreases the insulating quality of clothing and as sweat evaporates your body cools.

Adjust your clothing so that you do not sweat. You can do this by partially opening your parka or jacket, by removing an inner layer of clothing, by removing heavy mittens or by throwing back your parka hood or changing to lighter head cover. The head and hands act as efficient dissipators when overheated.

perature is below freezing; the sun's rays reflect at all angles from snow, ice and water. Extra sensitive areas of skin are the lips, nostrils and eyelids. You should apply sunburn cream or lip salve whenever you are out in the sun.

You can get sunburn more easily at high altitudes during the same time of exposure to the sun.

SNOW BLINDNESS

This is caused by the reflection of ultra-violet rays caused by the sun shining brightly on a snow covered area. The symptoms of snow blindness are a gritty feeling in the eyes, pain in and over the eyes that increases with eyeball movement, eyes watering and becoming red and a headache, which intensifies with continued exposure to light.

SNOW BLINDNESS

It is vital to protect your eyes in bright sun and snow. Wear your sunglasses. If you don't have any, improvise. Cut slits in a piece of cardboard, thin wood, tree bark or other available material. Putting soot under your eyes will reduce glare.

Prolonged exposure to these rays can result in permanent eye damage. To treat snow blindness, bandage the eyes until the symptoms disappear.

You can prevent snow blindness by wearing sunglasses.

CONSTIPATION

If you put off relieving yourself because of the cold, eat dehydrated foods, drink too little liquid and have irregular eating habits, you may become constipated.

Although not disabling, constipation can cause discomfort. Increase your fluid intake to at least two quarts per day and eat fruits, if available and other foods that will loosen your bowels. Eating burnt wood and charcoal may help!

HYGIENE

Although washing yourself daily may be impractical and uncomfortable in a cold climate, you must do it. Washing helps to prevent skin rashes that can develop into more serious problems.

In some situations, you may be able to take a snow bath. Take a handful of snow and wash your body where sweat and moisture accumulate, such as under the arms and between the legs, front and rear, and then wipe yourself dry.

If you cannot bathe, periodically wipe yourself dry in these areas. If possible wash your feet daily and put on clean, dry socks. Change your underwear at least twice a week. If you are

---

KEEP CLOTHING CLEAN

This is always important from the standpoint of sanitation and comfort; in winter, it is also important for warmth. Clothes matted with dirt and grease lose much of their insulation quality. If the air pockets in clothing are crushed or filled up, heat can escape from the body more readily.

A heavy down-lined sleeping bag is one of the most valuable pieces of survival gear in cold weather. Make sure the down remains dry. If wet it loses a lot of its insulation value.

unable to wash your underwear, take it off, shake it and let it air out for an hour or two.

If you are with natives or are using a shelter that has been used before, check your body and clothing each night for lice. If your clothing has become infested, use insecticide powder if you have some. Otherwise, hang your clothes in the cold, then beat and brush them. This will help get rid of the lice, but not their eggs, which will persist in the folds of your clothes.

SHELTER
Treeline Survival

The Arctic terrain of, for example, northern Norway restricts freedom of movement and is well suited to defence by small units. On the other hand transport of logistic support and reinforcements is very difficult. Even if you do receive re-inforcements you sill still be heavily outnumbered by enemy forces, and so there is a good chance that either alone or with your unit, you will find yourself in a struggle for survival as you try to evade the enemy.

If you are in the treeline, you may find that the snow is not deep enough to build snow shelters, but you can make brush-wood shelters. There are five basic designs which you can adapt to suit your purpose or the conditions:

1   Single lean-to shelter
2   Double lean-to shelter
3   Wigwam style shelter
4   Tree pit shelter
5   Fallen tree shelter

Basic building rules

The lean-to designs are the simplest, but the wigwam is the best, warmest and most comfortable. The tree pit and fallen tree are best used in tactical situations. If you have these basic designs in your mind, you can adapt them to most circumstances.

Build the main wall with its back to the prevailing wind, and weave it thickly with whatever wood or branches are available. A small wall can be built downwind to provide reflection for the heat from a fire. You can use snow to reinforce the woven wall, but it should not go too high up or it will melt into the 'bivi' from the roof.

If possible, dig down to ground level for the fire. If this is impossible, build a good solid firebase of mixed layers of logs, snow and brushwood. You can burn an open fire in all types of brushwood shelter except the tree pit, in this case the walls are inclined to melt back and the 'bivi' collapse.

The single lean-to shelter

The only problem with these shelters is that you must have a knife, saw or axe. The Eskimos have shown that with a knife you survive; without one you need a miracle.

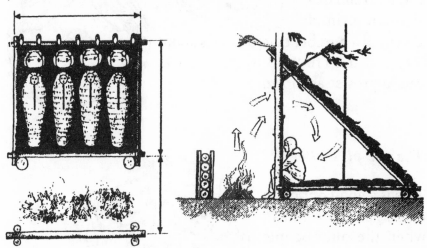

When building this lean-to make sure it is tactically located so that you can build a fire large enough to spread the warmth equally without the shelter. The shelter is improved by using a reflector of green logs with the fire.

With the reflector correctly placed, the warm air from the fire should circulate as shown. It is vital the sleeping shelf is insulated from the ground as without it you will rapidly lose body heat to the ground.

The double lean-to shelter

A larger group will be able to produce the more ambitious double lean-to which is a lot warmer than the single lean-to. It consists of two singles with the high, open sides facing each other across the fire. The fire reflector is not required. As with the single lean-to side walls can be added.

Teepee or wigwam shelters

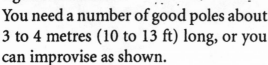

This is a tent construction which can be easily built using a parachute (paratepee). It is possible to cook, eat, sleep and make signals from inside. You need a number of good poles about 3 to 4 metres (10 to 13 ft) long, or you can improvise as shown.

The tree-pit shelter

This is a good option in an evasion environment when the only people looking for you are the enemy. The only drawback is that a fire tends to melt the walls and cause a collapse.

The fallen tree shelter

This is a mixture of the teepee and the tree-pit solutions and its design will contain greater of lesser elements of each according to the circumstances.

MAKING A FIRE IN THE ARCTIC

The skill to make a fire means the difference between death and survival. You should have waterproof matches in your kit.

1 Dig down to the frozen earth for your firebase. If this is not possible, build a base of logs over the snow. You need a layer of brushwood, a layer of snow, then another layer of each, finally topped off with good thick layers of logs.

2 Build your fire on this base

3 Use tinder to start the fire. If tinder is a problem, you can always find dry spruce twigs in the lowest branches, peel off birch bark, or use fir root. All contain high concentrations of tar and burn with a long-lasting flame. Fir root is especially good.

4 If you need to use fuel to help the fire along, dip your twigs in it and soak them. Don't waste fuel by pouring it on.

5 Use dead tree logs as the main fuel. It burns best.

TENTS AND TENTSHEETS

Tents can sleep five or 10 men and are large and bulky; they tend to be used in base areas, and generally have to be carried on a vehicle or on a 'pulk' – a man-towable sledge. The tents used by British forces are the Canadian single-pole or British ridge tent.

If you are working in small groups, you will not be able to carry a tent, so you will each carry at tentsheet. In its simplest form this is a diamond of canvas with buttons and buttonholes on each edge. They can be joined together to form a tent

THE TENTGROUP COMMANDER'S DUTIES

As commander, it is your responsibility to plan and organize the following:

1 Correct pitching of the tent or tentsheets
2 Allocation of sleeping space
3 Storage of weapons and equipment
4 Sentry roster and alert states
5 Routine for drying clothes
6 Fire precautions
7 Blackout drills
8 Track and camouflage discipline
9 De-icing of tent
10 Foot inspections
11 Overall welfare of your men

of almost any size, but normally it would be for eight to 10 men; the tent group.

Tentsheets give you a portable, windproof, lightproof, robust and flexible system that meets all the needs of survival and tactics. It takes time to construct a shelter using tentsheets, and you will need to be able to do it quickly when the temperature is 20° below freezing, so practise now. And learn to live in it.

Siting and pitching your tent

The tentgroup commander will direct this very simple drill for pitching a tent.

1 **Select the best site**

   Look for shelter from wind and the enemy, and make sure the snow is deep enough to dig your shelter in.

2 **Stow your kit**

   This should be neatly stowed to one side, normally to the left of the intended doorway.

3 **Level the site**

   Level to near ground level. The tentgroup commander will designate the area to dig.

4 Find insulation

At the same time, designated men find brushwood and undergrowth to use as insulation.

5 Install cooking kit

The designated cook unpacks the cooking kit, lights the stove and gets the rations ready for cooking. The lamp is lit.

6 Lay the tent

The tent is laid out with the door positioned away from the enemy (and, ideally, away from the prevailing wind) so that they will not be able to see any light.

7 Raise the tent

Peg the edges down and raise the tent on its own poles, if you have them; otherwise use brushwood poles. Do not use your skis or sticks except in an emergency. The cook takes the lamp, cooker, rations etc into the tent.

8 Settle in

Weatherproof the edges of the tent with snow (thrown over brushwood, which prevents icing and allows easy dismantling). The cook begins to heat the water (use clean, fresh snow, stored in plastic bags). Pass in sleeping mats and bags and lay them out. Make sure the floor is flat: or everyone will slide during the night and lose sleep, and the snow will harden into uncomfortable lumps. Dig a cold hole by the door.

9 Food and warmth

By now it will be pretty warm from the stove and the lamp. Two men will finish off the outside ski pit, weapons rack, fuel pit and latrine, but everyone else is thinking about food and admin, such as weapon and equipment maintenance. When you have eaten, night routine will begin.

It's −20°C but you have got your drills right and so you kept warm while the shelter was erected. Now you're inside you're comfortable in your shirtsleeves! It only took 15 minutes – and that's as good as a fully trained Arctic soldier

Once the tent is up, your immediate priority is camouflage.

Issue white netting gives good cover, but you must use poles to distort its outline and to avoid shadows formed by the shape of the tent. Snow walls around the tent provide cover as well as protection from the elements. The fighting position can be camouflaged with a few branches to minimize the shadow of the trench from the air.

The two-man tentgroup

The tentsheet is the basic unit from which you can make a simple two-man tent, using two sheets. Kit layout is all important. These tents are extremely cramped and you must decide where everything is stored so that you can move out at speed and your oppo can pack your kit when you are not there.

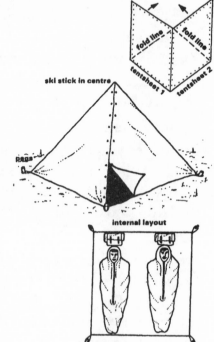

The four-man tentgroup

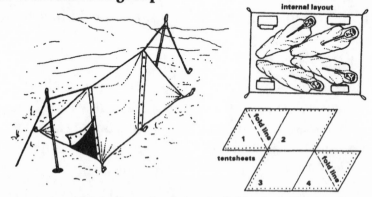

The ways in which the tentsheet is folded and joined to produce different-size tents is not obvious and must be thoroughly practised in dry training before you get out on the ground. Each man in the section must have an exact 'job description' so that the tent is erected as a drill.

TENTGROUP STORES

The commander must make sure that the following are carried, and that they work.

1. Pulk
2. Tent (5 or 10 man)
3. Snowshoes (if not being worn)
4. Snow shovels (2)
5. Stove and spares (2)
6. Pressure cooker
7. Lantern with case plus spares, including mantlets (1 or 2)
8. Machete (gollock) and case
9. Saucepan
10. Fuel funnel
11. Fuel containers: 2-gal, 1-gal or half-gal
12. Ski/pulk repair kit

Alternatives are:

1. Tentsheets (1 per man)
2. Fuel containers, 1 or 2 pint (5)
3. Two-man stoves (1 per 2 men)

Note: The amount of fuel carried will depend on the time to be spent in the field.

The five-man tent group

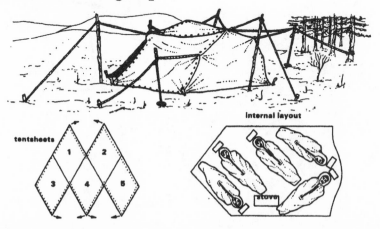

This is the usual half-section or fireteam layout complete with stove. Ideally you should not use ski poles in the construction of the tent as you may need them in a hurry.

TENTGROUP ROUTINE

The group will evolve its own routine depending on tactical conditions, but the commander and cook always sleep by the door. Cooking is also done by the door (in case of fire and to allow moisture to escape) or in the cold hole. Other points for comfortable tent life are:

1 **Control your kit**
   You will be cramped, so keep your kit packed unless you need it. Don't lose your gloves or hat.

2 **Keep clothes dry**
   Dry damp clothing by hanging it in the ceiling of the tent. When the heat is off, take it into your sleeping bag; this includes your boots.

3 **Check your feet**
   Your and your buddy should help each other to do this. Powder them and put on dry socks. If your feet are cold, rub them or, even better, warm them in your buddy's armpits! If they are seriously cold, don't rub them; just use the armpit method.

The seven-man tentgroup

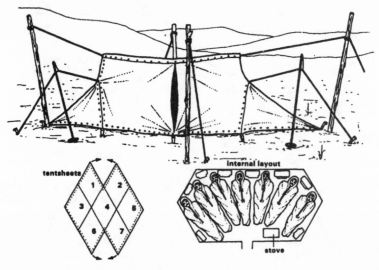

Everyone's feet face the door and the cook sleeps next to the stove. If you are operating a sentry stag, make sure the stag list is written so that the sentry wakes up the person who sleeps next to him, which means sentries do not have to trample over people looking for the next man on the stag list.

Layout of the eight-man tentgroup

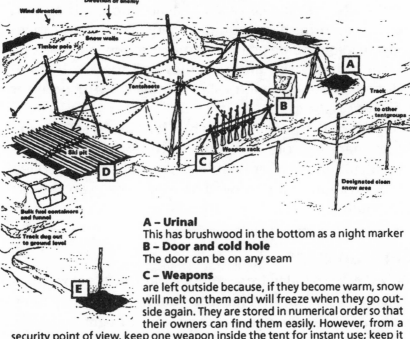

A – Urinal
This has brushwood in the bottom as a night marker
B – Door and cold hole
The door can be on any seam

C – Weapons
are left outside because, if they become warm, snow will melt on them and will freeze when they go outside again. They are stored in numerical order so that their owners can find them easily. However, from a security point of view, keep one weapon inside the tent for instant use; keep it free from snow.

D – Skis
are stored horizontally in a pit, again in numerical order, with brushwood or poles underneath so that they do not freeze to the snow. The pit will absorb any new snow during the night, leaving the skis exposed so that you will be able to find them.

E – Latrine
This is marked with brushwood and pole to make sure it can be found after a snowstorm.

Striking your tent or tentsheet

This is not difficult, but you must get it down to a fine art; you'll get cold if you find yourself standing around. Work out how long it takes you; this is your 'pull pole' time. It should be around 15 minutes when properly practised. This will help you make plans to go straight from the tent to work that keeps you warm.

Brush off ice and snow before packing away or you will be carrying unnecessary weight and it will take you longer to put the shelter up again.

THE JELPER SLEDGE AND GPMG PULK

The Jelper Sledge is the equivalent of the stretcher. It is the Arctic method of casualty evacuation, although it is also used for carrying light loads. The central sheet has an idiot's guide on how to make up the Jelper Sledge from ordinary skis and ski poles and the kit. It is designed to use one man's ski kit in its construction, for obvious reasons.

A specialist pulk is available for the GPMG in the sustained-fire role and enables the weapon and the huge quantities of ammunition it requires to be pulled into position and deployed at speed. You can fire off the pulk.

SNOW SHELTERS

You've been separated from your kit, but you've got your first- and second-line survival kit with you. It's a long way to base camp and there's only just over an hour of light left. A light snow is beginning to fall, and the wind's come up, but it's not too bad yet.

You haven't got a tent. You're facing the prospect of a night in the open in worsening conditions. This is an emergency survival situation. Stay calm. Think. You've got a number of options, and you've practised them all. And best of all, you've got your rations!

Shelters made of snow

The simplest way of building a shelter is to use snow. You can make a snow grave, a snow hole or an igloo; all three are better than a tent. Make sure the entrance is lower than the sleeping bench; this will trap the warm air in the living space near the ceiling. Even a burning candle will keep the temperature at about 0°C.

Always smooth off the ceiling to prevent dripping. This, though, will make the shelter airtight, which can lead to lack of oxygen especially if you are using a cooker, so punch a ventilation hole using a ski stick.

Keep a shovel in the shelter to dig yourself out if it blizzards or if the cave collapses; if the temperature is above freezing the snow conditions will not be quite right and the roof may start to fall in. For this reason, don't practise building snow shelters unless it's below freezing point.

Snow Trenches

You need about one metre of snow – the deeper the better – into which you dig a simple trench. Make the bottom wider than the top, especially if there are two of you. If it's not quite deep enough build up a bit at the sides.

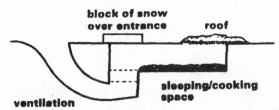

block of snow over entrance

roof

ventilation

sleeping/cooking space

Side view of a snow grave. Dig a trench, then make a tunnel from one end running back to the surface.

Now smooth off the sleeping bench, insulating it with brushwood, if you don't have your sleeping mat with you. Then dig a cold hole next to the door; this acts as a sump for the cold air. Then dig an entrance and move your kit inside, and put the roof on. This can be tricky, especially if your trench is too wide. The simplest way if the snow is compact, is to cut blocks and place them over the top, then add more snow. If you find you need support for the snow blocks use brushwood or tentsheets.

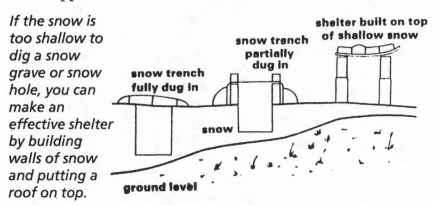

If the snow is too shallow to dig a snow grave or snow hole, you can make an effective shelter by building walls of snow and putting a roof on top.

snow trench fully dug in

snow trench partially dug in

shelter built on top of shallow snow

snow

ground level

You can use skis, but only as a last resort: if you do, put them in upside down, as this helps to stop them freezing in. Then add more snow.

Snow hole or snow cave

If there are two or more of you, you need a large bank or drift of snow about three metres wide and two metres deep. An avalanche probe will come in handy to gauge depth. Put on waterproofs if you have them as you will get wet.

There are two methods of digging: the tunnel method, and the block and cave method. The latter can be used when the snow is compact enough to be cut in blocks. Dig along the full length of the intended cave, using as many men as will fit, while one digs the entrance off to the side.

Once you have dug the sleeping benches, build up the open

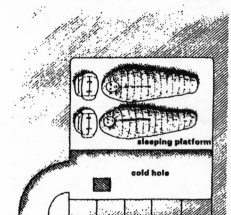

Block and cave method (top view)

The men sleep together on the raised sleeping platform, taking advantage of shared bodily warmth.

Tunnel method (top view)

You can build a raised sleeping platform to one side of the trench or, in this case, on both sides.

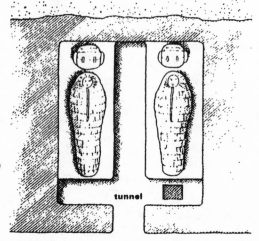

side of the cave with the excavated snowblocks until it is sealed in. Only the entrance remains open.

Using the tunnel method, only one man can work until the building of the sleeping benches is started; it therefore takes much longer than the block and cave method.

Snow house (igloo)

The igloo – the traditional home of the Eskimo – needs experience and practice to build, and snow must be of the right quality to cut into blocks. Loose snow is useless; and the more granular it is, the smaller the igloo must be.

Work from the inside, cutting out the centre and using your carefully cut blocks to form the base of the wall. Work progressively upwards in a spiral, shaping the blocks as you go, and leaning them just slightly further inwards with each spiral.

LIVING IN SNOW SHELTERS

Follow these rules for safety and comfort.

1 Strip off to avoid sweating; the sweat may freeze later. But wear waterproofs when digging or you will get soaked.
2 Make sure your shelter is adequately ventilated at all times.
3 Mark the entrance to your shelter so that you can always find it. This will also help rescuers if the cave collapses.
4 Brush loose snow from yourselves before entering. This prevents damp developing on your clothing in the warm interior of the shelter.
5 Take all your equipment in, ESPECIALLY a shovel.
6 Remove wet clothing and try to dry it overnight.
7 Take your boots into your sleeping bag and keep them near your stomach area. This will help to dry them.
8 Don't boil water for too long; its vapour will cause condensation and dampness.
9 Keep a candle burning to give light and warmth – but keep a watch on it.

Finally a key block is inserted – carefully – either by widening the centre hole or trimming the key block until it drops gently into place. The wall should be chest to shoulder high.

The entrance to your snow house should be small; a large doorway is simply an easy way for heat to escape. Ideally, it should be an S-shaped tunnel away from the prevailing wind. In deep snow, this can be underground. Construct sleeping benches inside and fill in any holes in the walls with loose snow.

Snow wall

In dire emergency a simple semi-circular snow wall will keep the worst of the weather at bay and provide shelter from the wind, allowing you to cook and sleep for a limited period.

These are your options. You will find a snowhole rather oppressive at first, but it is the most comfortable and warm form of shelter in the Arctic and much preferred by Arctic troops

FOOD AND DRINK

ARCTIC RATIONS

However tired you are, you *must* eat all your rations. In the Arctic you burn enormous amounts of energy, and your rations are geared to replace this loss fully. It's all freeze-dried for convenience and lightness, and you melt snow to add to it.

Meat/rice rations must be simmered for about 20 minutes to make sure they have completely absorbed the moisture – otherwise, when eaten, they may cause stomach pains and will certainly contribute towards dehydration. The diet in the ration pack is balanced and is very nutritious, with plenty of 'brews' in the form of tea, coffee and beef stock. Again, you must drink well, and one of the cook's main jobs will be to see that plenty of hot water is available to top up Thermos flasks.

You have four types of pack to choose from. Breakfast is always porridge and hot chocolate. The main meal is usually eaten in the evening, and you carry the snack pack in your windproof for eating throughout the rest of the day. You may get a little fed up with the chocolate, but eat it, it contributes as much as anything else to your diet and wellbeing. One little tip is to carry some curry powder with you to add to any food you're getting bored with.

DUTIES OF THE COOK

Follow these drills and responsibilities and you will ease congestion in your tent or tentsheet when you first pitch it. A familiar routine will also keep you spirits up! The cook should:

1 Be the first man in – with his cooker and lamp – and may raise the pole.
2 Arrange the sleeping mats and bags as they are passed in to him.
3 Arrange the collection of rations, and clean snow.
4 Cook the rations and with the help of other members of the tentgroup, arrange
   • The filling of stoves and lamps. Initially all stoves should be used, snow takes a long time to melt.
   • The collection of more clean snow and ice for melting
   • The collection of rubbish
   • A constant supply of hot water. Empty flasks are used for storage.
5 Organize a hot drink, if flasks are empty.
6 Use his imagination to make the ration as satisfying as possible; for example curry powder, onions and bacon all add flavour.
7 Have the next meal prepared, as far as possible; this saves time and effort later.

Remember the health and morale of your group hinges on your expertise and hard work as the cook.

Lamps and cookers

There are various types, but they work on the same principle. All burn deleaded petrol (naphtha), which is the only fuel that should be used, except in emergency. Leaded fuel causes poisoning and 'tenteye'. Even with naphtha you need some ventilation.

Your cookers are vital equipment. Check them constantly – nuts, bolts, and gaskets tend to come loose and carry spare parts in your pulk.

Light and fill cookers and lamps in the open – particularly in training. On operations, you may have to risk lighting them inside your shelter. Make sure the filler cap is properly screwed on, and use the filler funnel to avoid waste. Remember, the naphtha must live in its pit outside your tent.

THE ARCTIC PARAFFIN LAMP

- ventilator nut
- ventilator
- handle
- Pyrex globe
- mantle (very delicate: be careful not to damage it)
- gas tip cleaning lever
- fuel valve
- filler cap
- pump
- tank

1 Fill the tank and screw down the cap firmly.
2 Check that the mantle is undamaged
3 Lift the glass by slackening the ventilator nut and place four lighted meta blocks around the bottom.
4 Pump up the pressure vigorously while the meta blocks burn.
5 Switch the fuel on and if you have sufficient pressure the fuel will vaporize and the mantle will glow. If not you will end up with a small fire in the glass. If this happens, switch off the fuel and start again.

Most lamps and cookers need pre-heating to generate a gas pressure build-up before you can light them. Use 'meta' (methylated spirit impregnated blocks) to do this – never use naphtha.

Arctic tent group stores

The list below gives the usual cooking and lighting equipment for an eight man tent group. The kit is set up and used by the cook but is distributed throughout the group to spread the weight. Ideally it will be carried on a pulk, as the tent group can survive without it.

1 Paraffin fuel containers
2 Funnel
3 Paraffin lamp
4 Lamp carrying case
5 Saucepans for melting snow and ice for cooking
6 Pressure cooker
7 Peak fuel cooker
8 Issue fuel cooker
9 Saucepan and frying pan handles
10 Frying pans
11 Pressure cooker inserts
12 Snow melting tins
13 Meta fuel blocks (for lamps)

WATER

Thirst is a major problem in the Arctic; in order to conserve fuel for other purposes the survivor often deprives himself of drinking water from melting ice and snow, and the time and energy required to chop and collect ice for water also limits the supply. You may become dangerously dehydrated in the Arctic as easily as in the desert.

Remember

1 You need about 50 per cent more fuel to produce the same quantity of water from snow than from melting ice.
2 It is safe, within limits, to eat snow as long as you allow the

snow to thaw sufficiently to be moulded into a stick or ball.

3 Do not eat snow in its natural state; it will cause dehydration and chill your body.

4 Do not eat crushed ice as it may cause injury to your lips and tongue.

5 Any surface that absorbs the sun's heat can be used to melt ice or snow, e.g. a flat rock, a dark tarpaulin or a signal panel.

6 The milky water of glacial streams can be drunk once the sediment has been allowed to settle out.

Rules of health

1 *Keep fit* – You burn enormous amounts of energy just doing simple jobs. The fitter you are, the less energy you burn, and you can work without becoming exhausted. This reduces the danger of freezing.

2 *Drink plenty of water* – Dehydration causes tiredness. Drink even if you are not thirsty. Do not eat unmelted snow; it chills your body and can give you cramps.

3 *Eat your rations* – Even if you're not hungry, keep eating. Regular hot food will keep you at your peak.

4 *Maintain a positive attitude* – Keep alert and, above all cheerful. You can make it!

Elements for survival

The secret of successful travel in the Arctic is adequate clothing, sufficient food, rest and a steady pace. You must have your kit; unless properly equipped, the best course of action is to 'hole up' and hope that the friendlies find you before the enemy does.

Emergency Food

There is little to eat in the Arctic in winter, but in an emergency there are some possibilities. Look out for bird and animal tracks; these may lead you to their sources of food which will probably be safe to eat.

But beware; if you find berries or something you don't recognize, they may be poisonous. Try a small quantity on your tongue first of all, and if there are no ill effects eat a little; wait

24 HOUR ARCTIC RATION PACKS

Spare Arctic Ration packs are carried by each man as part of his survival kit. These rations will buy you the time to find help or find or catch food.

The packs contain:

1. Sugar packets
2. Powdered milk
3. Beef stock drink
4. Instant tea
5. Instant coffee
6. Instant dried apple and apricot flakes
7. Vegetable soup
8. Dehydrated beef curry
9. Rice
10. Dried peas
11. Tissues
12. Matches
13. Salt
14. Chocolate drink
15. Rolled oats mix
16. Sugar
17. Biscuits fruit AB
18. Nuts and raisins
19. Biscuits brown AB
20. Toilet paper
21. Milk chocolate
22. Beef spread
23. Chocolate and biscuit bar
24. Dextrose tablets
25. Chocolate covered caramels

up to eight hours and then eat a bit more. If after another eight hours you are all right, you can be reasonably sure that the food is safe. Be specially wary of fungi; don't touch them in training unless one of you is a real expert.

For safety, then you are limited to animals, birds and fish.

Animals

Arctic animals range from reindeer, moose and bear (brown and polar) to hares, rabbits, squirrels and lemmings (look under rocks for these). You will also come across wolves and foxes.

Look at the snow in the mornings and you will realize from the number of tracks just how much wildlife there is. The closer to the treeline or shoreline you are, the more abundant wildlife becomes, even in winter.

Hunting animals is a skill, but you will soon master it if your life depends on it. Points to remember are:

1 Always hunt up-wind (with the wind in your face)
2 Move slowly
3 Try to stalk from above
4 Crawl if you are on exposed ground; move while the animal is feeding and freeze when it lifts its head up.
5 Don't take too long a shot, and if using issue ammo (which has solid heads) shoot through the heart, although small ground game may have to be shot through the head.
6 A sharp whistle will cause most animals to stop; time enough to give you the chance of a shot.

Birds

The most common Arctic bird is the ptarmigan or snow grouse, which is relatively tame and can be killed with a stick or stone in a trap. There are owls and ravens too, but both are wily and you will need a baited trap. Near the coast, you will find gulls; these can be killed with a gorge hook. To trap birds you need some sort of cage system to be triggered as the bird takes the bait or by you from a hidden position.

Seals and walruses

These are found along the coastline or, on a good day, lying next to their breathing holes out on the ice. Both have large amounts of blubber, which is useful for cooking, heating and lighting, and is also edible, along with the flesh. You need to take great care when stalking a seal, and ideally you should shoot if through the head; this will make sure it cannot reach its breathing hole, and it will float if it's in the water.

Snares

If you do not have any customized snares you can use string or light wire. The secret of success is to make sure that the slide moves smoothly; you can improvise with bone or a button, or a spring-loaded system. Once it is set, run a flame round the snare, to reduce human smell. Set the snare on a natural game trail, preferably in a narrow place or gap. Use bait if you can.

Fish

There is an abundance of fish in the Arctic, not only in the sea but also under the ice of frozen lakes, generally towards the inflow or outflow. You will have to cut holes in the ice for your lines. Make hooks from safety pins, tin openers, bones, etc.

Bait can be inedible parts such as the entrails of animals or fish. The best fishing method is to put out night lines, which you check each morning, but where the bait needs to be moved about you must make 'jigs' using discarded food tins, silver paper or other shiny material. Cod will take your clasp knife!

For weights, use stones; for floats, a piece of wood. Animal tendons make very strong traces which are almost invisible and are ideal for attaching hooks to lines.

The automatic fisherman

Fish can be caught in winter, through a hole in the ice. Once you have cut it you can stop it freezing over by covering it with brush and heaping snow over the top. Fish tend to gather in deep pools, so if you are lake fishing cut your hole over the deepest part.

You will need several holes which you can fish simultane-

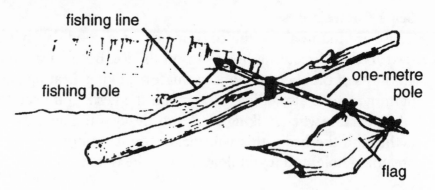

fishing line

fishing hole

one-metre pole

flag

ously using the 'automatic fisherman'. The fish pulls the flag upright. You need a one metre pole and enough line to reach well beyond the ice. Attach a spoon-shaped spinner from a ration pack can to the line and place a hook slightly below it.

IMPROVISED FISH HOOKS

Wood skewer
Buried in the bait this hook sticks in the side of the fish's mouth

Thorn
An awkward piece of thorn can be effective when buried in bait

Thorn
A thorn bush with large rearward pointing barbs is ideal

Bone
A sharp piece of bone can be fixed to a suitable piece of wood

Nails
Ordinary nails can be bent into shape or set into wood

Preparing fish

Bleeding
As soon as you catch a fish cut out the gills and large blood vessels next to the backbone

Scaling
Remove the scales by scraping with a knife

Gutting
Gut the fish by cutting it open and scraping out the guts.

Skinning
Some fish such as catfish, have no scales and can be skinned

Traps and Spears
Fall log trap for big game

rock weight

parachute buckle

bait

stockade

Large and medium-sized game is usually caught in deadfalls. However this method is only worthwhile if there are sufficient quantities of larger game available.

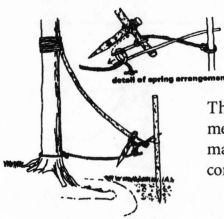

detail of spring arrangement

Spring and spear trap

The spear trap is another method of catching larger mammals but requires very careful construction to be effective.

Trip deadfall

A rock deadfall of this type stretched across an animal trail is effective as long as you are able to canalize the animal into the trap.

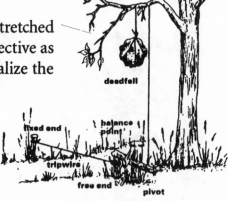

deadfall

fixed end

balance point

tripwire

free end

pivot

Harpoons and spears

You can make these from a piece of stout timber, their tips hardened in a fire , or with a knife or suitably shaped stone or bone

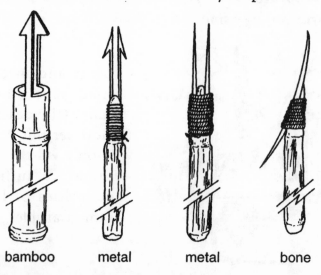

bamboo   metal   metal   bone

bound on to one end. They are best used to finish off an animal that has already been caught in a trap.

If you are near shallow water (waist deep) where fish are large and plentiful you may be able to spear them. Try to find a straight sapling with a solid core that you can sharpen to a point. If not, tie a bayonet or pointed piece of metal or sharp bone to the end. Next, find a rock or bank which overlooks a fish run and wait for the fish to swim past.

The Arctic is harsh but you can still live off the land as long as you have one or two basic items with you. Go for what seems to be plentiful; don't waste time or energy; and above all be patient and determined.

Travel in the Arctic

Deep snow means deep trouble if you're on the move. On foot or in an ordinary vehicle, you've got very little chance unless you've taken precautions beforehand. As well as the difficulty of moving through the snow itself, there are other less obvious things to worry about.

To start with, deep snow will change the appearance of the countryside, turning navigation by map into a nightmare. Secondly, the snow will hide all sorts of obstacles and dangers. Falling into a ditch filled with three metres of soft snow may sound like it could be fun, but the reality is deadly. You would find it very difficult to climb out before you were overcome by exhaustion and died of exposure. That is unless you drowned in the snow first.

Consider and conserve

So what can you do to make your way through Arctic, sub-Arctic or Alpine conditions?

Firstly you must stay calm and conserve as much energy and body water as possible. If you're carrying a heavy load of equipment, weapons and ammunition you'll be unable to travel far if there's more than half a metre of untrodden snow on the ground – even if the country is flat.

You have to spread the weight of your body and your load.

The two most usual ways of doing that both have their draw-backs – skis are hard to control unless you know how and anyway, are almost impossible to make from the sort of material you'll be able to gather. Snowshoes, the other real way to get about, are very tiring unless you're used to them, but they can be improvised using natural materials.

If you're properly equipped, of course, you'll have both available; skis to use when you're travelling any distance, and snowshoes for use in camp, where there are lots of people about – or in heavy brush or undergrowth, where two metres of ski on each foot would make you a little clumsy!

Ski into battle

A fit experienced skier can keep up a solid 10 kilometres an hour for days on end, even when carrying a full load of equipment. That's an awful lot more than you could manage on foot, and it requires a lot less effort, so there is much to be said for learning how to do it.

There are two main types of ski; Alpine skis are the shorter of the two types, and have fastenings for both the toe and heel of the boot; cross-country or Nordic skis are longer and narrower, with a hinged fastening at the toe only, so that the heel can be raised. This allows you to do a push/step movement that covers the ground remarkably quickly.

Military cross-country skis

The standard military issue ski is 208 cm (6ft 10in) long (big by alpine standard). They have holes in the tips to allow you to tow them in an improvised sledge, and are grooved at the heel to accept mohair 'climbers'.

To the non-skier it may come as a surprise to learn that you can actually walk uphill wearing skis.

Originally, people stuck strips of sealskin onto the soles of their skis, with the pile of the short, stiff hairs pointing backwards. The British Army uses mohair instead, but the effect is the same.

The length of a pair of skis isn't terribly important but the length of the poles is. They're much longer than the poles used in downhill skiing, coming to just below the shoulder. In the British forces they come in three lengths; 51 inches (130 cms), 54 inches (137 cms) and 58 inches (147 cms). Don't damage the points of your poles. They are intentionally sharp to allow you to get a purchase on hard ice.

Improvising snowshoes

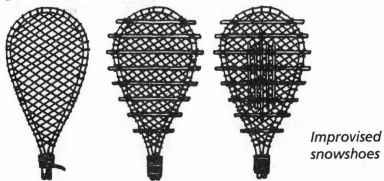

Improvised snowshoes

The traditional snowshoe looks a bit like a big tennis racket, but more modern versions are a rounded oblong shape, around 50 cm long and 25 to 30 cm wide, made up of a lightweight frame interlaced with straps of some sort.

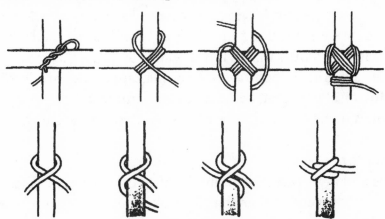

Lashings for straps

These straps can be made from any suitable material, and so can the frames, which means that at a pinch you can make a pair os snowshoes for yourself. Use stripped straight branches for the frame and webbing, animal hide cut into strips or even bark for the cross straps.

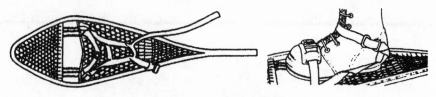

Conventional snowshoe and binding. The toe-hole allows the heel to lift freely

Improvised binding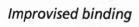

You don't need clever bindings on an improvised snowshoe, a single piece of rope, doubled and knotted twice around the foot and ankle will do fine. Do not bind the ankle to the snowshoe – allow it to lift in the same way as your heel lifts while walking normally.

Walking at night

In an operational or hostile situation, travel during darkness, unless the weather has closed in sufficiently during the day to hide you in low cloud or fog. Even then take care; bad weather can lift very quickly, leaving you exposed and unprotected.

And beware travelling in 'whiteout' conditions; the lack of contrasting colours makes it impossible to judge the nature of the terrain. And do not travel during blizzards – they are deadly.

Moving at night can be tricky, as any light from stars and the moon is made even brighter when reflected off the snow.

Plan your moves

Make a plan to work from one feature to another, for shelter and concealment, rather than to trek straight out into open country.

Sound travels easily in cold climates, so you should keep very quiet and stop to listen every so often.

Always cross a snow bridge at right angles to the obstacle it crosses. Find the strongest part of the bridge by poking ahead with a pole or ice axe. Distribute your weight by crawling or by wearing snowshoes or skis.

Cross streams when the water level is lowest. Normal freezing and thawing action may cause a stream level to vary as much as 2 to 2.5 metres per day. This may occur at any time, depending on the distance from a glacier, the temperature, and the terrain. You should also consider this variation in water level when selecting a campsite near a stream

Choosing your course

Consider rivers, frozen or unfrozen as avenues of travel. Frozen rivers are frequently clear of loose snow, making travel easier than on the land. Avoid snow covered streams, the snow, which acts as an insulator, may have prevented ice forming over the water.

Your course should be determined by your location and the terrain. In mountainous or wooded areas, it is advisable to fol-

---

CROSSING THIN ICE

If you have to cross thin ice, remember these rules:

1   One man at a time

2   Take your hands out of the loops on your ski poles

3   Put your equipment over one shoulder only, so you can shrug it off

4   Think about distributing your weight by lying flat and crawling

5   Bear in mind these thicknesses of ice and their corresponding capabilities:
      5cm supports 1 man
      10cm supports 2 men side by side
      20cm supports a half-ton vehicle

If you fall through the ice, get your kit off and up onto the ice; use your poles to help you out. Don't get too close to a team mate who has fallen through; you'll only end up in there with him. Throw him a line so that you can help him out from a safe distance. Hypothermia will set in very quickly after immersion, so carry out emergency re-warming straight away.

low rivers downstream towards populated areas (Siberia, where rivers flow northward to the high Arctic, is an exception),

When travelling cross-country, try to follow the contour of the land; however, note that valley floors are frequently colder than slopes and ridges, especially at night. Head for a coast, major river or known point of habitation.

Going the right way

Navigation is tricky in the Arctic. You're near the magnetic pole, so compass readings may be erratic; take more than one, and average them out. Use the shadow tip method or use the sun and stars to show you in which direction north and other points of the compass lie.

Nature itself can give you a few clues:

1 A solitary evergreen tree will always have more growth on its south side.
2 Bark on poplar and birch trees will always be lighter in colour on the south-facing side.
3 Trees and bushes will be bent in the direction that the wind normally blows, so if you know the direction of the prevailing wind you can work out north and south.
4 The snow on the south side of the ridges tends to be more granular than on the north.
5 Snowdrifts usually are on the downwind side of protruding objects like rocks, trees or high banks. By determining the cardinal points of the compass and from them the direction of the drifts, the angle at which you cross them will serve as a check point in maintaining a course.

In the Southern Hemisphere of course, the opposite polarity applies.

Pay attention to staying on the right track. You'll get some help in this during clear weather by looking back at your tracks in the snow.

But, of course, that's a sure sign to enemy forces that you're around. You have to be very cunning in the snow to cover up your tracks; stick to the treeline wherever possible, or use existing tracks and patches of broken snow. If you're travelling as a team keep in each others tracks.

Be careful how you plant your poles; always put them in the same holes as the guy ahead of you, then the enemy won't know how many there are of you. Alternatively, make lots of holes to confuse them.

Distance

It's very difficult to judge distances in the Arctic as there are so few visual clues, and the clear air makes estimating distances difficult; they are more frequently underestimated than over-estimated.

The simplest way of estimation is to pace out a given distance yourself, but this must be practised to be anywhere near accurate.

Another method is for rope or some signal wire of a given length (say 50 metres) to be strung between two men. The first man moves off, and when the slack is taken up the first man stops and the second man joins him, then repeats the exercise. Simple mathematics can be used to estimate the distance achieved after a number of repetitions.

Weather patterns

There is no fixed weather pattern in Arctic and sub-Arctic regions but the west coast of Scandinavia is affected by the meeting of the warm air masses off the Gulf Stream (which keeps most of Norway's ports ice-free) and the cold polar winds from the polar icecap and the land mass of the USSR. This leads to great instability along the coast, with considerable variations in temperature, high snowfall, rain and fog. Mountain flying is impeded by poor visibility, white-out and icing of rotor blades. High winds lead to drifting and snow build up on downwind (lee) slopes, with a strong possibility of avalanches.

When planning an operation, try to build up a picture of the weather you are likely to meet. As well as checking with weather stations, get the feel of local conditions. Observe the clouds; watch for a build-up in the mornings – particularly of layers of cloud on the mountain tops. Snow clouds are generally light in colour, with a slight yellow tinge. A watery moon or sun can also indicate poor weather to come. If the mountains look hard and clear, this too is a bad sign. A south or south-westerly wind or wind moving anti-clockwise towards the south, also portends bad weather. There are many other smaller indications, but these are the main ones and should influence your plans.

Avalanches are likely to occur after heavy snowfalls, often backed by a wind, or after a period of rising temperatures. Sometimes they happen for no apparent reason. 'Slab' avalanches consist of wet snow that has been heavily compacted by wind; soft snow avalanches involve loose powder snow travelling at up to 400 kilometres per hour and creating enormous pressure waves in front of them. Avalanches occur on slopes greater than 15 degrees and up to about 70 degrees. A powder avalanche may occur with as little as a third of a metre of snow at about 20-25 degrees, and wet avalanches on slopes as low as 15 degrees.

Arrive and perform

Special operations often take place far from any means of support. You may have to travel long distances in the harshest of conditions to reach your objective and you must be fit enough to do the job when you get there. Arriving as a casualty puts the whole team at risk, and not arriving at all means that the operation will fail. To be a successful Arctic warrior is more than survival; you have to be able to travel, fight and win.

AVALANCHES

Avalanches are difficult to predict, so avoid any slopes that look suspicious, especially when the temperature is rising or after blizzards. Avoid skiing in a traverse across the face, but if you have to, go as high as you can, and only one person at a time. Try to move from firm ground to firm ground if possible, to reduce the risk for example from a boulder to a clump of trees. Appoint someone as sentry to observe the crossing, at the bottom of the slope and to one side if possible, although this may not be tactically permissible.

Avalanche awareness

Avalanches come in four different types:

1   Soft slab; snow fallen on lee slopes which fails to bond with older snow.

2   Hard slab; a deceptively hard surface formed by high winds and cold air temperature.

3   Airborne; new snow falling on an already hard crust.

4   Wet snow; usual in spring thaw, often after a rapid temperature rise.

Some avalanches can reach 200 miles per hour and carry with them thousands of tonnes of snow, ice and rock debris, burying a victim up to 10 metres below the surface. Here are some basic precautions to keep you away from danger areas.

1   Stay high

2   Don't ski across rotten snow, new falls or very steep slopes.

3   Don't travel alone, but do keep a safe distance between group members.

4   Stay out of gullies – you never know what will come down from above.

5   Keep a close watch on the temperature, both of the air and of the snow; check them often, especially in the spring. Sudden changes bring about avalanches.

6   Dig pits from time to time to check on the condition of the snow lower down.

7   Watch for recent avalanche signs; they often come in groups.

8   Keep a very, very careful listening watch.

9   Don't assume, because one group's got across, that it is safe. They could have triggered an avalanche.

10 Avoid convex parts of a slope; this is where fracturing of the slab commonly occurs.

11 Keep below the treeline, it's generally safer.

12 Keep away from slopes of angles of between 30 and 45 degrees, which are often the most dangerous.

13 The deeper the snow, the greater the danger.

14 Avoid new snow, it takes a minimum of 2-3 days to settle.

15 Travel in the early morning before full sun up.

16 Do not adopt a 'lightening never strikes twice' attitude, or

assume that if there's been an avalanche the danger is past. Avalanches occur in the same place all the time.

17 On ridges, snow accumulates on the lee side in overhanging piles, called cornices. These often extend far out from the ridge and may break loose if stepped on, so do not stray unless you are sure of your ground.

Crossing a danger area

Do everything you can to stay away from areas that look or feel like they might be about to avalanche. There may come a time however when you just have to go through one!

Before you cross, loosen your bindings, hold your ski sticks in your hands only (no straps around your wrists) and be prepared to unclip your Bergen in a hurry. Do not rope up with your colleagues, but unravel your 30-metre avalanche (lavine) cord if available or your five metre cord. If you are buried, the cord may float on the surface and indicate your position.

Here are some rules that will increase your chances of making it safely – and some hints as to what to do if you get caught.

1 If you have to cross an avalanche area, travel across the slope one at a time.

2 Follow in the same tracks as the man in front of you.

3 Loosen your ski bindings and take your hands out of the loops on your poles.

4 Slip any rucksack straps off your uphill shoulder so that you can ditch it easily.

5 Fasten you smock hood over your nose and mouth to reduce the chances of drowning if you go down in powder snow.

6 Walk downhill; don't ski!

7 Go straight down, not in a traverse.

8 Keep high and stick to concave slopes.

Caught in an avalanche

If you feel or hear an avalanche coming, you must move fast but carefully – a fall now will almost certainly mean your death.

Don't panic. If you stay calm you have a good chance of coming out of it unscathed.

1 Ditch your kit
2 Find out where you are in relations to the avalanche. You may not be in its path. If its going to miss you, don't move.
3 Look out for your team mates. Remember their positions. You may have to dig them out.
4 Ski away in a steep traverse. Don't go straight down the fall line. The avalanche may be travelling at anything up to 200 miles per hour.

If you are in the path of an avalanche and cannot ski out of the way, try to find an anchor point (a boulder or tree) or sit down with your back to the slope, Bergen behind you, having kicked off your skis and sticks. Immediately the snow hits you, begin swimming, and try to stay on the surface.

The swimming action should help to clear an air space, which you must achieve as the avalanche comes to rest, and the snow resets. Remain as calm as you can; there is little point in wasting energy if you are trapped under the surface, where no-one will hear you.

1 If you get caught at the side of an avalanche, dig outwards – it's easier.
2 Make an airspace around your nose and mouth, but keep your mouth shut. In a powder avalanche, try to get a cloth over your nose to act as a filter.
3 Determine which way is up and down – perhaps by dribbling.
4 Start digging your way out before the avalanche has time to settle and freeze into position.
5 If you're covered in powder snow, try a swimming motion. Backstroke is the most effective.

Rescue

If attempting a rescue, you must start a systematic search immediately, in two phases. Post a sentry to watch for new avalanches, and send for help immediately. Organise a helicopter landing site close by, to which the rescue services can fly; this will often be the only way in.

Your buried person is likely to be somewhere in a vertical line from the point of disappearance to the bottom of the slope. The first phase of the search is a 'coarse' one; starting at the bottom, with a man every half metre, using avalanche search poles or ski sticks to probe the snow every 30 cms. Maintain a tight pattern on the search line and probe delicately so that you do not injure the lost person. If you touch something soft, dig. Mark the area as you search it.

Specially trained search dogs are available in most countries where avalanche risk is high, and they are invaluable. Ideally they should search the slope prior to any other human interference, but this will not always be possible as time is important; however, clear the slope of human searchers as soon as dogs become available.

Modern technology has also provided personal radio transponders and seekers. They are generally only available to troops who are at high risk, such as reconnaissance units, who work in small groups high in the mountains. The beacon works by sending a radio 'bleep' every second. Everyone's transponder is switched to 'send' at the start of the patrol. If anyone gets lost, all beacons are switched off except one or two that are switched to 'receive'.

Searchers then systematically quarter the site of the avalanche looking for the strongest signal, which strengthens as they get close to their target. At the location of the strongest signal, dig.

An injured man should be treated as for shock; make sure his airways are free, keep him warm and give him a warm drink. An unconscious man will need artificial resuscitation, and look out for other injuries that may not be obvious.

Transport

Helicopters
Helicopters are an invaluable asset, speeding movement over the inhospitable terrain, often where no roads or track com-

munications exist. They can undertake a wide range of roles and jobs – the ferrying of men and supplies, forward and flank reconnaissance, fire direction, liaison, casevac and if necessary, armed action. The main types used in the Arctic are the Puma, Sea King, Lynx and Gazelle; the USA uses the CH-53.

Helicopter operations are not easy at the best of times, and in the Arctic can be highly dangerous. Pilots, ground crew and the troops that are to be carried all need considerable training.

The biggest enemy of course, is the weather, affecting every aspect from flying to maintenance. For example, the helicopter will need 'pre-heating' before flying, which means blowing warm air into the engine and body from hot air generators. When flying visibility is crucial, and 'white-out' conditions where no depth or landmark can be seen by the pilot will curtail an operation. Another danger is icing up, caused by being caught in freezing rain or sleet.

All landing sites should, where possible, be flattened by an oversnow vehicle to create a hard landing pad. This avoids snow being churned around by the blades, which is hazardous to the aircraft and to everyone on the ground; the pilot can lose his bearings and high speed whirling air can cause frostbite within minutes.

To overcome the visibility problem, mark the landing site with a black, snow-filled plastic bag or with coloured smoke which stains the snow. If no markers are available, a marshaller will have to lie down to provide a marker. To avoid frostbite everyone on the ground must wear full protective clothing and masks, particularly the ground crew.

Maintenance

Maintenance is very difficult in cold temperatures, particularly at below –15°C, where skin sticks to metal. Heat is essential and is provided by a portable air generator inside a tent, or in the case of larger helicopters, a large cover such as a parachute. Fluid leaks are frequent as seals can contract and crack with the cold, so ground crew must be particularly alert.

Emplaning and deplaning

Drills for embarking and disembarking must be practised. Take great care to avoid damaging the helicopter with the large quantities of heavy, cumbersome equipment, such as skis and sticks that must be manhandled in difficult circumstances. In the Arctic, the technique is that the helicopter will land almost on top of you; your section will lie beside or on its equipment, acting as a marker, and the pilot will put down beside you. The section then emplanes through one door, equipment going in last. You strap in and raise your right arm to indicate to the loadmaster that you are secure; the helicopter then takes off.

When deplaning, Bergens and men are offloaded through both doors, but the pulk and skis always go through the starboard (right) door. Troops should adopt fire positions until the aircraft is clear, and they then go to cover, where reorganisation and ski fitting takes place.

Snow scooters

Most forces who operate in the Arctic make use of snow scooters as a means of easing travel in the snow covered terrain. In the military context, snow scooters have their plus and minus sides. They can carry out a variety of roles:

1 Liaison and communications (dispatches)
2 Casevac
3 Line-laying
4 Ammunition resupply
5 Route recce and deep patrols
6 Weapons deployment – off route, eg anti-tank weapons.

However, they do have a number of major disadvantages. Firstly, they are difficult to drive without considerable training and experience. Secondly, their engines are temperamental, although the modern machines are much more reliable and robust; they need constant maintenance, which may be difficult if deployed forward of their own troops. Thirdly, they need a reasonable amount of snow in which to operate successfully, so route planning is just as important as when moving vehicle-borne or ski troops to a target. They suffer high wear on open roads and off snow they are difficult to manoeuvre. A wheel can be attached to or in place of the front ski for road use.

Snow scooters are not particularly fast, but have powerful engines and a wide range of low gears to cope with snow, particularly heavy wet snow, which tends to clog the driving belts. The heavier machines, the 'workhorses' have twin tracks which give them greater grip and thrust through all types of snow and allow them to pull large loads.

Driving a snow scooter demands skill, which you often have to learn the hard way! The trick is to counterbalance the machine in the traverse – it will always try to slide down the slope, turning over on you if it can. Leaning into the slope while driving across it is physically and mentally demanding and takes confidence to master, particularly when pulling a fully laden sledge, but it is exhilarating and fun, and once mastered will allow you to use snow scooters as a significant contributions to Arctic operations.

Arctic Combat

Combat in the Arctic is probably the most challenging of all military skills. It is the soldier, either as an individual or as a team, against the cruellest climate in the world; a climate with no sympathy for men or machines. It requires constant practice, and minute attention to planning and detail, because if things go wrong there may be no way out. Arctic warfare demands the highest of conventional military ability, plus a whole range of extra skills.

Care of equipment

We will start by looking at the basics. You will have to learn to look after your equipment and pay special attention to the range of spares that you must carry. Because of the intense cold, equipment tends to be more brittle and may break more easily, and the harsh terrain also takes its toll. Among the most essential items that should be carried by each section are spare ski binding straps, poles and mittens together with emergency ski tips.

Weapons

Your weapons also require special attention. Some of the main problems that you may encounter when shooting are:

1 Working parts break more easily at low temperatures.
2 Ice may form on working parts after firing
3 Ammunition lethality is reduced and it may become fouled by ice or snow.
4 Your hands are less effective when wearing bulky mittens.
5 Weapons need a firm base to fire.
6 Fog that forms during firing may interfere with the optical sights.

The above problems can be overcome with maintenance becoming second nature. The muzzles of all weapons require a cover to prevent snow from entering the barrel and firing mechanism. Use light oil (normally a mixture of oil and naptha/petrol) to lubricate, but if this is not available, just dry clean your weapons. To overcome sweating and thus freezing, leave your weapons outside your tent sheet. Make a weapon rack and cover it if possible, but always remember to brush off any snow when picking up weapons. If the temperature is above freezing, the weapons can be put in the tent.

During pauses in firing you may find that the ammunition freezes in the barrel. To overcome this, work the bolt/cocking handle every few minutes until there is no possibility of freezing. This is painstaking work and could take up to an hour, but is well worth it. Ice fog which forms around automatic weapons during high rates of fire may force you to fire at a reduced rate. Alternative firing positions should be considered if possible. Also take care of your ammunition, keep it in its liner, remove any oil and avoid getting snow on it.

Always ensure that your mittens are dry. If your mittens are wet when throwing a grenade, it may freeze to them – think of the effect of that if you had pulled the pin! Another useful trick to prevent the grenade sinking in the snow is to tie it to crossed sticks or a board. It will then explode near the surface and have a much better effect. Remember that all your weapons will sink in soft snow and it will be difficult to attain muzzle clearance. You must put 'feet' on your machine gun bipods, light mortars, etc, and there are special techniques for rifle shooting using ski sticks to prevent your elbows from sinking into the snow. You can use snowshoes on the bipods but most light machine guns are specially equipped in Arctic trained units. Light mortars require a steel plate placed on the compacted snow, which the unit LAD (Light Aid Detachment) will make.

Radios

Radios and batteries should be looked after, particularly bat-

---

IMPORTANT ARCTIC WARFARE KIT

Kit to be kept in your pocket

First field dressing; earplugs; lipsalve; plastic spoon; snow goggles; plastic whistle on lanyard; survival/Silva compass; hat ECW; headover; toe covers; snowbrush; wristlets; contact gloves; survival bag (if bivi bag not issued); survival ration pack; Arctic mittens (if not worn); safety pins; ski scraper/waxes; M&AW safety guide; notebook & pencil; map and torch (remember to keep this warm).

Kit to be kept in your patrol pack

Wind proof trousers; Thermos flask; tent sheet; reversible-waterproof or Gore-Tex suit; jacket and trousers ('Chinese Fighting Suit'); shovel; 24 hour ration pack; snow shoes; No 6 cooker (one between two); fuel and matches; steel mug.

Belt order

Right/left pouch; rifle magazines; rifle cleaning kit (REK); bayonet; snowbrush (if not in smock); waterbottle pouch; emergency rations; string; candle; waterproof matches; steel mug; No 6 cooker and fuel (if not all in patrol pack).

Other items on belt

Avalanche cord (10 metres); survival knife (Gollock); rope and karabiner; bivi bag.

teries. These lose their power in half the time in Arctic conditions sometimes even quicker. So if a battery is not in use make sure that it is on charge or in a warm place – which may have to be inside your smock if you're on the move.

Individual camouflage

Camouflage starts with the individual and good use of a mixture of DPM and white overalls is important. For example if you are working in a forest a DPM suit is probably most suitable, whereas near the treeline/snowline a white jacket or white trousers may be worn. Above the snowline use the full white suit. Weapons and webbing must be camouflaged using white tape and special helmet and Bergen covers in white are available. Adjust your camouflage to suit your background, and use cover such as hollows, broken ground, trees and birch scrub as normal.

Movement is often the great giveaway, as it is very difficult to camouflage ski and vehicle tracks. Where possible use the shape of the terrain, moving in hollows and shadows. Tracks should run under trees if possible and sharp edges that might cast shadows in bright sunlight should be broken up by the last man or vehicle dragging a small pine tree along the track. In a camp where digging is necessary, remove snow from under the trees and throw it onto the tracks. This may deceive air recce but not ground patrols, although it all adds up to making it as difficult as possible for the enemy to spot you.

The disruption of sharp edges also applies to field defences, the entrances to tents and the tents themselves. Field defences should have rounded edges, smoothed to blend in with the shape of the ground. Fill in the bottom of trenches with snow to prevent black earth showing and remember that tracks within the position will need filling and smoothing daily. Pitch tents under trees, or if this is not possible, dig them in and camouflage with white nets or parachutes. Use track plans and discipline, particularly in camps, and try to set a series of deception tracks away from your position. Construct 'dummy' positions using spare tents to draw enemy fire and deceive the enemy about your strength.

Mountains

Mountains often contain vast tracts of open, unbroken snow fields, but the lower slopes are generally covered in pine and dense birch scrub. No amount of snow can fill all hollows or conceal all rock and scree, so natural cover does not exist. You will have to use deception extensively and reduce noise to a minimum, as sound travels over long distances in still air. There is also the problem of human-induced fogs of vehicle exhausts and cooking fires, as warm, damp air condenses in the cold conditions.

ARCTIC CAMP

We will now look at how the above techniques can be applied to set up an Arctic camp. Whatever the size of the camp, whether a patrol camp or a major formation base, the principles for setting it up are the same. Select the site carefully, considering concealment defence, routines and administration.

Initially you will set off with your recce party, which runs one or two hours ahead of the main body. The recce party will contain 2ICs and guides from all your sub units. What will you be looking for? A map study may have produced some likely areas to look at; you need an easily defendable area with good concealment, good snow cover for digging in and with the possibility of good administration. The position should avoid low-lying ground, which is likely to be on a marsh and may get very cold. Try to find a piece of forested high ground, or ground that is broken up with good fields of fire, limited access points or access routes which can be dominated by outposts. As far as administration is concerned you will probably have to consider fresh water, covered vehicle access from main routes, and helicopter landing sites.

Having made your selection, mark out the camp and brief your commanders and guides on areas, defensive work, sentry posts, arcs of fire, stand-to positions, track plans, areas for cutting brush-wood, latrines and a host of other measures.

The deception plan

Then consider your deception plan, which may require the

assistance of your main body. You will require a false trail beyond the camp area, and possibly a 'dummy' camp using spare tents. Vehicles may have to be used to produce long fake trails, creating confusing and large-scale defensive track plans.

The 'jump off'

For small units without vehicles the entry track to the camp will be a 'jump off' from the ski trail. A professional enemy may be able to detect the change in the track, and it is possible to tell from a ski trail how many men actually passed along it and in which direction by examining the number and angle of the ski pole plants in the snow and their compactness. The idea of a 'jump off' is that the patrol halts, but the lead skier or skiers lay a false trail beyond the 'jump off'. While they do this the remainder of the patrol leaves the main track often through a thicket or where the snow is broken. The skiers laying the false trail then return to the 'jump off', camouflage it (it may be disguised as a fallen man, and many similar dummy 'jump offs' will have been laid previously) and then rejoin the rest of the patrol. The job may of course be done by the main body, depending on the number of men you have and your SOPs.

Camp discipline

When the main body arrives at the camp, the sub-unit commanders are briefed, and work begins with the minimum of noise and disturbance to the snow. A track plan is established and should be used by everyone. Vehicles are tucked under trees and camouflaged; slit trenches are dug; tents and shelters are put up; weapon racks are built; and food and drink are prepared. At last light, patrols depart to lay mines and trip flares and to establish listening posts beyond the perimeter on likely enemy approaches. Each tent group has a man on sentry duty, connected to the tent group commander by a vine or string to ensure a silent call-out. Sentries are changed every hour, and in extremely cold weather as often as every 20 minutes. The camp then settles into night routine, which includes minimum movement (except for sentry changes and patrols leaving the camp), no lights and minimum sound – radios are on mute, but vehicles may have to be run occasionally to keep them warm and their batteries charged.

MOBILITY

Mobility is the key to successful Arctic operations. A thorough understanding of the capabilities of your vehicles and the techniques needed to overcome the problems you may encounter is vital to effective movement.

A variety of over-snow tracked vehicles is available to help you move around the difficult terrain of the Arctic. Two such vehicles are the BV202 and BV 206. The latter vehicle is relatively new, whereas the BV 202 has been in service for over 20 years. The infantry, engineers and artillery generally have one of these vehicles per section, but fewer in logistic units. The 206 can carry everything that is needed by a section, including all the men, but the 202 can only carry the section kit, although it will pull sledges and troops.

Skijoring

The technique of pulling troops is called 'skijoring' and requires a lot of skill to master. In skijoring, two 50 metre ropes are attached to the back of the vehicle at each corner. The troops attach themselves to the outside of the rope by twisting their ski sticks into it; the weight on the rope ensures that the ski sticks stay in place, and troops just hold on and are towed along. A 'guard' sits in the rear of the vehicle to make sure that the vehicle stops if any men fall, using a buzzer to communicate with the driver.

Once the technique is mastered troops can be moved very quickly with little exhaustion. But the reverse is true if the terrain and going are poor and can result in chaos; you must decide carefully, when to skijore or whether it would be quicker to ski. Broken birch country and forests are very difficult to skijore, but open snow fields above the treeline are ideal and you can cover up to 15 kilometres per hour.

Moving at speed through cold air can cause wind chill and frostbite and orders of dress must be given. You should normally wear the Arctic hat, with flaps down, a face mask and toe covers. Halts may have to be taken as frequently as every 20 minutes to allow blood circulation to be restored to reduce the risk of frostbite.

Vehicle mobility

The most likely problems you will come across are navigating, traversing a slope, ravines, ice crossings, rivers and icy roads as well as heavily-laden vehicles becoming bogged down on steep inclines. Route planning and preparation require a great deal of time, and large numbers of troops may have to be used for route construction and maintenance work.

To overcome some of the problems faced by vehicles you will have to learn a number of tricks. To traverse a steep hillside, dig a road to avoid shedding tracks or overturning. If you become bogged down, anchor your skijoring ropes to a tree and the other ends to the vehicle tracks; then simply drive out as the ropes wrap themselves around the tracks. Use this technique to maintain grip when heavily-laden vehicles slip on icy mountainous roads. Winching is another option, and many vehicles are now fitted with efficient winches that can be used with 'A' frames to solve most problems. (Another tip; if your Land Rover loses a back wheel, stick a stout log under the mudguard into the suspension unit until you reach safety; the end of the log simply slides on the ice-packed road.)

Crossing rivers

If your route involves crossing a lake or ice-covered river, an ice recce must be done. This involves drilling holes in the ice with an auger and measuring the thickness. Do this over the entire length of the crossing at 10-15 metre intervals and at smaller intervals if you think the ice may be rotten or unsupported. Sometimes you will find layers of water between the ice – beware, the load bearing capabilities are considerably weakened.

Make sure that crossing points avoid the inflow and outflow points on rivers and lakes. Lakes behind hydro-dams are particularly dangerous as the water level falls in winter leaving an enormous gap between the ice and water – sometimes up to 20 metres. You won't recover a man or vehicle if they go through the ice in these conditions.

Vision

Low light, flat light, or white-out blizzard conditions may also occur when drivers will be unable to distinguish the type of terrain, any obstacles or direction, even on a marked route. The main problem is that the driver has nothing to focus on, and no depth of vision. This is very dangerous as he may drive over a cliff. The only solution is to two skiers to go ahead of the vehicle and act as reference points so that he can judge the rise and fall of the land; they will also navigate for him. If the conditions are really bad the skiers should be changed every 20 minutes to stop them freezing.

NAVIGATION

The ability to navigate accurately in the Arctic is vital. It saves time and energy, and poor navigation could lead to death. The principles of navigation are the same as those in a temperate climate, but there are more problems; snow changes the shape and nature of the terrain and it is much more difficult to relate the map to the ground. Add to this white-out conditions, when it is impossible to judge relief and distance and freezing conditions, when it is difficult to handle both map and compass, and you can see the problems. It is also difficult to pace distance accurately, particularly on skis, so you must rely on obvious features – easier said than found!

The following techniques will help you. First select your route carefully from a map. This is vital to avoid obstacles such as steep ravines and slopes, forests and open water. Study the contours in detail as you draw in your route, trying to ensure gentle gradients.

En route, try to navigate parallel to a major feature or aim at a marker. For example, a river bed on a flank will act as a guide; or navigate towards a fixed feature such as a hut, tree or rocks. You can use a star for short periods (20 minutes), but remember that these move. If you are navigating towards a fixed feature, eg a hut on a road, aim to the right or left of the hut by

If you are caught out without a map and compass, you can navigate using the position of the sun and your watch. At 12.00 noon you will have a rough indication of north as shown above. You can then prepare a rough sketch map to hit a large feature eg a road by relating the map to the position of the sun.

a few miles. Then when you reach the road you know you are on one side or the other of your objective.

Distance is probably the most difficult element to judge,

particularly in white-out or at night, and on skis. Use the mile-ometer in your vehicle, or for more accurate measurement use two men tied together with a piece of rope of a known length (eg 50 or 100 metres). One man acts as anchor while the other skis forward to the rope's limit, then they swop roles and the anchor man skis past the skier. The distance is calculated by counting the number of rope lengths. This method is time consuming but can be vital in poor conditions.

Being lost can be very worrying, but don't let it affect your reasoning. Using a map and compass, select a linear feature and march on a compass bearing towards it – you should eventually hit it. Without a map and compass things are more difficult, and you will have to use your memory, your watch (if you have one) and try to relate your route to a linear feature. Make use of the sun (if it is up) or the North Star at night (this does not move). Draw a diagram on paper or in the snow, noting the position you want to get to, any roads or linear features, and the position of the sun at various times of the day, remembering that it rises in the east and sets in the west. Try to put in a north pointer. Then march in the direction you require, keeping your direction relative to that of the sun (at that time of the day) or to the North Star at night. It is not very accurate but that is not the point; you are aiming to hit a large feature and then refine your route from there, so trust your plan. If the conditions are not good, you may have to consider going into a survival situation with shelter, warmth and food.

Ice bridges

The requirements for suitable locations for ice bridges and methods for testing the quality of the ice using an ice auger were discussed earlier. In addition, avoid places with a fast in-flow or outflow, bends in rivers which accelerate the flow, and areas where banks are difficult to prepare.

Having made a sensible choice, you will still encounter problems throughout the crossing. The underside of the ice may melt and scour as the weather conditions change, and cracks will occur; cracks which are parallel to the direction of travel are the most dangerous, those at right angles less so. Cracks

CONSTRUCTING AN ICE BRIDGE OR FERRY

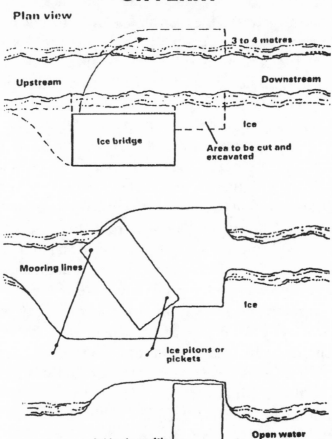

Plan view

3 to 4 metres

Upstream

Downstream

Ice bridge

Ice

Area to be cut and excavated

Mooring lines

Ice

Ice pitons or pickets

Bridge in position

Open water

Find a slow-flowing straight section or river away from any previous crossing sites and put out protection parties to cover the work party. Prepare and reinforce the banks and mark out a suitable block from the upstream bank. Once cut, using ice saws, the bridge can be floated into position using ice pitons and mooring lines. The bridge may weigh several tons and simple pulleys can be used to manoeuvre it. Once in position the bridge can be cemented in place by pumping water on to reinforcing material at the edges.

can be repaired by filling them with hay and straw and then pumping water onto the surface which freezes layer by layer. This is the principle for reinforcing any crossing that is deteriorating, but timber planks, steel mesh, trackway, hessian, brushwood and other materials can all be frozen onto the surface as reinforcement. The idea is to spread the load as widely as possible. This requires a great deal of effort and if the temperature is in the region of −10°C it is more economical to pump on layers of water to build up the depth of the ice.

Approaches to bridges will also deteriorate as the ice tends to be thinner at the banks. The bank and bridge should be reinforced with timber and frozen snow to form a base for an 'approach' bridge on to the ice. This relieves the load on the ice near the bank and maintains safe entry onto the main bridge. If there is open water between suitable ice banks you can cut a large section of ice and float it into position to bridge the gap. The ice should be good quality and of considerable depth – about 40-50 centimetres initially – and with temperatures below −10°C it can be reinforced like a standard ice bridge if it is needed for any length of time.

The most robust type of bridge is one that fits into notches cut into both banks. The notches should be cut with standard power saws and must be at least 20ft deep, so that the bridge can freeze into place or can be reinforced if it does not fit exactly. Lines attached through holes in the ice and toggled underneath are used to control the bridge as it is put into position. If the ice breaks, this technique can be used to make repairs, as the ice will quickly refreeze at low temperatures. Angle iron pitons can be used instead of toggle ropes, but these are not always readily available.

'Skewed' bridge

The previous type of bridge is probably the most stable but it is time-consuming to make. A 'skewed' bridge can be used as an alternative. The principles of its construction are the same, but the anchorage is less secure. The bridge has rounded ends which rest on both banks, which are again anchored by either toggled ropes or pitons. In the same way an ice ferry (an ice floe) can be constructed to move light loads; the load bearing/ floatation capacity can be worked out using a simple calculation. The ferry is hauled, using a hand or vehicle winch, across the gap collecting and delivering its load.

Remember, ice is dangerous. To use it requires a great deal of study and understanding, which is built up by many years of experience. Ice recce is extremely time-consuming because the ice engineer cannot afford to make mistakes; but ice is one of nature's phenomena that can be used to great advantage to speed up mobility in the Arctic.

Special Operations

In spite of the hostility of the terrain and climate in the Arctic, there is still a requirement for the specialist skills provided by the special forces. Troops who are specially equipped and trained in deep penetration behind enemy lines are often employed but very careful logistic planning and subsequent mission supervision is required for success. Like other troops, special forces will need acclimatization and they should also have the experience to operate independently. Most northern armies maintain such forces, some are assigned to land operations and others to operations at sea.

Soldiering in the Arctic requires determination, skill, and a great deal of hard work. Troops will be delivered to the target by boat, submarine, parachute or helicopter, followed by a long, hard ski march. Some armies use snow scooters, but these are only suitable if the terrain is reasonably flat. Most movement will be at night, and if a large unit is required to reach the target, infiltration tactics will be required. An individual's skiing ability and fitness must be exceptional and accurate navigation and survival skills are required.

Most special forces will be involved in strategic tasks. These encompass simple observation and reporting, target reconnaissance and attack, sabotage, ambush on lines of communication and beach reconnaissance, which is vital for successful amphibious landings.

Raids and ambushes

A typical raid by a Scandinavian special forces unit is pre-planned, with many small units infiltrating from temporary lying-up positions to the main RV in order to mount the operation. A classic ambush is to attack a convoy on a route, using 'stand-off attack' tactics to reduce casualties to their own men and making follow-up more difficult. The unit will covertly dig in about 150 metres from the route, and camouflage their position from both ground and air. The positions are well equipped as troops are likely to occupy them for considerable periods of time. Any tracks into the area should also be camouflaged and any likely follow-up routes booby-trapped and mined.

Remote control

A wide range of remotely-fired devices should be positioned in the main killing area to deal with armour, soft-skinned vehicles and personnel. The ambush may be initiated by blowing two culverts with improvised changes at each end of the convoy.

Anti-tank weapons of the LAW type or AT 64 are strapped between two posts or a tree and a post, and are aimed at a marker on the far side of the killing area. The firing mechanism is simply operated by a piece of string, attached to a piece of wood to give sufficient leverage to the trigger when the string is pulled and the rocket fired.

Various types of mine are also sown for both defensive and offensive use. The defensive mines will largely be anti-personnel, and there are two main offensive directional mines; firstly the well known Claymore type mine (No 13) which fires a large number of ball-bearings into a fixed killing area – ideal for soft-skinned vehicles and troops; and, secondly, the anti-vehicle mine, which will damage and immobilize most vehicles. If the killing area is properly mined and booby-trapped there would be little requirement for supporting fire from the main position. Once the ambush is over, a rapid withdrawal is undertaken through the usual RV's.

Attacking a railroad

To achieve the best effect when attacking a railroad both a train and a line should be destroyed together. In order to cause even more disruption and to delay the recovery of the train and

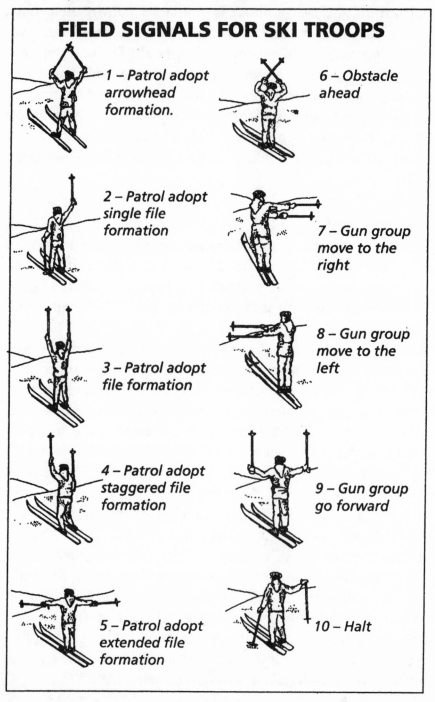

FIELD SIGNALS FOR SKI TROOPS

1 – Patrol adopt arrowhead formation.

6 – Obstacle ahead

2 – Patrol adopt single file formation

7 – Gun group move to the right

3 – Patrol adopt file formation

8 – Gun group move to the left

4 – Patrol adopt staggered file formation

9 – Gun group go forward

5 – Patrol adopt extended file formation

10 – Halt

repair to the line, the area around the ambush site should be booby-trapped.

The most suitable places to launch an attack are embankments or defiles or where the train is likely to be travelling at high speeds. The area should be ideally be covered by forest or brushwood, but the line should be visible from 100-150 metres. A further obstacle between the line and the firing position would also provide additional cover.

The mines are dug in under the rails into the track bed which may require the use of hammers and chisels if the ground is solid rock. The mines are then linked together with a detonating cord and a fuse is run back to the remote firing point, the base of a tree ideally, where it terminates in a firing cap pull switch. This in turn is attached to a pull cord. Great care must be taken to bury the mine and fuse and to camouflage any disturbances to the ground. Sometimes snow will have to be collected from an area well away from the line and used to fill any holes produced in laying the device.

Remember to position sentries linked by radio, well out to the flanks (400+ metres). The line may be patrolled or an unexpected train may use the line, and you must have early warning so that you can return to cover. Initiation is by pull which is followed by immediate withdrawal along a pre-planned route using the usual anti-tracking and anti-follow-up tactics.

As can be seen, special forces have their place in the Arctic, and they can have an effect which far outweighs the effort and resources committed to the tasks. It is vital, however, that any such operation is properly prepared and mounted, otherwise it will end in disaster and no more so than in the Arctic.

DESERT
ENVIRONMENTS

DESERT SURVIVAL

The very word 'desert' conjures up images of shimmering sand dunes and oases of refreshing sweet, blue water surrounded by vivid green palm trees – but in deserts like the Sahara reality is very different. Only 17 per cent of the Sahara's 3.5 million square miles consists of sand dunes. The rest is a mixture of broken plateaux, weird rock formations, endless gravel, dust plains and arid mountains. The Sahara, from the Arab word meaning 'empty place', is truly vast. Solitude and loneliness, coupled with fear, become a real test of your character and will to survive in this intimidating place.

Basic rules

If you're not acclimatized to the desert be extremely cautious during the critical first three or four days of working in summer heat. Sweating washes salts and other minerals out of the body, so make it your business to increase your water and salt intake to compensate.

Avoid salt tablets – they can cause damage to your stomach lining by lying undissolved against the stomach wall. Simple table salt taken with water is adequate. A guide to how much salt you need is taste. If the salt seems to have little or no flavour, increase your intake until it tastes normal.

Diarrhoea is doubly serious. While you suffer, fluids and essential salts tend to pass unused through the body. Cooling fluids fail to reach the skin surface in the form of sweat, your body thermostat fails and you'll have heat illness as well. Serious sunburn also damages the sweat ducts and so stops the skin surface cooling.

Choose lightweight, loose and comfortable clothes. The looseness provides insulation and prevents excessive evaporation of sweat. Sandals are common favourites for footwear, but beware of thorns, snakes and scorpions. If you expect the going to be rocky or difficult military pattern or lightweight desert boots are best.

Surviving the desert – a checklist

Survival in a desert as in any area depends upon your knowledge of the terrain and the basic climatic elements, your ability to cope with them, and your will to live. Every year the desert continues to kill the unwary, the unprepared and the foolish.

Types of terrain

Each type of terrain seemingly blends into another. There are five different types; mountainous, rocky plateau, sand dune, salt marsh and highly dissected rocky terrain called 'gebel'.

Sand dunes: these are usually extensive areas covered with sand and gravel. Some dunes may be over 300 metres high and 10 to 15 miles long; others will be completely flat. They can be devoid of plant life or covered in scrub up to two metres in height. Any form of travel through sand dune deserts should be avoided.

Salt lakes: If a large volume of water enters a basin, a lake may develop. However, the water has a very high salt content and is undrinkable.

Salt marshes: This type of terrain has a highly corrosive effect on boots, clothing and skin.

Rocky plateau deserts: These are characterized by many solid or broken rocks at or near the surface, and there may be sand dunes around the plateau. Rock outcrops may offer cover and shade. The rocks often form natural cisterns which collect water after rains.

TEMPERATURE CONVERSION

Most of the world's military use the Celcius scale, but some readers may be more familiar with Fahrenheit. Here are some approximate conversions.

50°C	120°F
30°C	90°F
20°C	70°F
10°C	50°F
0°C	32°F
-10°C	15°F
-20°C	-5°F
-30°C	-20°F

Mountain deserts: High altitude deserts have thin air and little or no vegetation. Sunburn is a real danger, and movement at altitude requires extra physical exertion.

Climatic elements

Temperature variation: The temperature may vary from as much as 55°C during the day down to 10°C at night; warm clothes are essential. Obviously, work or travel at night requires less water than day but may be more hazardous.

Rainfall: It does rain in the desert on high ground and, when it does rainwater runs off very quickly in the form of flash floods. The floods excavate deep gullies and ravines know as 'wadis'. Vegetation may appear after rain, but the water evaporates leaving the lands as barren as before.

The burning sand: The temperature of the desert sand and rock averages 15 to 20 degrees more than that of the air, so if the air temperature is 45°C then the sand would be around 60°C.

An individual first aid kit depends on personal choice and allergies. Seek your doctor's advice if you have any doubt about personal medications. You may also need a prescription for some of the items suggested. Your kit may contain some or all of the following:

Butterfly sutures

Surgical blade

Plasters – assorted sizes and waterproof

Potassium permanganate as general disinfectant

Mild painkillers for toothache, headaches e.g. Codeine phosphate

Intestinal sedative e.g. Immodium

Antibiotic cream and tablets

Antihistamine for bites, stings, irritant rashes, e.g. Piriton

Water sterilising tablets e.g. Puritabs

Anti-malaria tablets e.g. Paludrine, Daraprim, Mepachrin

You will be unable to walk around without adequate foot protection.

Your ability to cope

Convoy: Never attempt to cross a desert area in a single vehicle; always travel in convoy.

Movement by night: In most deserts, moving by night is so hazardous as to not be a viable option.

Equipment: Radios and other sensitive items of equipment are likely to fail when exposed to direct sunlight in the desert.

Dehydration: Keep activity to a minimum during the day to minimize water loss. Take sips of water often rather than normal drinking or gulping.

Animals and birds: Water sources are often indicated by animal trails and droppings or birds in flight.

Dehydration

The body absorbs heat from direct sunlight and from the atmosphere. You will also absorb heat reflected from the ground or from direct contact with the ground. Any increase in body temperature of three or four degrees C (six to eight degrees F) above normal (98.6°F/37°C) for any extended period can cause coma and death.

Your body attempts to dispose of this excess heat by sweating, which can lead to loss of body fluids and dehydration.

Drink early in the morning while temperatures are low. Remember, it is the water in your body that keeps you alive, not the water in your waterbottle. Don't ration your water intake to little sips. That will not prevent dehydration. If you drink only enough to satisfy your thirst you can still suffer from dehydration. Your water intake must remain sufficient to make you urinate three times daily. Healthy urine is a pale straw colour.

In summer in the Sahara, you will need to drink up to 6 litres/10 pints of fluid daily. Keep your clothing on, as the insulating effect of a layer of clothes will reduce evaporation of sweat and reflect direct sunlight.

If you lie up during the heat of the day, remember that ground temperatures may be as much as 15°C hotter than the air temperature. Break through the crust of the desert into soft sand and you will find the temperature is as much as 30° cooler at 45 cm deep. So try to rest in deep shade or about 45cms above or below ground level. Bushmen of the Kalahari Desert

BUILDING A DESERT SHELTER

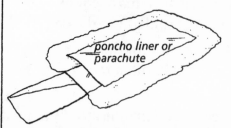

poncho liner or parachute

This shelter reduces the midday heat by as much as 15 to 20 degrees. However it does take more time and effort to build than other shelters so build it during the cool night to prevent increased dehydration during the day.

Construction

1 Find a low spot or depression between the dunes or dig a trench 45 to 60 cms deep and long and wide enough for you to lie down in.
2 Pile the sand from the trench around three sides to form a mound.
3 On the open end of the trench, dig out more so that you can get in and out easily.
4 Cover the trench with material such as a parachute or poncho.
5 Secure the cover in place using sand or rocks as weights.

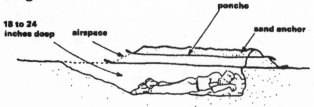

poncho

18 to 24 inches deep   airspace   sand anchor

You can reduce the temperature of the shelter further by adding an extra layer 30 to 45 cms above the first, creating an airspace between the two layers as shown.

urinate into holes in the ground and lie in them in the heat of the day to reduce sweating.

Don't smoke or breathe through an open mouth. This exposes the mucous membrane to the dry atmosphere, increasing your rate of dehydration. Reduce conversation for the same reason.

Finding water

If you are near a water supply stay there and set up ground-to-air distress signals. If you have to keep moving, look for signs that indicate the direction of a water supply.

Don't rely entirely on wild animals as a guide to water in the Sahara. Some are so adapted that they do not need a regular water intake as we do. Dorcas gazelles, jerboas and gerbils, for example, extract all the moisture they need from their foodstuffs. Foxes, jackals and hyenas, however do not stray too far from water.

Listen for the sounds of birds and baboons at early morning or evening. Quail fly towards water in the evening and away from it in the morning. Doves use the water both morning and evening but it may be along way off. Some turtle doves will fly 50 – 75 kilometres to water.

Man, on foot, and camels will eventually lead to water – but remember that a camel can walk vast distances between water stops. In camels, the water is stored in the stomach and Arabs in dire straits have been known to kill the animal and use this store of water.

Don't make the mistake of thinking that tyre tracks will lead to water – you could mistakenly follow your own tracks or those of someone else who is equally lost. In some parts of the Sahara the 'main' road is as much as 15 kilometres wide.

Study the rock in your surroundings; sandstone will absorb water after a rainstorm, basalt-type rocks will pool it on the surface. Dry stream beds, known as wadis, sometimes have water below the surface. Finding it is the problem. Look for greenery on the outside of a bend in a water course, and dig at its lowest point. You may have to dig deeper than your own height.

If you do find water, think before you camp in the wadi it-self. If it rains, wadis fill up with remarkable speed and become raging torrents.

Remember, survival in the desert is a matter of knowledge of the terrain, and minimising risks. As with all other extreme environments, you should not expose yourself to danger with-out proper training. The heat and the sun are your enemies; water and shelter are your friends. Without water you will be dead within a day; and if you can't find shelter, wear loose cloth-

---

SURVIVAL KIT

This could be combined with the first aid kit in a single pouch in the pack or on the belt. It is *not* to be treated as a kit to be opened only in an emergency. Use and familiarize yourself with the contents of your kits. Don't wait until you get into trouble before practising your survival techniques.

Wire saw with loop handles
Second compass (button or lapel type)
Fish hooks, line, weights and swivels
Strong needle and thread
Waxed non-safety matches that will strike on rough surfaces
Single large candle or three birthday-cake candles
Flint and steel
Cotton wool packing for use as fire starting aid.
Table salt in small container
Signal flares
Pen torch
Tube of Dextrose tablets
Heliograph
Ground to air recognition tables and Morse code sheet
Marker panel in fluorescent material
Whistle
Condom for water carrying

ing. Try to avoid exposing yourself to the sun; you don't see desert nomads working on their tans!

The desert still

The first attempts to extract moisture from air pockets within the desert sand were carried out simultaneously and independently at opposite ends of the world. Today, we accept the desert survival still as being a normal aid to survival in any desert.

To make a still, dig a hole roughly one metre square and 70 cms deep. Put a container at the bottom of the hole. Then put the end of a drinking tube at the bottom of the container. Cover the hole with a polythene sheet about 2m square threading the drinking tube under the edge of the sheeting. Then seal it all round the edge of the hole with sand or stones.

Let the sheet "belly in" – you can help by placing a stone in the centre of the sheet. This creates an inverted cone over the container at the bottom of the pit. The polythene must not touch the sides of the pit, or the container itself. If it does the condensed fluid will be wasted.

Theoretically, the sun's rays heat the ground inside the hole and cause the moisture trapped inside to evaporate. The moisture then saturates the confined air space and condenses on the cooler surface of the plastic sheet. This runs down into the container, where you can drink it through the drinking tube without having to destroy the still.

A still like this can produce up to a litre of water a day in some parts of the desert. In other areas very little is produced at all, unless you add greenery or urine in the evaporation space under the plastic sheet.

Purifying water

Treat all water in the desert, no matter where from, as suspect. Filter dirty water through several layers of cloth or a Millbank bag to remove solids. Even radioactive fallout can be removed in this manner.

Purifying the water involves killing the germs. To do this use purifying agents such as Puritabs, Halzone, Chloromine T, iodine, permanganate of potash, or simply boil it for between three and five minutes.

PROPRIETARY CHEMICAL PURIFIERS

Chloromine T: 1 cm/3/8th inch of matchstick loaded for 22 litre/5 gallon can

Tincture of iodine: 3 drops per litre of water

Household bleach: (5.2% sodium hypochlorite) 2 drops per litre for clear water, 4 drops for cloudy water. Water will taste of chlorine.

Puritab: 1 small tablet for 1 litre bottle. 1 large tablet for 5 gallon can.

Potassium permanganate: enough to colour the water pink.

The penalty you will pay for not purifying your water properly or neglecting to prepare food carefully or for lack of hygiene generally, is a severely upset stomach. This in turn can lead to dehydration and heat illness through loss of body fluids. Treat an upset stomach with a proprietary preparation, or if you don't have one, use crushed charcoal or burnt crushed bone. Neither taste very pleasant but both are effective. The tannic acid in a very strong brew of tea will also help. Continue to drink plenty of fluids during treatment.

Add charcoal while the water is boiling to remove disagreeable colours. Agitate it to restore its taste, or add a small pinch of salt.

There are many chemical purifiers, and the choice is a matter of personal taste. Generally, the water needs to stand for up to 30 minutes to allow the chemical time to act properly.

Carrying water

If you have any control over your circumstances, think about how you will carry your water supply. Always take 25 per cent more than you think you need, in several containers of unbreakable material. Glass and thin plastic containers are non-starters. Conventional military water bottles in tough plastic or aluminium are reliable, as are some of the civilian versions.

Avoid carrying single one or two gallon containers. Desert terrains are unforgiving – a slip can result in all your water supply being lost.

A condom from your survival kit (carried inside a sock for additional support) makes an excellent portable container.

Desert Hazards

Many of the creatures that live in the desert are potentially dangerous, from bats and snakes to scorpions and centipedes – and even dogs and spiders. Heat exhaustion, malaria and storms all offer their own hazards as well.

Bites
On your own in the desert, avoid suspect animals at all times.

Rabies virus is carried in the saliva of an infected animal and enters your body through breaks in the skin. Even a lick from a friendly but infected animal can infect you through a cut or abrasion. Potential carriers include dogs, cats, bats, and some types of rodents.

If you are bitten by *any* animal get a tetanus booster as soon as possible.

Scorpion stings
There are two common types of potentially lethal scorpion in the Sahara; *Androctonus australis* and *Buthus occiutanus* (also known as Fat Tailed scorpion because of its massive tail), which is often cited as the world's most dangerous. Drop for drop, their venom is as toxic as that of a cobra and can kill a man in four hours. If the scorpion stings in self-defence it will usually inject the maximum dose of poison.

The sting of a buthin scorpion produces intense pain at the site of the sting, often without discoloration apart from a small area of gooseflesh. A feeling of tightness then develops in the throat, so that the victim tries to clear imaginary phlegm. The tongue feels thick, and speech becomes difficult. The casualty becomes restless, with involuntary twitching of the muscles.

Sneezing bouts and a runny nose follow. There is an uncontrolled flow of saliva, which may become frothy. The heart rate will increase, followed by convulsions. The extremities turn blue before the casualty dies. The whole sequence of events may take as little as 45 minutes or as long as 12 hours.

Snakes

Snakes are permanent residents in most parts of the desert. They hibernate, however, and so you'll see fewer snakes in winter.

Most are venomous, so regard any snake bite as suspect and treat it as promptly as possible. Simple precautions against snake bite include shaking out boots and sleeping bags before you use them, and using a torch after dark.

Don't go barefoot; certain types of snake actually bury themselves in the sand, leaving only their nostrils and eyes showing. They ambush their prey – including you – in this fashion and are extremely difficult to spot.

If you get bitten by a snake, study the pattern of teeth punctures. If there are two well-defined punctures, the bite will be that of one of the viper group. Non-poisonous snakes with solid fangs, and mildly venomous back-fanged snakes, make a horseshoe shaped row of teeth marks.

It takes only 5 mg of venom from the Saw Scale Viper to kill a man. As with scorpion stings, defensive bites tend to contain the maximum amount of venom.

However, not every snake bite is fatal. You're more likely to survive a bite to the shin than one deep in the muscular tissues of the thigh or calf.

Treatment for snake bite

Ideally a snake bite casualty should be immobilized and given sedatives. Ice is put on the bite site, and a tourniquet applied and loosened at frequent intervals, and the casualty evacuated to hospital for treatment with anti-venene, adrenalin and plasma. The snake is killed for hospital identification.

In reality, you will probably be able only to attempt to restrict the amount and rate of venom entering the blood stream by applying a tourniquet between the bite and the heart. The tourniquet must not cut off the blood supply entirely – this can cause tissue damage and possibly gangrene and kidney failure. Release the pressure each half hour until you get help.

The patient must also be rested as much as possible, and kept calm. Panic can become a major problem – it increases the heart rate and so speeds the circulation of the venom in the blood. Physical exertion must also be avoided.

Opinions differ on whether to "cut and suck" or not. This treatment may worsen the situation, as any wound inside the mouth will allow the venom to enter into the system.

When you're on your own, there may be some value in cutting and bleeding as an alternative to simply sitting and hoping that the snake was not venomous. You can easily shed a pint of blood without any ill effects, and this may be all you need to do to save your life.

DANGEROUS WILDLIFE

Egyptian cobra
Typically about 2 metres long, the Egyptian Cobra can be black, brown or yellow. Some are light brown with darker crossbands. They like cultivated land, rocky hillsides, old ruins and even rural villages. Their venom is a very powerful neurotoxin; it attacks your nervous system, making it hard to breathe.

Sand Viper
Well camouflaged and only about 60 cms long, the sand viper is found throughout North Africa, its venom is haemotoxic; it attacks your circulatory system, causing tissue damage and internal bleeding.

Camel spider
The camel spider or 'wind scorpion' as it is known to the Arabs, grows to 15-20 cms in length and has some very anti-social eating habits. When not eating its fellows, the camel spider will eat beetles, scorpions and even small lizards at great speed by injecting a venom that dissolves the internal organs of the prey and then sucking out the resulting juices.

Simply cut yourself deep enough to bleed freely with a clean knife at both entry points. Then wash the cut in a solution of potassium permanganate. Do not urinate into the cut.

Overheating and water loss

The maximum water loss your body can tolerate is probably as high as 20 per cent. However 12 per cent is a more practical maximum. You won't be capable of making rational decisions after losing a fifth of your body fluids.

Upset stomachs can be a major cause of dehydration. On your own in the wild, you can quickly find yourself very ill indeed. Crushed and ground charcoal, chalk or bone will provide a cure. Similarly, the tannic acid in a very strong brew of tea will help.

Two conditions can arise from overheating; heat exhaustion and heat stroke.

Heat exhaustion usually affects people performing strenuous physical exercise in hot, humid climates. It's caused by loss of salt and water from the body. It will be aggravated by stomach upset, diarrhoea or vomiting.

Remove the casualty to a cooler environment and replace lost fluids and minerals. Seek medical aid.

Heat stroke is caused by a very high environmental temperature or a feverish illness (such as malaria) and leads to a greatly increased body temperature. It develops when the body can no longer control its temperature by sweating and can occur quite suddenly.

Reduce the casualty's temperature as quickly as possible and get medical help.

Malaria

This very debilitating illness is caused by the bite of the female *Anopheles* mosquito. The insect breeds in stagnant water. Take a course of anti-malaria tablets before you enter into an area where the disease is endemic, continue the treatment throughout your stay in the country and for the medically advised period on your return.

See your doctor for advice on the type of anti-malarial treatment recommended for the area. In an emergency, quinine is an effective if unpleasant treatment.

Dust storms

Generally, these are either limited to a height of about 6ft or rise to hundreds of feet in the air. In either case, if visibility is restricted, seal all equipment likely to be affected and be prepared to sit it out. This is preferable to getting lost or even injured in the poor visibility.

During severe dust storms, the air temperature can soar up to 58°C (135°F), while simultaneously the moisture content will drop to only a few per cent. A long lasting dust storm can cause serious dehydration; you can lose up to a quart of moisture in sweat in one hour in these conditions.

A side-effect of a prolonged severe dust storm is the rise in atmospheric electricity due to sand friction. This can cause severe headaches and nausea but can be neutralized by 'earthing' yourself to the ground.

Magnetic compasses will be affected in these conditions. The wisest course will be to stay where you are. Always carry a spare compass.

EMERGENCY SURVIVAL

When you find yourself stranded in the Sahara, you'll have to make up your mind whether to stay where you are, or try to move on. It's a decision governed by circumstances. If you've been travelling by aircraft, the pilot will have filed a flight plan. Similarly, employees of oil and water prospecting companies and similar organisations file a route plan with an estimated time of arrival. In the event of your non-arrival, a search and rescue plan will be put into action. Clearly, the best course here will be to remain with the aircraft or vehicle until help arrives.

The problems arise if you're stranded while engaged on military activities for real or on expeditions to more remote regions, where the chances of rescue are slim at best. In one region of the Sahara, some 43 people died in a single year. These are recorded deaths; the actual figure may be higher.

VITAL SKILLS

To improve your chances of survival in the desert, learn and practise these basic skills before going abroad. The average soldier will be familiar with most of the following but may find one or two techniques that aren't in the Army manual.

- Map reading
- Compasses, bearings, back bearings and variations
- Direction-finding using sun and stars
- Direction-finding using shadow stick methods
- Water location, extraction and purification
- Heat and its effects and how to avoid them
- First aid
- Signals – ground to ground and ground to air

In temperate or tropical zones the environment is relatively kind. The survivor is rarely far from materials water, foodstuffs and people to assist in an emergency. The desert militates against this and the decision to say or move is much more difficult to make.

You must consider your assets, equipment, physical state, mental state, navigational skills and equipment, water, food, location and the size of your party. Then you must weigh these against the distances involved, the terrain, your chances of rescue, weather, temperatures etc.

How far can you go?

By walking slowly and resting for 10 minutes every hour, a man in good physical condition can cover between 20 and 30 kms (12 and 18 miles) per day if he has sufficient food and water. If you plan on walking during the day, you may get 16 kms (10 miles) to one gallon of water. At night, you could possibly double that distance, since you will dehydrate less. If a lack of water is a problem then moving at night is more sensible. The disadvantages are that you may bypass water supplies and habitation.

Choose the easiest route. Go round obstacles, not over or through them. Zigzag to prevent over-exertion when climbing. Visibility for a man six feet tall is limited to between five and six miles when standing on a flat plain.

The sea shore

Your choices of direction are reduced to two since you can be certain that people will be living along the coast somewhere. You can also be sure of finding fresh water where rivers discharge into the sea. (The term 'fresh' means non-salt, rather than drinkable). All water will be heavily polluted, so take all precautions to make sure the water you drink is sterile.

You can also get 'fresh' water by digging several beach wells. Dig the holes a safe distance above the high-water mark, and

---

SIGNALS

You should carry a copy of the Morse alphabet in your survival kit and try to memorize the May Day signal along with the newer Pan signal. This is a lower priority signal recognized by all international maritime and aircraft crews.

May Day — • — • — • •

Pan • — • • — •

Include in your kit a set of ground-to-air signals as follows (see page 185):

Require doctor – serious injury

Need medical supplies

Unable to proceed

All is well

Do not understand

Am moving in this direction

Indicate direction to proceed

Need compass and map

No

Yes

deep enough to permit water to collect in the bottom. Skim off and use only the top layer of water – this will be less salty than the denser sea water below it.

The sea shore also has plenty of things living or growing on it that you can eat.

Signals

Set signal fires in threes, arranged in a large triangle with sides approximately 20 metres long. In daylight the glare from the ground and from the air reduces the visibility of wood fires as wood in the desert is so dry that it is smokeless. Add oil, rubbery plastic, or green plants, if available to generate smoke. You can also use mirrors for signalling over long distances in the desert.

Set ground signals too. These last a long time and need little or no maintenance. Lay out a large SOS in stone, preferably of contrasting colour to the ground, but at least large enough to cast a well defined shadow. There is an international system of ground-to-air signals which is worth carrying in your survival kit.

Fluorescent signal panels are a useful addition to your kit. Learn the international distress signal, and the reply. The distress signal is six flashes of light, six blasts of a whistle or six waves of a signal flag followed by a break of one minute before repeating the sequence. The response is three long blasts, waves or flashes.

The heliograph

The Mk 3 signal mirror issued to US forces is a handy heliograph which you can hang around your neck when not in use. Make sure the reflective side is against your chest when not in use.

1 Reflect sunlight from the mirror on to a nearby surface like a rock or your hand

2 Slowly bring the mirror up to eye-level and look through the sighting hole . You will see a bright spot of light which is the aim indicator.

SIGNALLING WITH AN AIR SIGNAL PANEL

Air panels are light, easy to carry and should be carried by at least two members of a patrol. The US issue VS-17 signalling panel is a simple plastic sheet which is violet on one side and orange on the other. Use the orange side to initially attract the pilot's attention. Flashing the panel will make it easier to spot. You can then use the panel to pass information as shown. You can use any reasonable substitute for the panel e.g. liferaft sails, bright-coloured rain jackets etc.

on land and at sea
OK to land (arrow shows landing direction)

on land and at sea
need medical attention

on land and at sea
do not attempt landing

on land and at sea
need gas and oil; plane is flyable

on land
need warm clothing
at sea
need exposure suit or clothing indicated

on land
indicate direction of nearest civilisation
at sea
indicate direction of rescue craft

on land and at sea
plane is flyable; need tools

at sea
need equipment as indicated (signals follow)

on land
need quinine or atabrine
at sea
need sun cover

on land and at sea
need first aid supplies

on land
should we wait for rescue plane?
at sea
notify rescue agency of my position

on land and at sea
need food and water

have abandoned plane
on land
walking in this direction
at sea
drifting

3   Hold the mirror near to your eye and move it so that the aim indicator is on the target.

CAUTION: Don't flash the mirror rapidly. In a combat zone, a pilot might mistake the distant twinkling for groundfire and treat you to a rocket attack! Don't hold the light on someone's cockpit either, or you could dazzle the pilot.

Mirror signals can be seen for many miles, even in hazy weather, so keep sweeping the horizon even if nothing is in sight. In a combat zone where you could attract the enemy attention you must obviously wait and positively identify an aircraft before signalling.

Navigation

With a map and compass you should be able to establish you position. Without these, you will have to improvise.

To find north, first establish south by pointing the hour hand of your watch towards the sun. Then find the mid point between the hour hand and the 12 o'clock position. The line from the centre of your watch to here points south.

Remember that if you are in a desert in the southern hemisphere the procedure is slightly different. Point the 12 o'clock position towards the sun and bisect the angle between the 12 o'clock position and the hour hand. This points north.

A digital watch can be used for the same task, despite opinion to the contrary. Either mark with a grease pencil or imagine the conventional watch face and hands showing the time, overlaid on the digital face. Then continue as above.

Remember that the sun rises in the east and sets in the west to within a few degrees. Remember also that in the northern hemisphere the sun is to the south of us and in the southern hemisphere the sun passes to the north of us.

The east-west line

Place a one-metre stick vertically into the ground and mark the top of its shadow with a stick or stone. After 15 minutes, place another stick or stone to mark the tip of the new shadow position. Then the straight line that joins these two points indicates roughly, east, west.

The north-south line

Put a stick in the ground in the morning and mark the tip of its shadow on the ground. Using a piece of string anchored to the base stick, draw an arc. The arc must be the same length as the shadow line you've just drawn. In the afternoon, when the tip of the shadow touches the drawn arc once more, draw a further line from the arc to the base stick. Bisect the angle formed between the two lines and the resulting line will indicate north-south.

Night navigation

If you move at night, you will need to be able to recognize certain star constellations, that either point the way north or point to the North Star (sometimes known as the Pole Star). The constellations to learn are The Plough, Orion and Cassiopeia. They appear at different times during the night throughout the year and revolve, so they may well appear upside down when compared with conventional star charts.

You must learn your constellations before you set out on any journey that involves the risk of being stranded. And *practise* all your survival skills before you need to use the.

Survival tips

Staying where you are

Aircraft wrecks: In some desert areas there are many aircraft wrecks left over from the war. These usually have 'wreck' painted across the wings. Make sure your aircraft cannot be mistaken for a wreck by having at least one signal operative at any one time. If you can, put out a large SOS in wreckage or stone on a stretch of the beach.

Aircraft kit: All commercial aircraft must carry a dinghy if they are travelling over water. In addition you will have the survival kit in the dinghy, a first aid kit and what you can salvage from the aircraft itself.

Air panel: Make sure you carry a fluorescent air panel in your survival kit. These can be used not just to draw the initial attention of a rescue aircraft but also to pass messages to the aircraft (see page 145).

Signal fires: Signal fires should be set in the shape of a triangle with the fires 20 metres apart. These are useless in the intense sunlight of the day unless you use plant material or oil to produce smoke. Smothering a fire with leaves tends to produce white smoke and oil produces black smoke. Make sure you produce a colour that contrasts with the background.

Limit movement: Any essential work should be done at night. During the day, get under cover, put something between you and the hot ground and stay there.

Stay in the shade: If you stay in the shade quietly, fully clothed, not talking, keeping your mouth closed and breathing through your nose, your water requirement will drop dramatically and consequently you will last a lot longer.

Conserving sweat: In this situation you are not going to have unlimited amounts of water, so if you cannot control the amount of water you take in you have to control the amount your body loses. This means complete body coverage. Roll your sleeves down and cover your head and neck. This will protect your body from the hot sand-laden winds and the direct rays of the sun. Your clothes will absorb your sweat and keep it against your skin so you gain the full cooling effect.

'Voluntary dehydration': When you are thirsty you will generally drink only 65 per cent of your daily requirement. To avoid this voluntary dehydration at temperatures below 35°C/100°F drink one pint of water every hour, at temperature above 35°C/100°F, drink two pints every hour.

Food discipline: If water is scarce, do not eat. Water is required for digestion of food and you need that water for cooling.

Health hazards: The sudden and extreme temperature shifts from day to night can cause chills, chest infections and even pneumonia.

Insects: Lice, mites, wasps and flies which are drawn to man as a source of water and food are extremely unpleasant and may carry disease. Old buildings, ruins and caves are favourite habitats for spiders, lice, scorpions, centipedes and other wildlife that can make life unbearable. Take extra care when sheltering in these areas. Always wear gloves and do not sit down or lie down without visually inspecting the area first.

Moving out

You must prepare for every eventuality; that includes having to walk out. Do it with a 5 gallon water jerrycan mounted on an aluminium rucksack frame with shelter kit and sleeping bag fixed on top.

Estimating distance: If you do decide to send off a party to find help remember that things always seem closer than they are in the desert by a factor of three. So a rough guide is that anything that looks one mile away is in reality three miles away.

Night marching: Although you will conserve water by moving at night visibility on moonless nights is extremely poor and travelling is very hazardous. Dangers include getting lost, falling into ravines and missing water sources. Conversely, moonlit nights are usually crystal clear, with none of the problems associated with daylight moves; winds die down and haze and glare disappear, you will be able to see lights at great distance and noise will carry further.

Sandstorms: Sandstorms or sand-laden winds occur regularly in most desert areas; for example the "Siestan" or desert wind of Afghanistan and Iran can blow up constantly for up to 120 days. Wind speeds in the storm could reach 70 to 80 miles per hour by early afternoon. Major dust storms can be expected at least once a week. When confronted with this you should take cover and mark its direction of travel. These storms will effect radio transmissions.

EVASION, CAPTURE
AND ESCAPE

There are any number of situations where you as a soldier will need the skill to evade. For example:

1   A breakout from a PoW camp or holding area.
2   An escape from a surrounded position in small numbers or as an individual.
3   As a result of the disruption of boundaries, between units after a tactical nuclear exchange.
4   As a result of becoming lost on patrol and straying into the enemy positions.
5   When your defensive position is overrun and not cleared.

EQUIPMENT

Could you survive and fight if you were captured and lost all your equipment except the clothes you stand up in? What if you were searched by an enemy soldier and had everything in your pockets taken away from you? He might not be thorough enough; though and you have had the foresight to conceal enough equipment in your clothing to enable you to escape.

If you are captured the man searching you is going to be so interested in retrieving stuff such as notebooks, maps and knives that he will not even think about looking in the other places where small items of equipment can be concealed.

Hiding places

He will find the tobacco tin containing your survival kit, and it is probably best not to hide any equipment in your jacket or smock as this will probably be taken off you straight away. Your shirt, jersey or trousers are, however ideal hiding places for escape and evasion equipment.

The most useful item of E & E kit is something you can usually guarantee not to be without: your brain. No-one can take away your skill or experience so prepare now. Useful things to conceal are:

1   A wire saw
2   A compass
3   A sharpened hacksaw blade

4   A fishing kit

5   A sewing kit

6   Condoms

7   Scalpel blades

8   Map

9   Firelighting oil

You can usually feed the wire saw into the waistband of your combat trousers; remove the rings from the saw, and replace

SURVIVAL RIFLE

A Ruger10.22 silenced semi-automatic rifle complete with folding stock and 4 x 40 scope will definitely keep the larder stocked.

SAS BELT ORDER

Sabre squadron troopers always carry E and E equipment, as part of their belt order. This is not the definitive layout, individuals are allowed to carry what they like once they are on squadron

1   Belt, pouches and water bottles
2   SLR magazines
3   Rifle cleaning kit
4   Purse net
5   Fishing kit
6   Snares
7   Mess tin lid and rations
8   Torch and filters
9   Button-compass
10 Wire saw
11 Fire starting kit
12 lock picks (note these are illegal in UK)
13 Clasp knife
14 Prismatic compass
15 Miniflares
16 Millbank bag for filtering water
17 Field dressing
18 Survival ration
19 Heliograph
20 Silk escape map

them with bootlace or nylon cord. Likewise you can feed fishing line into the seams of your clothing or under the collar of your shirt. Some soldiers remove all the buttons on their trousers or pockets and re-sew them using fishing line.

Fishing hooks are, however, a different problem. If you sew them into clothing unprotected, they may pierce the cloth and injure you; wrap them in PVC first. The same applies to needles and scalpel blades.

Boots are often cited as good hiding places for escape and evasion equipment, but beware. Walking is probably the only way you will be able to travel and if your boots are uncomfortable or unable to protect your feet you will be in trouble.

If you have very thick shock-absorbent insoles in your boots you can hide things beneath them, but check regularly to make sure the insole is not being worn away. Obviously only very thin items can be concealed this way, and nothing over about

---

CONDOMS
CAN BE USED AS:

1 Water carriers
Each one will take about one and a half pints. Remember to put the whole thing in a sock for support.

2 Surgical gloves
Bullet wounds are usually already highly contaminated, but if you are clearing out a wound put condoms on your fingers to reduce the chances of further infection.

3 Signalling devices
Useful for ground-to-air signalling; simply blow them up and place them on the ground in the desired pattern.

4 Waterproof containers
You can use them to protect kit or maps and for hiding things internally, and for keeping water out of weapons and radio equipment.

REMEMBER

1 Every piece of kit you smuggle through the first search will help you to escape.
2 If they keep searching, eventually they will find everything.
3 Make sure the piece of kit can be retrieved once you have escaped e.g. that it is not so well sewn in that you can't get at it.
4 Make sure you know how to use the kit you've hidden.

8cm long, as it may puncture the insole and your foot when the sole of the boot flexes.

Condoms also need to be concealed with care; if they are unprotected the plastic wrapper will eventually wear and damage the contents, so when you come to use one in a survival situation it has a hole in it! Wrap them in PVC tape (ideally, a minimum of five should be carried).

If you can conceal a flint and steel firelighter in your clothing so much the better, but make sure you know how to use it before sewing it in otherwise the space is wasted.

Small compasses are fairly easy to conceal and the small RAF button compass can even be swallowed and retrieved at a later date! However these compasses only really give an indication of magnetic North, and are not accurate enough for bearings.

Rough maps of your operational area are not as difficult to construct as you may think. Pilots and Special Forces are often issued with elaborate maps, printed on cloth or silk and disguised as handkerchiefs or sewn into the lining of clothing.

Your escape map should be a very simple affair, with only large towns, major roads, railways and rivers marked on it. Any other detail would be useless and confusing. Combined with your simple compass, it just makes sure you walk in the right direction. It is best drawn on rice paper or airmail paper, folded and wrapped in cling film or seran wrap and sewn behind a unit or rank patch or hidden under the insole of your boot.

EVADING DOGS

Every breath you take, every move you make, a dog can detect it. Perhaps as much as a mile away under the right conditions. And an attack dog, trained to silence, can be on you literally before you know it; travelling at 15 metres a second and weighing anything up to 45 kilograms, it is as lethal as any bullet. What can a man working behind enemy lines do to protect himself against these killers? In this section we're going to examine some of the dog evasion techniques taught to British Special Forces units.

Dogs of war are trained to do specific jobs. Guard and attack dogs are trained to detect, engage and, in some cases, to savage intruders or evaders either under the command of a handler or running free.

Search dogs are adept at picking up and finding the source of airborne scents and are allowed to run free, going over an area of ground yard by yard. Tracker dogs, on the other hand run on a long leash with a handler. Ground scents are the trackers' speciality. Search and tracker dogs lead their handlers to their target, but do not usually assault the fugitive, leaving that to the attack dogs, to the handlers or their combat back-up.

Eyes, ears and noses

Like most mammals except man dogs have very poor eyesight. They don't see colours at all, only shades of grey, and then not very clearly. They can see you moving of course, and this is very likely to attract their attention. Because their eyes are low down to the ground they're quick to see movement above the skyline.

If a dog's eyesight is only half as good as man's its range of hearing is twice as good. How far away they can hear you is affected by weather conditions, especially wind and rain. If the wind is blowing away from you and towards the dog, he's a lot more likely to hear you. Rain creates a background noise and makes individual sounds much more difficult to pick out. So take advantage of rain to get on the move.

It's not just that a dog can hear you a long way off, he can also hear sounds that man can't. High-pitched squeaks and whistles that you don't know exist are part of a dog's everyday life. So tape loose pieces of equipment to stop them rubbing and catching. Think about the way you use radios and other items of hardware. A clink of cooking utensils, a match being struck, even the sound of the flame when you're cooking your meal can give away your position to a well trained dog.

In fact if you were cooking a meal the chances are that he would smell you first – from anything up to a couple of miles away under the right conditions! Because while a dog's hearing is a lot keener than ours, his sense of smell is many thousands of times better.

The strongest human body odour comes from the sweat glands, especially under the arms. Moving quickly, particularly when carrying a heavy load and wearing too many clothes, makes you sweat heavily. So does being tense, nervous or frightened. Eating various types of strongly flavoured food makes it worse, and so does not washing regularly.

And it's not just the natural smells of our bodies that provide a target for the tracker dog's nose. Clothing especially when it's wet; soap and deodorants; leather; tobacco; polish and preservatives; petrol; oil; and many, many more smells that are a natural part of our everyday lives can give a dog a clue to your presence.

A dog picks up scent in two different ways; from the air, and from contact with the ground, trees, plants and buildings. Airborne scents do not last very long; they are blown away by the wind quite quickly.

Traces of movement

A ground scent, on the other hand, may be obvious to the dog for anything up to 48 hours. Ground scents are caused not just by you leaving your own smell on things you touch, but also by the movement itself. If you're walking on grass or pushing through vegetation you will crush leaves and stems with every movement.

Even on bare ground you will release air and tiny quantities of moisture that have been trapped in the soil, which smell quite different from the fresh air above the ground. From the scent 'footprints' that you leave behind a dog can even tell in which direction you're moving.

And because you push off each step with your toes, the front of the footprint is more obvious than the heel, and it only takes a few steps for a dog to work out which way you're travelling.

Just as each person's footprints look slightly different to the eye, so to a dog is the mixture of scents in the smell footprint slightly different. The dog recognizes this difference and so may be able to track one person even where there are a number of people travelling together, or where there are animals present.

Methods of evasion are detailed in the special sections, but remember the general point; although a dog can outhear, outsmell and outrun you, you can out-think him. To do that you must assess the skills of the dog opposing you, and use your wits and tactics to confuse all or most of its senses. Out-wit the dog or handler and you may escape where others may not.

Combatting Attack Dogs

Guard dogs and attack dogs either operate with a handler or are left to run free in a confined area. A dog that is running free in a compound may not even recognize his handler, but will attack absolutely anyone who comes into his territory. But whether the dog is on a leash or running free its training is designed to do just one thing – catch anybody who shouldn't be there.

You do have one slight advantage when dealing with a guard dog – he's fixed in one place, more or less.

1   Always approach from down wind.
2   Take it slowly and easily to minimize exertion, and thereby cut down the amount of smelly sweat you secrete.
3   Keep as low as possible and use natural features of the ground. Windborne scent doesn't quite travel in straight lines, but any natural obstacle will help.

4   Approach along paths used by other people.

5   When you get within 200 metres of the objective, don't stop for anything – dogs have been known to pick up scents even against the wind at this sort of distance.

6   If you're dealing with a dog guarding a building, try to get above the ground floor if you can; dogs have difficulty detecting people way above their heads.

7   If you find yourself close to a dog and handler unexpectedly, keep still. Guards have been known to pass within 10 metres of an intruder who's keeping perfectly still without detecting him.

Try to get above the dog's level; this will make his job more difficult.

Sacrificial defence

If you can't evade the dog you have to immobilize him. And you can't do that effectively until the dog is within attack range. You have to let the dog bite you. Wrap protection around the forearm of the hand you don't use by choice. Arrange it in three layers. A soft one on the inside as padding; a hard one next to

Protect your forearm with three layers of padding

Allow the dog to grab your protected arm. If you're still standing you can club the animal.

If the dog leaps on you, roll over with him and keep his body tight to yours. Work your way around onto the top and back of the dog to immobilize it.

stop the dog's teeth penetrating; and lastly another soft layer to give the dog something to get his teeth into.

Don't discourage the dog from attacking you, but make sure

he takes the offered target; he will be more difficult to deal with the second time. When he's sunk his teeth into the padding, he's within reach, and you can deal with him.

Evading Tracker Dogs

So what can you do to fool the dog? Let's split the mission up into four phases; lying up, pre-contact, distant contact, and close contact.

Lying up

If you have to spend any length of time in a lying up place always obey these simple rules, even if you have no proof that a search dog is operating.

1   Keep as close to the ground as possible.

2   Put most of your clothing over you so that the ground absorbs your scent rather than letting it out into the open air.

3   Breathe down into the ground or at least into the vegetation.

4   Keep as still as possible.

5   Bury rubbish under where you are lying.

6   No smoking, no fires wherever possible.

7   If you're discovered by anyone move away as fast as you can.

Pre-contact

Use all the normal physical camouflage tricks to blend into the environment, plus a few that are designed to throw the dog off the scent.

1   Travel over ground already used by other people or by animals. This makes the dog work much harder to keep on your track.

2   If you're travelling as part of a group, split up from time to

time. Double back on yourself. Leave a false trail wherever possible.

3   Use streams and running water to confuse the dog, but don't try to walk for too long in the stream itself – it will slow you down too much. Instead cross the stream diagonally, doubling back perhaps two or three times so that the dog can't tell which of your exit tracks is the real one and which ones are dummies.

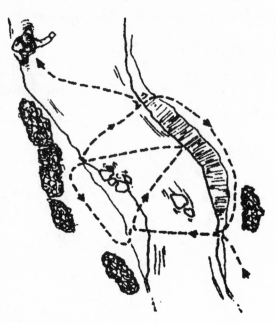

4   When you're preparing food, pay close attention to the direction of the wind. You must bury all wrapping and containers, but remember too to handle them as little as possible. The smell of the food is one thing, your smell on the wrappers tells the dog that it was your food. When you bury the remains, don't touch the

ground with your hands. Use a metal tool of some sort. Whenever you can, sink the rubbish in deep water. The same goes for urine and faeces.

Distant contact

If you're sighted from a distance, speed becomes important.

1   Try to tire the dog and handler team; it will be easier to destroy their confidence in each other if they make mistakes through tiredness.

2   If you're part of a group then split up straight away, and arrange a rendezvous for later.

3   Make for hard ground. A road or a rocky surface makes and holds much less scent than a soft one.

4   If you are in wood country or scrub, double back and change your direction as often as you can.

5   The tracker dog will be on a long lead. If you can get him tangled up you can increase the distance between you and him and maybe break off the contact entirely.

Close contact

If the dog catches up with you you're in deep trouble. Not so much from the dog, he's done his job in finding you. Now you're in trouble from the handler and whatever combat back up he may have available.

1   Forget the dog for the moment. You'll know from the look of him whether he's an attack dog or a tracker. If he's a tracker, he probably won't come near you.

2   Move as fast as you can. Get out of sight of the handler.

3   Get rid of loose pieces of clothing, food (especially food – the dog may be distracted by it when he comes looking for you) and any other pieces of kit that aren't vital to your mission or your survival.

4   If the dog sticks with you, you must kill or immobilize it.

Evasion and Capture

To be taken prisoner is the worst thing that can happen to a soldier. Death is quick; a wound will see you evacuated to a field hospital for treatment; but capture exposes you to a nightmare of torture, indoctrination and exposure. An army is a part of a nation, an arm of government, and every government goes to great lengths to protect its soldiers from every danger, including that of mistreatment as a prisoner of war.

Techniques in which Special Forces are trained are not widely published, but reliable sources applying to all soldiers do exist. The United States Army issues Field Manuals – FM 21-76 and FM 21-78 – that deal only with evasion, escape and survival. This section is taken from those manuals. It deals with evading enemy forces and how to behave if you're captured.

The manuals put a new word into the English language – the evader. A man, probably on his own, being hunted by enemy troops in unknown country. The chances against him are enormous, but if he keeps his head and remembers his training, he just might escape – against all the odds. Evaders are split into two types; short-term and long-term.

Short-term evasion

You're a short-term evader if you or your unit is temporarily cut off from the main body of your forces. This can happen quite frequently while you're on patrol, for instance, and is actually the way of life of long range patrol units (known as LURPS in the US military).

When you know you're going to be separated from the main force, navigation and fieldcraft are your best friends. Knowing where you are and which direction you're heading in is going to help save your life, and your own skill in moving cross country or through town will finish the job.

Long-term evasion

Very few people have to evade the enemy for long periods of time or cross long stretches of enemy held territory. The only people likely to have to undertake this most difficult and arduous task are aircrew who have been shot down, and escaped prisoners of war, though patrols are sometimes sent so far out that the same principle applies to them.

Try to relax. Fear and tension will only force you into making mistakes. Time is on your side. It doesn't matter how soon you get back to your own people, as long as you do get back. This may mean lying up for weeks or even months and applying all your survival skills.

Under military law, a soldier must make every effort to return to his unit. If captured, it is his duty to try to escape – though few ever do so successfully. Getting 'home' will be a lot easier before you're captured. You must use all the tricks of camouflage and concealment to say hidden from the enemy.

Rely on your own resources. Don't trust civilians unless you absolutely have to. Their whole way of life will be strange to you. A gesture that in your home town might mean 'welcome' could mean the very reverse in enemy territory.

It's not a good idea – ever – to try to disguise yourself as a native. Even if your colour and clothes don't give you away, and you happen to speak the language, the smallest gesture will be enough to show an experienced observer that you're not what you're pretending to be.

If you have been lucky enough to make contact with a friendly local group, be guided by them – but remember that no conventions of war apply to them. Any civilian found helping you will probably die for it.

Take every opportunity to distance yourself from your helpers. If you have to travel with a member of a local resistance group, for instance, don't sit together. Arrange a system of simple signals so that you don't have to speak.

Be ready to go it alone at any moment, and don't carry anything that could point a finger of suspicion at anyone who might have helped you. No names and addresses written down; no marked maps. Remember that you're a representative of your country – perhaps the first one the natives have actually met. Even under the hardships that an evader must endure, it's up to you to make a good impression. Remember, you're fighting a war that requires their cooperation.

9 POINTS FOR SUCCESSFUL EVASION

1 Large groups are easily detected. If there are a lot of you, split into four-man teams, which are a lot harder to detect.

2 As long as you are wearing your uniform you can attack enemy military targets, but not civilians.

3 Do not disguise yourself as a local unless you can do so convincingly. Amateur disguises and ignorance of local language and customs will quickly betray you.

4 If you landed by parachute, you should assume that the enemy spotted your descent and get out of the immediate area as fast as you can.

5 Observe the basic rules of camouflage, concealment and movement at all times.

6 Take your time when travelling; hurrying makes you less alert and tires you out.

7 Avoid populated areas and busy routes wherever possible. If approached by strangers pretend to be deaf, dumb or just half-witted; it often works.

8 If you are being helped by the local population, do not make any marks on your map; if you are captured with it the enemy could work out who was assisting you.

9 Observe enemy troop movements, military positions, weapons and equipment if you have the chance – but do not write anything down, or you risk being treated like a spy.

Communicating

If you do get the chance to talk to natives and feel secure enough to ask them for help, communicating is going to be a big problem. The chances are you won't speak each other's language, so you'll be reduced to making signs and gestures. To make this easier, the US, for example, issues each soldier with what is known as a 'Blood Chit'. A Blood Chit is an American Flag, printed onto cloth, with a message in English, and all the other languages you are likely to come across in the area in which fighting is taking place. The last, and most important feature of the Blood Chit is a unique number that identifies the person it was issued to.

The message asks for help and assistance. It promises that this will be rewarded. Don't give up the Blood Chit itself. Anyone who helps you will get their reward just by quoting the number. Give them the number but don't give them the chit itself.

If you lose your Blood Chit, report it straight away. It's a very

REJOINING YOUR UNIT

If you're out on patrol there will be an established method of rejoining your own forces – direction of approach, safe periods, recognition signals, password and all the other ways of making sure that you don't come under fire from your unit. You won't have the benefit of these safeguards, so you must follow basic rules when rejoining.

1   Get in a position close to the front line
2   Watch and wait for a friendly patrol
3   Let them come to you
4   Don't give away your position – or that of the patrol – to enemy forces.
5   Show a white cloth
6   Shout out an unmistakeable greeting
7   Don't fool around. The patrol will believe you're the enemy trying to trick them until you prove otherwise.

If you get caught without map, compass or other navigating equipment, use your memory. Orient yourself by listening to the fighting. Use your time behind the enemy lines to gather intelligence. Take a prisoner if you think you have a reasonable chance of making it back to your own lines with him. You must think positively all the time. Fear is your worst enemy.

valuable document. If it falls into the hands of the enemy's Intelligence Section, they could very easily use it to discover which members of the local population are likely to be friendly to you and this will probably get them shot. It will certainly make sure that no-one trusts the chit – or you.

It may be possible for your own people to rescue you, most likely from the air. To stand a chance of this being successful you must know the standard ground to air distress signals.

Don't call down a rescue attempt unless you are absolutely sure that the area is safe. Remember that a helicopter is most vulnerable to attack when it's taking off and landing. Make sure that any signals can be removed or covered up very quickly in case an enemy air patrol should appear.

Save the wounded

If there are casualties, make sure they get off first. If you do have seriously wounded men in your party, you must always consider whether their best chances of staying alive are to surrender (United States law allows that). Obviously, local conditions will be important – a man with a light wound surrendering to troops who are known to kill all prisoners, despite the Geneva Convention, is not helping himself!

Intelligence of all sorts – and evidence of the blood-thirstiness of enemy troops is only one sort – is really vital. Use every means you can to learn about enemy troop movements and placement, and the attitude of local non-combatants.

Try to keep abreast of the progress of the war as a whole, too. You may be hiding for nothing! Remember that some Japanese infantrymen were still living concealed in the jungle of the South Pacific islands 25 years after the end of World War II because they didn't know it was all over.

If the worst does happen and you face capture, your first decision will be whether to try to fight you way out. If you're alone and unarmed, this is not likely to be an available option, but if you're with your unit and your armament is up to strength, you may stand a very good chance of wining a fire-fight even against a larger enemy force, because surprise will definitely act in your favour – the last thing the enemy force will expect is an armed and trained group of soldiers behind its own lines.

If you are captured, you are required to tell the enemy, only four things – your name, rank, serial number and date of birth. Say nothing else. Don't refer to your unit by name, don't talk about your superior officers, don't identify the leaders of your group. The smallest piece of information may be useful to the enemy.

Searching and handling a prisoner

This is how you can expect to be treated by an enemy who plays by the rules.

Standing position: arms stretched, body relaxed. They work from top to bottom and will check your clothing carefully

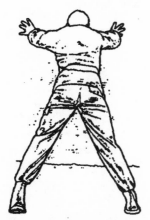

Stress position: with your weight on your fingertips and toes, you cannot react quickly. Expect your groin and armpits to be checked as well.

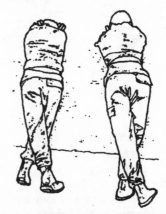

If you are caught in a group they may position you like this to prevent fast reaction against a search.

Again, if you are in a group, you will be placed close together and your captors will not move between you.

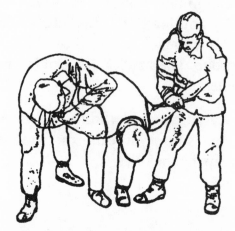

A two-man arrest position: one fixes you with an armlock while the other applies pressure points.

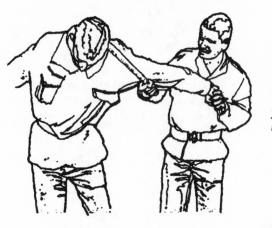

One way of using a baton to support an armlock: with the baton under your arm and behind the neck you are immobilized.

Arresting method with a baton: by pushing this between your legs and grabbing you by the neck, the guard can move you easily by pushing your neck and raising his right arm.

Ejecting Behind Enemy Lines

You know what is likely to happen if you have to abandon your aircraft over the sea – but what would you do if you were forced to eject over land? Whether you crash or bang out, and whether you're over friendly or enemy territory, the basic rules of survival are essentially the same. Obviously, your prospects are better if you land in a friendly country. Things become slightly more complicated should you be unlucky enough to get shot down by the very people you have just been trying to kill. The *basic rules* of survival remain the same but, with enemy troops now looking for you, you will need to use considerable guile and cunning.

Escape and Evasion (E & E) is a subject all aircrew should be

---

THE 'GO-PACK'

Irrespective of whether you fly in a single seat jet or a multi-seat aircraft, you will always carry emergency survival equipment. The Personal Survival Pack (PSP) carried underneath your seat holds the bulkier, heavier kit. However the PSP my well get lost if you are forced to bang out in combat. In the event of coming down behind enemy lines you may have little or no time to retrieve it.

For this reason, all aircrew should carry a 'Go-Pack'. The official RAF version contains: a 7ft x 3ft polythene sleeping bag, firelighting kit, 4 grips, a compass, 4 rubber bands, an instruction sheet, 6 plastic ties, 15ft x 150 lb nylon cord and three 6 in x 10 in polythene bags. However most aircrew prefer to make up their own Go-Pack – the contents of which are often carried in a container such as an Emergency Flying Ration tin. For those who can afford a little extra room, a container measuring approximately 18 cms x 10 cms x 4cms can accommodate: a 7ft x 3ft sleeping bag, a candle, a melinex sheet (space blanket), fishing kit, firelighting kit, fire blocks, a compass, needles, a scalpel, water purification tables, cotton wool, nylon cord, brass wire, wire saw, water carriers (ie *unlubricated* condoms), instruction sheet and a couple of Tampax (ideal for firelighting).

EMERGENCY FLYING RATIONS

Mark 9 27.P/38 Instructions

These are the RAF's instructions on what to do with your rations.

1 All food components in this pack may be eaten ONLY when about three pints of drinking water per man per day are available.

2 Used efficiently the ration will provide sustenance for a number of days, even when doing hard work, provided that fresh water is available.

3 The circumstances in which you find yourself must decide the amount to eat each day. Plan this carefully, endeavouring to eat a portion of each food each day. As a general rule, it is not necessary to eat very much on the first day of the survival period.

4 It is not essential for most men to drink water during the first day of the survival period. Obvious exceptions are those who are injured or losing body water at an excessive rate by sweating, vomiting or diarrhoea. If possible each man, after the first day, should drink at least one pint, (half a litre) of fresh water per day. Under some circumstances this may be impossible. However even three quarters of a pint per man per day can sustain life for quite long periods, depending upon the climatic conditions and other circumstances.

5 At all times conserve body water, for man can survive longer without food than he can without water. During survival at sea, and in very hot climates, utilize shade and breeze where possible and avoid unnecessary exertion. If marching move by night if possible.

6 NO MATTER HOW THIRSTY YOU ARE DO NOT DRINK SEA WATER AND DO NOT ADD SEA WATER TO FRESH WATER RATIONS. However if a few drops of sea water get into your fresh water rations by mistake this is not serious.

7 Fresh water should be purified before it is consumed. This can be achieved by boiling or using the water purifying tablets provided. Sea water cannot be purified by either of these methods.

------------------------------CONTENTS------------------------------

DRINKS

Beef Stock 'Cubes' – half a 'cube' to a lidful of water (Note sterilisation of water)

Coffee or Tea – if the water has not been sterilized with Puritabs, or previously boiled, then it must be boiled during the making of coffee or tea.

Milk Powder – add to drinks as required

Sugar – use as preferred

──────── **FOOD PACKS** (Flavoured bars or tablets) ────────

Remove carefully from the laminate pouch so that these can be used again to store water or food.

  Eat the food portions only when hungry

  Not more than eight portions a day

  Eat one tablet at a time. Chew slowly and well.

Salt – when doing hard work, and sweating vigorously AND WHEN PLENTY OF DRINKING WATER IS AVAILABLE salt should be taken. Do not take salt if water is in short supply. If you take extra salt you need extra water. The salt will also help to remove leeches when applied to their point of attachment.

Spatula – all purpose mixing utensil. This can also be used as a drinking straw for the water pouch.

──────────────── **BOX** ────────────────

Use the box and lid as cooking pots. Use the empty food bags for storing water and food components. The four lengths of wire make 'loop' handles for the box. The ends of a length of wire should be place in the holes at one end of the box and bent in the form of a hook.

Note: The box holds about three quarters of a pint of water when full to the holes for the wire.

──────────── **STERILISATION OF WATER** ────────────

Fresh water must be sterilized before drinking using either of the two methods below:

  If water is muddy it should be filtered through a handkerchief, piece of sheeting, or other available material.

  The tablets are the first method of choice.

a   Water purifying tablets

  These are found in the survival kit.

  Add 1 tablet to the polythene bag or lid full of water then wait 10 minutes before using.

b   Boiling

  Heat water until it boils. Boil for as long as is practicable. If stored keep in a clean bag or other clean container.

SEA WATER IS NOT PURIFIED BY BOILING OR
PURITAB TABLETS

taught. The actual term can be misleading and should perhaps read Evasion and Escape. This is because you are *escaping* only when you reach a neutral country. Prior to this you are *evading*. Evasion begins from the moment you arrive on enemy soil. Imagine that your Harrier aircraft has been hit during a low-level interdiction raid. Luckily, there is just enough time for you to eject. You find yourself drifting down towards a vast open plain. Seconds later, you thud into the ground and quickly get out of your parachute harness, to stand, shaken but unhurt. Hastily, you gather up your parachute and sling the heavy bundle across your back. There is no time to bury it and, besides, it will be useful later on.

Get moving

Dusk is rapidly falling yet in the east it looks as though dawn is just breaking. However, the red glow on the horizon is not of nature's doing, but the results of countless fires caused by your own bombs. To the west, the setting sun is partly obscured by a pillar of dark, oily smoke rising from the twisted wreckage of your crashed aircraft.

It is essential that you now put as much distance between yourself and the place where you have landed before the enemy come searching. You decide to head south, away from the burning target area and the Harrier crash site. Besides, your map shows a huge forest beyond a range of low hills just visible in that direction. You can hole up there for a couple of days.

The excitement of the moment results in an excess of adrenalin – so you can maintain an energetic pace despite the weight of your parachute. After a while, however the reality of the situation begins to tell, and your pace slows to a walk. It is late at night by the time you reach the first hill. You do not arrive at your destination until early in the morning.

Stay in hiding

By travelling just five miles you increase the enemy's area of search to some 75 to 80 square miles, and you estimate that you have covered a good 10 to 12 miles. Excellent! The next priority is to remain hidden for at least 48 hours, thus rendering obsolete any tactical information you might have. Also the longer you can stay free, the greater your chances of remaining free. A search party's eagerness will naturally diminish as time passes.

The effort of lugging your parachute pack all through the night now begins to pay off, as you can use the material to make a shelter. During survival training you will have been taught how to build a variety of shelters. However not all are suited to an evader in enemy territory. A well-constructed parachute tent will certainly shield you from the elements but not from the eyes of hostile civilians and enemy soldiers.

When you're weary, it is all too easy to ignore the basic principles of camouflage. But unless you camouflage your position and do it well, you will be caught!

A soldier will be extremely respectful towards a pilot seated in the cockpit of an aircraft. Yet that same soldier is fully aware that outside his element a pilot is a different bird indeed. If detailed to search for downed air crew most soldiers, especially those from the more professional units will take the task as a challenge to their skills. If they were at the receiving end of your attack, they will have another good reason for finding you!

Their task may well be made easier by the attitude of some airmen. Because of his own 'elite' status, a pilot might be tempted to underestimate the infantryman. Don't! Once on the ground you must exercise extreme care if you are to evade your searchers, for you are now treading in *their* territory – literally.

Use your common sense when choosing a site for your shelter. Ask yourself, if you were in a search party, where would *you* look? Don't hide in caves or choose isolated cover. Pick an unlikely spot that stands a good chance of being overlooked. If possible, try to hide out fairly close to a water source, and go for high rather than low ground.

Once in position, avoid making tracks. Use the same route in and out. Don't leave the shelter unless you have to. Keep still and quiet, and stay alert. If you are a smoker, throw away your cigarettes so that you are not tempted. The aroma of burning tobacco can be detected for a considerable distance. Bury all refuse, and when you eventually move out, don't leave any traces of your stay.

Moving on

After two or three days you might consider moving on. Before doing so, bear in mind the 'Five Ps': Prior Planning Prevents Poor Performance. Decide where you are going and, if possible, plan on the route. Take only what you need. By now you will have an idea of what is essential. Conceal everything else. As always use your common sense. Move only at night and avoid people, built up areas and roads.

During your trek across enemy terrain you could be presented with an opportunity to hit at the enemy. You will definitely be in a unique position to observe him at first hand. Remember anything that might be of use to Intelligence. This is assuming that you can pass on that information within a reasonable span of time.

You may be aware of an escape net operating in the country you are in. If you manage to contact such an organisation, you will, initially, probably be treated with distrust. This is understandable, as such people survive by being extremely cautious. Once contact is made be prepared to be left alone while they observe your reactions. You will probably then be blindfolded before being taken away for questioning.

If the escape organisation is satisfied by your replies, you can then expect them to help you. Of course, the enemy could impersonate such a group, so never give away classified information, and take care not to implicate anybody else.

In exceptional circumstances you could be in for a long journey before reaching the safety of a neutral country. You could be shot down in the middle of summer – and find yourself still on the run at the onset of winter. Your trek to freedom could take months, even years. One German paratrooper, captured by the Russians during World War II, took *three years* to reach his homeland during his escape from Siberia!

Keep up your spirits

If the prospects of a long uncomfortable journey, fraught with danger, seems too grim, try to remember why you should continue:

1   It is easier to evade than to escape.
2   You will be better clothed and equipped before, rather than after capture.
3   If captured, you will be moved to a prison camp far away from safety.
4   An evader is a *free man!*

And if that is not reason enough, bear in mind that according to regulations:

'Any person . . . shall be guilty of an offence against the appropriate section if . . . he . . . fails to take . . . any reasonable steps to rejoin HM Service which are available to him.'

MAINTAINING THE WILL TO SURVIVE

Knowing that you may have to travel hundreds of miles over a period of months may be a little upsetting; having to survive alone in a strange environment for this period may make dying look like the easy option.

The determination to survive must be maintained at times by sheer willpower; most of the obstacles you will have to overcome will be mental rather than physical. The factors that make all the difference are:

1   A sense of responsibility, loyalty to your unit and a sense of duty.
2   Family and home ties; having something worthwhile to survive for.
3   Self control; thinking the problem through rather than panicking.
4   Planning; preparing a plan that makes use of all available resources.
5   Endurance; pain, discomfort and other unpleasant conditions must be accepted as normal.
6   Leadership; the strong help the weak.
7   Knowledge of escape and evasion and survival techniques.

In other words it is your duty to survive, to escape to fight again!

Urban Evasion

Urban evasion, like its rural equivalent, varies according to the climate and wealth of the country you are operating in. For example, a country with strong family or local loyalties or with a restrictive political regime will be harder to move about in than one in which there is a large 'floating' population, a high level of personal wealth and public transport and facilities. The important considerations will be the sense of national threat and suspicion that has been generated by war.

A large Western city can be a very anonymous place. Even to members of ethnic minorities it offers a level of concealment. Citizens will keep to themselves and as long as your manner and appearance do not attract attention you can move fairly freely. Always include a shaving kit in your E & E gear – unshaven men will always attract attention. Trains, entertainment centres etc, can offer protection from the weather by day and sometimes by night; evasion is not helped by standing around.

Movement by day

Generally, moves by day are not a good idea, but are sometimes unavoidable. If you have to move by day;

1   Be confident; look as if you know where you are going, do not loiter and do not appear furtive.
2   Obtain some unobtrusive clothing and try to assume a definite identity; e.g. steal a donkey jacket and carry a spade.
3   Keep clean, and shave if possible.
4   If you can get hold of a bike you are doing well, but assess the risk before you steal it. Use public transport if you are completely confident that you know how the system works.
5   Keep away from stations and bus terminals.
6   Rivers are an excellent escape route, but the larger ones will be watched.
7   Watch out for children and dogs. Children are not bound

MOVEMENT BY NIGHT

Virtually all evasive moves should be made at night. Do not be over confident; remember the enemy has night vision devices. You will always have to compromise between choosing the easiest route and not going where the enemy expect. Remember:

1 Learn the route.
2 Unless you have foolproof documentation and the right clothes, never move on roads.
3 Never cross bridges; use improvized rafts or swim.

---

by grown-up conventions of social behaviour, and when they see something peculiar they will point it out loudly.

Checkpoints

If you have to pass through an area covered by a checkpoint, imitate the silhouette of the enemy sentries as far as possible, especially headgear, which is a common recognition feature. Learn at least one phrase in the local language along the lines of 'Don't shoot you idiot, it's me!' – and make sure it is fluent.

Weapons

You will have a good chance of bluffing your way out of a stop and search check if you have the right document and kit and know the language. In this case, do not blow your chances by carrying a weapon. If you have no chance of bluffing then consider carrying a weapon; silenced firearms are ideal, but otherwise choose something that is concealable or not in itself harmful e.g. a screwdriver or chisel. Silenced firearms are ideal, but realistically a meat skewer is more the sort of thing you can hide in your kit.

Capture

If you are caught in civilian clothes you will not be able to claim protection as a PoW; you will probably be treated as a spy and eventually killed.

Slumming it

One way of surviving is by becoming a vagrant. This is not as easy as it may sound. In many cities there is a well-developed underworld of vagrants and drop-outs and your arrival among them will not go unnoticed. The vagrants may include informers or drug addicts, who are an easy target for pressure by the police or enemy security forces.

If you can degenerate to a low enough level you will become an unlikely suspect. You may have problems with your health and in protecting yourself against bad weather if you adopt this technique.

Foraging for food is easy in a wealthy environment as long as you are prepared to examine the contents of café and restaurant dustbins. This type of odd behaviour will also add to your cover as a vagrant.

Dustbins are an excellent source of food and useful kit. Use the lid to sort through the stuff or lay it out on some paper so that you do not make a mess. If you take things away you must fill the bin with newspaper and try to leave the top layer undisturbed; people notice how full their dustbins are.

The vagrant approach to urban evasion depends on the society in which you are on the run. A European vagrant could be the object of great interest in some African or Far Eastern cities, and this would not assist your attempts at concealment. But in North America and all of Western Europe you could easily pass as a victim of war or civil disturbance. In this environment you can effectively pretend to be insane.

Deep Cover

Food can be a problem, depending on how you intend to work. If you go into deep cover and remain concealed in a 'safe house', you will depend on your hosts. There may be problems where food is rationed or controlled.

Within the house you will, as in an OP, need a look-out position and, most importantly, a place to hide. Many modern houses are built to well known specifications; a search team will perhaps have plans, they will at least have a good knowledge of the type of house. Older houses, on the other hand may have common roof space that allows you to move from house to house in a run of terraced buildings. Flats that have been converted from larger buildings offer good hiding places, but may be less sound-proof.

The ideal hiding place should be small so that its presence does not detract from the space or comfort of the house. However it should not be so small that prolonged occupation becomes uncomfortable. Water and a bucket for waste matter are the basic priorities and good ventilation is essential. A bench or seat is welcome.

The walls of the hide should be thick enough not to sound hollow. Various types of sound insulation can be added to the inside to give the impression of a solid structure. Lay in a store of simple foods that will not deteriorate over time and which have basic wrappings.

When you have prepared the inside you should practise a 'crash move' – getting into the hide from 'a standing start' from somewhere else in the house or flat. When you are under cover, the householder will have to remove any trace of your presence in the building. This can include extra food, and plates, books and magazines, clothing of the wrong size or sex and even the extra toothbrush or towel in the bathroom.

This type of concealment assumes that your evasion is assisted by relatively well-paid people with a circle of reliable contacts. Such people do not normally have a traditional fear of authority but nor do they have the skills of deception and concealment.

The grey man

The mid-way approach to evasion is to adopt the 'grey man' technique. Here you aim to have as anonymous an appearance as possible. Clothing should be neutral and your behaviour will have to be that of a 'solid citizen' – such people do not sit around in public parks or search through dustbins; they are on their way to or from work.

But this can be very tiring, and you will need a good command of the local language. The advantage is that unlike the vagrant you are less vulnerable to assault by other vagrants or bored members of the enemy police force. Your travel through the country is less likely to be questioned, but – and this is critical – you will need the right paperwork, work permits, identity cards, even documents for travel in restricted areas such as the border and you must also have money.

It may be that you can make the transition from deep cover to a grey man role. During your time in cover you will be able to learn some language and local knowledge before venturing out.

Seasonal advantages

Though evasion and escape can be easier in the country in spring, summer and early autumn, the city can have attractions in the winter. The major disadvantage is that contact with enemy citizens or even occupying powers is inevitable, and this can compromize you.

Jungle Evasion

Evasion in an environment such as tropical jungle, savannah grassland or deep temperate forest can be a case of survival rather than evasion. Enemy hunters may find searching for you or your group as difficult as locating the proverbial needle in the haystack. But your movements may be predicted by shrewd hunters and they can place ambushes or stop lines on features.

You will probably have a compass and basic survival kit and even if you escape from a PoW camp or convoy you need a sense of direction, particularly if moving by night. Hunters will try to put stops between you and friendly forces or an open border or sea coast. They will also look at the easy routes, for instance tracks or river lines. Roads and railways are often covered by transport police or civil security forces.

Security vs speed

You will be faced by a trade-off between security and speed. Movement by day is faster, and in deep jungle movement by night is almost impossible. But grassland should be covered at night since helicopters or fixed wing aircraft can cover large areas very easily by day.

Jungle varies between primary and secondary, and though the high canopy of trees in primary may obscure the horizon and make navigation difficult, it is excellent cover from the air, and the going on the ground is easy. However it does not adequately conceal you from enemy troops.

Secondary jungle gives excellent cover, but is very hard going on foot and can house dangerous plants and animals. But among these threats to life and health there will be edible plants and scope to make animal traps – you have to wait for the trap to be sprung, and it may be found by local people who will report its presence to the enemy.

Finding water

Water can be collected from plants or as rainfall, but avoid streams unless you have sterilising tablets in a survival kit. There are a vast number of killing or incapacitating organisms in rivers.

Savannah and bush have water holes and do give you a better chance to kill game, but remember that you will have to cook it. Cooking takes time, requires a fire and the trade-off of the nutrition of the meat against time and vulnerability is a decision that you or your team will have to make on the ground. Dried or smoked meat is one way of making the most of game that you may have killed.

Talking to the locals

You may be obliged to enter a village, perhaps because you need urgent help or simply through bad navigation. Most villages have dogs and dogs bark. This will warn the locals that there is a stranger about. Avoid crossing rivers downstream of the village; there may be sewers as well as the 'launderette'. Remember that infection can enter your body through your skin as well as you mouth.

You will be an object of great interest to the locals, but not necessarily an object of hostility. Your colour, clothing and equipment will be observed.

APPROACHING THE LOCAL PEOPLE

As an evader, getting the local population on your side is of paramount importance. If you are going to approach a village a thorough recce is essential. Before going in, decide whether you stand a reasonable chance of winning if you do have to fight. If you come to the conclusion they would easily kill you, do not risk provoking them; stash your rifle where it can be retrieved later.

When you approach the village, do so openly so that they have plenty of warning and will not be forced into a snap decision, such as killing you. Take off your helmet, and bin anything that makes you look like a spaceman. They are less likely to kill you if you look vaguely like them.

Items such as survival knives and water bottles or footwear will be examined; be prepared to demonstrate them in the spirit of mutual interest – the locals are professional hunters who kill to live, and should be extended respect and courtesy.

Village leaders

It is a fair bet that the older men are the village leaders. Treat them with respect and you will ensure that the village will respect you – if you are brash, threatening, or offhand with them you will probably find enemy troops on your tail within hours of your exit from the village.

Local hospitality

It is worth remembering that not all villages in remote rural locations or deep jungle see their government as friendly. You may have more in common with them than they with the soldiers, and a lost, perhaps wounded and frightened man will merit traditional hospitality extended to any stranger. But do not overstay your welcome – the villagers' resources may be limited, your presence will become known through tribal gossip and sweeps by enemy soldiers may pick you up.

GROUND AIR EMERGENCY CODE

If friendly forces are going to be looking for you, all means of communication are important, so do not assume the radio will work. This signalling system will work wherever you have air superiority; hilltop village sites are usually clear enough to set this up.

NOTE: leave a space of about three metres between each element where possible

1   Require doctor, serious injury

2   Require medical supplies

3   Unable to proceed

4   Require food and water

5   Require firearms and ammunition

6   Require map and compass

7   Require signal lamp with battery and radio

8   Indicate direction to proceed

9   Am proceeding in this direction

10   Will attempt take-off

11   Aircraft seriously damaged

12   Probably safe to land here

13   Require fuel and oil

14   All well

15   No

16   Yes

17   Not understood

18   Require engineer

The longer you stay, the more vulnerable you make the villagers to enemy reprisals. One night – or a brief stop – can always be explained away to the enemy; they can say you were armed and threatened them. If you stay longer it will be obvious that they co-operated with you.

Respect for women

An important rule when visiting a village is to extend a dignified respect to the women – whatever their age. It is very unlikely that they have the same values as your culture. If you are in a group, keep an eye on anyone who is likely to breach the social etiquettes.

Disguise your route

If you discuss your proposed route with the villagers, do not tell them which one you decide on, and do not leave in the direction you intend to travel. Go west if you plan to go north, and change route after you are away from sight. The villagers may wish to guide you on your way; accept with gratitude and when they have gone cover your tracks. Even if they have been friendly, they may be naive people who will subsequently betray you.

Interrogation

To the army on the move, taking prisoners is more than a waste of time, it's a waste of precious manpower to guard them and rations to feed them. It's often only some respect for the laws of warfare and the fear that they would be treated the same way themselves that keep them from shooting everybody.

To the intelligence specialist, though, the prisoner is not a waste of time. He's precious. He may be pure gold. The information about troop strengths and positions that he has in his head – perhaps not even realising that he has it – could be the difference between a battle lost and a battle won.

The US Army knows this, and spends a lot of time training its men how to combat enemy interrogation techniques. Field

Manual FM 21-76 is the source for this section on how to get through a hostile interrogation while giving away as little information as possible.

The laws of war

The news of your capture is supposed, under the Geneva Convention to be passed to a body called the Protection Power, often the Red Cross/Red Crescent, so that they can pass it on to your own government. That's the only reason for giving away even such simple information as your name, rank, number and date of birth.

If you're captured by a terrorist group, they probably won't do this – even some governments don't which is why so many US prisoners of the Viet Cong and Pathet Lao are still recorded as MIA (Missing in Action) following the war in South East Asia.

The Geneva Convention

The Geneva Convention is an international agreement first formulated in 1864 to establish a code of practice for the treatment of wartime sick , wounded and prisoners of war. These are the major elements of the Geneva Convention as it affects prisoners of war.

1 *Interrogation*
   A PoW is required to provide only his name, rank, service number and date of birth. The use of physical or mental coercion to obtain information from PoWs is prohibited.

2 *Movement*
   PoWs must be moved under humane conditions.

3 *Environment*
   The internment environment must not be unhealthy or dangerous.

4 *Food*
   Food must be of sufficient quality and quantity to maintain good health.

5 *Clothing*
   Suitable clothing must be provided.

6   *Health, Hygiene and Wellbeing*

The detaining power must ensure that adequate hygienic facilities are provided. The PoW is entitled to treatment by medical personnel from their own country, where available. The seriously wounded or sick are entitled to special treatment and may be transferred to a neutral nation.

7   *Protected Personnel*

Captured medical personnel and chaplains are treated as protected personnel and are to be free to circulate among the PoWs tending to their spiritual welfare and health.

8   *Religion, Recreation, Education and Exercise*

Each PoW has the right to practise his religion, and to engage in physical exercise, education and recreation.

9   *Work*

All enlisted personnel below NCO rank are subject to work details, but these shall not be dangerous or unhealthy. NCOs may be called up to work in a supervisory capacity; officers may work voluntarily. The Geneva Convention prohibits the use of PoWs for mine clearance and lays down working conditions, pay, fitness for work and the treatment of PoWs working for private individuals.

10   *Outside Contacts*

PoWs have the right to write to their families on capture. The convention outlines postal privileges and rights pertaining to the receipt of packages.

11   *Complaints*

PoWs have the right to complain to the military authorities of the detaining powers, and to representatives of the neutral protecting powers recognized by both sides.

12   *Representatives*

The senior PoW will be the prisoners' representative. In a camp where there are no officers or NCOs the representative will be chosen by secret ballot.

13   *Legal Proceedings*

PoWs prosecuted and convicted for offences committed before capture retain the protection afforded by the convention. They may not be tried for any action which becomes illegal after the act is committed. The captors may not use force to gain a confession.

14 *Punishment*

Cruel and unusual punishments, torture, collective punishments or unfair punishments by a biased court are prohibited.

15 *Escape*

Attempted escapes, or non-violent offences committed only to aid escape and not involving theft for personal gain, the wearing of civilian clothes or the use of false papers are subject only to laid-down disciplinary action.

Your conduct

You don't have to tell them what branch of the service you're from, though they may be able to guess that themselves from your uniform and equipment. Some personnel traditionally get a hard time, notably members of Special Forces units and fliers.

Try not to get noticed and singled out for interrogation. Don't exhibit bravado or humility. Just fade into the background.

There's no point in not being respectful and polite – in fact, to behave in any other way is extremely stupid. It will only earn you harsher treatment and probably get you beaten up and deprived of food.

At the same time, don't give the interrogator the idea that you might be willing to co-operate. All you'll succeed in doing is to prolong the interrogation.

There's a world of difference between acting ignorant and acting dumb. The interrogator may say something like 'We know there's a build up of troops at such-and-such a location. Does it contain armour?' If your answer were 'I don't know, Sir, I've never been in that location,' it sounds a lot more convincing than 'Piss off'. But beware of seeming to be trying to be helpful.

Watch out for apparently innocent enemy personnel such as doctors, nurses, orderlies and cleaners. Never talk in front of them; they could well be intelligence agents, operating under-cover – perhaps not even revealing themselves to other enemy agents on the spot.

The enemy interrogator will be very keen to turn you into a collaborator too. The two main methods are threats – of physical torture or death, to you or to another member of your squad or promises – of better treatment, medical attention for someone badly wounded and not treated properly or almost anything else that seems attractive. After all, they can promise you anything – you're not going to get it anyway.

The Interrogator's skill

The interrogator prepares himself before interrogating his pris-oner. He adopts a three phase approach:

1 **Research**: He gathers all the information he can about all his prisoners.
2 **Selection**: He chooses which prisoners to interrogate and determines the information he wants.
3 **Extraction**: He puts into operation his varied mix of ex-traction techniques.

1 Intelligence
The interrogator studies any information he may have acquired from initial searches, overheard conversations and background material gleaned by intelligence workers operating in the cap-tive's own country.

2 Weak or strong?
He also builds up a picture of the PoWs makeup; is he weak or strong? Can he take punishment? What gets to him? Is he cold or emotional? How has he adjusted to PoW life?

3 Softening up
You'll be softened up, either by rough treatment, starvation, thirst, sensory deprivation, sleeplessness or solitary confine-ment. The interrogator will set up the place where he'll ask his questions so that it's intimidating and unfriendly.

4 Disgrace

He will try to destroy your confidence by disgracing you in the eyes of your fellow prisoners or your family or comrades at home or will simply try to make you feel ashamed of yourself.

5 Lesser of two evils

The captor will give you a choice between two evils, one of which is less damaging that the other. He knows that you will choose the least damaging and that is the one he can use for his own purposes.

6 The File

Your interrogator may start by asking you a harmless question about yourself. If you give a false answer he checks his intelligence file on you and gives you the right one. You begin to think this guy knows everything. 'What's the use of holding out?' Don't give in. He is telling you the little he does know; if he knew everything he wouldn't have to question you further.

7 Hidden eyes and ears

You may have looked and found nothing, but the enemy has probably bugged the camp, so watch what you say, everywhere.

8 The silent treatment

You may be put into solitary confinement or held in a room with an interrogator who says nothing. Don't be afraid of silence; come to terms with it.

9 Repetition and monotony

Your interrogator may ask you the same question in the same tone over and over again. Let him, if you get riled he'll win; if you maintain control the psychological victory will be yours.

10 What's the use?

'Why hold out?' 'Why suffer?' 'You are at our mercy.' 'We'll get the information out of you anyhow.' 'Make it easier on yourself.' These are all statements that you must learn to resist.

The double game

As well as trying to convince you that other prisoners have been cooperating he will try to get information from you about them which in turn will allow him to put subtle pressures on anyone you talk about. Don't give out any information about any of your comrades. Don't admit to being in the same unit with them.

Be on guard

Watch out for false questionnaires 'for the Red Cross', for instance. The aid organisations need to know nothing more than your name, rank, number and date of birth. Any information you provide on a form like this is only for the enemy intelligence officer's use.

Never make any statement of any kind. Not in writing, nor spoken where it might be recorded.

Don't try to impress the interrogator by boasting about things that you and your unit have done whether they're true or not. He's not going to let your go because you make yourself out to be some sort of superman!

At the same time, don't try to deceive him by volunteering false information, no matter how subtly you think you do it. He knows the wide intelligence picture and will ask you the same questions over and over again, perhaps with days in between. He'll record everything you say, and look for differences in your answers.

Don't look into the interrogator's eyes. You may give away information without meaning to. Pick out a spot between his eyes or in the centre of his forehead and concentrate on that.

Once he has you talking, it won't take a skilled interrogator long to get the truth out of you. Don't put yourself into a position where you find that you're having a conversation with him. Let him do all the talking, and limit your answers to 'No' and 'I don't know anything about that'.

Never drop your guard. You can be taken off for further interrogation at any time, at any hour of the day or night.

Try to win a victory every time you're interrogated, no matter how small. Having worked out how, pass it on to your fellows, so that they are morally stronger.

The longer the interrogation goes on, the safer you are. More prisoners will be arriving and needing your interrogator's time and your information will become more and more out of date.

What will prolong the nightmare is your partial co-operation. One snippet of useful information will convince your interrogator that he may be onto a good thing, and he'll carry on until he gets the lot, no matter what it takes.

Forcing co-operation

These are some techniques that PoWs have been subjected to in recent times.

1 Torture

Technique: extreme dislocation of body parts e.g. arms, legs, back etc by twisting or pulling; beating, slapping, gouging, kicking; inserting foreign objects such as bamboo slivers under the fingernails; electric shocks.

Effect: crippling; partial or total temporary or permanent loss of use of limbs and senses; loss of normal mental functioning; extreme pain; lowering or breaking of ability to resist captor's demands. TORTURE IS THE MAJOR MEANS OF FORCING COMPLIANCE.

2 Threats

Technique: threats of solitary confinement, non-repatriation, death or beatings to oneself or other PoWs; threats regarding future treatment; threats against family.

Effect: unreasonable anxiety; loss of hope and confidence; despair.

3 'Now and then' treatment

Technique: occasional favours such as release of food packages and better living conditions; promise of big rewards for helping captors.

Effect: tempts the PoW to go along with captors; presents the captors in a favourable light; makes resistance to questioning seem a bad idea.

4 Isolation or solitary confinement

Technique: total or partial isolation by rank, race, degree of compliance etc or total solitary confinement.

Effect: keeps PoW away from anyone who can give any kind of support, moral, physical, psychological.

5 Hints that captors are in full control of everything in camp

Technique: use of information from other sources to make PoW believe the captors know more than they really do.

Effect: makes PoWs suspicious of each other and makes resistance seem futile.

6 Show of power over life and death

Technique: use of executions or torture; introduction and withdrawal of better conditions and medical care; complete control over physical aspects of camp.

Effect: breeds extreme caution and the belief that the captor is boss.

7 Deliberately-caused physical deterioration

Technique: extremely long interrogation sessions; long periods in leg irons and stocks; bad food.

Effect: drastic lowering of resistance to interrogation.

8 Enforcement of minor rules and commands

Technique: overly strict demands for compliance with instructions and expected courtesies; forcing PoW to write or verbally repeat nonsensical words or phrases.

Effect: causes automatic obedience to commands

9 Lowering of self-respect of PoW

Technique: lack of privacy; ridicule and insults; prevention of washing; keeping living conditions filthy, insanitary, full of vermin etc.

Effect: humbles PoW and makes giving in an attractive prospect.

10 Control over physical senses

Technique: placing in isolation with no stimuli or giving extreme stimuli such as no light or sound or too much light or sound; dripping water on forehead.

Effect: makes PoW think that captors have total physical control; causes extreme discomfort and distress.

Surviving as a Prisoner

A prisoner-of-war camp can be anything from a huge barbed wire compound holding tens of thousand of men to a crude shelter in a jungle clearing and one or two men in a bamboo cage. Once your interrogation is over you're of very little use to the enemy, unless he can exploit you for political purposes.

You're just a drain on his resources. The men he has to use to guard you, the food and medicines he has to send to keep you alive; all of these could be better used on the battlefield. So it's going to be tough. The US Government has spent a great deal of time and money to find out what gives its soldiers the best possible chance of getting through a period spent as a PoW. US Army Field Manuals 21-76 and 21-78 are the source for this section on life as a prisoner of war.

Strength through unity

No matter how few of you there are you must have an organisation. One man must be in command. Chances are that your captors will try to force someone of their choice on you.

If they try to set up an organisation amongst the prisoners, then the best thing to so is to appear to go along. But you'll know who really is the Senior Ranking Officer. He, not the enemy's puppet, will appoint his Adjutant, his Quartermaster, his Welfare, Education and Entertainments Officers and set up the rest of the PoW infrastructure.

Eat the food

You will get less, worse and stranger food than you have ever had – a poor version of the stuff the enemy eats. If you are a finicky eater, get over it. Many men have died in a short period of captivity because they could not adapt to the food – they have starved themselves to death.

Add to your diet with roots, weeds, bark, a hidden garden, animals or reptiles. Ants and grasshoppers are good sources of protein. Cat, dog and monkey meats are staples of many diets.

Steal from your captors. If your Senior Ranking Officer approves, trade with the enemy, and share with those PoWs who need it at least as much as you do. If it's edible, eat it.

The enemy knows that lack of enough food or the right kinds of food decreases mental and physical powers, making you less able to resist and easier to manipulate. Therefore he will withhold food to make you do what he wants.

Drink the water

You must drink, even though your water smells bad, is dirty and is alive with bugs. Strain or purify it with chemicals or by boiling if you can. Make a still to obtain water or suck the juices from fruits. Tomatoes are an excellent source of fluid as are some plants, such as cacti. Catch rain or snow. If you think, you'll drink; if you panic, you'll dehydrate.

Exercise for survival

Try to take some sort of exercise every day. Keep up your muscle tone, but don't overdo it – you won't be getting the proteins and carbohydrates in your diet that will allow you to do strenuous exercise.

Keep your mind active too. Try to be learning something new all the time. If you're in a large camp, with lots of other people, the chances are that you'll be able to learn pretty much anything you can think of. You'll have skills that others will want to learn too.

Play can be just as important as work. Not just physical games and sports, though these are very important, but entertainment of all kinds. Painting and drawing and writing need very little in the way of materials, and they don't just keep you busy – they allow you to express yourself, your inner thoughts, in an important way.

Remember, it may be hard work trying to stay fit and healthy, but it's nothing compared with the job you've got if you lose your health and fitness and then have to get it back again. Your captors will like it a lot better if you just sit around doing nothing all day and every day, weakening your own morale and destroying your will to stay awake and alive. Don't do it! Your life is in your own hands.

Join in

The men appointed to the jobs of Sports, Education and

Entertainments Officers will want to set up as many activities an events as they can. Get involved in these activities. It doesn't matter if you're not too good at whatever it is – what matters most is that you get busy and active and stay that way.

The folks back home

Keeping in touch with your family and friends is very important for both sides. You need to know you're not forgotten and they need to know that you're as safe and well as possible.

Letters and photographs are the only way you'll be able to keep in contact, and the enemy will know this and use it to weaken you. Be ready to share your letters, photographs and parcels, if you get them, with the people around you. The SRO will put someone in charge of mail, and keep an accurate list of letters sent and received.

Outgoing letters are often a source of intelligence for the enemy. Try to restrict yourself to a brief note like 'I'm alive and well' and if you're in any doubt about the value to the enemy of something you want to say in a letter home, ask the SRO's advice – that's another one of the many things he's there for.

Make sure that you circulate any scraps of news that you get in your letters. The best way is for a group of people to produce a camp newspaper. It needn't be more than a handwritten sheet that get passed on from person to person around the camp. If that's not possible, then you'll have to do it by work of mouth.

Get one over

Let no chance go by to 'get one over' on the enemy, and make sure that everyone knows about every little victory. Give all the guards and camp personnel nick names – the crueller the better! Don't use them to their faces of course, but in private use every chance you have to make fun of them. Leave them in no doubt of what you think of them.

Camp communication

There are many ways to communicate with other prisoners. The PoW isolation barrier and enemy-imposed ban on communication must be broken. If you can see, hear or touch other PoWs, or if articles are brought into and taken out of your place of confinement you can communicate.

Sign language
The standard deaf-mute language may be learned, but it is difficult. There is a simple variation that is quicker to learn, using hand signals. Either hand can be used. Numbers are rotated to indicate that they are numbers and not letters. The code uses the standard US Navy hand signal numbers; zero is shown

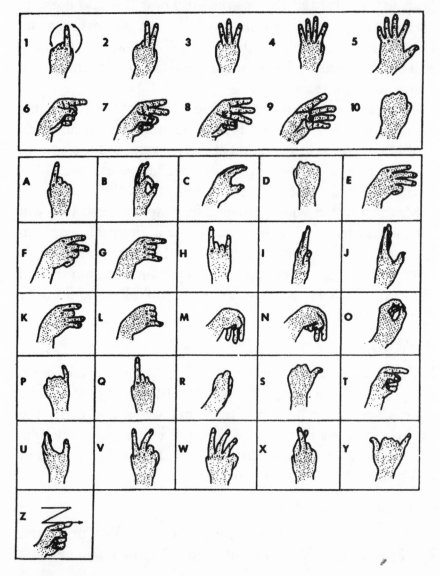

by rotating the letter O. Let your hand drop slightly after each series of letters or words.

To indicate 'I understand', the receiver may nod slightly in a prearranged manner. Different body movement such as blinking the eyes, flexing the hands or arms, shrugging the shoulders etc; all natural and meaningless to the enemy – can be worked out in advance to indicate different responses.

Tap codes

The morse code can be learned quickly. But it has a serious drawback; it consists of dots and dashes that sometimes cannot be distinguished. There is a better system that consists of a square marked off in 25 subsquares; 5 across and 5 up and down, with the letters of the alphabet in the subsquares (the letter K is not used because it sounds like C). The squares running from left to right are rows; the squares from top to bottom are columns.

Taps are used to identify the letters. The first series of taps

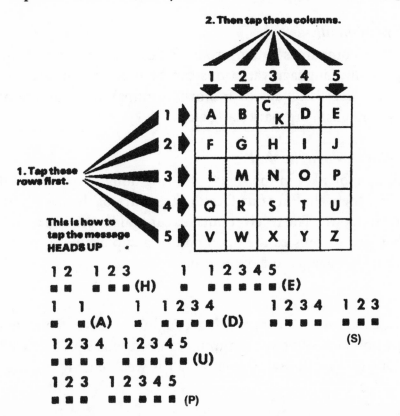

gives the row; after a short pause the second series of taps gives the column. The letter is in the block where the row and column meet. To find the letter O for example, three taps would designate the third row (L-M-N-O-P); a slight pause followed by four taps would designate the fourth column (D-I-O-T-Y); the row and column meet at the letter O.

A longer pause indicates the end of a word. Two taps indicate that the word has been received. A series of rapid taps indicates that the word was not received or not understood. When a receiver has enough letters to know what the word is, he gives two taps and the sender goes on to the next word. Each time the code is broken by your captors you can rearrange the letters.

The methods of getting a message across with this code are almost unlimited. The code can be tapped, whistled, winked, coughed, sneezed or hummed; you can nudge the guy next to you; you can use finger movements, eye movements, twitches, broom strokes, pushups; or you can bang objects together.

Word of mouth

This can sometimes be dangerous. To disguise the content from the enemy, language variations can be used; subculture language (street language of minority groups), for example or pidgin English, ordinary slang etc.

Talking through the wall

Roll up a blanket in the shape of a ring doughnut and put it against the wall. Put your face in the centre of the doughnut and talk slowly. The receiver puts his ear against the wall on the other side or presses the open end of a cup against the wall with his ear against the other end.

Different noises

Various sounds such as grunting, coughing, sneezing, blowing your nose, whistling or humming can be used as prearranged signals to pass messages such as 'all is well', 'enemy around', 'stop' 'go' etc.

Writing messages

You will not usually have writing materials available, but you can improvize; use charred wood, fruit juices, ashes mixed with any fluid etc. Use any pointed object as a writing implement. Leaves, wood, cloth, toilet paper and any material can be used as a writing surface.

Mail deliveries

As well as personal deliveries, messages can be left in any hiding place – latrines, trees, rocks, crevices, holes etc; the best places are those that the enemy would expect you to visit normally. The hiding places should be changed frequently and couriers should deposit and collect their dispatches at different times.

Escape

The first hours

The best chances to escape will come straight after your capture. You'll still be close to your own forces, and so you'll know which direction to head in, and you may even be familiar with the country. You'll be fitter and healthier than after any time in captivity, and if you can keep your wits about you, you may be able to take advantage of the confusion that is usually to be found just behind the fighting front, with reinforcements and resupply trying to go forward and medevac an empty resupply units trying to move back.

You'll be in the hands of combat troops, not people trained in holding prisoners, and their inexperience may give you opportunities. But at the same time they'll be psyched up for battle, so will probably shoot rather than ask questions. They might just shoot you for the fun of it.

For all these reasons every army has a plan for dealing with prisoners of war, for getting them out of the combat zone as quickly as possible, so that they can be interrogated while the information they have about troop strengths and movements is still worth something.

The chances are that if you're captured on your own, or as part of a small group, you will be held somewhere like the regimental command post, and then transferred to the rear echelon headquarters run by intelligence security units, military police or internal security troops. This will not be far from the fighting front.

In transit

When enough prisoners have accumulated, you'll be moved back, being kept to open country and avoiding towns and villages. The enemy is likely to be short of motor transport – or, at least, will give a very low priority to the transportation of prisoners, so you may well find yourself evacuated on foot.

He'll be short of personnel too, so the PoW column may have too few guards, who may even be unfit for active duty – walking wounded perhaps, themselves on their way to rear echelon hospitals. That mens that there will be more chances to escape.

If the guards are placed at the head and tail of the column, as is often the case, pass the word through the ranks of prisoners to spread out and make the line of marching men as long as possible.

Keep the pace as slow as you can. At a bend in the road, you may suddenly find that the head and the tail are out of each other's sight, which means that men in the centre of the column can slip away to either side of the road and get quickly into some kind of cover.

The larger the number of men who make the break, the greater are the chances of their absence being noticed straight away. One or two men missing probably won't be noticed until the next head count is made, and that may not be until the end of the day.

Take advantage of any diversion, too. Artillery bombardment and attack from the air or extreme weather conditions, for instance, are likely to cause a lot of confusion, and may permit men to slip away while the guards' attention is distracted.

If you're being transported by truck out of the combat zone, you will probably be moved by night. If the guards are not alert and you are not locked inside the vehicle, you may get a chance to jump for it when the truck slows down – climbing a hill, for instance, or negotiating a section of damaged road. Try to sabotage the vehicles – put sugar or sand in the petrol, for example – so that they are forced to stop. Once again, an air raid may give you the necessary cover.

Permanent PoW camps are usually placed as far away as possible from the battlefield and from borders with neutral or enemy territory, so the last move will probably be made by train. Large groups of prisoners in transit are usually locked into freight cars, the guards relying on the physical security of the locked wagons to stop escape attempts.

The conditions inside these cars especially during a long journey in the middle of summer or winter can become lethal, and the fact that you'll probably be packed in very tightly doesn't help. Even so because you'll have long periods without observation this may provide your best chance. Try to break though the floor, the walls (especially at a window or a ventilator) or the roof.

If you're travelling in passenger coaches, then you have two other advantages, even though you may have guards to worry about; it's much easier and quicker to break out through a window than the solid sides of a freight wagon, and you'll probably be able to communicate in some way with prisoners in other compartments or even in other carriages.

Don't relax for a moment, but always stay alert to any possibility, because you never know if you'll ever get another chance. If you're not in a position to escape yourself, help others to do so even if it means that you'll be punished for it later.

In the camp

Escaping from an established prisoner of war camp is a much more difficult task than making a break from a train or from a column of marching men.

The camp itself will have been built specifically to keep you in; barbed wire, electronic surveillance, floodlights, watch towers, dogs and thermal imaging for tunnel searches are just some of the weapons at the enemy's disposal. And even if you do succeed in getting out of the camp itself, you're still faced with

RESCUE

As technology takes over from human observation and scrutiny, escape has become more and more difficult. But what technology has taken away with one hand it has given back with the other. Spy satellites and high-altitude observation flights give intelligence officers a clear view of every part of the Earth's surface. That means you have a way of signalling to your own people, no matter where on Earth you may be.

There's no need to rush it. You can trace out the letters of a message in the soil of a compound -or even stand around in groups that shape the letter in human bodies – in such a way that the enemy won't even be aware that you're doing it. Make certain that each arm of each letter is at least two metres long or it might not be seen from above. But remember, it's as likely to be seen by enemy satellites as your own.

Once your position has been identified either by this method or by a successful escaper being de-briefed, a coded letter getting through, or an enemy national selling the information – it may be possible for a rescue mission to be put together. Even if you're four or five hundred miles from the nearest friendly border or sea coast, your own authorities may be able to get a rescue force through.

The odds on a successful rescue will be a lot greater if there's a channel of communication from the would-be rescuers to you, and that probably means coded radio messages. There have been many cases of prisoners building radio receivers in camps, and here technology lends a hand once again, modern radio receivers being small enough to be easily hidden in all sorts of places.

Any information should include a validation code, such as mention of a pre-arranged subject such as trees or weather, or even the days of the week. Leave this code off only when under duress.

Every piece of information that you can exchange with the people planning the rescue attempt will increase its chances of success. One of the most vital will be to set up the signalling system you'll use to call the rescue force in at the last moment.

The chances are that it will be helicopter borne and the pilots and mission commanders will need to be shown exactly where to land to be most effective, wind direction, where to expect resistance, and perhaps even where the prisoners they've come to rescue are to be found.

a difficult and dangerous journey through enemy territory, where just your physical appearance may be enough to give you away.

The escape committee

Part of the prisoners' secret organisation in the camp will be devoted to the business of escaping. There will be very few ways of making an escape from a camp, and each time an attempt is made it will cut down those possibilities even further.

The escape committee will coordinate escape attempts, to try to ensure that each one has the best possible chance of success and also set up the infrastructure that each will need – tools, diversions, false documents, intelligence and so on. You should collect and hoard everything, even useless articles; these will mask the useful ones if you are searched by camp guards.

Most escape attempts will need this sort of organisation – but that doesn't mean that you shouldn't go for it on your own if a chance presents itself unexpectedly, perhaps from a labour party working outside the camp.

IMPROVIZED SIGNALS TO AIRCRAFT

Unless aircraft are flying slowly at low altitude you will probably not be seen. To attract the attention of friendly aircraft you need to make a large sign which will stand out; letters should have arms of not less than two metres. Alternatively you can send the emergency 'SOS' signal in Morse code. Look around for any useful material; stones, fertilizer sacks, anything that can be arranged into a shape to catch the pilot's attention. Or when on parade in PoW camp, form your parade up so that it spells out the letters 'SOS' as shown above.

Documents and disguises

Before you get too far in your escape planning, you have to think how you'll cross the enemy territory that lies between you and neutral or friendly forces. There are two methods – either you try to blend in with the local population, or you try to stay hidden.

If you try to fit in, you'll need clothing, documents, money and at least some knowledge of the language, all of which will either have to be produced inside the camp or stolen once you get outside.

In order to forge documents, you have to know what they look like to start with, and you must have the right sort of raw material available – paper, inks and dyes, pens and so on, not to mention the skill to do it. And as magnetic encoding like that used on credit cards gets more common, the chances decrease of producing forged documents that will pass any sort of examination.

The other option is to travel in secret using your survival training to keep our of enemy hands. In many ways this is more practical and at least you know where you are when you depend only on your own skills.

The SCUD-Hunters

In 1990 the ministry of Defence once again called on the 22nd Special Air Service Regiment's special service and sent it to fight Saddam Hussein in the Gulf War. It was almost a homecoming for the Regiment, for it had been raised in the desert fifty years before. And as the story of the 22 SAS patrol codenamed 'Bravo Two Zero' shows, the intervening years had done nothing to diminish the professionalism and physical capability of the SAS trooper. John Amos tells of the hunters of Saddam Hussein's Scud Missiles.

The 22nd SAS Regiment was alerted for action within hours of Saddam Hussein sending his armour rolling into oil-rich Kuwait at 02.00 (local time) on 2 August 1990. At Stirling Lines, the SAS camp situated behind a nondescript 1950s red-brick housing estate on the edge of Hereford, a small batch of troopers was issued desert kit and briefed. They were flown out to Saudi Arabia later that month, carrying hand-held designators (which 'paint' targets for the laser-guided bombs of Allied aircraft), as part of the United Nations' Operation 'Desert Shield', the securing of the Saudi border from further Iraqi encroachment.

More teams of SAS followed. Initially, it seemed that the SAS would be employed in their role as hostage rescuers. The commander of the 40,000 strong force which made up the British contribution to the anti-Saddam Coalition, Lt-General Sir Peter de la Billiere ('DLB'), had previously fought with 22 SAS in Oman and Malaya, and commanded the Regiment during the Falklands conflict. He had also planned the 1980 seizure of the Iranian Embassy at Prince's Gate. Now, in the Gulf, he was faced with another hostage situation, Saddam's use of 'guests' as human shields at important military installations. Eventually however, de la Billiere ruled out an SAS mass rescue mission. The hostages were constantly moved and the intelligence inside Iraq was not good.

Meanwhile the number of 22 SAS at the regimental holding area in Saudi Arabia grew steadily. By early January 1991 the force assembled totalled 300 badged SAS soldiers, plus 15 volunteers from the elite reserve team of the part-time Territorial Regiments, 21 and 23 SAS. It was the biggest gathering of the unit since the heady days of World War II.

For an agonizing period, however, it looked as though the unit would be given no role in Operation 'Desert Storm', the Allied offensive to remove the Iraqis from Kuwait. The SAS were gathered like so many racehorses before a race, but not sure if they would be allowed to run. The Commander-in-Chief of the Allied forces, US General H Norman 'Stormin' Norman' Schwarzkopf, intended to degrade Saddam's military capability by a huge air campaign, while finishing him off with a completely conventional – if tactically brilliant – infantry and armoured envelopment. Also, like many senior military figures, the irascible Schwarzkopf was no admirer of Special Forces. Reputedly, he had met a contingent of US Special Forces in the Gulf with the greeting: "I remember you guys from Vietnam . . . you couldn't do your jobs there, and you didn't do you job in Panama. What makes you think you can do your job here?" However, de la Billiere, the only non-American on Schwarzkopf's planning staff, CENTCOM, was determined to find a job for his old Regiment. In the second week of January, de la Billiere identified a task for 22 SAS, to cut roads and cause diversions in the enemy rear, thus pulling troops away from the front. After a presentation by the SAS themselves, Schwarzkopf gave 22 SAS the go-ahead. They would cross the Iraqi border right at the beginning of the air campaign. This was scheduled to begin on 29 January. The SAS was in the war.

As the Regiment made itself ready at its holding area, the world was hypnotized by the deadline by which President Bush insisted Iraq implement United Nations Resolution 660 (Iraqi withdrawal from Kuwait), midnight on 16 January. Saddam refused to blink or budge.

The Regiment was as surprised as most other people when hundreds of Allied aircraft and Tomahawk Cruise missiles began bombarding targets in Iraq just before dawn on 17 January. Within twenty four hours the Iraqi airforce was all but wiped out and Saddam's command and communications system heavily mauled. Allied commanders retired to bed at the end of D-Day most satisfied.

The only nagging area of Allied doubt was Iraq's Scud surface-to-surface (SSM) missile capability. Though an outdated technology, a Soviet version of Hitler's V2, the Scud was capable of carrying nuclear and bio-chemical warheads. It could be fired from a fixed site or from a mobile launcher. Could Saddam still fire his Scuds? Would he? On the second night of the air campaign,

Saddam answered all speculations by launching Scuds (all with conventional warheads) at Saudi Arabia and Israel. The six which landed in Israel injured no one, but they were political dynamite. If Israel responded militarily the fragile coalition, which included several Arab members, would be blown apart. Israel declared itself to be in a state of war, but frantic diplomacy by the Allies managed to dissuade Israel from taking immediate punitive action. Batteries of Patriot ground-to-air missiles were dispatched to Tel Aviv, Jerusalem and Haifa. The Allies diverted 30% of their air effort to Scud hunting. But in the expanses of vast Iraqi desert all too often the air strike arrived to find the Scud fired and the mobile launcher elusively camouflaged. Previously, the US military had believed that its hi-tech satellite observation system could detect Scuds before launch. Now it was finding that the Scuds could be many minutes into flight before being betrayed by the flare from their motors. Asked by the media on 19 January about the Scud menace, the normally upbeat Schwarzkopf was obliged to say that "the picture is unclear", and to grumble that looking for Scuds was like looking for the proverbial needle in the haystack.

If the C-in-C was unclear about what to do, the Scud factor gave 22 SAS an absolutely clear-cut mission. De la Billiere signalled 22 SAS that "all SAS effort should be directed against Scuds". That very same day, 19 January, the SAS was rushed 1500 km from its holding area to an FOB just inside the Saudi border with Western Iraq. The move was made in a non-stop 24 hour airlift by the RAF Special Forces flight.

The Regiment decided on two principal means of dealing with the Scud menace. It would insert into Iraq covert 8-man static patrols to watch Main Supply Routes (MSRs) and report on the movement of Scud traffic. There would be three such patrols, South, Central and North. When Scud sites and launchers were identified, US F15 and A10 airstrikes would be called down to destroy them, directed to the target by the SAS patrol using a tactical airlink. (Though the SAS patrols carried laser-designators to 'paint' targets for Allied aircraft they only used them infrequently.)

Alongside the road watch patrols, there were four columns of heavily armed vehicles, 'Pink Panther' Land Rovers and Unimogs, which would penetrate the 'Scud Box', an area of western desert near the border with Jordan which was though to contain around 14 mobile launchers.

As is traditional in the SAS, the decision how to deploy was left to the patrol commanders and reached after democratic discussion.

The South and Central road watch teams were inserted on 21 January, and both found that the eerily flat, featureless desert offered no possibility of concealment. The South road watch patrol aborted their mission and flew back on their insertion helicopter. The Central team also decided that the terrain was lethal, but before 'bugging out' in the Land Rovers and stripped down motorcycles called down an air strike on two Iraqi radars. After a four-night drive through 140 miles of bitingly cold desert the patrol reached Saudi Arabia. Four men needed treatment for frostbite.

Road Watch North, codenamed 'Bravo Two Zero' had the most isolated insertion, landed by RAF Chinook 100 miles north-west of Baghdad. The weather was appalling, driving wind and sleet, the worst winter in this part of the Iraqi desert for thirty years. Led by Sgt Andy McNab (a pseudonym), the patrol took food and water for 14 days, explosives and ammunition for their 203s (American M16 rifles with 40 mm grenade-launchers attached), Minimi machine guns, grenades, extra clothes, maps, compasses and survival equipment. Each man was carrying 209 lbs of kit. Watching a main supply route, the patrol saw a Scud launch and prepared to send their first situation report ('Sit Rep') to base. In the first of several fruitless efforts, Bravo Two Zero's signaller, Trooper Steven ('Legs') Lane prepared the radio antenna, encoded Sgt McNab's message and typed it ready for transmission. There was no answer and no amount of adjusting the set got a response.

On the second day an Iraqi military convoy rumbled across the desert towards the team and sited a battery of low-level anti-aircraft guns only yards from where they were hunkered down. The team was now in grave danger of compromise. In mid afternoon the compromise came. A young Iraqi goatherd looked down into the patrol's lying-up place (LUP), a shallow wadi, saw the troopers and ran off towards the Iraqi soldiers. Bravo Two Zero rapidly prepared to move, checking equipment and gulping down as much water as possible. They had a "fearsome tab" (march) in front of them.

There were further frantic efforts to radio base that they were now compromised and requested "exfil asap". There was again no response, The F radio was being rendered near useless by ionospheric distortion. The men loaded their bergens and moved quickly westwards. As they cleared the bottom of the wadi they heard tracked vehicles approaching from the rear. They dropped into a depression and turned to face the enemy. An Iraqi Armoured Personnel Carrier (APC) opened fire with a 7.62 machine gun. With a scream of "Fucking let's do it!", the SAS patrol fired off a fusillade of 66 anti-armour rockets, rifle grenades and Minimis. They held off the Iraqis twice, destroying armoured personnel carriers and infantry trucks and cut down scores of troops.

It started to get dark and the patrol decided to get out of the contact area, moving as fast as they physically could manage with their heavy bergens. As they cleared a slope the Iraqi Triple-A battery sighted them and opened fire. A 57 mm ack-ack round hit one trooper in the back, ripping open his bergen. When extracted from it he was found to be uninjured. The rest of the patrol voted to 'bin' their bergens for more speed, and eventually lost their enemy in the gloom. At a rallying point, Sgt

McNab decided to use their four personal short-range TACBE (personal rescue beacons) to get in touch with an orbiting AWACS plane to bring strike aircraft down on the Iraqis. Again there was no reply. McNab did a quick appreciation of their situation. The Iraqis would expect them to make south for Saudi Arabia. Jordan was due west but was a non-combatant ally of Saddam Hussein. A hundred and twenty kilometres to the north west was Syria, a member of the anti-Saddam coalition. McNab decided to go for Syria.

Moving fast towards the Syrian border, Bravo Two Zero walked 50 miles that night through driving sleet, pausing to rest only four times. Two troopers were in a parlous state, however. Sgt Vince Phillips had fractured a leg in the contact with the Iraqis and was finding it difficult to move. Trooper 'Stan' was becoming dangerously dehydrated.

The sound of aircraft high overhead prompted another call on the TACBE. Finally, they got a response. An American pilot on a bombing mission acknowledged their call. The message was relayed to the British Special Ops HQ in Saudi Arabia. British and American helicopters went into Iraq to search for the patrol, but a specific run to a pre-arranged rendezvous was ruled out as too dangerous.

The stop to use the TACBE proved unlucky. In the swirling, raining darkness, Sgt Phillips, Cpl 'Chris' and Trooper Stan carried on walking and became separated from the rest of the patrol.

Sgt McNab and his four companions had no option but to continue on without them, hoping they would meet up later. The rain turned to snow. During rests they huddled together for warmth. In their soaked clothes the wind-chill was starting to kill them. Throughout the night they slowly made their way to the Syrian border. Resting during the next day they decided that, if they were going to make it, they would need to hijack a vehicle, preferably something inconspicuous. Watching by a main road they ignored military trucks. In the gathering darkness of evening they spotted the lights of a single vehicle and flagged it down. The incident has already entered Regiment folklore. Instead of the hoped for 4WD, they found before them a bright yellow New York taxi proudly sporting chrome bumpers and whitewall tyres. The five SAS men pulled out its amazed occupants and hopped in, putting the heater on high. They made good progress towards the border, their shamags pulled up around their faces to conceal their Caucasian identity until they became confused in the lacework of roads near the border. Along with other traffic they were stopped by Iraqi soldiers at a vehicle checkpoint. An Iraqi 'jundie' (squaddie) knocked on the driver's window to ask for their papers. Trooper Legs Lane shot the Iraqi in the head with his 203. The SAS men leaped out, shot two more soldiers and ran off into the desert.

By now the lights of a town across the border were clearly visible. As they neared the border they again ran into an anti-aircraft battery. Shells and small arms fire landed all around. There were now over 1,500 Iraqi troops looking for them. The SAS men had barely six miles to go, but the moon was bright. An Iraqi patrol found them hiding in a ditch. A running firefight broke out in which the SAS soldiers killed scores of Iraqis, but became separated from each other in the process. Trooper 'Mark' was wounded in the elbow and ankle and captured. Another Trooper, Robert Consiglio, a Swiss-born former Royal Marine was hit in the head as he covered the withdrawal of Trooper 'Dinger' and Lance-Corporal Lane. Consiglio was the first SAS soldier of the campaign to die from enemy fire. He received a posthumous Military Medal. Lane urged 'Dinger' to join him and swim the Euphrates, then in full icy flood. Lane emerged on the far bank in a state of collapse. His companion stayed with him and hid him in a nearby hut. When it became clear that Lane was going to die from hypothermia 'Dinger' attracted the attention of a civilian working nearby. By the time the Iraqi retrieval team got to Lane he was dead. He, too was awarded a posthumous MM. 'Dinger' tried to escape but was captured.

Sergeant McNab was discovered the next morning in a drainage culvert. Along with the other SAS men captured alive he suffered a month of imprisonment and torture. The latter was brutal physical and, ultimately, counterproductive. It only made the SAS men more determined not to talk. Though the Iraqi military imprisoned the men together they failed to even covertly monitor their conversations.

As for the trio missing in the desert, Sergeant Phillips was lost in driving snow on the night of 26 January. His companions, 'Stan' and 'Chris' turned back for him but could not find him. His body was eventually found by Iraqi soldiers and handed to the British authorities at the war's end. Later the next day, Stan went to see if he could hijack some transport. As he approached a parked lorry an Iraqi soldier came out of the house. The Iraqi tried to pull a weapon out. Stan shot him with his 203. Six or seven other Iraqi soldiers came running out. Stan shot three of them but then his gun jammed. The Iraqis did not kill him, only beat him unconscious with their rifle butts. When Stan failed to return to the LUP, Chris decided to set out on his own. He would be the only man from Bravo Two Zero to escape to safety.

Massively dehydrated, his feet and hands turning septic from cuts and, at one point falling unconscious and breaking his nose, Chris managed to cross the Syrian border on 30 January. He had covered 117 miles, evading hundreds of Iraqi searchers, with only two packets of biscuits for nourishment.

During the final two days he was without any water. He had filled his bottles from a small stream. When he came to drink the water his lips and mouth burned instantly. The stream was polluted from a nearby uranium processing plant.

Inside Syria, Chris was initially treated with hostility. As he neared the capital Damascus, however, his treatment became more cordial. A civilian pin-stripe suit was run up for him as he bathed in the HQ of the Syrian secret police. That same night he was handed over to the British Embassy. It was the first anyone at SAS HQ in Saudi Arabia had heard of Bravo Two Zero since infiltration. The seven day walk of Trooper Chris across the desert is considered by the Regiment to be at least equal to that of Jack Sillitoe, an SAS 'Original', who crossed the North African desert in 1942 drinking his own urine to survive. In a Regiment where the remarkable is standard, Chris's epic trek is still considered one of the most amazing escapades ever recorded.

The eight members of Road Watch North, Bravo Two Zero, killed nearly 250 Iraqis in their fight and flight across northern Iraq.

After the attempt to insert the static patrols, 22 SAS effort shifted to the four mobile fighting columns. Drawn from Squadrons A and D, the columns – which contained about a dozen Land Rovers or Unimogs together with motorcycle outriders – were the biggest overland fighting force put into the field by the SAS since 1945. The columns had their own Stringer anti-aircraft and Milan anti-tank missiles, plus .5 Browning machine guns, 7.63mm general purpose machine guns and 40 mm grenade launchers. One team found a sledge hammer most useful. The freebooting columns, soon operating in broad daylight, scored spectacular successes as they sped into the Iraqi desert flying enormous Union flags to identify them to friendly aircraft.

An Iraqi deputy commander of a gun battery taken POW proved to have on his person a map giving positions of Iraqi front line units. On 29 January SAS columns called down F15E airstrikes on two mobile Scud launchers, plus one fixed site. On 3 February in the Wadi Amij ('Scud Alley') locality, a patrol from D Squadron called down an airstrike on a Scud convoy. Only one airstrike hit the target, so the SAS patrol hit the convoy with wire-guided missiles, an inspired last minute addition to the SAS armoury.

These SAS attacks were the first military actions on the ground in the war except for the minor Iraqi cross-border attack on Khafji, Saudi Arabia on 29 January. Group 2 from D squadron called an airstrike on a Scud convoy on 5 February and on the same day fought two firefights with Iraqi troops. Increasingly the SAS destroyed Scuds and launchers themselves, since some were escaping in the gap between their targeting by the SAS and the arrival of the airstrike.

To service the Land Rovers and Unimogs, the SAS organized a supply column ('E Squadron') which formed a temporary workshop deep inside Iraq. Everywhere the SAS teams went they caused mayhem, and not only to the Scuds. Saddam (courtesy of the time when the West regarded him as a friend) had an advanced communications network, consisting of buried fibre optic cables. The weak point in the system was that the signal needed to be boosted at above-ground relay stations. A team from 22 SAS blew up seven of these stations alongside the highway from Baghdad to Amman. When the SAS Land Rovers returned to Saudi Arabia at the end of the war, they had covered an average of 1,500 miles and spent between 36 and 42 days behind the lines. The front wings of the Land Rovers were decorated with scores of silhouettes of 'kills', including mobil Scuds and communications towers.

The SAS had also provided valuable advice to US Special Forces, operating in a 'Scud Box' north of the Regiment's. It is a measure of the success of the SAS that General Norman Schwarzkopf, the 'enemy' of special forces, praised the Regiment's "totally outstanding performance" in the Gulf. No less than 39 awards and honours for bravery and meritorious service were given to the Regiment for its part in Operation Granby, the Gulf War.

There was of course, a price to be paid for the Regiment's achievement. In addition to the three SAS soldiers from Bravo Two Zero who were killed, Trooper David Denbury from A Squadron was killed on 21 February during the ambush of a Scud convoy in North West Iraq. A sapper attached to the regiment was also killed in action.

HEALTH AND MEDICAL SKILLS

AVOIDABLE HEALTH RISKS

Personal hygiene and concern for your immediate camping or training environment are important. It is also advisable to avoid substances which actively increase the probability of ill health, and harm the body, such as alcohol, tobacco and drugs. All these substances are addictive, and once you've started it's very hard to stop. The degree of addiction can vary, but anyone can become hooked.

Smoking

For many years smoking has been known to be harmful even the tobacco companies acknowledge this. The addictive element is the nicotine. The major harmful effects are caused by other substances such as tars and carbon monoxide that are produced by burning tobacco.

Smoking mainly attacks the lungs and heart. Lung cancer, heart attacks and bronchitis are all linked to smoking.

Lung cancer

The commonest form of lung cancer normally occurs only in smokers. This does not mean that all smokers will get lung cancer; the great majority will not. What it does mean is that non-smokers will almost certainly not suffer from the disease.

Heart disease

The largest single preventable cause of early death is coronary heart disease. Smokers have a very much higher chance of heart attacks, often leading to death, than do non-smokers; this is particularly so in men in their early 40s and even young male smokers probably run a greater risk than non smokers. Again not every smoker will have a heart attack, and not every heart attack victim is a smoker. It is, however absolutely clear that smokers run a very much higher risk of serious heart trouble than non-smokers. The sooner a smoker stops smoking the better his chances, the longer he leaves it, the greater the risk of permanent damage.

Alcohol

Alcohol has fewer addictive qualities than nicotine and in moderation, has relatively few ill effects. It is, however, a poison. It has a depressant effect on the brain, but at first appears to be stimulating because the first thing it depresses are your inhibitions, making you more lively and talkative.

As the dose increases, so does the depressant effect. It is less easy to control personal behaviour, so fighting becomes more likely and the control of machinery is more difficult. One of the biggest problems is that it is almost impossible for an intoxicated person to realise and accept that their driving ability has been seriously impaired.

The poisonous effect of alcohol becomes more obvious the larger the amount taken. A blood level of about 400mg/100ml is often fatal in itself. The after effects are proportional to the amount consumed. Hangovers are due to a variety of factors – a combination of the toxins acting on the brain, dehydration from the diuretic properties of alcohol and a low blood sugar level. The liver is an organ which is especially sensitive to the effects of alcohol, because it is where the alcohol is broken down and detoxified. Long term alcohol intake can lead to permanent liver damage, known as cirrhosis of the liver.

Drinking moderately is not normally a health risk, but there are circumstances when it should obviously be avoided. Any time you need to keep a clear head, such as walking or climbing in the mountains, your life and the lives of others could depend on your having absolute control, unclouded by alcohol.

Drugs

There are a wide variety of controlled drugs ranging from the relatively innocuous cannabis to the potentially lethal heroin and cocaine. There are claims that cannabis is less harmful and addictive than tobacco, but there is no doubt that it clouds the judgement, which is particularly dangerous in a combat situation or training exercise when errors of judgement could be fatal.

Once you start experimenting it can be difficult to resist the temptation to move on and try harder and more dangerous drugs that are being pushed by the same dealers.

Heroin and cocaine are much more addictive than cannabis or alcohol. You can get hooked the first time you try it. Say no. Once you are hooked, it is extremely difficult to get off. Your health will rapidly be destroyed. In addition to the effects of the drug itself, injecting with dirty needles can give you infections, septicaemia, hepatitis and AIDS.

Some trials have been done, mainly in America, on drugs that have a stimulant effect. It was thought that such drugs might help soldiers to perform more effectively in battle but the results were so unpredictable with soldiers attacking their friends and so on that these ideas have been totally abandoned.

SEXUALLY TRANSMITTED DISEASES

Staying healthy will enable you to perform much better in combat, on exercise or in sport. Sexually transmitted diseases, like many others, can all be avoided; they will not occur unless you have had sexual contact. But advice to refrain from sex is easier to give than to take, so make sure that you know something about sexually transmitted diseases and how to minimize the risks.

Venereal disease

Venereal disease (VD) is a legal definition relating to various sexually transmitted diseases. This is now an outdated term and has been replaced by 'Sexually Transmitted Disease' (STD). Among the most important of these diseases are syphilis, gonorrhoea and non-specific urethritis.

Syphilis

Syphilis is much less common than it used to be, and can be treated with penicillin, but remains a potentially serious disease. It can be transmitted to a baby in the womb, but again this congenital syphilis is now very rare. Acquired syphilis passes through three stages, primary, secondary and tertiary syphilis. The secondary stage occurs within a few months of the primary stage but many years may go by before the tertiary stage appears.

A sign of primary syphilis is a painless ulcer about 1 cm across which shows up about a month after infection. In men it is usually on the penis, in women it can occur on the genitalia but is often deeper inside and so may not be noticed. More rarely, it may occur on the lips or in the mouth. Even if it's not treated the lesion will seem to heal but that doesn't mean all is well. A few months later, secondary syphilis occurs.

Secondary syphilis is characterized by a skin rash of varying appearance, plus a sore throat, a slight temperature and swollen lymph nodes. In the mouth there are painless, slimy greyish ulcers. Again these may seem to clear up, but the disease re-appears years later as tertiary syphilis.

The tertiary disease is accompanied by the localized swellings that may break down into ulcers. They may occur anywhere in the body, on the surface or deep within. The disease may affect the brain or the circulatory system leading to mental breakdown, insanity or fatal illness.

Gonorrhoea

This again causes differing symptoms in men and women. In men, within about three to ten days of infection there is a slight burning sensation on passing urine, which is soon followed by a yellowish discharge from the end of the penis. If treatment is not given the infection may spread deeper, causing pain and a fever. There may be swelling of the lymph nodes in the groin, sometimes including the testicles.

In women, passing urine may be painful and frequent and there may be a vaginal discharge. Often however, the infection may be deeper in the genital tract, and will not be noticed.

The usual treatment is with penicillin, but there is increasing resistance by the infecting organism, so other drugs may have to be used

Non-specific urethritis (NSU)

This is now much commoner than syphilis and gonorrhoea. It can be caused by a variety of organisms and occurs mainly in young men. The symptoms are similar to those of gonorrhoea, the passing of urine may be frequent and painful and there may be a discharge from the penis. The disease can show up anything from a few days to two or three months after infection. Treatment depends of the causative organism.

AIDS

Acquired Immune Deficiency Syndrome (AIDS) was first recognized in 1981. It is a disease affecting the body's immune system, which means that the body cannot combat certain illnesses, including infections and some cancers. People with AIDS die of these infections and cancers, not of AIDS itself.

When AIDS was first recognized the cause was not known, but it was found to occur particularly in homosexual men. Since then it has been found in drug abusers, those who have had blood transfusions with infected blood or blood products (such as haemophiliacs), and more recently in those who have had heterosexual relationships.

In the USA and UK the disease is still one primarily of homosexuals and drug abusers. In some parts of the world however, males and females are equally affected, particularly in some countries of Africa, where the disease is widespread.

AIDS can follow infection by a virus known as HIV. This virus affects one type of white blood cell. HIV infection is NOT the same as AIDS; AIDS is an illness that results from HIV infection. Not all those affected with HIV will develop AIDS, and the average time between HIV infection and the development of AIDS is five to seven years or even longer. So far about half those affected with HIV have developed AIDS. It is not known whether everyone with HIV infection will develop the disease; the probability is that at least a proportion of HIV carriers will not.

Even if a person does not have AIDS but only HIV infection, they can still infect someone else. HIV is transmitted from person to person either by sexual intercourse, or by transmission of blood. It is not transmitted by shaking hands, by kissing or by any normal social relationships, so there is no danger in working or going to school with someone who is HIV infected.

Infection through sexual intercourse is much commoner in male homosexual relationships and this is the commonest means of transmission in the USA and the UK. But the experience in Africa indicates that we can expect an increase in transmission through normal heterosexual intercourse, which means that both men and women can be affected.

Drug abusers are susceptible to HIV infection if they inject themselves with needles used by others, because small amounts of blood will be present in the needle and syringe from the previous user. Remember that many prostitutes are intravenous drug abusers and may therefore pass on HIV infection through their sexual activities.

All blood and blood products used in the UK and USA are now screened for HIV infection and there is no chance of catching the infection through blood transfusion. Unfortunately this is not necessarily the case in other parts of the world.

HIV infection itself causes no symptoms. Infected people appear quite well and neither they nor anyone else will know if they are infected. Blood tests can be carried out to find out if people are affected, but there is no other way of telling, so an infected person can infect someone else without either of them knowing anything about it. The other great problem with HIV infection is that there is no cure, and it does not look as if one will be available for quite some time, if ever. Nor can anyone tell who will go on to develop full-blown AIDS and who will not, so prevention is all-important.

Prevention

Avoid high risk groups; avoid homosexual intercourse, and intercourse with partners of homosexuals; avoid drug abusers and their partners; avoid prostitutes. Also, avoid the enthusiastic amateur. Again, the more partners you have, the higher the risk. A steady couple who only have intercourse with each other will not become infected.

The second preventative measure is the use of condoms. Even if other contraceptive measures are being taken, a sheath should still be worn if you are indulging in casual sex. Both partners should insist on the man wearing one, and both should be prepared. Condoms are now openly available. You should not feel embarrassed about buying them, even if you are, this is better than having to worry about AIDS. But remember; a condom reduces the chance of infection, but is not 100 per cent effective.

FIELD SANITATION

In war, the number of casualties due to enemy action has always been exceeded by the number caused by illness, and similar problems often arise on expeditions and military exercises. Very often this is due to bad hygiene leading to stomach upsets and diarrhoea.

You can avoid illness by taking proper preventive measures. You must be fit to start with, maintain personal hygiene and change into clean clothes as often as possible. Pay attention to food and water, and dispose of waste carefully.

General health
Before setting out on any form of expedition or training you must be in good general health; if you are suffering from flu or a stomach upset, for example, these are likely to get worse. Also if you are suffering from or just recovering from an infectious

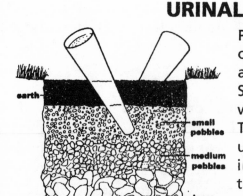

URINAL

earth

small pebbles

medium pebbles

large stones

Piss tube (should discharge into the pit about 60cm down)
Side view of a gravel pit with piss tubes drawn in. This sort of pit allows urine to drain quickly into the earth rather than create a foul-smelling swamp in camp. Place some obvious marker on the spot so you can find it at night.

disease you may get worse yourself and will almost certainly pass it on to others.

Make sure your teeth and gums are in good condition. Many a soldier on operations or training has had to be evacuated because of dental trouble.

Personal hygiene

1 Keep as clean as possible, paying particular attention to your feet, these must be washed daily and dusted with powder.
2 Clean your teeth regularly.
3 Continue to shave every day, even though it's easier not to bother. But avoid after-shave, not just for practical reasons but because it will dry on your skin and make it sore.
4 Change into clean clothes as often as possible, and change your socks every day. Natural fibres such as wool and cotton will breath and allow sweat to evaporate. If you are out for any length of time you will have to wash your clothes; you can buy travellers clothes-washing liquid in a tube, which will work in cold water.

Water

In Britain and the USA you can drink tap water, but this is not

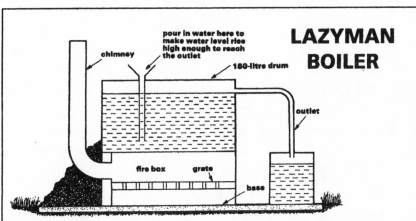

The lazyman boiler is an elegantly simple solution to an age-old problem. You start heating a tank of water, go away while the fire does its stuff and come back to find some lazy bastard has used up all the water. By constructing your boiler as shown anyone wanting water must pour in an equal amount of fresh water.

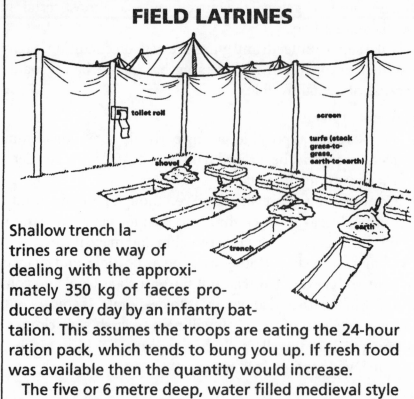

FIELD LATRINES

toilet roll

screen

turfs (stack grass-to-grass, earth-to-earth)

shovel

trench

earth

Shallow trench latrines are one way of dealing with the approximately 350 kg of faeces produced every day by an infantry battalion. This assumes the troops are eating the 24-hour ration pack, which tends to bung you up. If fresh food was available then the quantity would increase.

The five or 6 metre deep, water filled medieval style pit works fine until some idiot pours disinfectant in, killing the bacteria that make the pit work.

necessarily the case in the rest of the world. Even in Europe, although most indoor taps are safe, those in farmyards may not be.

Never assume that river or stream water is safe, even if it looks clear. Any water that you cannot be sure about must be purified by boiling or by adding water purification tablets. These will be on issue or you can buy them from camping shops.

All water that is used for drinking and cooking should be treated. It is not necessary to purify water for washing, but avoid it if it's obviously polluted.

HEALTH IN COLD CONDITIONS

Working in a cold climate can cause major health problems. The physical effects of cold cause real difficulties, but in addition the loss of morale caused by the cold can in itself lead to further trouble. Problems with the cold are not confined to the Arctic or mountain regions. They also happen in relatively mild climates, especially when associated with wetness. Exposure causes a substantial number of casualties and even some deaths on exercises in the UK.

Dry cold

Dry cold is typical of Arctic regions and is characterized by very low temperatures and often biting winds. The temperature may be down to − 30°C or even lower.

Wet cold

Wet cold occurs in more temperate regions where the ice and snow melts, and there may be rain. The temperature is rarely as cold as in Arctic areas for more than occasional short periods.

Cold Illnesses: Hypothermia

Hypothermia simply means sub-normal body temperature. It is often called exposure when it happens outside and hypothermia when it affects old people indoors, but it is the same thing.

There are a number of factors that may lead to hypothermia.

1   *Lack of food*
    Food provides the energy for the body to produce heat. To combat cold, the calorific value of the food needs to be increased. Lack of food will lower the ability to cope with cold.

2   *Poor clothing*
    In cold weather, you need extra clothing. Multiple layers that trap air are the most effective way of retaining body heat. You lose a lot of heat through your head and feet, so make sure you have proper headgear and footwear.

3   *Dirty clothing*
    Wet, damp and dirty clothing is a poor insulator and increases heat loss. Keep your clothes clean, and remove damp or wet clothing during rest periods and dry it out. This

apples particularly to footwear, socks must be changed and boots allowed to dry as much as possible.

4 *Alcohol*

Alcohol causes the blood vessels in the skin to dilate which increases heat loss. Alcohol may make you feel warmer, but in reality it has the opposite effect.

Treatment

The casualty should be warmed slowly. Change any wet clothes and place him in a warm environment in a bed or sleeping bag. It may be necessary for someone else to get in as well to provide gentle heat. Cover his head to reduce heat loss. Moderately hot, sweet drinks will provide energy and gradually raise the temperature. DO NOT GIVE ALCOHOL. Evacuate the casualty as soon as possible.

Snow blindness

This is a temporary blindness caused by direct and reflected light. Snow is a very good reflector and will exacerbate the effects of the sun. The eyes become sensitive to glare, blinking increases and the eyes begin to water and feel irritable. Sight begins to have a pinkish tinge and eventually the vision is covered by what appears to be a red curtain. At the same time the pain increases, so it can be a very frightening condition. Fortunately, the eyes will recover, given time, if they are covered with pads and rested. It can be avoided altogether by wearing proper sunglasses.

Sunburn

Just as the light effects of the sun on the eyes are increased in snow, so are the tanning effects on exposed skin. You may need to use cream, especially on your lips.

Frostbite

Frostbite is what happens when body tissues freeze, and it is your extremities that are most vulnerable to attack. Unfortunately the onset of frostbite can often go unnoticed until it is too late. The freezing prevents body fluids reaching the affected tissues and they will eventually die. When this happens they will slowly turn black and drop off, but the damage is done long before this stage is reached. In the early stages the affected parts are cold, firm, numb and marble white. It is essential to recognize frostbite at this stage to avoid lasting damage.

Treatment

Use body heat to warm the affected part, while encasing the whole body in a sleeping bag. Hot drinks may be given and the casualty should then be evacuated.

DO NOT:
1 Rub the injured part.
2 Expose the injured part to fire or similar heat.
3 Exercise the injured part.

Frostbite can be prevented if the proper clothing is worn, especially on the hands and feet, which are the parts most at risk.

Immersion foot

Immersion foot, also known as trench foot, is caused by a lack of blood circulation and prolonged exposure to wet conditions. There are three stages.
1 The feet become white, numb and cold.
2 The feet become red, hot and painful.
3 The feet can become swollen, develop cellulitis (a form of inflammation) and eventually gangrene.

Prevention

You can take various measures.
1 Keep your circulation going by exercise.
2 Do not restrict your circulation with tight trousers or with tight binding round the bottom of trousers.
3 Keep your feet as dry as possible.
4 Change socks daily and use powder on your feet.
5 Keep your feet clean.

Properly cared-for feet should give you little trouble.

Treatment

1 Remove boots and socks and warm and dry the casualty's

feet, handling them gently. Do not rub or massage them or expose them to fire.

2 Elevate the feet.

3 Put the casualty into a sleeping bag.

4 Give hot drinks

5 Give Paracetamol

6 Evacuate the casualty as a stretcher case.

HEALTH IN HOT CLIMATES

A lot of military training is still carried out overseas. Years ago, troops went out by sea, and the long voyage would give them time to acclimatize to the tropical environment. Nowadays, flying out means that you can be deposited in a tropical country without any period of acclimatization. Heat related illnesses can be a danger even without exceptionally hot weather. Strenuous training when unfit in warm weather can cause it – and heat exhaustion can kill.

Body temperature

The body temperature must be maintained close to its norm of about 37°C to say healthy, in addition to heat from the sun, and reflected heat from the sun, and reflected heat from the ground and surrounding objects, any physical activity produces heat. To maintain the normal body temperature, this heat must be lost. This is done by sweating, which causes heat to be released from the body as it evaporates. In a climate where the temperature is over 30°C a man may lose 10-15 litres of sweat a day, even without exerting himself. This amount of water needs to be replaced.

In addition to the water loss, there will be salt lost in your sweat. If the body is not acclimatized, this loss can be serious and can result in heat cramps. Salt added to food should be sufficient to replace this, but it should not be added to water without medical advice. There is however a safe alternative which can be added to your water bottle. This is Dioralyte, a compound of the minerals and salts lost through sweating.

Prevention of heat illness

It is much easier to prevent heat illness than to treat it.

Acclimatization

A period of acclimatization helps the body to adjust to the heat; the main effect is to reduce the salt loss in the sweat to about half its previous levels. The blood vessels on the skin dilate, so increasing the amount of heat loss. This normally takes about three weeks.

Fluid intake

No-one can be trained to do without water; it's dangerous and will make you ill. Obviously, your liquid intake does not have to be restricted to pure water. Fruit juices and tea are just as good. Be careful with alcoholic drinks, since alcohol is a diuretic and causes you to pass more fluid as urine than you take in. It is possible to raise your body fluid levels before an arduous exercise by drinking more than normal (but not alcohol) in the 12 to 24 hours before the start of the exercise.

Shelter

Your shelter should be light in colour to reflect the heat, and should allow air to circulate and provide shade.

General health

Your general health is important. Personal hygiene is essential, and you must pay particular attention to your skin and feet. If you're overweight your body will be less able to respond effectively to heat; strenuous physical activity can cause heat illness even in temperate climates for those who are unfit or unused to it.

Heat illnesses: Sunburn

Sunburn is a form of superficial burn that can be prevented. One day in the sun will not give you a tan, but it could give you serious burns. Wear clothes that cover as much of your skin as possible, and do not spend too much time in the sun; half an hour on the first day is more than enough.

Prickly heat

Some people are more susceptible than others to this irritable condition of the skin. Your skin needs to be kept very clean, but soap can make it worse, so rinse it off thoroughly after washing. Hair must also be regularly washed but well rinsed. Loose clean clothing should be worn, including clean under-clothes.

Heat cramps

Heat cramps are caused by a lack of salt in the body. They can happen in any part of your body and can be quite severe, but are easily prevented by ensuring that there is adequate salt in your diet. If they do occur, seek medical advice.

Heat exhaustion

This can happen when you're working hard in relatively high temperatures and is more likely to happen if you're overweight or unfit; excessive sweating causes abnormal fluid and salt loss, leading to circulatory failure. This results in

1 Headache nausea and dizziness
2 Pale clammy skin
3 Weak, rapid pulse progressing to hot, flushed, dry skin and full bounding pulse.
4 Cramps.

The casualty will have the signs of shock plus heat cramps. The body temperature may be normal or slightly raised. If not treated the casualty may become unconscious.

Treatment

Lie the casualty down in a cool place. Remove as much of their clothing as possible and give them frequent drinks of water to which salt has been added; half a teaspoon of salt or sodium bicarbonate to a litre. Get them to drink as much as you can and get medical help as soon as possible. In combat, if the casualty is unconscious, insert the rectal drip set to restore the fluid balance, since at least 60 per cent of water is absorbed by the colon.

Heatstroke

Heatstroke is a very serious condition that if not recognized and treated quickly can result in severe brain damage and death. The heat regulating mechanism of the body ceases to work and the temperature keeps on rising. The brain literally cooks. The signs of heatstroke include:

1 Disturbed behaviour
2 Delirium, partial loss of consciousness and coma
3 Tiredness, headache and irritability
4 Nausea and vomiting
5 Reduced or absence of sweating
6 Strong, bounding pulse
7 Hot, flushed and dry skin

The casualty's temperature must be reduced by whatever means are possible. He should be moved into a cool dry place and have his clothing removed and then sponged down with tepid water, or if possible wrapped in a wet sheet. In both cases, fan the body to assist cooling. Give frequent small drinks of water. Get him proper medical help without any delay.

FIRST AID IN COMBAT

If you get hit, sort yourself out if you can. Otherwise, whoever gets to you first will help you. In a tactical situation lightly wounded men can carry on fighting after being given first aid, and must be encouraged to do so.

Each section contains a combat medic who is trained in combat first aid; he is however, primarily a rifleman and may well become a casualty himself. So you must not only know the life-saving techniques, but must be practised in their use. There is nothing worse than watching one of your mates die because you don't have the skill or the knowledge to save him.

Dealing with a casualty while in contact with the enemy will be covered in the orders issued before every operation. But the following applies in general to various phases of war.

The attack
Once you are across the effective fire line, winning the firefight and fire-and-manoeuvring forward, you cannot afford to stop.

If someone gets hit and you are near him there is a strong temptation to go and help, especially if he is making a lot of noise. The result is that more and more people are drawn into casualty handling, less fire goes down on the enemy and his fire gets heavier and more accurate.

As more people get hit, you lose the firefight and the attack fails. Withdrawing from the EFL is as expensive as fighting through, so you might as well remove the source of injury by killing the enemy and let your reserve platoons give first aid as they move up behind you.

Patrols

Casualties incurred on the route out will be left with a guard, if your patrol has sufficient strength and the standby patrol tasked to collect them. If you're on the route back, you take your casualties with you. If you're in contact with the enemy, you must take your casualties back with you as you break contact. If you are going to leave them, you must be 100 per cent sure that they are dead.

Generally recce patrols will not be large enough to take many casualties and go on with the mission. Fighting patrols are intended for combat and are therefore large enough to take casualties.

Defence

If someone in a four-man main battle trench gets hit, one of the others gives first aid while the remaining two continue to fire. If however, the enemy has closed to within grenade chucking distance, it's not a good idea for anyone to stop firing.

Do not move around the position to help other trenches unless you have dug communication trenches. Forward slope positions are very difficult to move casualties back from, compared to reverse slope. The best approach is to carry out immediate first aid in situ and make the casualty as comfortable as possible in the shelter bay until rounds stop flying.

Internal security

The terrorist or insurgent uses casualties to create more casualties; he will aim to injure or kill one man or unit to draw the remainder into an ambush command-detonated mines or a sniper. Watch out!

The four Bs

When carrying our first aid, remember the four Bs – Breathing, Bleeding, Breaks and Burns. You must deal with breathing first, because if a casualty has an obstructed airway and cannot breathe he will die, however well you treat his other injuries.

The human brain starts to suffer permanent damage after about four minutes without oxygen, so you must get a casualty breathing again as quickly as you can.

Check his mouth

A casualty with an obstructed airway may have stopped breathing completely but you are more likely to find him choking. First, look into the casualty's mouth and extract anything obstructing his throat. You must not be squeamish; remove whatever is there, even if it is covered with blood or vomit. Be positive and don't fiddle about.

Obstructing tongue

Sometimes the tongue can fall back and block the throat. You clear the casualty's airway by extending his neck; with him flat

---

THE FOUR BS

First of all decide which casualty to treat first. The order of priority of injuries to treat is
1. Stoppage of breathing
2. Bleeding wounds
3. Broken bones
4. Burns

This is the rule of the four Bs – Breathing, Bleeding, Breaks and Burns. Remember also that the casualty who is making the most noise is rarely the most seriously injured; don't make the mistake of treating a broken leg while a head injury case quietly dies.

on his back, tilt his head right back. If he doesn't start to breathe then you must resuscitate him; otherwise, treat him as an unconscious casualty.

There are five main causes of an obstructed airway.

1. Suffocation
2. Teeth, including false teeth
3. Swelling of the mouth or throat
4. Blood, water or vomit
5. Bone or tissue injuries

The unconscious casualty

You must place an unconscious casualty in such a position that no further harm will come to him. An unattended, unconscious casualty can easily die by choking to death on his own vomit. To keep his airway clear, place him in the recovery position.

If the casualty is unconscious, tuck his nearside hand under his body and the other over his chest. Cross the far foot over the nearer one. Then, supporting his head with one hand, grasp his clothing on his hip and roll him towards you.

Check that his airway remains clear and make sure that he cannot roll right over onto his front and that his neck stays extended. By placing him in this position his airway will stay clear even if he vomits and he will not swallow his tongue.

Check his pulse every 15 minutes and examine the rest of his body for obvious injuries. Remember that anyone with neck or spinal injuries cannot be moved, and you will need further assistance. Casevac an unconscious casualty as soon as you can, and never leave him alone.

For all casualties

1. Assess the tactical situation; do not endanger yourself. If the enemy are still in business continue firing, keep under cover and look out for falling masonry, mines, booby traps etc. If a vehicle is involved, switch off the fuel supply.
2. Assess the casualty; check him out completely and remove him from danger if possible. At least drag him into cover, and give protection if necessary from chemical weapons.

WHEN YOU COME ACROSS A CASUALTY

1	LOOK	3	THINK
2	LISTEN	4	ACT

3. Deal with priorities – remember the four Bs

4. Reassure the casualty, no matter how revolting his injury, and tell him what you are doing while you work on him.

5. Try to keep him warm and dry

6. Give morphine only for pain

7. Never leave the casualty alone

8. Take the casualty's ammo and any specialist equipment he may be carrying

RESUSCITATION TECHNIQUES

CAUTION

These techniques can harm a casualty if improperly performed. The information given here is for familiarisation only and formal training should be obtained before you attempt to use them.

Exhaled Air Resuscitation (EAR)

The best way to get a casualty breathing again is to use the Exhaled Air Resuscitation (EAR) method. This is best learned on the Ressusi Anne type of dummy; do not practise on another person.

Is he asleep?

First make sure that the casualty is indeed not breathing. This may seem obvious but there have been cases of people trying to resuscitate someone who is simply asleep. Look carefully at the casualty.

1 Is he/she unconscious?

2 Can you wake him up?

3 If not is his chest moving?

Do not spend too long making up your mind; every moment is vital. Follow the procedure given here, and make sure the casualty's chest is rising each time you blow. If it isn't, you are not doing it correctly.

Pulse

Check the casualty's pulse at his carotid artery. If his heart has stopped you will need to perform cardiac compression as well as resuscitation,

Airway

To perform resuscitation, place the casualty on his back and extend his neck by tilting his head back. Check his airway and remove any obstructions.

Loosen any tight clothing around his neck

Inflate his chest

Pinch his nose, take a deep breath and breathe hard into his mouth, hard enough to make his chest rise. Then remove your mouth and allow his chest to fall. Repeat every six seconds and continue until he begins to breathe. If EAR is still not working, check that his airway is still clear and that his neck is extended properly.

Don't be squeamish

The most difficult part of EAR is getting started. The casualty may have other injuries; there may be blood and vomit in and around his mouth. He may even be dead. But apart from a quick wipe around his mouth there is no time to be lost; without prompt EAR, the casualty will die.

When the heart stops

If a casualty has stopped breathing his heart may have stopped too. When you first examine the casualty, check his pulse by feeling the side of his windpipe; you should be able to feel the carotid artery at work. This is the best place to check, as a weak pulse is difficult to detect at the wrist.

Combining EAR and ECC

If someone's heart has stopped beating; their breathing will soon cease and you will have to carry out artificial respiration as well as cardiac massage. Ideally, two people should treat the casualty; one doing EAR and the other External Cardiac Compression (ECC). However, you might have to do both on your own until help arrives. If you do, then use 15 compression of the heart to two expansions of the chest. Remember to keep the airway clear.

WARNING

You must never practise External Cardiac Compression on a real person because it is very dangerous. Never start or continue to give cardiac massage to a casualty whose heart is beating, no matter how faintly.

External Cardiac Compression

Check pulse

Check the casualty's pulse at his carotid artery and if there is no pulse commence ECC. NEVER perform ECC on someone whose heart is still beating.

Position

Position the casualty as for EAR; neck extended and airway clear. Now find the lower end of the sternum (breastbone).

Your hands

With both your hands palm down, place one on top of the other with the fingers interlaced. Place the heel of the lower hand three fingers width up from the bottom of the sternum.

Commence compression

Push down with the weight of your body, pushing the casualty's breastbone towards his spine. Lift your hand to allow the chest to recoil. Repeat 60 times per minute, checking the pulse every fifth push.

CONTROLLING BLEEDING

When you've got the casualty breathing again, you can turn your attention to controlling any bleeding; the second most common cause of death from injury. Bleeding may be in the form of a slow ooze from the very smallest of blood vessels, or a much more rapid loss from a major vessel. If it's spurting out, it is coming from an artery and this is very serious.

Occasionally, bleeding stops of its own accord, either from retraction of the blood vessels or clotting of the blood, but this is likely only with small or superficial wounds.

First steps

These simple measures will help to control bleeding in most cases. Points 2 and 4 apply to injured limbs. The most important factor in dealing with bleeding is speed! But make sure that you are treating the most serious wound. Check over the whole body and, in the case of gunshot wounds, do not expect the exit hole to be in line with the entry point.

1 *Place the casualty in a comfortable position*
   This reduces the blood flow as his heart will be making less effort to pump blood.

2 *Raise the limb*
   This also reduces the bleeding but think careful before doing this in case you cause further injury, if in doubt, don't!

3 *Apply pressure to the bleeding wound*
   This will often stop the bleeding completely; place a dressing over the wound and apply pressure with the palm of your hand. Make sure the dressing is big enough, and use a sterile one if available; but any piece of clean material will do. If you can't find a dressing big enough to cover the wound, press it down where the bleeding is worst. If bleeding continues despite pressure, apply a second dressing on top of the first. Do not lift the first one to see what is happening! You can apply up to three dressings, and none should be removed until the casualty gets to hospital.

4 *Immobilize the limb*

Pressure Points

Any place where an artery crosses a bone close to the skin is a pressure point, pressure applied at these areas will, in theory interrupt the blood flow. If the pressure point is between the heart and the bleeding point, you may be able to stop the flow altogether.

In practice, only two pressure points are of much use; the brachial and femoral areas. Direct, firm pressure at these points can be used to stop bleeding in the arms and legs. To carry out the procedure:

1   Place the thumb or fingers over the pressure point.
2   Apply sufficient pressure to stop the blood flow and hence the bleeding.
3   After 15 minutes, slowly release the pressure.
4   If bleeding has stopped dress the wound.
5   If bleeding starts again, repeat the process.

The release of pressure after 15 minutes is essential to allow blood to reach the tissues beyond the pressure point; if this is not done they may be damaged. Resist the temptation to release pressure in under 15 minutes to see how you are getting on, as bleeding will not yet have been controlled.

Internal bleeding

Internal bleeding is harder to deal with. It may have been caused by a severe blow to the abdomen, a crush injury to the chest, or by the blast effects of an explosion. Also if a bone is broken, especially a large one such as the femur (thigh bone) there will be bleeding in the surrounding tissue. Internal bleeding can cause any or all of the following symptoms.

1   Pallor
2   Cold, clammy skin
3   Rapid, weak pulse
4   Restlessness and weakness

Treatment is difficult and depends on rapid evacuation to hospital. In the meantime, talk to the casualty and make him as warm and comfortable as you can.

TREATING SHOCK

Shock is a term that is very often misused and misunderstood. How often have you heard of people being admitted to hospital suffering from shock after an accident? In the vast majority of cases they are suffering from no such thing. What has actually happened is they have had a nervous reaction to the accident; they are not suffering from shock in the medical sense of the word.

True shock is a major cause of death after injury, and is the reaction of the body to a loss of circulating body fluid, which in most injury cases means a loss of blood. In the case of burns the casualty may lose a substantial amount of fluid from the burn itself.

Recognising the symptoms

A casualty suffering from shock will show several of these symptoms

1 Paleness
2 Cold and clammy skin
3 A fast, weak pulse
4 Rapid, shallow breathing
5 Anxiety
6 Faintness, giddiness and blurred vision
7 Semi-consciousness or unconsciousness

He will also have a low blood pressure although it is unlikely that you will be able to measure this.

These signs are the result of the body's attempt to keep up the blood pressure and so maintain an adequate supply of blood to essential organs such as the brain.

Unfortunately the signs of a purely nervous reaction can be very similar; people can be pale sweating and indeed sometimes unconscious. If in doubt treat for shock.

Treatment

There is very little the first-aider can do: evacuation to proper medical assistance is essential, as the casualty will need intravenous fluids or blood. But while waiting for this, you can take some immediate steps.

1 Lie the casualty down
2 Make sure his airway is clear
3 Look for and stop any bleeding

Raise the casualty's legs so that they are higher than his heart, but check his legs for fractures first.

Keep the casualty warm. Remember to insulate him from the cold ground; don't just pile a blanket on top

If you are forced to leave the casualty or if he is unconscious, tilt his head to one side so that he will not choke if he vomits.

4   Raise his legs above the level of his head
5   Support any injured limbs with splinting
6   Protect the casualty from exposure to wind and rain
7   NEVER give the casualty alcohol
8   Reassure the casualty

Battleshock

This is a temporary psychological reaction to the stress of battle which can produce similar symptoms to shock; heavy casualties or prolonged bombardment can cause physically sound soldiers to become unable to fight effectively. During World War I 'shell shock' was not sufficiently understood, and some victims found themselves charged with cowardice. In fact, if detected early and treated as far forward as possible, battleshock can be overcome. Those most at risk are inexperienced troops or newly arrived replacements who are not yet 'part of the team'. However, courage can be a consumable resource, and if a combat veteran exhausts his reserves he too can fall prey to battleshock.

Symptoms

Most people in action will show some signs of fear, so sweating or trembling are not reliable indicators of impending battleshock. Watch for the following:

1   Physical symptoms without actual injury
2   Severe restlessness
3   Overwhelming despair
4   Panic reaction to sound
5   Indecision among officers or NCOs

Treatment

Casualties from battleshock are best treated forward rather than sent to the rear away from their own unit. Respite from the worst of the battle, sleep, hot drinks and the chance to relive experiences with friends all help repair the psychological damage. Getting a casualty busy with some simple but useful task is also helpful. Avoid medication or alcohol.

Hysteria

A fatal combination of youth, inexperience and poor discipline can lead to some troops becoming hysterical and going berserk. Treatment is:

1   Remove the casualty's weapons and make them safe.
2   Administer Diazepam tablet from the cap of the casualty's Combopen. Repeat at 30-minute intervals if necessary.
3   If tactically necessary, administer morphine.
4   Casevac the victim. The stretcher bearers should take the casualty's personal weapon.
5   At all times be calm and reassuring

CHEST WOUNDS

Chest injuries can be very serious and must be recognized and treated urgently; prompt evacuation to proper medical care is essential. You can treat superficial injuries like any other wound, with a clean dressing, but watch out for these serious problems.

Crush injuries

The casualty may have fractured ribs, often in several places. At the site of the injury the chest wall will no longer be rigid, and breathing becomes difficult as the chest is no longer effective in pumping air in and out of the lungs. Worse, air could be getting moved from one side of the chest and back again rather than up and down the windpipe. The casualty tries to overcome this by taking deeper breaths, which only makes matters worse.

Recognising the symptoms

Look for the following
1 Abnormal movement of the chest
2 Painful and difficult breathing
3 Distress and anxiety
4 Cyanosis (blueness) of the lips and mouth
5 Signs of shock.

Treatment

The aim of the treatment is to stop the abnormal movement of the chest wall. If the casualty is unconscious, you should:
1 Check and clear his airway
2 Place him in the three-quarters prone position
3 Place a hand over the injured area to provide support
4 Place a layer of padding over the area and secure it with a firm, broad bandage.
5 Treat for shock
If he is conscious, carry out steps 3 and 4 with him sitting upright.

Open chest wounds

If the wound is severe enough there may be a hole in the chest wall. Air will get in and the lung will collapse, and air will go in and out of the hole instead of up and down the windpipe.

Recognising the symptoms

Look for the following:
1 Shallow and difficult breathing
2 The sound of air being sucked in and out of the chest wall
3 Bloodstained fluid bubbling from the wound
4 Cyanosis of the lips and mouth
5 Signs of shock

Treatment

The aim is to prevent the air going in and out of the chest wall. Quite simply, you must plug the hole. Whether the casualty is conscious or unconscious you should:

1 Make sure his airway is clear

2 Seal the hole in his chest by placing a large dressing over the wound and fixing it in place with a firm, broad bandage. Make sure it completely covers the wound forming a seal

3 Place the casualty on the injured side to help maintain the seal.

4 Treat for shock

Bleeding into the chest

Crush or open wounds may be accompanied by bleeding into the chest. It may also happen without obvious external signs of injury, particularly following an explosion when the casualty suffers what is know as blast injury.

Recognising the signs

You should suspect bleeding into the chest if the casualty:

1 Shows signs of shock

2 Is coughing up blood

3 Has difficulty in breathing

Treatment

Unfortunately there is very little a first aider can do about internal bleeding into the chest apart from general measures for the treatment of shock. The important thing is to recognize that there is a problem and to arrange for urgent evacuation

TREATING ABDOMINAL WOUNDS

WARNING:
Casualties with abdominal wounds should not be given anything by mouth.

The abdomen, the part of the body between the chest and the pelvis is often mistakenly referred to as the stomach. The stomach is just one of the contents of the abdomen; other important organs are the bowels, liver, spleen, kidneys and bladder. An abdominal injury may result in severe shock and the majority of cases will require surgery.

As well as injury to internal organs there may be considerable internal bleeding. A further cause of trouble is infection, which is particularly likely if the gut is penetrated or torn.

First aid treatment is very simple. All you can do is make the patient comfortable and cover the wound.

Recognising the symptoms
An abdominal wound is usually obvious and part of the guts may be sticking out. There may be severe bruising to the abdomen or lower chest, back or groin. The injury may be the result of a direct blow or the casualty may have suffered a blast injury. Other signs are:

1   Pain or tenderness in the abdomen
2   Vomiting, which may contain blood
3   Tense abdominal muscles
4   Shock

Treatment
Make the casualty lie down on his back with his knees drawn up. This will help to relax the muscles and ease the strain on the abdomen. If the patient is not suffering too much shock, the head and shoulders may also be raised.

Cover the wound with a clean dressing. If any guts or tissues are sticking out, don't try to push them back in; just leave them as they are and cover with the dressing. Also don't try to remove the debris from the wound or you make matters worse.

Do not give the casualty any food or drink, but protect him from further injury and from wind and rain and keep him warm. Arrange for speedy evacuation

TACKLING BURNS

Burns are the last of the four Bs. They are an increasingly common type of injury, particularly in tactical military situations where damage to vehicles often results in fire or explosions. Burns range from the superficial and small to those involving extensive tissue damage.

> NEVER APPLY BUTTER OR SIMILAR FAT; THIS WILL INSULATE THE AREA AND CAUSE FURTHER DAMAGE.

People with extensive deep burns may eventually die from them, but the great majority of fire deaths result from damage to the lungs by smoke and fumes or by the heat of the fire. People who have this sort of damage may have little or nothing in the way of visible breathing. In these cases you should try expired air resuscitation until medical help can be obtained, but unfortunately this is often unsuccessful. However, that's no reason for not trying.

Types of burn

Burns used to be described as first, second, or third degree, but this system is no longer used; burns are now classified as superficial, or deep. Superficial burns will appear red, swollen and tender.

Deep burns will be surrounded by very red skin and will be blistered and swollen. In the most serious instances the skin may be pale and waxy and even charred, and the casualty may not feel much pain due to destruction of the nerve ends.

Treatment

The first thing to do, as with any injury is to remove the

Your first priority is to extinguish the flames if the casualty is on fire. Use water if available, or a blanket to smother the flames. If indoors and the building is not at risk, stay inside. Rushing out would only make the flames worse.

Wrap the casualty in a heavy material which will not catch fire and lay him on the ground. Then remove any clothing which has been soaked in boiling fluid, but leave cooled, dry burnt clothing alone.

casualty from the source of danger. Hopefully, someone else will extinguish the fire, while you deal with the casualty.

A burn is a wound like any other, and is treated in the same way – with a clean dressing. Cover the whole area to prevent infection getting in and more fluid leaking out. Burns can cause extensive fluid loss and this must be reduced as much as possible. Leave any blisters intact; they are performing a useful function in keeping fluid in. They may be removed later in hospital, but it's not a first aid job. Also, do not attempt to remove any burnt skin.

Do not remove burnt or charred clothing unless it is continuing to be a source of heat. If clean water is available immerse the burn area to cool it. This reduces further heat damage and reduces the pain.

Even the smallest burn can be very painful. Paradoxically, some large deep burns can be surprisingly pain free because the nerve endings have been burnt away.

Splints and slings may help to keep the patient comfortable and will therefore reduce pain. Prepare them in the same way as for fractures.

SIX STEPS FOR DEALING WITH BURNS

1. If the casualty's clothing is on fire, lay him down and extinguish the flames with water, a fire bucket or similar heavy material that will cut off the air from the fire.

2. Cool the burn area using clean water or other harmless liquid for example milk, beer etc. It is important to stop the 'cooking' effect of the heat; do not apply fat, cream or ointments.

3. Cover the burn with a sterile dressing

4. Do not break any blisters or remove burnt clothing (unless it is hot)

5. If the casualty has facial burns, make a mask with a clean dry cloth, and cut holes for nose, mouth and eyes.

6. Immobilize a badly burned limb as for a fracture.

FRACTURES

When you've dealt with the casualty's breathing and bleeding, the third priority is broken bones. Fractured bones can cause serious injury or death, but can often be successfully treated and a complete recovery achieved. A great deal depends on the first aid you give the casualty before he is evacuated for treatment. Before he can be moved you must immobilize the fracture; the basic principle of splinting is to immobilize the joints above and below the break.

Immobilising fractures

You must keep the fracture still to prevent the sharp edges of the broken bone moving about. This achieves three things:

1   Stops further damage to tissue, muscle, blood vessels and nerves.

2 Reduces pain and shock

3 Stops a closed fracture becoming an open one because of bone fragments penetrating the skin.

Rules for splinting

1 Remove watches, rings and garments from the limb or these may reduce the flow of blood to the hand or foot when the injured part becomes swollen.

2 If the tactical situation allows it, splint the fractured part before moving the casualty and without any change in the position of the fractured part. If a bone is in an unnatural position or a joint is bent, leave it as it is.

   If circumstances force you to move a casualty with fractures in his lower body before you can apply a splint, tie the injured leg to his other leg. Grasp the casualty beneath his armpits and pull him in a straight line. Do not roll him or move him sideways.

3 Apply the splint so that the joint above the fracture and the joint below the fracture are completely immobilized.

4 Place some padding between the splint and the injured area. This is especially important between the legs, in the armpits and in areas where the splint rests against the bony parts such as the wrist, knee or ankle joint.

5 Bind the splint with bandages in several places above and below the fracture but not so tightly that it interferes with the flow of blood. Do not bandage across the fracture. Tie bandages with a non-slip knot against the splint.

Signs and symptoms

Symptoms of a fracture include pain when slight pressure is applied to the injured area, and sharp pain when the casualty tries to move the area. Do not move him or encourage him to move in order to identify the fracture because the movement could cause further damage and lead to shock. Other signs are swelling, unnatural movement of the limb, bruising and crepitus (the distinctive sound of fractured bone ends grating together)

Types of fracture

1 Open fracture
   An open fracture is a break in the bone and in the overlying skin and flesh. The broken bone may have punctured the skin or a bullet may have penetrated the skin and broken the bone.

2 Closed fracture
   In a closed fracture the bone is broken but the skin remains intact. There may be tissue damage and the area is likely to swell and later bruise. It may only be a sprain, but you should assume the worst and treat it like a fracture

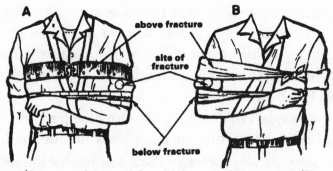

If you have nothing with which to construct a splint, immobilize an injured arm by securing it to the casualty's chest. Slings can be improvized from belts or bits of shirts or blankets. Remember to put some padding between the splint and the injured arm.

FIELD FIRST AID – IMPROVISATION

There might come a time when your oppo has been hit and you haven't got the kit to help him. But most 'official' first-aid kit is unnecessary, so you should not be tempted to burden yourself with a vast collection of equipment. Every soldier is trained in first aid. The only pieces of equipment he carries are dressings; everything else has got to be improvized.

Dressings

A field dressing is a large pad of gauze with a bandage attached; ideally it should be in a sterile packet, and each soldier should carry at least three. A lot of dressings that are commercially available are frankly too small; a dressing cannot be too large. If you cannot find a proper dressing the next best thing is a suitable gauze pad held in place with a crepe bandage. Failing this, any clean material will do; clean cotton is best, so use handkerchiefs or shirts folded to make a pad or torn into strips to make a bandage. If you can't find anything very clean, use the cleanest part up against the wound and the less clean further away. Remember, most gunshot wounds are highly contaminated anyway by the bullet; bits of cloth have been pushed into the wound and dirt sucked in as the temporary cavity caused by the wound repressurizes.

Splints

Splints can be made from anything that is reasonably rigid, wooden planks, branches or metal sheeting. Items of military equipment might be suitable, but if you decide to use your rifle pay attention to the tactical situation first. Inflatable splints are carried by the combat medic.

Leg Splints

See illustration for how to apply improvized splints for a frac-

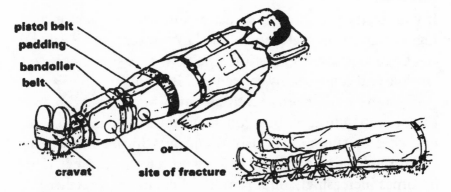

You can use the uninjured leg as a splint for the fracture; pad out the gaps between the legs before you start tying them together. Leave the boots on and tie them together firmly at the base and the top of the boot. There should be no shortage of things to use as strapping; the picture shows just a few ideas. They must be placed as shown and this is the minimum number that will be effective.

ture of the lower limb or ankle. Note that the knots are against the splints, not the leg.

Arm splints

The aim of splinting is to immobilize the limb and prevent the break getting any worse. Both diagrams show methods of splinting a broken arm or elbow where the elbow is not bent. Try to pad the splint so that the casualty feels comfortable and immobilize the whole arrangement by strapping it down to the chest.

The binding or cravats should be firm enough to prevent movement but not so tight that they limit the blood flow. Use a piece of cloth or bandage so that it does not cut in. Remember to immobilize the joint above and below the fracture.

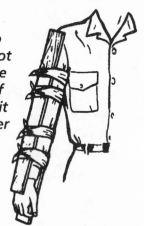

Stretchers

If you need to evacuate a casualty you will need a stretcher. Lightweight rope stretchers, as used in climbing, are ideal and can be carried, one per section. The new issue stretcher is collapsible and can be easily carried in a Bergen.

If you have to improvize, things such as doors and planks are obvious choices, but you may have to make do with branches or rifles. Obviously whatever you use must be as comfortable as possible for those who have to carry it. This becomes increasingly important the further the stretcher has to be carried.

If you do not have a stretcher and haven't time to improvize, you may have to carry the casualty in, for instance, a fireman's lift. There are several ways of making things easier for yourself, particularly in getting the casualty up on to your shoulder.

From the recovery position haul the casualty up onto your

knee and balance him there while you change grip to under his armpits. Then heave him on to his feet, leaning against you.

Hold out the casualty's right arm and then duck under the arm. Put your head against his chest and your left arm between his legs, holding the right knee in the crook of your elbow and swing him up onto your shoulders. The higher up you carry him, the easier it is. Hold his right arm and leg together in your left hand and carry your rifle in your right hand.

CASUALTY CARRYING TECHNIQUES

'Stretcher bearers' always seem to be on hand in the movies, but the truth is that they will always be thin on the ground forward of the company aid post. In most cases you will have to move your own wounded back via platoon headquarters.

Wounded are usually controlled by the platoon sergeant. The lightly wounded should be given first aid and encouraged to fight on, and the walking wounded should move to the CAP under their own steam if possible.

The rest can roughly be divided into the conscious but immobile, and the completely out-of-it. There is a wide range of carrying techniques to deal with the different categories, so learn and practise them now. In any future European war there will not be sufficient helicopter assets for casualty evacuation.

Types of carry
The drag
This is for conscious or unconscious casualties and requires a good deal of upper body strength. With the casualty on his back adopt an all-fours face to fact position over him with his arms tied together and looped around your neck. Tie the arms of the casualty around your neck at the elbow to make the task easier. Then only his legs will drag in the dirt. This is a good technique if you are under fire.

The side drag
This, with its variations, is the method you will use when in close contact with the enemy and where cover is limited (when

the rounds start flying you will pick it up naturally). With one hand grasp the casualty's shoulder webbing and with your feet alongside him, lever yourself along on elbow and thigh. You can also try looping your foot through his webbing and dragging him on the end of your boot.

The fireman's lift

This is comfortable to the carrier but hell for the patient. It does tend to make you a large target, and it is difficult to get the unconscious casualty onto your shoulders without help.

The piggy back

This is really only useful if the casualty is conscious and can use both his arms. It can be quite comfortable if you sit the casualty on your webbing, transferring his weight onto your shoulders.

Webbing carry

This method is best for short distances in place of the fireman's lift for a casualty who can't be doubled over. Hold the casualty on your back, his head next to yours and facing the same way, by grasping his shoulder, or webbing, with your hands close to your neck.

Webbing stretcher

Sit the casualty in his webbing the wrong way round with his feet through the shoulder straps to produce an improvized sit harness.

The seat

By crossing and linking your arms in this way, you can carry a casualty who is unable to walk. As a third soldier will be needed to carry the wounded man's weapons and kit, it is easy to see how a couple of casualties can paralyse a unit.

The sit

This method provides back support but less of a seat. Two men hold hands so that one handgrip is below the casualty's knees and the other behind his back with his arms grasping the carriers' shoulders.

Extracting casualties from vehicles

You should be familiar with most Army MT and AFVs and know the positions of all the hatches, the fire extinguishers and the fuel cut-off.

Casualties in vehicles are often severely injured with multiple wounds, burns, etc so practise the techniques now.

BATTLE CASUALTY EVACUATION

The first man in the casualty evacuation system is the soldier who has been wounded. The first thing he has to do is to stabilize his injury – in other words, stop the flow of blood, move into a position that prevents his lungs flooding or throat

---

BATTLE CASUALTY MARKING

When treating a casualty you can make the medic's job a great deal easier and prevent complications further down the line of casualty evacuation by marking the casualty's forehead with the relevant information. The section medic will label the casualty when preparing him for casevac, but labels can be lost; information on the forehead cannot. The symbols are:

X	Emergency evacuation necessary
T	Tourniquet applied with the date, time group written underneath
H	Haemorrhaging
M	Morphine with the date and time of the injection written underneath
C	Gas – contaminated chemical casualty
XX	Nerve agent poisoning
R	Radiation sickness
P	Phosphorous burns

clogging, or simply keep broken limbs supported so that simple fractures don't become compound. Your buddy may also assist if he is nearer than the section medic.

The section medic will then check the casualty on orders from the section commander – remember that in contact with the enemy the medic may himself become a target. Next, the platoon medic will be brought in to prepare the casualty for evacuation, and, while this is happening, platoon HQ will contact company HQ with a request for a casualty evacuation.

The company stretcher bearers then evacuate the casualty to the Company Aid Post. The stretcher bearers will be moving backwards and forwards between the platoons in contact and the company and, as long as they are not badged up with red crosses, can also be used to move up ammunition. They can't do this if they are protected by the red cross, because they are engaged in humanitarian work and cannot give material support to the battle – a convention normally respected by both sides. In an infantry battalion medics are normally members of the band (or buglers or pipers) who combine their skills as musicians with first aid training.

The company medic ensures not only that the casualty goes on his way to the Regimental Aid Post (RAP) in a stable condition but also that medical supplies are fed back down to the section from the RAP.

Out of the battle

In transit, you must protect casualties from the weather, chemical agents and enemy weapons. Shock can kill, and it can be accelerated by wet and cold. Casualty bags have been produced for work in an NBC environment, but it may be necessary to make repairs to the casualty's NBC suit as an expedient.

The casualty will retain his weapon while he is evacuated though the section medic will probably have removed and redistributed ammunition and grenades. The weapon will need to be made safe, and you should search for other weapons at an early stage.

Enemy casualties are evacuated in the same way, but they are disarmed when they are captured. Security is the unit responsibility, though a wounded PoW is unlikely to wish to escape or cause trouble.

The Regimental Aid Post varies in size depending on the type of battalion, but a typical team comprises a Regimental Medical Officer (RMO) and eight assistants. They will document casualties and dead – the dead are brought in, in the same way as casualties. The usual daily work of the RMO is to treat the battalion sick.

From the RAP, the casualty will be evacuated by ambulance to the Dressing Station in the divisional administrative area, where he is treated for further evacuation, or return to his unit. He will not receive any surgery here.

Field surgery

Surgery in the field can be brought forward to the casualty, rather than the man having to make a long journey to the rear. Helicopters have made evacuation fast and reliable, but the turn-around time can be critical. Battle injuries have some uniquely unpleasant features – blast and fragments can produce extensive damage. Though a gunshot wound may be precise, the track of the round after it has entered the body can be unpredictable, and the exit hole can be larger than the entry hole. Dirt, clothing and fragments enter the body with the round, and tissue is damaged by the passage of the round through the body.

The only advantage that the field hospital surgeon has is that the casualty is basically a fit man. There is no danger of heart attack, respiratory collapse, or thick layers of subcutaneous fat to be penetrated. Recovery can be fast, with sleep and proper nursing, since a man in his late teens or early twenties is the 'ideal' patient. The problems lie in psychological adjustment to permanent disablement or the death of close friends.

Triage and survival

A uniquely grim feature of battlefield surgery is the triage system. Developed by the French in World War I, triage is the classification of incoming casualties by types. T1 can have his life saved by emergency surgery, T2 can await treatment, T3

CASUALTY EVACUATION

In battle, the most important priority after achieving the unit mission is the successful management of combat casualties.

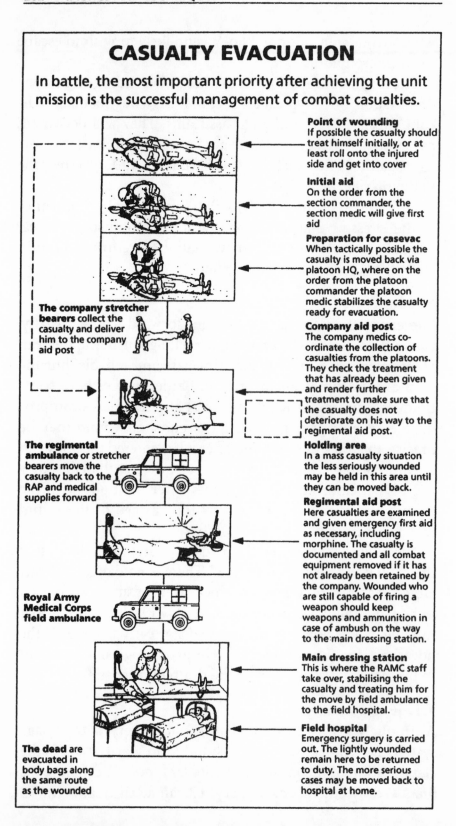

Point of wounding
If possible the casualty should treat himself initially, or at least roll onto the injured side and get into cover

Initial aid
On the order from the section commander, the section medic will give first aid

Preparation for casevac
When tactically possible the casualty is moved back via platoon HQ, where on the order from the platoon commander the platoon medic stabilizes the casualty ready for evacuation.

The company stretcher bearers collect the casualty and deliver him to the company aid post

Company aid post
The company medics co-ordinate the collection of casualties from the platoons. They check the treatment that has already been given and render further treatment to make sure that the casualty does not deteriorate on his way to the regimental aid post.

The regimental ambulance or stretcher bearers move the casualty back to the RAP and medical supplies forward

Holding area
In a mass casualty situation the less seriously wounded may be held in this area until they can be moved back.

Regimental aid post
Here casualties are examined and given emergency first aid as necessary, including morphine. The casualty is documented and all combat equipment removed if it has not already been retained by the company. Wounded who are still capable of firing a weapon should keep weapons and ammunition in case of ambush on the way to the main dressing station.

Royal Army Medical Corps field ambulance

Main dressing station
This is where the RAMC staff take over, stabilising the casualty and treating him for the move by field ambulance to the field hospital.

Field hospital
Emergency surgery is carried out. The lightly wounded remain here to be returned to duty. The more serious cases may be moved back to hospital at home.

The dead are evacuated in body bags along the same route as the wounded has relatively minor injuries and can look after himself: finally T4 has serious multiple injuries. In surgical terms T4 may not be worth working on. He may die after surgery and, meanwhile, a T1 may slip into a T4 while this operation is under way. A US army surgeon recalled his first encounter with T4 in Vietnam, when he saw an unconscious casualty apparently neglected in the corner of the ward. When he started to work, a colleague told him not to bother. Raising the soldier's head, he showed the young surgeon that half the man's brain was spilling out of his smashed skull.

Educational role

Despite this, it is vital that men should know that when they are asked to put their life on the line, they are backed by an efficient evacuation and treatment system. They will fight more effectively. The RMO has an important 'educational' role within a battalion explaining the system and ensuring that everyone understands basic first aid. The panic and terror that can ensue after a man has been hit will be reduced if he knows what to do and what will be happening to him now that he has become a casualty.

HIJACKS AND HOSTAGE RESCUE

PERSONAL SURVIVAL

You switch on the 6 o'clock news and once again you see an airliner parked at the end of a runway. It shimmers in the heat reflected from the concrete and you can see armoured cars and troops lurking by the control tower. The terrorists' demands seem wearily familiar and there's no comment yet from the White House. But hijacks don't just happen to other people. One day it might be you.

You can survive some hijacks, like some ambushes, by careful planning and thinking ahead. Don't just follow the crowd; think through your schedule, the different routes to your destination and the airlines you might fly with.

Are you a target?

The very first priority is to establish if you, or anyone you might be with, is a potential target. Remember that you are more likely to be singled out because of what you represent than who you actually are: terrorists often attack people just because of their nationality. If they simply want Western hostages, you might fit the bill very nicely just because you happen to be in the wrong place at the wrong time.

Choose your carrier

The second area of prior planning is the booking, route, carrier and seat. Make two bookings on different airlines, but only pick up one. Collect these tickets at the airport, so that your movements are known to a limited number of people. Choose an airline like Swissair or SAS which has no political associations. Some of the US carriers are obvious targets, as are Middle East airlines. Go for the neutrals – even countries with former colonial empires can be targets.

If you are flying to a potential trouble spot some airlines are noted for their high level of security – El Al insists on searches of baggage as well as electronic and body checks of passengers. It is also one of the many airlines that now operate with 'sky marshals'. El Al may be a target, but it is a 'hard' target.

Avoid stop overs

Try to make sure that you have a direct route with no stop-overs – this is particularly important with the Middle East. Some airports have very sloppy security, and while you may have had a thorough search when you boarded at your departure, other passengers at other stops may board less thoroughly checked.

If there is a stop-over, a walk around the terminal will get you away from the vulnerable aircraft – some terrorists have boarded aircraft disguised as cleaners during stop-overs, so a stroll reduces your chances of being caught in the hijack.

Pick your seat

Your seat could be a lifesaver – aisle seats put you within reach of the hijacker. Window seats are safer and exit seats may give you the chance to escape if the aircraft is on the runway of an airport.

'Neutral' seating in tourist class is less likely to attract attention than first class. If the terrorists wish to show their determination they may shoot hostages, and these are likely to have been chosen from passengers who are obviously important.

Be a grey person

Your dress and manner will also make you a target. In some countries blue jeans are seen as Western clothing, and so are suspect. Ex-army clothing is to be avoided, combat jackets being the most obvious. Baggage also draws attention either by its opulence or by being service issue, for example kit bags or rucksacks.

Labels should only have a business address, and the baggage should not sport hotel labels from around the world (incidentally, these precautions also reduce the chance of theft at airports). Jewellery, striking T-shirts and obvious ethnic clothing can also be a liability and reduce your ability to be the 'grey man', a neutral unnoticed among the passengers.

Finally your passport and wallet can contain a goldmine of information. Try to avoid collecting visa stamps from countries that have a terrorist problem – many countries will stamp entry and exit visas on a separate piece of paper if you ask.

HOW TO AVOID AND SURVIVE A HIJACK

1. Travel with an airline that has no or few political enemies.
2. Do not wear Army or ex-Army clothing
3. Do not carry your luggage in service-issue kit bags or rucksacks
4. If the plane is hijacked keep quiet and do not draw attention to yourself.
5. Observe the terrorists' activities very carefully: if you do escape you'll be able to help the security forces.

Your job description can be a major liability – government or service personnel are seen as 'targets' by many hijackers and natural targets for hostage executions.

Photographs of relatives and children are always worth including in your wallet/passport. You will be seen as a family man or woman with dependents and thus a less suitable person for execution. At the other extreme, the bathing-costume picture of a wife or girlfriend may cast you as a corrupt and decadent Westerner in the eyes of some hijackers.

Action

If the worst happens and you are on the aircraft that has been hijacked, follow the old army adage: 'Keep your eyes open, your mouth shut and never volunteer for anything'. The last part can be modified if it allows you to escape.

As the hijack is taking place the armed men and women will be very nervous, and rapid or unexpected movements from the passengers may produce violent reactions. They may assault you, note you as a future execution victim, or kill you as a suspected sky marshal.

By quiet observation you will be able to build up a picture of the numbers of hijackers and their mode of operation. In a large aircraft they may collect everyone together, or position themselves at different points around it to cover the passengers.

Tiredness and tension

As time passes everyone will be affected by fatigue and the need to perform bodily functions. This will increase tension and the presence of children will further aggravate this.

The hijackers will probably release women, children and elderly people if the aircraft has landed at a location where negotiations are taking place. These released passengers will be able to give details of the hijackers to the security forces, assuming that the aircraft is in a reasonable pro-Western country.

If you have a seat by the door there may be an opportunity to escape. However if you are travelling with a group this may make them potential execution victims. Note how the hijacker is armed – if he has a handgun you have a better chance of surviving, and there may even be a chance to overwhelm him.

The most dangerous situation is a group with automatic weapons and explosives. The explosives may be positioned around the aircraft, with the threat that they will be detonated if there is an attempt at rescue; and automatic weapons are notoriously inaccurate in untrained hands, and could cause casualties if a firefight with a sky marshal developed.

If there is a firefight, stay as low as possible. Window seats give better cover, though they are less easy to escape from. The sky marshal will probably have a low-velocity weapon with ammunition that will not damage the fuselage, but the hijacker may be using a 9-mm high-velocity weapon – and if this punctures the aircraft fuselage there may be decompression.

Rash rescue attempts

However, the aim of the hijacker is to get the plane to a place where the bargaining can begin. There have been examples where hastily mounted 'rescue' operations have caused more casualties than were expected when the rescuers stormed the aircraft. If a rescue operation takes place the most likely course of action will be for the assault team to order the passengers to keep down. In this way they can identify the hijackers, who are likely to be on their feet in the aisle.

Your best course is to keep down and wait for the shooting to stop: the assault team will be looking for any violent or unexpected movement. They will have preceded the assault with stun grenades, and both passengers and hijackers will be suffering from temporary shock. The team will then aim to have the passengers off the aircraft as fast as possible so you should follow their instructions.

Keep cool

If, however, the aircraft arrives at a neutral or 'friendly' country where the hijackers can negotiate, the advisable course is to assess the situation. There may be friends of the hostages at the airport who will take over the negotiations with a friendly power and be more rational than the men and women who hijacked the aircraft. In this situation, a leader for the passengers may emerge; he could be the pilot or a mature and experienced passenger. Such a person will be able to make representations about the health and welfare of the passengers.

By this stage the aircraft and passengers will have become bargaining counters and their safety will be more important. Now it may be a time for patient waiting. If you find you are moved from the aircraft to hotels or holding areas, try to take some hand luggage or toiletries – there may be nothing when you arrive. Staying clean and presentable will also sustain your morale.

The inflight comforts will stop almost at once if a hijacking happens, since the stewardesses and stewards will be seen as conduits for information as they move around the aircraft. It is advisable therefore to keep hand luggage that contains simple toiletries and any medication you may need ready to hand.

For many people hijacks, like other man-made or natural disasters, are experiences that happen to other people and which are reported on the news. But they could happen to almost anyone, even if they see themselves as 'Mr Average': they may be on the flight with an important traveller, or they may just be unlucky.

Ever since the series of 'skyjacks' in the late 1960s, anti-terrorist units have been refining a series of methods for storming a plane on the ground. It is not easy task. The terrorist have every advantage in their favour; they usually have a

SWEATING IT OUT

Some hijacks are over in hours. But others can last for days, as the aircraft is directed from international airport to international airport.

While in flight, the air conditioning will work and the physical conditions will not be too bad. On the ground however, the aircraft will be reliant on its Auxiliary Power Unit (APU) and so it can become hot and not very comfortable.

The passengers' discomfort will be one of the bargaining counters that the hijackers will use as they talk to the control tower. Lavatories will become blocked and food will be reduced to light snacks from the galley. Though the staff at the control tower may be able to send food as the negotiations continue, this cannot be relied on. These points will help you to get through a trying and frightening time.

1. Avoid provoking the hijackers by unnecessary demands or by eye contact that may be seen as critical.

2. If you have hand luggage that can be reached without creating problems, you may be able to use your sponge bag to keep clean and refreshed.

3. Eat any snacks or sweets you have packed but avoid snacks that will make you very thirsty.

4. Try to contact your neighbours and take an interest in them. It will take your mind off your own situation and may even enable you to place some leverage on the hijackers – for instance, if your neighbour is sick or elderly he may be evacuated from the aircraft as a humane gesture.

5. Contact with your neighbours will also allow you to work out any plan of action that my present itself – thus the single hijacker may lay himself open to attack by the passengers if he turns his back on them as he moves along the aisles.

6. Avoid a rash attack on a hijacker. You may be happy to be a hero, but if you fail the attack puts everyone at risk. Random shots may penetrate the fuselage or kill or injure passengers. The hijackers may also see the whole aircraft as a threat and attempt to destroy it in revenge.

Attempts to disarm hijackers should be left to the skilled experienced and brave, not the amateur and enthusiastic.

clear field of view and can slaughter the passengers in a matter of moments. If you are going to make a rescue attempt it must be planned to the last detail and executed with split-second timing.

Ending a Hijack

In some instances hijackers have released men and women who are sick or very young or old. These people will be vital since they will give information on the hijackers' numbers and their weapons and equipment. They will also provide more information on their level of training and motivation though some of this will have been gleaned from the conversations with the control tower.

Wear them down

You will need to know how close you can approach without alerting the hijackers. Disguise as ground crew is good cover, though ladders and weapons and equipment can be difficult to conceal. Night is the obvious time when the hijackers will be fatigued and there is reasonable cover.

If the APU (Auxiliary Power Unit) cuts out through lack of fuel, the internal lights, air conditioning and other power will cease, putting the aircraft in darkness. If the ground crew from the previous stop-over can advise on fuel states and it seems that there might be a breakdown, then an attack can be planned or the hijackers warned that the aircraft will be without power due to failure of the APU. Timing must be perfect: it was a failure to co-ordinate an APU breakdown that caused heavy casualties at Malta airport when Egyptian special forces attacked an airliner that had been hijacked.

Talking them out

The negotiating team can induce fatigue in the hijackers if they can keep them talking, although this must be balanced against the risk to the passengers, as well as their continuing discomfort. Sometimes the negotiators will be able to talk the hijackers out of the aircraft with no need to assault it, and no loss of life.

Losing patience

However, once hijackers lose patience with the negotiating team and start killing hostages to show that they mean business, then the assault team must be ready to move in fast.

Since hijackers are not likely to have weapons with rifle-calibre ammunition, your team could wear body armour, which will provide sufficient protection: the new lighter weight Kevlar armour can be worn without reducing efficiency. The use of body armour is also important for the morale of the assault team.

Weapons for the assault team

The weapons for the job can include a linear cutting tape charge, stun grenades and automatics. Linear cutting tape is a flexible metal or plastic tube with a notch running along one face and when correctly positioned, acts as a charge to cut through an aircraft fuselage to gain entry. It can be fixed magnetically or with adhesives, according to the target.

Weapons for the firefight

The handguns favoured by anti-hijack teams vary. The Delta Force in the USA originally used the venerable .45 M1919A1; the big slug will knock a man down without penetrating the aircraft fuselage. Hollow-point ammunition that flattens when it hits a target has a devastating effect on soft tissue, but will not ricochet or cause damage to internal controls and fittings in the aircraft.

New ammunition

Some new plastic ammunition will slow down after a short range, but is lethal over the short distances in which the action will take place. Automatics with large-capacity magazines like the Browning High Power will give enough ammunition for the short but violent action that will follow the entry into the aircraft. However, you should carry spare magazines where they can be quickly loaded if there is a sustained firefight.

Entering the aircraft

If the hijackers are divided, with some on the flight deck and

NINE QUESTIONS THE ASSAULT TEAM MUST FACE

1 How many hijackers are there?
2 Where is each one stationed in the aircraft?
3 What are they armed with?
4 Have they prepared any explosives to destroy the aircraft?
5 How fit and motivated are the hijackers?
6 How many passengers are aboard, and what is the seating plan?
7 Can the hijackers be tricked into gathering together in the cabin for a discussion with the control tower?
8 How many entry routes does the aircraft have?
9 Can the assault team practise on a similar aircraft first?

others amongst the passengers, then you will need to attack in two teams and stage the assault so that one team fights towards the front and one towards the back of the aircraft. This way you should avoid firing into your own men. Entry must be preceded by stun grenades, which will temporarily disable the enemy but not severely injure the passengers.

Stun grenade effects
When a stun grenade explodes in a confined space like an airliner, anyone standing nearby will be completely deafened and if you are very close your eardrums will be shattered. The flash leaves you temporarily blinded and if you were looking towards it when it went off the image will be burned onto your retina for at least 10 minutes, making it very hard for you to shoot straight.

Speed means success
However the rehearsals went, you must be ready for anything when you get inside the aircraft. The hijackers may not be where you expect them, and its tempting to fight your way forward cautiously. But your attack will only succeed through speed.

The volley of stun grenades and the suddenness of your assault throws the hijackers off balance and you must not give them time to recover.

Shout at the passengers to lie down. This will keep them out of the line of fire and should make the hijackers better targets. As you move through the smoke-filled aircraft hunting a handful of terrorists amongst hundreds of passengers it is horribly easy to shoot the wrong target.

Standing targets

This the moment all your training is for, when life or death hangs on your split-second reactions. If Intelligence managed to provide you with photos of the terrorists, at least you have some means of identifying you target; if not, then you must sweep through going for anyone standing or armed.

The passengers can be removed from the aircraft as soon as the hijackers are cleared from a major exit. Station members of

HOSTAGE SURVIVAL

Keep low

As soon as the action starts slide to the floor under your seat and stay there. Do not move into the aisles, any assaulting troops will flatten you in their rush to dominate the aircraft.

Obey all orders from the assault team without question or protest. They'll treat everyone as potential threats so you'll be handled very roughly until positively cleared.

Tear gas will probably be used, so bury your head in the seat cushions. Do not rub your eyes – especially if you wear contact lenses.

Non-provocative stance

Do not pick up weapons as you flee the aircraft – you may be shot as a suspected terrorist when you get outside. As you exit, fall to the ground as though injured with your arms outstretched, and stay there until instructed to move by security forces.

your team by the exits to make sure no hijackers try to sneak out the same way and to co-ordinate the security forces outside the aircraft. There have been cases when escaping passengers were shot by mistake as they fled from the fighting.

Assault team moves out

After the hijackers have been dealt with and the aircraft declared 'clear' the assault team moves out. It is sensible to keep a low profile, because you do not want your arrival during a future crisis to be observed by the press and blasted over the TV and radio. This is why all special forces preserve the anonymity of their men. It may save their lives one day — and it may save yours.

◉ SIEGE AT PRINCES GATE

The Special Air Service of the British Army burst into the world headlines in May 1980 when it stormed the Iranian Embassy in London to free 26 hostages held by Arab gunmen. It was an unusually public appearance for the SAS, most of whose operations since its foundation in 1941 have been deep behind enemy lines, or in the more shadowy areas of counter-revolutionary warfare. Jon E Lewis gives the following account.

At 11.25 am on the morning of Wednesday 30th April, 1980, the tranquillity of Princes Gate, in London's leafy Kensington district, was shattered as six gunmen wearing shamags over their faces sprayed the outside of No 16 with machine gun fire and stormed through the entrance. The leading gunman made straight for an astonished police constable standing in the foyer, Trevor Lock of the Diplomatic Protection Group, while the rest, shouting and waving their machine pistols rounded up the other occupants of the building.

The gunmen — Faisal, Hassan, Shai, Makki, Ali and Salim — were members of Mohieddin al Nasser Martyr Group, an Arab group seeking the liberation of Khuzestan from Ayatollah Khomeini's Iran. No 16 was the Iranian Embassy in Britain. The siege of Princes Gate had begun.

The police were on the scent almost immediately, alerted by an emergency signal from Trevor Lock, and were soon followed by Scotland Yard specialist units including C13, the anti-terrorist squad, and D11, the elite blue beret marksmen. The building was surrounded, and Scotland Yard hastily began putting in motion its siege negotiation machinery.

While no siege is ever the same as the one before or after it, most follow a definite pattern: in stage one, the authorities try to pacify the gunmen (usually with such provision as cigarettes and food), and allow the release of ideological statements; in stage two, the hostage-takers drop their original demands, and begin negotiating their own escape; stage three is the resolution.

The Princes Gate siege moved very quickly to stage one, with Salim the head Arab gunman announcing his demands over the telephone just after 2.35 pm; autonomy and human rights for the people of Khuzestan, and the release of 91 Arab prisoners held in Iranian jails. If his demands were not met he would blow up the Embassy, hostages and all, at noon the following day.

The SAS meanwhile had been alerted about the siege within minutes of its start. Dusty Gray, an ex-SAS sergeant now a Metropolitan Police dog handler, telephoned the Officers' Mess at Bradbury Lines, the SAS' HQ next to the River Wye in Hereford, and said that the SAS would probably be required at the Iranian Embassy where gunmen had taken over. That night SAS troopers left for London in Range Rovers, arriving at a holding area in Regent's Park Barracks in the early hours of Thursday morning. The official authority from the Ministry of Defence approving the move of the SAS teams to London arrived at Bradbury Lines some hours after they had already left.

Over the next few days the Metropolitan Police continued their 'softly, softly' negotiating approach, while trying to determine exactly how many hostages were in the Embassy and where they were located. Scotland Yard's technical squad, C7 installed microphones in the chimney and walls of No 16, covering the noise by faking Gas Board repairs at neighbouring Ennismore Gardens. Gradually it became clear that there were about 25 hostages (as they discovered at the end of the siege, the exact count was 26), most of them Iranian embassy workers. Also hostage were PC Trevor Lock and two BBC sound engineers, Sim Harris and Chris Cramer. The latter, who became seriously ill with a stomach disorder, was released by the gunmen as an act of good faith. It was a mistake by the Arab revolutionaries; a debriefing of Cramer gave the SAS vital information about the situation inside the Embassy as they planned and trained in a new holding area only streets away from Princes Gate itself.

Inside the holding area a scale model of the Embassy had been constructed to familiarize the SAS troopers with the layout of the building they would assault if the police negotiations were to break down. Such training and preparation was nothing new. At the Bradbury Lines HQ, SAS Counter Revolutionary Warfare teams use a Close Quarter Battle house for experience of small arms fire in confined spaces. (One exercise involves troopers sitting amongst dummy 'terrorists' while others storm in and riddle the dummies with live rounds).

As the police negotiating team located in a forward base at No 25 Princes Gate (of all places, the Royal School of Needlework) anticipated, the gunmen very quickly dropped their original demands. By late evening on the second day of the seige, the gunmen were requesting mediation of the siege by Arab ambassadors – and a safe passage out of the country. The British Government, under Margaret Thatcher, refused to countenance the request. To the anger of the gunmen, BBC radio news made no mention of their changed demands, the broadcast of which had been a concession agreed earlier in the day. Finally, the demands were transmitted – but the BBC got the details wrong.

For some tense moments on Saturday, the third day of the siege, it looked as though the furious Salim would start shooting. The crisis was only averted when the police promised that the BBC would put out the demands accurately that evening. The nine o'clock news duly transmitted them as its first item. The gunmen were jubilant. As they congratulated themselves, however, an SAS reconnaissance team on the roof was discovering a way into No 16 via an improperly locked skylight. Next door at No 18 the Ethiopian Embassy, bricks were being removed from the dividing wall, leaving only plaster for an assault team to break through.

On Sunday 4 May, it began to look as though all the SAS preparation would be for nothing. The tension inside the Embassy had palpably slackened and the negotiations seemed to be getting somewhere. The gunmen's demands were lessening all the time. Arab ambassadors had agreed to attend a meeting of their COBRA committee in order to decide who would mediate in the siege.

And then, on the morning of Bank Holiday Monday, 5 May, the situation worsened rapidly. Just after dawn the gunmen woke the hostages in a frustrated and nervous state. Bizarrely, Salim, who though he had heard noise in the night, sent PC Lock to scout the building, to see whether it had been infiltrated. The hostages in Room 9 heard him report to Salim that there was nobody in the Embassy but themselves. Conversations among the gunmen indicated that they increasingly believed they had little chance of escape. At 11.00 am Salim discovered an enormous bulge in the wall separating the Iranian Embassy from the Ethiopian Embassy. Extremely agitated, he moved the male hostages into the telex room at the front of the building on the second floor. Forty minutes later, PC Lock and Sim Harris appeared on the first floor balcony and informed the police negotiator that their captors would start killing hostages if news of the Arab mediators was not forthcoming immediately. The police played for time, saying that there would be an update on the midday BBC news. The bulletin, however only served to anger Salim, announcing as it did that the meeting between COBRA and the Arab ambassadors had failed to agree on the question of who would mediate. Incensed, Salim grabbed the telephone link to the police, and announced: "You have run out of time. There will be no more talking. Bring the ambassador to the phone or I will kill a hostage in forty-five minutes."

Outside in the police forward post, the minutes ticked away with no news from the COBRA meeting, the last negotiating chip of the police. Forty-two minutes, forty-three minutes ... The telephone rang. It was Trevor Lock to say that the gunmen had taken a hostage, the Iranian Press Attache, and were tying him to the stairs. They were going to kill him. Salim came on the phone shouting that the police had deceived him. At precisely 1.45 pm the distinct sound of three shots was heard from inside the embassy. The news of the shooting was immediately forwarded to the SAS teams waiting at their holding area. They would be used after all. Operation Nimrod – the relief of the Embassy – was on. The men checked and cleaned their weapons, 9mm Browning HP automatic pistols and Heckler & Koch ('Hockler') MP5A3 submachine guns. The MP5, a favourite SAS weapon, first came to prominence when a German GSG9 unit used it to storm the hi-jacked airliner at Mogadishu. It can fire up to 650 rpm. The order for the assault teams to move into place was shortly forthcoming.

At 6.50 pm, with tension mounting, the gunmen announced their demands again, with the codicil that a hostage would be shot every forty-five minutes until their demands were met. Another burst of shots was heard. The door of the Embassy opened, and a body was flung down the steps. (The body belonged to the Press Attache shot earlier in the day. The new burst of shots was a scare tactic.) The police phoned into the Embassy's first floor, where the telephone link with the gunmen was situated. They seemed to cave in to Salim's demands, assuring him that they were not tricking him, and that a bus would be arriving in minutes to take the gunmen to Heathrow Airport, from where they would fly to the Middle East. But by talking on the phone Salim had signalled his whereabouts to the SAS teams who had taken up their start position on the roof, and in the two buildings either side of No 16, the Ethiopian Embassy and the Royal College of Physicians. At around this time, formal responsibility – via a handwritten note – passed from the Metropolitan Police to the SAS.

Suddenly, as the world watched Princes Gate on TV, black-clad men wearing respirators appeared on the front balconies and placed 'frame charges' against the armoured-glass window. There was an enormous explosion. The time was exactly 7.23 pm. At the back of the building and on the roof, the assault teams heard the order "Go. Go. Go." Less than 12 minutes had elapsed since the body of the Press Attache had appeared on the Embassy steps.

The assault on the building came from three sides, with the main assault from the rear, where three pairs of troopers abseiled down from the roof. One of the first party accidentally swung his foot through an upper storey window, thereby alerting Salim to their line of assault. The pair dropped to the ground and prepared to fight their way in, while another pair landed on the balcony, broke the window and threw in stun grenades. A third pair also abseiled down, but one of them became entangled in the ropes, which meant that the rear assault could not use frame charges to blow-in the bullet proof glass. Instead a call sign from a rear troop in the garden sledgehammered the French windows open, with the troopers swarming into the building on the ground floor. They 'negotiated' a gunman in the front hall, cleared the cellars, and then raced upwards to the second floor and the telex room, where the male hostages were held by three gunmen. Meanwhile the pair who had come in through the rear first floor balcony encountered PC Lock grappling with Salim, the head gunman, who had been about to fire at an SAS trooper at the window, and shot the gunman dead.

Almost simultaneously with the rear assault, the frontal assault group stormed over the balcony on the first floor, lobbing in stun grenades through the window broken by their frame charges. Amid gushing smoke they entered and also moved towards the telex room. Another SAS team broke into the building through the plaster division left after the bricks had been removed from wall with the Ethiopian Embassy.

Outside, at the front, the SAS shot CS gas cartridges into an upstairs room where one of the gunmen was believed to be hiding. This room caught fire, the flames spreading quickly to other rooms. (The trooper caught in the abseil rope suffered burns at this point, but was then cut free and rejoined the assault.)

The SAS converged at the telex room as planned. The gunmen had started shooting the hostages. The Assistant Press Attache was shot and killed and the Chargé d'Affaires wounded before the SAS broke in. By then the gunmen were lying on the floor, trying in the smoke and noise to pass themselves off as hostages. What then happened is the subject of some dispute, but the outcome was that the SAS shot two of the gunmen dead. Afterwards, some of the hostages said that the gunmen tried to give themselves up, but were killed anyway. In the event, only one gunman escaped with his life, the one guarding the women in Room 9. The women refused to identify him as a terrorist, and he was handed over to the police.

After a brief assembly at No 14 for emotional congratulations from Home Secretary William Whitelaw the

SAS teams sped away in rented Avis vans. Behind them the Embassy was a blaze of fire and smoke.

The breaking of the siege had taken just 17 minutes. Of the 20 hostages in the building at the time of the SAS assault, 19 were brought out alive. The SAS suffered no casualties. Although mistakes were made in the assault (part of the main assault went in via a room which contained no gunmen and was blocked off from the rest of the Embassy), the speed, daring, and adaptability of the SAS proved the regiment an elite amongst the counter-revolutionary forces of the world.

LANDINGS AND RAIDS ON ENEMY TERRITORY

AIRBORNE LANDINGS

Special Forces teams take the battle to the enemy on his own ground. Working behind the lines, their missions can vary from intelligence-gathering to sabotage, and organising guerilla resistance movements against the enemy. It is a war without rules. The Special Forces soldier can expect no mercy from the enemy.

Many operational techniques are made up on the spur of the moment, to take advantage of a tactical opportunity. But that doesn't mean there's no formal training. The US military forces all have special detachments and they all take as their guide FM 31-20, the US Army Special Forces Operational Techniques field manual on which this article is based.

Because they are 'Special Forces', their job is impossible to describe without listing all the possibilities. It is safer to say that as a member of Special Forces team you have to be prepared to tackle just about anything that comes up. One of the most important tasks is intelligence-gathering – eg locating hidden 'Scud' missile sites in western Iraq. Another is the instruction of locally recruited guerrillas in military and other techniques, anything from personal hygiene to farming methods. The aim is to prove to the local population that you have their best interests at heart.

Winning the battle for the hearts and minds of the people is really much more important than taking an objective by armed force. But you can't win either of them until you get to the battlefield itself. Inserting agents into hostile territory has been a front-line intelligence task for thousands of years. There are two main methods.

1. False identities and disguise
2. Covert operations.

False identities

The biggest advantage of the first approach is that once you have got through the identity checks at the frontier you will be able to live openly in enemy territory. You will be living a double life, with slim chances of survival if the enemy identify

INFILTRATING SPECIAL FORCES TEAMS

When preparing a team for infiltration by parachute, remember the following:

1. Aircraft load capacity may limit the equipment and personnel you can take.
2. The presence of a reception committee on the drop zone makes 'sterilising' the area and hiding your parachutes less of a problem.
3. You must ensure you take the equipment needed for your initial tasks
4. The detachment commander places himself in the best position within the stick for controlling the team.
5. Team recognition signals and signals for contacting the reception committee must be decided in advance.
6. The primary assembly point should be 100 to 200 metres from the drop zone and you should have a secondary point 5 to 10 kms from the DZ for use in an emergency.

you – but no-one said Special Forces work would be easy. Disguising your identity is peacetime is essential if you are to succeed in such a task; this is why the US Special Forces do not allow their personnel to be filmed after they complete basic training.

Covert operations

Covert operations involve entering the enemy's territory without his knowledge. It can mean trekking across a border in remote frontier regions or parachuting from an aircraft at very high altitude to freefall most of the way.

Insertion from an airborne operation is popular because no area is inaccessible by air; it's quick and, when organized properly, minimizes the risk both to the carrier and to the passenger and his reception committee. There are three normal variants.:

1. Low and normal altitude parachuting

2   High Altitude Low Opening (HALO) parachuting

3   Air Landing operations

The objective is to insert agents without the enemy's knowledge, so you must take his capabilities into account. How good is the enemy radar? Are adequate drop or landing zones available? Are there personnel on the ground who could act as a reception committee and help transport people and supplies to safe locations and 'sterilize' the drop zone after use?

You must consider many of the same factors when planning an infiltration from the sea. First of all, what sort of coastal areas are available, and how vigilant are the enemy defences? Do you have the right sort of marine craft to hand? Do you have the facilities to make sure that sea water can't affect vital pieces of equipment? Submarines are widely used to land Special Forces. Modern submarines are difficult to detect and Special Forces personnel can exit underwater and stay that way until they reach the beach.

Infiltration overland is very similar to a long range patrol in enemy-held territory and can be the most secure way of all of getting the Special Forces team into place, especially if time is not crucial. Distance is not necessarily a problem to fit, well-equipped Special Forces personnel, trained to use their skills, wits and resources.

Local assistance

Where you can get help and assistance from 'friendlies' already in place, to provide food, shelter and intelligence, overland infiltration is often the most effective of all. Because drop zones and landing zones are unlikely to be next door to the area of operations, both air and seaborne insertions will probably end up as overland journeys as well. So there is a lot to be said for relying on your own two feet rather than on technology; man can escape detection a lot more easily than a machine.

One factor is common to all three methods of insertion that we've looked at so far – the availability of people on the ground to act as porters and guides and to provide security for the infiltrators. But it may not always be that way. In some cases the members of your team will have to go in 'blind', relying exclusively on your own skills and resources – not to mention a degree of luck!

Planning Airborne Operations

Airborne operations are the arteries and veins of Special Forces operations in enemy-occupied territory. In most cases, it's just not possible to get men and supplies in and out of operational areas by any other means, and so a great deal of effort goes into making them as safe, secure and simple as possible. This section, taken from the US Army's handbook introduces you to the methods that are used.

The DZ or LZ

The first stage of any airborne operation is the identification and selection of Drop Zones (DZs) or Landing Zones (LZs).

Drop zones and landing zones must please both the aircrew who are to fly the mission and the reception committee who will be there to meet the consignment and passengers. From the aircrew's point of view the zone should be easy to identify from above and the countryside around it relatively free of obstacles.

All round access

Flat or rolling countryside is best, but if the Special Forces operation being supported is located in mountainous country, this may not be possible. In that case, it's best to choose sites on broad ridges or plateaux. Small enclosed valleys or hollows, completely surrounded by hills, should be avoided whenever possible.

To give the aircrew as much flexibility as possible in the route they will take to the zone, it should be accessible from all directions. If an approach can only be made from one direction, then the area should be free of obstacles for five kilometres on each side to give the aircraft space to perform a 'flat' turn.

Even particularly tall trees can be a potential danger to an aircraft doing a low-level drop. Where the operation is to take place at 130 metres or less, the safety requirements are that there should be no obstacle higher than 30 metres within eight

LEVEL TURNING RADIUS

Drop zones with a single, clear line of approach are acceptable if there is a level turning radius of 5 km each side (1.5 km for light aircraft). Remember that these are minimum distances and if you reduce them the aircraft may be endangered or may fly higher than desirable when making the drop, leaving your supplies drifting on the wind away from the DZ.

1 The general area surrounding the drop zone must be relatively free from obstacles which might endanger the aircraft. Flat or rolling terrain is the best, but plateaux in hilly country can be suitable.

2 Small valleys surrounded by hills should not be used for drop zones.

3 For night operations you must avoid using drop zones with ground rising to 300 metres within 16 km of the site level.

TAKE OFF & APPROACH CLEARANCES FOR FIXED WING AIRCRAFT

Minimum landing zone sizes

Light aircraft: 305 m x 15 m

Medium aircraft: 920 m x 30 m

Add a 15 metre cleared strip each side as a safety margin

kilometres, if possible. Where the aircrew have no choice but to put up with such obstacles in the immediate area of the DZ, their location must be well known.

Dispersion

The DZ should be equally accessible from all direction, so the best shape is round or square, even though the various packages that make up the consignment will land in a line parallel to the course of the aircraft. Dispersion – the distance between the points where each component will hit the ground – is mostly controlled by the speed of the aircraft over the ground, and the time it takes to get the whole consignment out through the hatch.

The rule of thumb for low-level operations is that half the speed of the aircraft in knots (nautical miles per hour; 100 knots/115 mph) multiplied by the time it takes to get the whole consignment out of the aircraft, will give the dispersion in metres on the ground.

DISPERSION PATTERN

release point

forward throw

last bundle

first bundle

wind drift

release point marking panels

dispersion pattern

The first man or package out of the aircraft will obviously tend to land some distance behind the last man out. You can calculate the dispersion as follows: half the speed of the aircraft in knots multiplied by the exit time in seconds, equals the dispersion distance in metres.

The dispersion distance is the absolute minimum length of the drop zone.

This is the critical distance, because it determines how long the zone needs to be. If possible add at least 100 metres to each end as a safety factor. Sometimes it may be impossible to find a potential DZ as wide as it is long that meets all the other requirements

Drop zone axis

If you have to use an oblong DZ, it must have its long axis in absolutely the right direction to allow the pilot of the aircraft the best possible chance of completing his mission safely and delivering the consignment into the right hands. It must make some allowance for sidewinds, because this will dictate how far to the side of the aircraft's track the drops will land. It's not sufficient to expect the pilot to compensate completely for sidewinds by 'aiming off'.

The surface

The surface of the DZ should be level and free from obstructions such as rocks, fences, trees and powerlines. Where personnel are to be dropped at high altitude (15,000 metres and higher), try to locate DZs in soft snow or grassland. Parachutes fall faster in the thin, high air, and so the passenger will hit the ground harder.

Dangerous drop zones

Swamps and marshy ground, including paddy fields are suitable both for personnel and bundles of goods in the wet season and for bundles when they are dry or frozen. Water-covered DZs are particularly dangerous to heavily-laden personnel; in the airborne landings on D-Day in Normandy for example, on 6 June 1944, the American 82nd and 101st Airborne Divisions lost so many men drowned in flooded fields that their combat efficiency was badly reduced. They were carrying more than a normal equipment load.

It is possible to drop into water providing special precautions are taken. The water should be one and a half metres deep; it should be cleared of obstructions both on and below the surface; it must be 10°C or warmer; it must be free of swift currents and shallow areas and there must be a foolproof recovery system that ensures that personnel don't stay long in the water.

One particular problem that dropping into water minimizes is that of cleaning up the DZ after use, so that no tell-tale signs of the operation are left. Be particularly careful when dropping onto agricultural land. If the fields in question are cultivated, it will be next to impossible to eradicate all traces of the drop.

Landmarks and way-points

The further an aircraft has to fly on a compass course, without way-points (visual checks on position) the more likely it is to be off the correct course. The main causes are tiny inaccuracies in the compass and other instruments and external factors such as wind.

Special Forces re-supply missions rely on being pinpoint accurate first time; the pilot hasn't time to fly around the countryside looking for the drop zone.

The usual procedure is to select an easily identified landmark somewhere between eight and 24 kms away from the DZ itself. The pilot then takes his bearings from this point and flies on a compass heading for a predetermined time to bring the aircraft over the zone.

Features that stand out from the ground may well not make good landmarks from the air especially at night. These are the sort of things you should be looking for.

1 Coastline in distinctive stretches, especially with breaking surf or white sand beaches, river mouths over 50 metres wide, or sharp promontories or inlets.

2 Rivers more than 30 metres wide. Heavily wooded banks will reduce their visibility.

3 Canals. Their straight course and consistent width make them easy to spot, except where the surrounding countryside follows a uniform pattern.

4 Lakes at least a square kilometre in area with a distinctive shape or feature.

PARA DROPPING BEHIND ENEMY LINES

Resupplying Special Forces teams that are operating behind enemy lines is a very difficult business. Because radio communications can be detected, the supply drops often have to be at pre-planned times. Since the Special Forces teams cannot guarantee their arrival at a specific drop zone either, the US Army units have a system for area supply drops. The aircraft arrives at point A and flies to point B. Below the flightpath there are several possible drop zones, but the aircraft does not need to know which one the ground troops want to use. The aircrew simply fly along the route and drop their supplies when they see DZ markings. The distance between points A and B should not exceed 25 kms and whatever DZ is chosen should not be more than 1 km away from the line of flight.

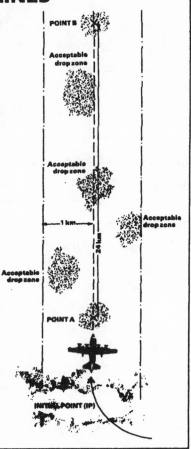

5 Woods and forests a square kilometre and more in size with clear-cut boundaries or some special identifying feature.

6 Major road and highway intersections

7 Railways especially when there is snow on the ground.

How to send an airdrop message

Whenever you use a radio, keep the three principles of use in mind: Security, Accuracy and Discipline (SAD).

Security

Remember the eternal triangle of sender, receiver – and enemy monitor. Keep your transmissions as short as possible, always encode your own and enemy grid references and be careful not to use names or appointment titles on the radio. If in doubt, encode it into battle code (BATCO). Watch your speech mannerisms; these can also give you away and are a vital source of long-term intelligence.

Accuracy

You must encode and decode accurately. BATCO leaves no room for mistakes. Corrections take up valuable seconds that could lead to a message being intercepted and a traumatic experience; for example in a 40-second fire mission a battalion of Soviet BM-21 multi-barrelled rocket-launchers can deliver 14 tonnes of HE (high explosive) or chemical agent onto your position.

Discipline

You must obey radio net discipline, provide constant radio-watch and answer calls correctly and quickly. Use correct voice procedure, apply the rules of BATCO and this will help prevent enemy electronic warfare units from breaking in on your net.

Radio voice

You must be aware of your radio voice. It should differ from normal speech in the following respects, Rhythm, Speed, Volume and Pitch (RSVP).

1 Rhythm
   Divide the message up into logical portions, and deliver it at an even rhythm with pauses; remember the recipient has to write it down.

2 Speed
   BATCO delivered too quickly will lead to mistakes; delivery must be slightly slower than normal speech.

3 Volume
   Speak slightly louder than normal but don't shout; this just distorts the message.

4 Pitch
   Try to pitch your voice slightly higher than normal; this enhances clarity.

A typical drop zone report

Your report might look like this:

Code name:
DZ HAIRY

Location
THREE TWO TANGO PAPA TANGO SIX FOUR ONE TWO FOUR THREE

Open Quadrants
OPEN ONE THREE ZERO DEG TO TWO TWO ZERO DEG AND THREE THREE ZERO DEG TO ZERO ONE TWO DEG

Recommended track
TRACK THREE SIX ZERO DEG

Obstacles
RADIO TOWER ZERO EIGHT SIX DEG SIX KM

1 The code name would have been decided on and briefed prior to the mission
2 The location of the centre of the drop zone is given as a partially encoded six-figure grid reference.
3 The open quadrants give the boundaries of the drop zone. Note these are in degrees not mils.
4 The recommended track is the approach route, again in degrees.
5 The aircraft would be warned of any potential obstacles and their position on or near the track.

Marking drop zones

Even if his navigation is excellent and his instruments spot-on, the pilot should still be helped in the final stages of the approach by signals from the ground. At night these can be made by electric flashlights (torches), flares, small fires or vehicle headlights.

In daylight, the best DZ marking method is the square panels that are supplied as sets to Special Forces units. If they're not available, use bedsheets or strips of coloured cloth, but make sure they stand out against the background. The squares or strips are used to make up distinctive shapes or letters which

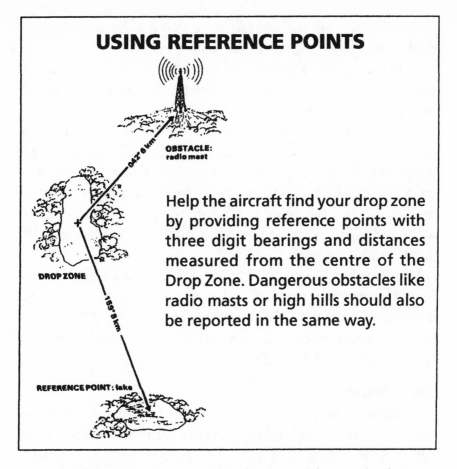

USING REFERENCE POINTS

OBSTACLE:
radio mast

042 6 km

DROP ZONE

159 8 km

REFERENCE POINT: lake

Help the aircraft find your drop zone by providing reference points with three digit bearings and distances measured from the centre of the Drop Zone. Dangerous obstacles like radio masts or high hills should also be reported in the same way.

are changed every day according to the unit's Standard Operating Instructions.

Smoke grenades or simple smudge pots of burning oil aid identification considerably.

Radio homing devices become more and more popular as the technology that supports them improves but remember that they need to emit a radio signal to operate. Any signal that you can pick up, the enemy can pick up too.

Ground release points

The ground party has a much better chance of computing the Wind Drift Factor (the distance that bundles and personnel will be carried by the wind) than the pilot does, so they allow for it when marking the Ground Release Point.

The wind doesn't start to act on the load immediately it leaves the aircraft. The rule of thumb is that the load will travel in the same direction as the aircraft for around a hundred metres before starting to slip off to the side.

Drift is calculated by a simple formula; aircraft height in feet times wind velocity in knots times a constant – three for bundles, four for personnel.

Release Point Markers can then be offset according to the likely wind drift. Obstacles along the flight path might prevent the pilot from seeing the markers, and to reduce this possibility there must be a clearance on the ground of 15 metres for every metre of the aircraft's height above the ground. An obstacle 30 metres high mustn't be closer than 450 metres from the ground markings.

Markers should be sited in such a way as to be visible only from the direction from which the aircraft is approaching. This may mean screening them on three sides placing them in pits with the appropriate side sloping, or in the case of panels, mounting them at an angle of 45 degrees.

Unmarked drop zones

In particularly sensitive operation it may be necessary to make deliveries of personnel and equipment to unmarked drop zones. This usually means a daylight or full-moon drop into a zone that has a particularly well marked geographical feature to identify it.

Because of the need for security, the ground party will have no way of communicating with the aircrew. The pilot will have to calculate wind drift himself, using the latest available weather reports as a guide and make allowances accordingly.

Electronic homing devices should be used whenever possible to help the aircrew recognize the DZ, but very careful arrangements are necessary to keep transmissions to a bare minimum.

High Altitude Low Opening

Precision skydiving, an increasingly popular sport, grew out of a Special Forces infiltration technique known as HALO – High Altitude Low Opening – parachute infiltration. Dropping from around 1000 metres, the parachutists fall free, controlling their

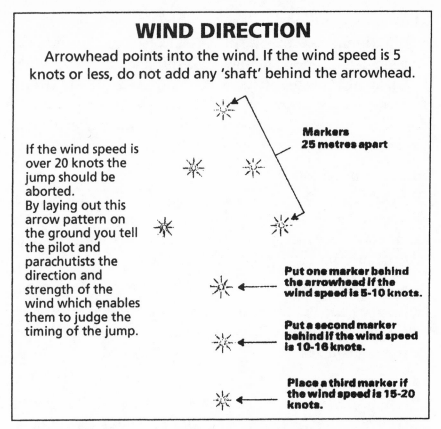

WIND DIRECTION

Arrowhead points into the wind. If the wind speed is 5 knots or less, do not add any 'shaft' behind the arrowhead.

Markers 25 metres apart

If the wind speed is over 20 knots the jump should be aborted.
By laying out this arrow pattern on the ground you tell the pilot and parachutists the direction and strength of the wind which enables them to judge the timing of the jump.

Put one marker behind the arrowhead if the wind speed is 5-10 knots.

Put a second marker behind if the wind speed is 10-16 knots.

Place a third marker if the wind speed is 15-20 knots.

direction with hand and arm movements that act in the same way as the control surfaces of an aircraft.

DZ markings indicate the landing point itself in this technique, because the parachutist is able to make corrections for windage. In the last few hundred metres of the descent, however, he will be subject to the same forces that act during a normal descent, and so it is necessary to show wind speed and direction by arranging the target marker in the shape of an arrow pointing into the wind. Up to five knots of wind are indicated by an arrow head, adding one additional marker to form a tail, for every further five knots of wind speed.

Using sophisticated electronics, it is not necessary for the target area to be visible from the aircraft, so the HALO jump can be made from above cloud or at night. Equipment can be free fall jumped too, using altimeter triggered or timed parachute release and the same aiming techniques used in high altitude precision bombing.

Helicopter Landing

For maximum effective use of the helicopter you should position the landing zone to allow take-off and landing into the wind. At night the helicopter will usually have to land to transfer personnel or cargo, but during daylight hours it can fly a couple of metres off the ground and the team can leap out of the back.

Altitude and temperature

Remember that at high altitudes and high temperatures the density of the air is sharply reduced. This means the helicopter cannot carry as much cargo and will need a longer distance to take off and land.

Approach path

Helicopters need at least one approach path 75 metres wide. For a night landing a helicopter requires a minimum space 90 metres in diameter.

Surface and slope

The surface chosen for the landing zone must be relatively level and free from obstructions such as logs, rocks, ditches or fences. The maximum ground slope permitted is 15°. In dry conditions it is a good idea to dampen the area to reduce the tell-tale dustcloud which also hampers the pilot's visibility.

Noise

The noise of a large helicopter such as the Chinook coming in to land will reveal your position to any enemy forces nearby. For this reason, helicopter landings must be conducted away from the enemy unless you have a powerful security detail in position.

Water landings

Helicopters like the Chinook can land in a water course provided the bottom is firm and the water no more than 46 cm deep.

The reception committee

The reception committee is split into five parts, but a single person may, of course, take on more than one role. The five functions are

1   *Command Party*, to control and co-ordinate the operation and provide medical support.

2   *Marking Party*, which sets out and collects markers and assists in recovering equipment and personnel and sterilising the site.

3   *Security Party*, which ensures the unfriendly elements don't interfere with the operation.

4   *Recovery Party*, ideally two men for each bundle or parachute. They should be spread out along the drop axis at the same interval as the drops are expected. Any back up should be stationed at the far end of the drop track, because the drop is more likely to overshoot than undershoot. The recovery party is also responsible for the clean up 'sanitisation' of the drop site, and that includes briefing all members of the reception committee on proper procedures. A surveillance team should keep watch over the DZ for 48 hours after the operation to warn of enemy activity.

5   *Transportation Party*, responsible for getting personnel and

---

STERILISATION PROCEDURES

The reception committee will clean up the drop zone after the operation. Here's a basic check list:

1   Collect cigarette ends and food wrappers; mislaid equipment; human waste

2   Collect rigging straps and parachute line

3   Count all items of equipment out and in

4   Bury any waste or unwanted equipment, preferably in a number of different places, at the base of large bushes.

5   Erase drag marks, footprints and impact marks. Use a leafy branch and disguise the freshly-cut end on the tree with mud.

6   Avoid trampling vegetation, especially in cultivated areas.

7   Maintain security on the way in and out of the DZ.

LOLEX

Vital cargo can be dropped without landing with a technique known as Low Level Parachute Extraction Resupply System (LOLEX). The aircraft flies a couple of metres above the ground and a parachute fitted to the cargo pulls it out of the rear door.

equipment away from the DZ according to a pre-arranged system. the transportation party will usually include all members of the command, marking and recovery parties.

Security

Because security and concealment is so important to Special Forces operations, you must pay a lot of attention to those considerations when selecting reception zones. Three factors are important; freedom from enemy interference on the ground; accessibility by means of concealed or secure routes for the reception committee; and proximity to areas suitable for hiding supplies and equipment.

Avoiding the enemy

It goes almost without saying that the aircraft's route into and out of the DZ must avoid enemy troop installations. There must be a very high level of patrol activity around the DZ for some time before the operation is due to take place. When the aircraft is actually scheduled to land, rather than merely drop a consignment from the air, vehicles with mounted automatic weapons should be available, to keep pace with the aircraft on both sides during landing and take-off (bear in mind that the vehicles will have to be moving and up to speed at the point where the aircraft will touch down). If incoming fire is received the crews of these vehicles must be in a position to suppress it immediately.

WATERBORNE LANDINGS

Landing from the sea

Special Forces Operations often start and finish on a beach.

Even though airborne insertion is faster and more flexible, when safety and secrecy are the first considerations the unit commander will often opt to go in by ship or submarine, landing his men from inflatable boats or getting them to swim.

Submarines are self-contained, safe from prying eyes. They mean that amphibious special operations can be mounted at extremely long range: from the other side of the world if necessary. The long journey time can be an advantage in itself, because it allows the operation to be studied, pulled apart and put back together again until it is close to foolproof.

The first consideration is the type of boat available to carry the team to the landing site. When security comes first, this will usually be a submarine, but that choice will put a severe limitation on the amount of equipment that can be carried, which may mean that a resupply mission will be needed. However, for infiltrating small groups of people into existing operations, or for mounting hit-and-run raids, the submarine is ideal. Space is very limited in submarines, but there is room in flooding compartments for kit such as inflatable boats and that is where they are carried.

The mission can be split down into four stages.

1. Movement to the disembarkation point. This part of the operation is normally under the control and charge of regular navy personnel.

2. Transfer from ocean-going vessel to the landing craft and movement to the landing site.

3. Disposal of the landing craft. This may mean destroying it, hiding it or navy personnel ferrying it back to the mother ship.

4. Sanitisation of the landing site and movement to the operational area.

Keep fit

Physical exercise plays a bit part in the shipboard life too, to ensure that the team is in top condition for the operation. This is a particular problem when the mother ship is a submarine making a completely submerged passage. The modern generation of submarines routinely crosses oceans without ever surfacing and there's not a lot of space on board for callisthenics or aerobic exercises!

Transferring at sea

From a surface ship, the transfer procedure is quite simple. The landing craft are inflated and sent over the side. A scrambling net is let down, and the operational team instal themselves in the inflatables, stow their equipment and set off on their long journey to the beach.

And it will be a long journey. To maintain security, the mother ship will never come above the horizon as seen from the shore – maybe a distance of more than 20 miles.

Outboard engines are notoriously noisy. There are electric versions which are almost silent, but they have a very limited range. To get around this problem the landing craft may be towed in close to shore by a purpose built tug – low to the water and fitted with a heavily-silenced inboard engine. The landing craft then make their way the last two or three miles to the beach under their own steam – or rather, by the muscle power of the Special Forces team who are paddling.

Transferring from a submarine to the landing craft is either a lot easier, or a lot more difficult, depending on which one of the three methods is chosen. If the submarine can come to the surface, the inflatables can be dropped over the side, the landing party boards, and away they go. In one interesting variation to this method the boats are placed on the deck of the submarine and the crew get aboard then the submarine submerges gently beneath them.

Submarine landing

Alternatively, the submarine commander comes up to just below the surface, exposing only the very tip of the conning tower and presenting a very small picture, even to enemy radar. The landing party exits and either swims to the landing point, on a compass bearing, or inflates the boats in the water and paddles in.

6 POINTS FOR LEAVING A SURFACED SUBMARINE

1   Crew members and troops should be fully briefed on the debarkation plan.

2   Inspect all your kit before the debarkation.

3   Wait for the crew to man their debarkation stations first before going to yours.

4   Swimmers debark in pairs from the conning tower of the submarine, which will surface with its decks awash.

5   Form up in the control room with all your kit. If there is space the first pair can be in the conning tower ready for the submarine to surface.

6   If possible, rehearse the whole debarkation procedure before you do it in a tactical situation.

The most secure technique of all requires the landing party to exit the submarine underwater, usually with the boat completely stationary and sitting on the bottom. Team members wearing SCUBA (Self Contained Breathing Apparatus) then emerge from a hatch connected to an air-lock and swim under water to the landing place.

Special Forces personnel who undertake missions like this have to be highly trained and very, very fit. If it's necessary to use this 'locking out' technique with technicians or mission specialists of any kind, then the lead pair will exit with inflatable boats and set them up on the surface. The rest of the team can then make 'free ascents' using the submarine's ordinary escape hatch, join up with the divers, and make their way to the beach in the normal way.

Underwater infiltration

As radar and anti-aircraft weapons become increasingly effective, underwater infiltration has become an increasingly important method if infiltrating Special Forces troops. The key to any successful infiltration may be summed up as Short,

Simple and Secure. Underwater operations using SCUBA equipment provide an extremely secure method of infiltrating short distances by water.

Shallow depth

Try to make you approach at the shallowest possible depth so that your air supplies last longer, and you and your equipment do not suffer the problems associated with sustained diving at great depths. There is another reason, swimmer detection systems find it harder to detect people at shallow depths.

Security

Part of the team should land ahead of the main body to check

PRECAUTIONS AT SEA

1 Is the area used frequently by passing enemy patrol boats?
2 Fishing boats can cause embarrassing confrontations and must be avoided.
3 Rocks and any other hazards that are likely to make navigation difficult have to be noted and passed on.
4 Sometimes underwater obstacles will be in the way, so a route through to the shoreline has to be checked.
5 A close check on weather conditions is important and prior to the raiding force landing a met report should be sent back.
6 You need a secure landing point that will enable the raiding force to disembark safely and without making any noise.
7 The reconnaissance team will have been given a time and a date for bringing in the raiding troops and by this time all their work must be complete. They should know the lie of the land like the back of their hands and in particular which routes afford the best cover. Having checked the state of the sea and sent their met report back they will then stand by at the landing area to receive the raiding troops.

that the beach is clear. Surfacing and removing their masks outside the surf zone the security team goes ashore and signals 'Clear' to the rest of the troops when it has examined the beach area.

Combat loads

Combat loads must be light and small and should include only equipment, weapons and ammunition needed for the mission. You must have a proper equipment unloading plan and preferably have it rehearsed before landing.

Swimmer delivery vehicle

The furthest reasonable distance the swimming team should have to cover is 1,500 metres. If the submarine cannot approach this close to the target area then swimmer delivery vehicles should be used to reduce fatigue.

On the way in

In anything but a flat calm it will be impossible to see the shore for most of the journey in, except when you get up onto the crest of a wave. Even then you probably won't have time to get a fix on your objective. You have to navigate by compass and that's satisfactory as long as you know where you are.

Unfortunately, the seas and oceans never stand still. Except for a very short period at high and low tides (called 'slack water'), they are constantly in motion – and not just straight in to the beach and out again either. On top of that there are coastal currents with which to contend, and though they may run in the same direction all the time they certainly don't always run at the same speed.

These factors are much worse in some parts of the world than in others. The Mediterranean, for example, has no tides to speak of, while the Bay of Fundy and the Bristol Channel have up to 15 metres between low and high water. And around the Channel Islands there are four tides a day instead of two!

It's impossible to compensate for all this, and the commander of the mother ship will have calculated the transfer point to take account of all the known factors. Even so, the landing party will have to work hard to keep on course and will be grateful for all the help they can get.

Choosing a landing place

The ideal site for a sea-borne landing has very similar features of a good airborne drop zone; it's easy to identify from a distance; is free of obstacles; has good and secure access and evacuation routes for both the transportation group and the reception committee and is largely free from enemy activity. The main differences lie in the sea and under it.

Any reasonably competent observer can evaluate an inland drop zone just be looking around carefully. To do the same for a seaborne landing requires a certain amount of training in the science of hydrography. Tides and currents are more difficult to deal with than underwater obstacles – at least these don't move around all the time!

Navigation at sea or even on inland waterways is much more difficult than on land, chiefly because it's difficult to know exactly where you are at all times. Modern small radar equipment can solve this problem but leaves you exposed if the enemy detects the radar emissions.

A better solution is offered by satellite navigation (satnav) hardware, which will tell you where you are to within 100 metres anywhere on the earth's surface. Because it's completely passive (it transmits nothing itself but only receives) you don't risk giving away your position when you use it.

Find the beach

If there's no reception committee on the beach, the landing party will navigate for themselves, using the compass, sun or star sights and shoreline observation and will be rather lucky to hit the beach at precisely the right place except under the easiest possible conditions.

If there is a beach party it can help with visible light, well shielded and only allowed to shine out to sea; infra red beacons, which the boat party can pick up using special goggles; underwater sound; and radio.

The surf zone doesn't stretch very far out from the shore.

When the landing party are close to its outer limit they stop and maintain position. Scout swimmers get into the water, approach the beach and check it out. When they are sure there's no enemy activity they signal the rest of the party to come in.

There are no exceptions to this procedure. Even though there may be a reception committee waiting with established perimeter security and reconnaissance patrols, the landing party still performs its own reconnaissance.

The raid goes ashore

The transit to the area may take some time and distance will depend entirely on fuel consumption. The troops must also be prepared for a wet and bumpy ride and must wear adequate clothing.

At a certain distance from the objective the boats slow their engines to cut down on noise. At this point their greatest ally will be wind and the crash of the sea, which will disguise any noise they make. From there they move slowly up to a rendezvous point, within a visible distance of their landing site. It is important to note that good radar can pick up and identify small boats and you should remember this when planning the route.

Once at this RV point the troops wait for a pre-arranged signal from the reconnaissance team ashore to notify them that all is clear to move in. It may be that something has occurred ashore and therefore no signal will be given, in which case the boats will return.

Having received the signal, the boats move in with engines cut and the troops paddling. This depends on the weather conditions, but it is essential that from here on as little sound as possible is made. One man in each boat has a gun trained on the shore as a precaution. Once in, everyone disembarks as quickly and quietly as possible and moves to a given area to await the next stage. Meanwhile the boats wait in the most concealed area, along with a guard force, their bows pointing back out to sea.

The raiding force commander and his team leaders are then given a final brief by the recce team commander. This gives everyone an opportunity to confirm any last minute details and to make any changes. Once everyone is satisfied, the team leaders carry out a briefing for their teams and then at a given time, they move off.

It may be necessary at this stage for teams to split and approach the target from different angles. In this case each team is led by one member of the recce force, who takes them up to a starting line. Quite often the recce team acts as a fire support group giving whatever help they can when required.

RIVER RAIDING

Infiltration is by no means the only type of amphibious operation. There are lots of important military targets underwater, in the water or close alongside and all of these are vulnerable to attack from combat divers either operating submerged or approaching secretly, landing and approaching the target from an unexpected – and therefore poorly guarded direction.

Breathing apparatus

Underwater operations like this generally require the diver to stay submerged for some considerable time, and that means breathing apparatus. There are two types of SCUBA: open circuit where the bottles are filled with compressed air and the outbreath is vented into the water, and the closed circuit system where the diver breathes the same air over and over again, each breath being 'topped up' with pure oxygen carried in the tanks and exhaled carbon dioxide absorbed by a special chemical.

Closed circuit SCUBA is particularly difficult and dangerous to use and even preparing the equipment is risky in itself – pure oxygen is highly explosive in the right circumstances. The advantage is that it doesn't leave a stream of tell-tale bubbles to give away the diver's position.

Even with the danger of being spotted, open circuit SCUBA can sometimes be used, but the surface of the water must be broken and turbulent to minimize the risk. The advantage is in its ease of use and much greater safety.

As well as laying demolition charges, the combat diver may be called upon to reconnoitre minefields and other underwater obstacles, check out harbours, docks and dams, establish and recover underwater caches of equipment and find essential equipment that has had to be abandoned in an emergency.

Because it's bulky and difficult to conceal, equipment for underwater missions will have to be air dropped to established undercover Special Forces teams as they need it.

Small boat operations

In many countries rivers and inland waterways take the place of roads as the prime communications routes, and Special Forces with their comprehensive training are very well equipped to make good use of them.

River craft and small inflatables are better suited to transportation than for use as fighting vehicles, though you must always be prepared for ambushes, for example, which will force you to fight from the boat. This possibility will influence the team leader's decision when it comes to choosing between boats or travelling overland.

The one great advantage to travelling by boat is the speed. It's quite in order to estimate average speeds of 35 to 30 miles per hour (55/60 km/hr) in areas where the waterways are widely used and kept free of debris and other obstructions

Inflatable boats

Inflatables, which ride on top of the water, are much more manoeuvrable than displacement craft, which may draw anything up to two-thirds of a metre. They are also very light in weight, and so can be carried for short distances if necessary.

Purpose built inflatable assault boats do have their disadvantages however. There's no disguising them; their outboard engines make an awful lot of noise, and they are very easily damaged by waterlogged trees and other debris floating on or close to the surface.

When he decides whether or nor to use boats in a particular operation, the team leader has to think of the operation as a whole, and choose the ways and means most likely to get the job done successfully and in the shortest possible time.

The rule of thumb must be: use boats when they offer a quicker way of getting from place to place; abandon them and set off across country when that looks like the better solution. The same applies to using divers; hit the enemy where he's weakest, from the direction he'll least expect.

This training in small boats and underwater operations is just one more example of the flexibility of the Special Forces soldier, ready to go anywhere and do anything at a moment's notice.

RAIDS AND AMBUSHES

Special Forces units operate deep in the heart of enemy-occupied territory, undertaking both active and passive missions. A typical passive operation involves moving into position in the utmost secrecy, setting up a concealed and secure observation post, and then passing information about enemy troop strengths and movements back to HQ.

It may be months before the observers can be extracted or even re-supplied, so their training has to make them self sufficient, allowing them to operate in the most hostile environments where one false move, day or night, could give the whole thing away.

Active operations such as raids and ambushes call for a different sort of courage. Daring instead of patience, decisiveness instead of caution. This section on Special Forces Operational Techniques looks at the way active clandestine operations are planned and executed, and takes FM 31-20, the US Army's field manual for Special Forces, as its source.

A Special Forces raid is a surprise attack on enemy force or installation. It breaks down into four parts:

1 Clandestine insertion
2 Brief, violent combat
3 Rapid disengagement
4 Swift, deceptive withdrawal

Raids may be mounted to destroy enemy equipment and installations such as command posts, communications centres and supply dumps; to capture enemy supplies and personnel; or simply to kill and wound as many of the enemy as possible. They may be used to rescue friendly forces or partisans too, and can also serve to distract attention away from their operations.

Organising the raid

The purpose of the mission, the type of target and the enemy situation will all have a bearing on the size of the raiding party. But whatever its size it will always have two basic elements – an assault group and a security group.

The assault group conducts the operations itself. They are the troops who go in and demolish installations, rescue the prisoners, steal the plans and code books or whatever the objective may be. As well as out-and-out fighting men, the group may include demolition experts, electronics technicians, and whatever specialist may be needed – pilot, for example, if the object of the operation were to steal a specific enemy aircraft.

The security group is there to protect them, to secure the area and stop enemy reinforcements from becoming involved in the action, to stop any would-be escapers and to cover the withdrawal of the assault group.

FIVE POINTS FOR A SUCCESSFUL AMBUSH

1 Set the ambush in a site you can move into and out of unobserved.
2 Use a night ambush if the mission can be accomplished by a short intensive burst of fire.
3 Use a daytime ambush if a follow-up is required.
4 Choose a site where the terrain forces the enemy to bunch up.
5 Bear in mind that you may need a secondary ambush if enemy reinforcements can reach the scene quickly.

Special Forces units have a well-deserved reputation for aggressiveness. Not one man amongst them will want to be idling away his time, and so they are always on the look-out for potential targets. Before operation planning can begin, each one is assessed for importance, accessibility and recoverability, taking into account distance and terrain and the strength of raiding party required.

Local repercussions

Another important factor is the likely effect on friendly natives and others as a result of the raid. There are countless examples of tens of local people being executed for every one occupying soldier killed. Planning for this possibility always forms part of the back up organisation to the raid, and psychological operations experts (psyops) will also be ready to exploit any successes to the full.

Keep it simple

Although it should be accurate down to the last detail, the plan must be essentially simple. If success depends on a large number of factors coming together at the right time, any one of them going wrong will probably blow the entire operation.

Time – of day and of year – is a crucial factor in the plan. When the operation is straightforward and the physical layout of the target is well known, it's probably better to operate during the hours of darkness. Where intelligence is less complete, go for dawn or dusk.

Launching a raid

1 Whatever the mission and whatever the size of the raiding party, the principles of a guerilla-style raid are the same. The actual assault team must be protected by security elements who will prevent enemy interference with the operation.

2 As the explosive specialist lays charges underneath a railway, for example, on the spot security is provided by a small team of Special Forces soldiers. This team will take out any sentries on the objective, breach or demolish obstacles and provide close protection for the main mission.

3   After the target has been destroyed the security groups provide cover on the flanks for the assault team to retreat. If
the enemy follow the raiders, one security group should try
to draw them away from the main assault force.

Withdrawal

Dusk is the best time for withdrawal; it gives you the advantage of the last minutes of daylight to exit the immediate area
of the operation and darkness to slow the enemy down during
any follow up. But in any event, choose the time very carefully,
to give yourself the greatest possible advantage.

Withdrawal after a large raid can be conducted with the party
split up into small groups. This denies the enemy a large target
for an air or ground strike but an alert and aggressive enemy
may be able to mop up the force one unit at a time.

In some circumstances it is safer for the entire party to
stay together and operate as a fighting column, but it will all
depend on the situation of enemy forces, the terrain and the
distances to be covered. An overt withdrawal, with no attempt
at secrecy will require a great deal of external support. There's
very little chance that the extraction force, it their is one, will
escape enemy attention.

Intelligence

It may seem obvious, but it's impossible to over-stress the value
of accurate intelligence. There are three main sources.

1   Local agents
2   Reconnaissance
3   Satellite and high level flights

Local knowledge is of the utmost importance. Whenever possible friendly locals should be recruited to act as guides, and
may even be employed in the raiding party itself if security
considerations permit.

In the movement towards the objective, take every precaution so as not to alert hostile troops to your presence. Avoid
contact, but make sure that the enemy suffers one hundred
percent casualties if the worst does happen.

Test your weapons

Where conditions allow, conduct a weapons and equipment test before the assault phase, replacing any pieces of kit that may be faulty. Personal belongings should be 'sanitized' at the same time, even down to removing clothing labels if necessary.

Size of raiding party

Well defended objectives sometimes demand large raiding parties perhaps in battalion strength or greater. Surprise is just as important as in a smaller raid, but will be much more difficult to achieve. A large raiding party will usually split into small groups and move towards the objective over a number of different routes. That way, even if some components are detected the enemy may still be in the dark as to the real target.

Control and co-ordination of a large raiding party is more difficult, too, especially with regard to timing. Only a high degree of training and excellent standards of equipment operation can make it easier.

CRATERING CHARGES

This mixture of five charges at 1.5 m and 2.1 m depth will blow a crater approximately 2.5 metres deep and 7.5 metres wide in any road.

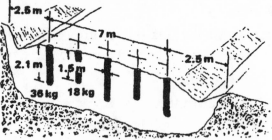

Timber cutting charges

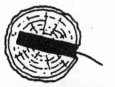

If you can drill into the wood and place the explosives inside, you can use a much smaller charge for exterior explosives calculate the charge using the formula D^2 divided by 40. (D = least dimension in inches). This gives the number of pounds of TNT needed

Raiding a shore installation

The first priority when mounting a raid on the enemy coast is to carry out a thorough recce of the target area; it is unusual for you to have enough information available without sending in a reconnaissance team. They will be looking for the following.

1   The exact location, size and structure of the target.
2   Any fortifications, minefields, searchlights and wandering guard patrols, checking their routines.
3   The nature of the surrounding terrain
4   The best route from the sea to the target
5   A place where the boats can come in and be hidden while the attack goes in.
6   A position to place any covering fire or mortar teams.

Blowing up bridges

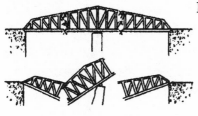

1   For complicated structures, two sets of cutting charges are required to cause collapse of the bridge. These should not be placed equidistant from the centre of support

2   Cutting charges must be placed on beams and crossbraces as well as on the floor plating.

3   Stone arch bridges are best demolished by placing a charge to blow out the keystones. A larger gap will be created using three charges placed as shown.

4   Small stone arch spans are easily demolished by a row of cutting charges across the centre, which destroys the integrity of the arch.

The diagrams show where to place a line of charges on some typical bridges. Remember that only one person should prepare, place and fire explosive charges, never divide responsibility, that is how expensive mistakes can occur. To destroy a bridge abutment use 18 kg TNT charges in holes 1.5 metres deep at 1.5 metre intervals across the width of the bridge and 1.5 metres behind the river face of the abutment.

Ambush

An ambush is a raid on a moving target. The only real difference is that the timetable of the operation becomes much sketchier and unreliable. Even excellent intelligence sources can't really predict the enemy's operational delays, and so the raiding party will often be in position for some time before the target comes along, considerably increasing the chances of detection.

Ambushes are conducted to destroy or capture enemy personnel and supplies or block their movement. A systematic approach can channel the enemy's communications and resupply operations, and force him to concentrate his movements onto main roads and railway lines, where they are more vulnerable to attack, especially from air strikes.

Railways and waterways

Railways themselves are always relatively open targets. Just removing the rails will bring the system to a halt. The attacking force tries to derail as many wagons and carriages as possible and leave the wreckage blocking the track. This maximizes the damage to stock, passengers and material and slows down the work of repairing and reopening the permanent way.

If the attack party is large enough they assault the train with automatic weapons and grenades. Part of the raiding party's security element will remove sections of the track in both directions, some way away from the scene of the ambush. Explosive charges should be used to destroy the level railbed itself. This will prevent any possibility of reinforcements arriving unexpectedly.

Traffic on inland waterways – barges and smaller craft – can be disrupted in much the same way as railway trains, and the same technique is used against columns of vehicles on roads.

PERSONAL SKILLS
AND
TECHNIQUES

SPECIAL FORCES PERSONAL PROTECTION

It now costs around £1 ($1.5) million to train a Special Forces trooper, so any money spent on keeping him alive is money well spent. The trouble is that such personnel are prone to all types of attacks and aggressive or defensive counter-measures, so it is difficult to decide exactly what to protect an individual against.

The result has been a wide array of protective clothing with each item proof against something or other, and designed in isolation from anything else. This often means that when all the various items are worn together they do not integrate: NBC respirator face seals may be broken when a helmet is put on, weapons cannot be sighted through respirator lenses, bulletproof garments interfere with movement and so on.

The IPPS

This integration problem has been overcome by five British companies which have got together and developed a protective outfit that is proof against most threats to special forces personnel. It is known as the Integrated Personal Protection System (IPPS) and has been tested by Special Forces. The IPPS is not just a design venture: it has been developed using all manner of practical combat experience and the result is a superb protective outfit.

Starting from the skin outwards, the basis of the IPPS is a set of carbonized viscose 'long john' underwear. The material is light and comfortable to wear but is flame retardant, as is the main overgarment, a one piece assault suit also made from carbon fibre material, in this case Nomex 3. The suit incorporates flame retardant pads at the elbows and knees, allowing the wearer to crawl safely over hot surfaces such as aircraft engines during hijack hostage rescue missions.

Incidentally, the suits are very similar to those being worn by tanker crews currently operating in the Persian Gulf, but theirs are coloured bright orange; the IPPS is usually black.

Armoured vest

Over the flame-retardant garments the IPPS features a bullet - proof waistcoat made of soft fragmentation armour and with a built-in trauma liner to absorb shock. Without this liner internal injuries could occur even if a bullet is stopped by the armour. The soft armour protection is enhanced by inserting curved ceramic plates at the front and back: these can stop .357 Magnum bullets at a range of three metres. A groin panel can be added if required.

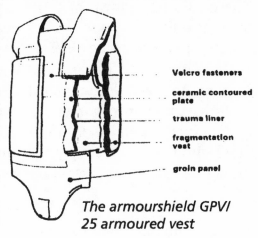

Velcro fasteners

ceramic contoured plate

trauma liner

fragmentation vest

groin panel

The armourshield GPV/ 25 armoured vest

The helmet

Further armoured protection is provided by a special helmet known as the AC 100/1, a National Plastics product made from layers of a Kevlar-type material. This can withstand the impact of a 9-mm bullet at close range and to ensure the wearer's head is not knocked off by the impact, the helmet uses a bullet trauma lining.

An optional fire-retardant leather waistcoat can be worn over the suit and armour protection and is used to carry special

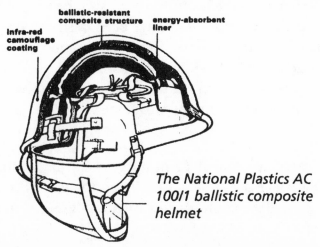

ballistic-resistant composite structure

energy-absorbent liner

infra-red camouflage coating

The National Plastics AC 100/1 ballistic composite helmet

equipment such as an assault axe, stun grenades or rescue knife, all in specially-fitted pockets or leather loops.

Respirator

These days some form of respirator is worn operationally by most special forces, so the IPPS uses a specially developed respirator known as the SF10, a variant of the Avon S10 used by the British Army. The SF10 has an internal microphone, but its most prominent features are the outset darkened eyepieces. These have been incorporated to cut down the flash produced by stun grenades or other bright lights. The SF10 can also be fitted with its own air supply from an air bottle carried in the leather waistcoat or an extra filter canister can be worn.

Communications

The respirator microphone connects into an assault team communications harness known as the CT100 which has a chest or respirator microphone and press-to-talk switches located on the wrist or anywhere handy. The communications system uses electronic earphones that are designed to cut out sound produced by grenades or gunfire (ie high air pressure) but which allow all other sounds to be heard normally. The earphones are connected into the communication harness to allow the wearer to listen in to a team command net.

The main feature of the IPPS is that all the components are designed to work together. For instance the IPPS helmet does not interfere with the respirator seal, and the ear defenders fit under helmet ear lobes that have been designed for just that purpose. The darkened eyepieces permit almost any weapon to be aimed and fired without difficulty, and even though the protective waistcoat can stop most fragments or bullets it still allows complete freedom of movement.

Belt kit

A belt carrying combat or other gear can be worn, and an abseiling harness has been developed for use with the IPPS which provides an indication of the degree of movement available.

PERSONAL CAMOUFLAGE AND CONCEALMENT

Good camouflage and fieldcraft are almost as important as good marksmanship – in fact, a well camouflaged man who is a poor shot will probably survive longer than the badly concealed sniper. In an escape and evasion operation, camouflage and concealment are paramount. The hunted man will conceal himself and sleep by day, and move by night – and here even the cover of darkness will not negate the importance of camouflage.

Personal camouflage (PC) has certain simple rules that will defeat the most obvious sensor on the battlefield – the human eye.

Shape

Your helmet, web equipment, rifle and other kit such as manpack radios have a clear, often square shape – and – there are no squares in nature. Break up straight lines by the addition of scrim – neutral-coloured strips of cloth in browns and greens. Camouflaged elasticated pack covers exist, and these can be stretched over packs and radios.

Rifles and LMG/GPMGs have a clear shape, and are often black. Though scrim can be used to break up their line, it is not advisable to fix it to the stock – it may slip when you are firing and by shifting your grip cause you to shoot inaccurately. It is better to cover the weapon with camouflaged tape, or even green masking tape (tape is a useful aid to PC – see 'Sound').

A discarded vehicle camouflage net is a very useful source of camouflage for PC. It will have nylon 'scrim' that has been treated to give an infra-red reflection similar to vegetation. Fixed to the back of packs and webbing, or in the netting on a helmet, it breaks up shape very well and enhances the chlorophyll-based infra-red camouflage treatment (see also 'Silhouette').

Shine

In the old days of brass buckles, soldiers were told these should be allowed to grow dull, or be covered with masking tape.

However, most web equipment has plastic or alloy fittings that do not reflect – but there are still shiny surfaces even on a modern battlefield.

Binoculars and compass surfaces, even spectacles, can catch the light. There is little that can be done about spectacles, but when using binoculars or a compass make sure that you are well concealed: like radios, they are 'signature equipment' and attract attention. Stow binoculars inside your smock, and take care that your map is not opened up and flapping about – a drab map case with the map folded so that it gives the minimum working area is all that is needed. Take care also that the clear cover to the map case does not catch the light.

Shine also includes skin. At night it will catch moonlight and flares, and even black soldiers need to use camouflage cream.

Silhouette
Similar in many respects to shape, silhouette includes the outline of the human form and the equipment it is carrying. The

---

FACIAL CAMOUFLAGE

1 The first coat
First get rid of all that white shining skin. Mix a small quantity of camouflage cream with spit in your hand and rub it all over your face, neck and ears. This gives a full light coverage of camouflage. Then cover your hands with the cream.

2 Breaking up the shape
Now break up the outline and shape of the eyes, nose and mouth. Any pattern that breaks up this familiar format will do; use more if you're going in night patrol. Don't forget your neck and eyes.

3 Finishing it off
Fill in the rest of your face with earth, loam and green colours, then spit in your hands and rub them over your face to blur it all together. On the move you will probably sweat heavily so you must top-up your face cream as you go along.

shape of the head and shoulders of a man are unmistakeable and an unscrimmed helmet attracts attention.

The use of vegetation as garnishing helps break up the silhouette. Thick handfuls of grass tucked into equipment can remove the shape of the shoulders, and garnishing on the helmet breaks the smooth curve of the top and the line of the brim.

Silhouette also includes fieldcraft – however well camouflaged you may be, it is little help if you 'sky line' by walking along the top of a hill, or stand against a background of one solid colour.

Smell

Even the most urbanized man will develop a good sense of smell after a few days in the open. He will be able to detect engine smells, cooking, body odour and washing.

HELMET CAMOUFLAGE

1   Kevlar helmet
    The new issue Kevlar helmet comes complete with a cover of DPM – standard military camouflage colours – and straps for local camouflage.

2   Disguising the shape
    Cover the helmet with strips of scrim and cloth

3   Adding local camouflage
    Insert local vegetation under the elastic. Use plenty, make sure it stays in and make sure it matches your background.

Some smells are hard to minimize. Soaps should be scent-free and activities such as cooking confined to daylight hours when other smells are stronger and the air warmer.

One of the greatest giveaways is smoking: its refuse has a unique smell. Rubbish produced by cooking as well as smoking should be carried out from the operational area and only buried as a second choice. Buried objects are often dug up by animals and this can give a good indication of the strength and composition of your patrol or unit as well as its morale. The disciplines of refuse removal are important.

Sound

You can make a lot of noise while out on patrol. Your boots can squeak, your cleaning kit or magazines may rattle in your ammunition pouches. Even your webbing can creak if it is heavy. Fittings on your weapon may rattle. Radios can have background 'mush'. Coughing and talking can carry for long distances in the darkness of a clear night.

You must become familiar with a 'silent routine' in which field signals replace the spoken word, or conversations are conducted in a whisper.

Proper stowage of kit, taping of slings and other noisy equipment and a final shakedown before a patrol moves out will reduce noise. If a position is being dug, sentries should be positioned at the limit of noise so that they can see an enemy before he hears the digging.

Colour

Though most modern combat uniforms are now in a disruptive pattern camouflage, there may be times when this is less helpful. If you are evading capture and are unarmed, drab civilian outdoor clothing will be less conspicuous if you encounter civilians.

The trouble with camouflage-type clothing is that in the wrong environment, like cites, it seems to do the opposite and say 'Hey, look at me!' In fighting in built up areas a camouflage of greys, browns and dull reds would be better. The use of sacking and empty sand bags as scrim covers would help here.

Natural vegetation used to garnish helmets and equipment (see 'Silhouette') will fade and change colour. Leaves curl up and show their pale under-surfaces. You may have put grass into your helmet band and now find yourself in a dark wood: or be wearing dark green ferns when you are moving across a patch of pale, open grass land. Check and change your camouflage regularly.

The most obvious colour that needs camouflaging is that of human skin, and for that you need camouflage cream. As mentioned, even black or brown skin has a shine to it. A common mistake is to smear paint over the front of the face and to miss the neck, ears and back of the hands.

Camouflage cream needs to be renewed as you move and sweat. A simple pattern is to take stripes diagonally across the face – this cuts through the vertical and horizontal lines of the eyes, nose and mouth. Some camouflage creams have two colours, in which case you can use the dark colour to reduce the highlights formed by the bridge of the nose, cheek bones, chin and forehead. The lighter colour is used on areas of shadow.

Association

The enemy may not see you, but he might spot your equipment or refuse and associate that with a possible unit on the move. A cluster of radio antennas shows that a company HQ is on the move or dug in. The cans stacked near a vehicle park, perhaps with white tape around them, are likely to be fuel. To a trained observer the unusual – a flash from a plastic map case, or the smell of cooking – will alert him and he will bring his own senses to bear on the area.

VEHICLE CAMOUFLAGE

Good camouflage and concealment is often a trade-off against good fields of fire or good positions for observing enemy movement. Radio communications work better with line-of-sight but sitting on top of a hill is very public. And if you are trying to evade or escape you will need a vantage point for a sentry to observe likely enemy approaches, and may be observed yourself.

Assuming that you are part of a group of six to 12 men and that you have a light vehicle like a Land Rover or jeep, how would you conceal your position while evading capture?

Siting

Avoid the obvious. If the enemy are looking for you they will sweep the countryside, and if there are not many of them they will concentrate on rivers and woodland, farm houses, barns, known caves and natural cover. All are on maps, and the first move that an enemy search team will make is to do a map reconnaissance and look at likely locations.

Track plan

A track plan is essential if you are going to stay in the location for any length of time. Trodden grass and footprints will show clearly from the air, and large areas of normally lush undergrowth can be flattened in a way that attracts attention.

Vehicle tracks are even more dramatic from the air – bad drivers will carve a path across a field in a way that no farmer would dream of driving. Track planning means attempting to copy the normal routes adopted by animals, farmers or the locals. Thus vehicle tracks along the edge of a field and a footpath that might also be used by the inhabitants will pass unnoticed by the enemy.

IR signature

As with personal camouflage, the infra-red band is the most difficult to avoid. Thermal imaging will penetrate cover, and activities like running a vehicle engine to charge batteries or simple tasks like cooking become a major problem since both will show as a very strong hot point in an otherwise cool terrain.

Though a cave may not be ideal if it is on the local map, it will give good thermal screening. Parking the vehicle under cover will also reduce its IR signature – but again remember that barns and farmhouses are very obvious and may attract attention from the air or ground.

Sound and smell

As with personal camouflage, sound and smell are important. If you run your engine to recharge batteries you will make noise and exhaust fumes (and take care that fumes do not blow into the vehicle if the exhaust pipe is blocked by the camouflage). Use a flexible metal extension pipe to reduce the noise.

If you are in a convoy, the sound of your vehicles will attract attention and so will your radio traffic.

Smell will come from cooking as you prepare your evening meal and the smell of fuel is also distinctive. Spilled fuel and the wrappings from rations are a calling-card for an alert enemy.

Association

Association is also important – radio antennas around a position or on a vehicle show that it is of significance. Antennas can also catch the light and show up as long, hard shadows in an otherwise concealed position. Most antennas can be situated away from the set, so put them on a reverse slope where they are not only invisible to the enemy, but also have some of their signal screened. Failing that, locate them against a building or tree.

Camouflage is a complex and sometimes contradictory skill. There is a reduced TI signature in a building under cover; but buildings attract attention. Hessian should be used on a vehicle among cold buildings; but not in warmer woodland. If you want to remember one rule to camouflage, it is that you should not give the enemy the signal that will make him look twice.

Concealing your position

Don't make the mistake of thinking you're safe as long as you have dug your position. A good hide or bunker should be invisible even at close quarters; if you have dug it well and are careful in your movements, it may pass unnoticed. But the enemy can still spot you if you haven't been careful enough, so keep the following in mind.

1 The colour of soil that has been dug from lower than about a metre is lighter than the topsoil, and a trench has a strong

shadow at the bottom. Conceal earth by covering it with turfs; and put light-coloured straw at the bottom of the trench to reduce some of the shadow. This will also be more pleasant to walk on and live in.

2 In a tropical environment, cover can grow very quickly, so replace plants and creepers around your position and it will soon be concealed.

3 A simple basha made up with poncho or basha sheet can be square, shiny and noisy. Do not put it up until after last light, although you can position it flat on the ground before dark. Carry a length of old camouflage net; it will break up the shape and shine.

4 When you are cooking or brewing up keep your opened kit to a minimum; you might need to make a quick getaway. Also, avoid littering tins and wrappers around the position that may catch the light and be seen from a distance.

5 It is commonly thought that a hand torch with a red filter does not show at night. It does; it's certainly less obvious than a white light, and it does not impair night vision, but it shows. Do not use a torch at all; by last light you should have set up your position so that your kit is packed and you can reach for your weapon, webbing and pack without needing one.

Concealing your vehicle

Any vehicle will be under suspicion. If you are moving in convoy, take care to avoid bunching. Vehicles close together are very recognisable from the air, and make easy targets for enemy aircraft. And remember the following points when finding somewhere to position your vehicle.

1 If you are near buildings, for instance on a farm, try to get the vehicle close to a wall or under cover in a barn. A camouflage net will attract the attention of a nearby enemy. Use hessian and local materials to disguise the vehicle.

2 If you park in the country, try to find the shadow of a hedge to disguise the vehicle's hard shape. But remember that in northern and southern latitudes the sun moves, and the

VEHICLE CAMOUFLAGE CHECKLIST

1 Site selection: Choose a harbour area away from the edge of the wood, away from tracks and with good cover overhead as well as at ground level. Try to pick a 'hull down' or 'dead ground' position. Remember to back the vehicle in, you may have to exit fast.

2 Hessian sacking: All the principles of personal camouflage apply equally to your vehicle. Black hessian destroys the shine from windows, headlights and number plates and disguises the general shape of the vehicle.

3 Net poles: A good selection of net poles is essential to hold the camouflage net off the vehicle to disguise its shape. Chicken wire can also be used. You must not cut poles from trees around your position; the cut-off shoots will give you away. Harbouring two vehicles together with nets over both can be helpful in producing a more natural shape. Remember, you cannot afford to leave any equipment lying about; concealment is an ongoing task, as the threat of discovery is ever-present. Plastic bags and uncovered windscreens are asking for trouble.

4 Camouflage net: Use the surrounding trees as well as the poles. The ideal situation is to create a camouflage 'garage' you can drive into and out of without having to remove net, poles etc.

5 Two-sided net: There are two sides to a camouflage net, with different colour combinations, so use the side that best matches your surroundings.

6 Shell scrapes and track plan: As soon as the position is occupied, a route around the site must be marked by cord and cleared. By using this trackplan, disturbance of natural ground is minimized. Shell scrapes must be dug in 'stand to' positions.

shadow of the morning can be the sunlit field of the afternoon.

3   Late evening can be particularly difficult with low sunlight catching the glass fittings of your vehicle. As a short-term precaution cover the windscreen and lights when you stop, not forgetting the reflectors.

4   If your vehicle is military, it will have been painted with IR reflective paint and you should not cover this with hessian, which will produce a blue-grey colour on any infra-red device that the enemy might be using. You should cover the reflective surfaces and then deploy a camouflage net.

5   A camouflage net should stand clear of the vehicle, partly so that you can get in and out and also to disguise the vehicle's shape. It should also stretch far enough to contain any shadow that the vehicle might cast. Ideally, it should also have a 'mushroom' on the top; a frame of wire about the size of a domestic saucer. This gives a smooth line when the net is stretched over. Make sure that the net will not snag on the vehicle or underbrush or trees, preventing any quick exit you might need to make.

BOOBY TRAPS

A booby trap is designed to cause sudden and surprise casualties and to reduce morale by creating fear, uncertainty and suspicion. You will only be able to counter booby traps if you understand how they work, in what circumstances they are employed and what they look like.

Booby traps are used in various terrorist situations but are more likely to be used in a jungle environment than anywhere else, mainly because they are more easily hidden but also because the materials to make them are readily to hand.

Jungle traps

The jungle guerrilla will be restricted in the operational employment of booby traps only by the extent of his imagination. The range and variety of traps used by the Viet Cong was bewildering and was responsible for lowering the morale of government forces in Vietnam. Guerillas will continue to use booby traps along obvious lines of communication, forcing troops to move cautiously or to deploy engineers and assault pioneers to clear routes – which is very time consuming – or to move deeper into the jungle where the going is appreciably more difficult.

The sides of roads, rivers and streams and any track or ridge line are likely targets. When they are on the defensive, guerillas will use booby traps to protect a bunkered camp, a defended village or a tunnel system. They will be laid in conjunction with

THE WAY THE ENEMY'S MIND WORKS

A guerilla will follow some common-sense rules when he is setting up his booby traps.

1 He will go to enormous lengths to conceal his device. The charge and mechanism will be concealed or made to resemble some harmless object.

2 He will usually choose a constricted location where you are channelled into his trap. Any defile or enclosed space such as a room or tunnel is a potential booby trap site.

3 Traps are usually laid in groups so that when you come across them you are likely to spring at least one of them. There will be dummy booby traps to confuse you; having disarmed an obvious trap, the idea is that you will be sufficiently off your guard to blunder into a second one.

4 Guerillas often place traps on obstacles. The removal of the obstacle, which may be a road block of some kind, sets off the trap. Similarly traps can be placed on attractive items such as weapons, food or potential souvenirs.

5 When you think you have discovered a booby trap and the method of setting it off, beware a second method!

obstacles, wire, conventional mines and roadblocks to deter any detailed reconnaissance of their position and to give advance warning of an attack. They will also use booby traps to cover their withdrawal.

But, despite the very real and unpleasant threat of booby traps, there is something you can do about them. First, learn all there is to learn about booby traps. Knowledge dispels fear; know your enemy and you're halfway to beating him. Five examples of jungle booby traps are:-

1   *The barbed spike plate*

This is a very common trap. It is easily made and can be placed anywhere and is difficult to detect before the damage is done. The spikes are often tipped with poison such as human excrement.

2   *The punji bear trap*

The trap is concealed under brushwood or leaves on the track. When you walk over the trap, your leg plunges down into the pit, pivoting the boards, which close on your leg spiking it above the ankle.

The punji bear trap is a refinement of the basic pit trap to counter the steel plate in the bottom of the issue jungle boot. This arrangement leads to damage to the unprotected area of the calf above the boot.

3   *The overhead grenade trap*

A grenade is suspended in the overhead foliage. As you trip a wire, the pin is pulled from the grenade suspended above you. You have

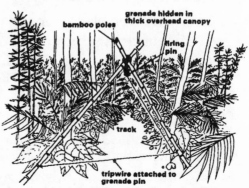

3-5 seconds to get out of range of the blast; difficult because the shrapnel from the grenade is likely to travel a great distance due to its height above the ground. It is particularly effective at night. By day, the tripwire can be removed to allow the enemy or civilians to use the track.

4 *The cartridge trap*
This trap is easily set up and is very effective. It is buried so that the head of the round is only partly exposed; pressure on the tip sets the round off.

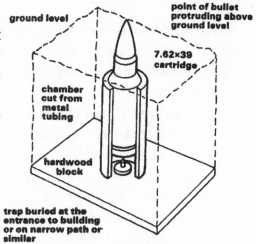

ground level

point of bullet protruding above ground level

7.62×39 cartridge

chamber cut from metal tubing

hardwood block

trap buried at the entrance to building or on narrow path or similar

5 *Grenade daisy chain*
The trip wire is camouflaged across the track and when pulled, the first grenade explodes. This breaks the wire to the second grenade, which has had its pin removed, and releases the lever. The second grenade explodes, breaking the wire to the third grenade and so on.

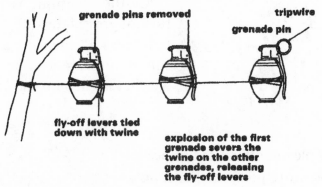

grenade pins removed

tripwire

grenade pin

fly-off levers tied down with twine

explosion of the first grenade severs the twine on the other grenades, releasing the fly-off levers

Detecting booby traps

These booby traps are operated by a pull, pressure, release or delay mechanism, or a combination of more than one method. When looking for booby traps, there is no substitute for sharp eyesight and awareness. Among the many things you can look out for are loose dirt or newly filled areas; loose or taut wires; rope, strings or vines or sticks and stones in unnatural-looking positions, providing marker indicators. The foliage may be disturbed or damaged or camouflage may look out of place or have died.

Look out for plastic wrapper materials protruding from the ground. Look in particular for any electrical lead wires. And, of course, look for irregular tread patterns and footprints on roads and tracks.

Marker indicators may give you the best warning that a booby trap is in the area. Guerillas have traditionally marked their booby traps to warn their own men and sympathetic locals to avoid the area. The sort of indicators they have used are piles of stones, crossed sticks, broken saplings or marks on the trunks of trees. One specific marker they have used is a stick balanced in the fork of a tree. This is surprisingly difficult to detect  and has been known to indicate a mine or booby trap some 10-20 metres away.

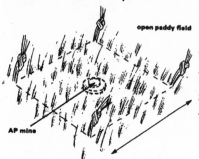
open paddy field

AP mine

Another example is knotted tufts of grass: four tufts of knotted grass at each corner of a square indicate a mine or trap within the encompassed area.

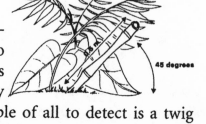
45 degrees

A simple but often used indicator is a short piece of bamboo stuck into the ground at 45 degrees and pointing towards the booby trap. Perhaps the hardest example of all to detect is a twig threaded through a leaf to indicate the very close presence of a trap.

Dealing with booby traps

If you are aware of these methods of detection and recognition, you stand a very good chance of avoiding a booby trap. If you detect a booby trap you should ideally call in an expert to deal with it – an engineer or assault pioneer. But sometimes a device has to be neutralized quickly and there are two things you can do to disarm the device – providing you use your common sense.

First, by pulling with a cable and hook from a safe distance and from behind cover you can either set off the device intentionally or disrupt the mechanism. Secondly, you can destroy the device by placing a charge next to it and then detonating it from a safe distance. But never attempt to disarm a device by hand.

Avoid the obvious

The best way of combatting booby traps is to avoid tracks and roads whenever possible. But if you have to use tracks, avoid setting a pattern; it is unlikely that the guerillas will be able to booby trap or mine *every* track or road. Locals can be a useful source of information; even if they are not willing to help you directly, their behaviour can provide clues. If they are avoiding an area, it's for a good reason. And if they show signs of anxiety or agitation at the close proximity of troops, this is a sure indicator that something is amiss.

Any future jungle enemy will continue to employ booby traps. Find out everything you can about his likely booby trap methods, types and procedures, and understand the disciplines for coping with the threat. If you become 'jungle wise', a booby trap is unlikely to surprise you.

Mines and large-scale booby traps

Mines are often deployed as booby traps or combined with other explosives as nasty surprises for the unwary. This is particularly common in counter-insurgency, so it is especially important to take precautions and to understand the sort of devices you may encounter. Most booby traps exploit haste, carelessness or curiosity. By staying alert to the danger, you increase your chances of survival. There are eight general precautionary measures which should be observed at all times.

1 Never leave any of your own equipment behind where hostile forces could make use of it. In Vietnam, careless

RUT TRAPS

Keep out of old ruts. The puddles and mud could conceal an excavation under a tarpaulin with a wire anchored on one end with the other attached to a grenade. The grenade can be used as the booster charge to initiate a secondary explosion inside a pot filled with explosive and scrapyard confetti. This type of mine was commonly used by the Viet Cong.

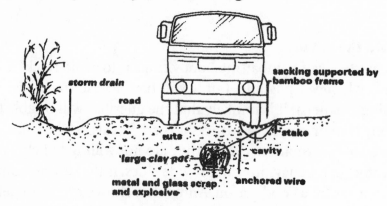

RUT GRENADE TRAP

Puddles and muddy ruts in the road can be used to disguise a simple pressure plate of wood or wire mesh that, when stepped on or driven over, acts on the two anchored wires attached to the operating rod threaded through the grenade pins.

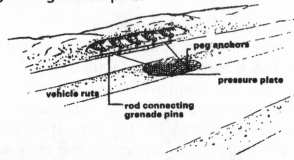

American troops left a trail of valuable equipment behind them. Grenades slipped into webbing by the lever may look good in the movies, but many fell off and were literally handed to the enemy. Similarly, US landing zones were often littered with everything from empty cans (ideal for grenade traps), rifle magazines, loose rounds and many other items useful to the needy guerilla. British readers need not be smug: the British Army was guilty of the same thing in South Africa during 1900/1901.

2   When on the move, maintain proper spacing. Mines have a limited radius of effect, so dispersed formations suffer less damage. Men or vehicles that bunch up are asking for trouble.

3   When driving, drivers should follow the tracks of the vehicle in front. If he is safe, then so are you. Conversely, don't drive in old tracks you know nothing about. They are a favourite spot for an anti-tank mine

4   If a unit on foot sustains casualties to mines, approach the wounded with caution: secondary mines or booby traps are often used against those who rush in to assist a mine victim.

COMMAND-DETONATED ROCKET ATTACK

Most rockets from the 66-mm LAW to single BM-21 rounds, can be fired as booby traps or command-detonated devices. The only way to defend against this type of attack is not to bunch up and not to drive at constant speed. Foot patrols should be used to clear any potential firing points.

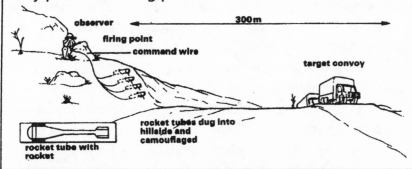

observer
firing point
command wire
300 m
target convoy
rocket tubes dug into hillside and camouflaged
rocket tube with rocket

5   Vehicle floors can be sandbagged and a thick rubber mat over the sandbags will further reduce blast and secondary fragmentation if you detonate a mine. Keep your arms and legs in.

6   Mines can be command-detonated i.e. someone watching from the bushes presses the plunger as you drive past the bomb. This is a favourite IRA ambush technique. One answer is to vary the speed and the spacing of vehicles to make it hard for the terrorist to judge the right moment to set it off.

7   Never allow single vehicles out on their own. They are an easy target and very tempting for terrorists/guerillas who regard small units of troops as a potential source of weapons and equipment.

8   Key personnel are an obvious target for command-detonated mines. A conspicuous command vehicle bristling with radio aerials is easily singled out, so do not place all the HQ personnel in the same APC. The same 'eggs in one basket' principle applies to medical and other specialists.

Detection and search techniques

Detecting mines and booby traps is hard, slow work which demands careful observation and a great deal of concentration. There are certain areas worth particular attention an various clues which will help you survive. Once again, get into the habit of thinking. 'If I were going to booby trap this area, where would I lay the tripwire?' Expect a trap and you may well find it.

Observe the movement of the local people: guerillas usually aim to single out the security forces in the familiar 'battle for the hearts and minds'. If the farmer suddenly stops using one particular gate, there could be a very good reason. Gates and places where paths pass through dense undergrowth are favourite spots for a booby trap, and don't forget to look above you and to the flanks for grenades or shells in the trees. Entrances to buildings, caves or tunnels require special caution.

You have been warned about leaving kit behind for the

BRIDGE TRAP

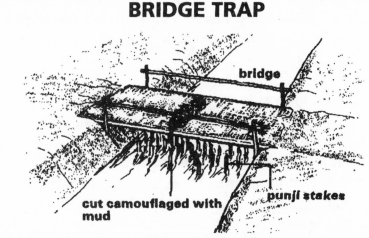

bridge

cut camouflaged with mud

punji stakes

Sawing through a native bridge with a drop onto some punji stakes concealed by the water of a drainage ditch will produce a difficult casualty. Even a simple fall for a soldier fully laden with equipment can produce a broken leg.

enemy. Be very cautious if the enemy has been so obliging as to leave weapons or supplies lying about for you. They may well be wired to something nasty. Check all items which would make good souvenirs: they also make good booby traps.

Bridges, drainage ditches, culverts and streams are common sites for mines and booby traps and they should be checked. Look out for any signs and markings which the enemy may be using to mark his mines – this could be anything from knotted grass to the positioning of stones. If you can learn his signs they will act as sign posts in the future.

Disarming methods

The first step to surviving the mined battlefield is to detect, recognize and locate mines. Having done this, your safest bet is to bypass the area you know to be dangerous, but in certain circumstances this will not be possible. In combat you may need to maintain the momentum of an attack. Engineer units will have to destroy mines in place to allow the safe passage of friendly troops and the rest of the mines will be neutralized later by EOD (Explosive Ordnance Disposal) teams.

Making a mine safe means displacing or replacing safeties in the firing assembly and separating the main charge from the detonator. If this is not possible, the mine must be destroyed in place.

Destruction in place

A mine can be deliberately detonated if the damage is acceptable and the tactical situation permits. For example, a mine by a roadside can be detonated without much trouble, but if you deliberately explode a powerful enemy mine on a strategically vital road bridge you may have some explaining to do.

Before trying to remove a mine, probe around the main charge with care to locate any anti-handling devices which have to be neutralized. Identify the type of firing mechanism and replace all safety devices. If you have any doubts about neutralising the mine, pull it out with a grapnel or rope from behind cover. Wait at least 30 seconds after extracting it in case it has a delay-action fuse. Only trained specialist should attempt to disarm a mine by hand unless the device and appropriate disarming techniques are well known.

NON-EXPLOSIVE SPEAR TRAP

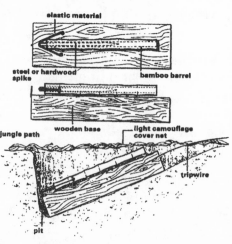

Improvized traps may take many forms that may seem alien to Western eyes, but such traps are still widely used in the jungle environment for trapping animals such as bush pigs. The Viet Cong simply scaled up their traps to deal with a larger prey. This trap uses a bamboo hollowed out barrel and a steel dart propelled by a car fan belt secured to a block of wood and connected to a trip wire.

Non-explosive traps

Not all booby traps are explosive, but you should follow the general principles above, being especially alert for further mines and booby traps near a trap you have found. Also, a trap may be several booby traps together: you find one wire, think you are safe and walk round it straight into the punji pit. If you bypass a trap, mark it clearly for any following troops. Loose spike-type devices and bear traps which have been sprung should be picked up and disposed of so they cannot be re-used after you have gone. Spike pits should be exposed to view and later dismantled and filled in.

Be particularly careful when clearing or neutralising traps activated by tripwires. This includes such devices as log or ball maces, angled arrow traps, suspended spikes and bamboo whips. Clear all troops from the area and set off the device from a safe place using a grapnel.

Falklands booby trap

Hundreds of booby traps were left in the Falklands by the Argentine forces. These can be divided into two main categories, those that used the M5 grenade and those improvized using available components and explosives. Many booby traps were improvized in the field by military engineers using available components: most used a trip wire to release a spring-

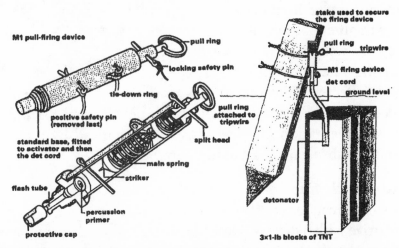

The Argentine booby trap was fitted with the US M1 pull-firing device. A pull of 3 to 5lb on the tripwire will fire the device.

loaded striker to fire a detonator. The main charge was normally American-made TNT demolition blocks buried in the ground.

Occasionally the TNT blocks would be used to initiate an item of explosive ordnance such as a large artillery shell; one such device was discovered in a culvert near Port Stanley connected to a 1,000lb-aircraft bomb. Other variations include attaching a short wire to an innocent looking object such as an ammunition box. This would explode if the item was removed by the victim. A recent find was a trip wire with a TNT charge at each end.

Viet Cong and IRA traps
Bamboo bomb

Any tube, such as a bicycle frame or section of bamboo, can be used as a container for explosive. These could be used

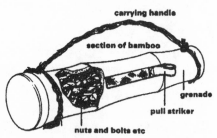

as booby traps or as grenades packed with metal scrap. The Viet Cong packed explosives in growing bamboo on the side of a known patrol route; in the same way the IRA made mines out of cast iron drain pipes on the sides of houses.

The Coconut mine

Any non-metallic mine will produce fragmentation that will now show up well on an X-ray of the victim. The Viet Cong made highly effective IEDs out of hol-

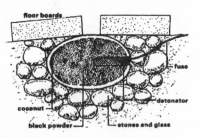

lowed out coconuts packed with black powder and a detonator. Fragmentation effect was usually enhanced by placing stones and broken glass round the mine.

Anti-Vehicle traps

Tank crews can see very little when buttoned up and will therefore drive with hatches open when out of contact. This type of grenade booby trap is designed to injure the crew and any infantry riding on the tank or in trucks or other soft skinned

vehicles. The grenade bodies are tied to the main wire and the pins are tied to stakes driven into the ground. More than two grenades are usually used the whole arrangement is camouflaged; in the trees lining a road for example.

Helicopter landing site trap

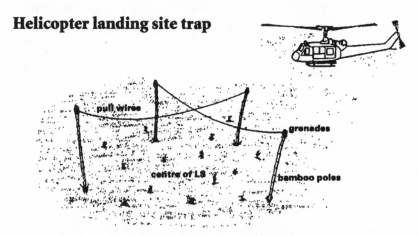

Where there is a limited number of helicopter LSS, such as in the jungle or if you get into the habit of using an LS more than once, you could find this waiting for you. The grenades or charges on the poles would usually be hidden in the trees.

MINES

The war is over and the soldiers departed. The odd rusting tank or water-filled crater bears mute witness to years of bitter fighting, but civilian traffic now passes over rebuilt roads and bridges. As you pass across a field towards the edge of the village there is a dull boom from across the track. The plough stops dead, the ox stands patiently – but the farmer lies in a bloody heap. The troops may have returned to barracks, but their mines remain on duty.

Combat zones and old battlefields the world over are dominated by minefields.. Vietnam, Laos and Cambodia remain littered with mines: the old infiltration routes along the borders were showered with air dropped mines by the US Air Force and unexploded ordnance in the south continues to inflict casualties. Afghanistan has been similarly treated by the Soviet forces and more recently by the opposing sides in the civil war.

Throughout North Africa the desert still conceals lethal leftovers from World War II, and in the western Sahara the Polisario guerillas and the Moroccan army both sowed new fields. In the Falklands, tiny plastic anti-personnel mines are moved out of the marked danger areas by the winter storms and continue to present a serious hazard. You may be lucky and never need to know how to survive the mined battlefield; but if by accident or design you find yourself tip-toeing across eggshells in some foreign field, a knowledge of mines could mean the difference between life and death.

A bewildering selection of mines confronts any soldier trying to learn how to counter them. Different nations manufacture mines that produce similar effects but are of totally different construction. The only general preparation you can make is to learn how mines are used, how they are constructed and how armies mark minefields and make them safe for themselves.

But if you're on operations against an unexpected opponent, you won't have a chance to become familiar with his mines prior to hostilities. This is what happened to the sappers of the Falklands Task Force, who had little idea of the type of mines used by the Argentines. In the end, young sappers had to infiltrate booby-trapped minefields and recover examples of live mines.

Mines are being developed with increasing sophistication to keep phase with their primary target – the battle tank – and have an enormous psychological as well as physical impact on an enemy. If you are to survive the mined battlefield, you must appreciate that you are in as much danger from 'friendly' devices as you are from your enemy's. Remember, the mine is a double edged weapon.

The basic principles

A mine is made up of a fuse, a detonator, a booster (sometimes), a main charge, and a body or case. An initiating action causes the fuse to function and this starts the explosive train, whereby a flame or concussion is caused by electrical or mechanical means and is applied to the detonator. This then sets off the booster, if there is one, or the main charge. A variety of initiating actions can set off the process:

1 Pressure (downward force caused by a man's foot or the wheel or track of a vehicle).

2 Pulling (on a tripwire attached to the fuse)

3 Tension release (release of tension such as cutting a tripwire, that prevents the fuse from acting).

4 Pressure release (release of pressure that prevents the fuse from acting).

5 Electrical (closing a circuit that activates the fuse).

6 Timer rundown (a preset timer arrives at a point that activates the fuse).

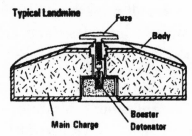

Typical Landmine

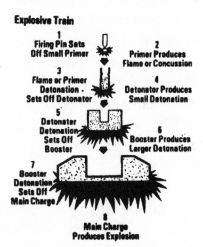

Explosive Train

Other types of initiating actions include vibrations, magnetic influence, frequency induction and audiofrequency.

Types of mine

There are three main types of mine, anti-tank, anti-personnel and chemical. Anti-tank mines, designed to damage or destroy tanks and other vehicles and their occupants can be blast-type, disabling wheels or tracks; vertical penetration, attacking the bottom of a vehicle; or horizontal effect, placed off routes to attack the side of vehicles.

Anti-personnel mines are designed to disable or kill personnel. The blast type have an explosive charge and detonate when stepped on. Fragmentation types contain shrapnel or have a case which fragments when the main charge fires, and are divided into static mines (which detonate in place), bounding mines (which bound into the air and explode several feet above the ground), and horizontal effect mines (which expel a spray of shrapnel in one direction).

Not all mines are harmful. You may come across phoney mines – dummies planted to make the enemy think they have found a live one, and waste time tackling it or avoiding it.

Handling mines

Like any other explosive material, mines and their fuses must be handled carefully. Most mines have safety devices to stop them going off by accident or prematurely, but as a soldier you may also find yourself having to improvize mines in the field, so get used to taking great care.

Any amount of explosive can be fused and placed as a mine. Grenades and some demolition charges already have fuse wells for installing firing devices; bombs, mortars and artillery shells can be used; and incendiary fuels in containers can be rigged as flame mines. The aspects of handling mines are:

1 Fusing

This means installing the detonator and fuse assembly. Fuse wells should be clean and free of foreign matter when the fuse and detonator are put in.

2 Arming

When the fuse is installed, you arm the mine by removing all safety devices. The mine is then ready to function.

3 Safing

In general, this is the reverse of arming. If you put the mine in place yourself and kept it in sight the whole time, you can remove it from its hole for safing. If not, attach a long rope or wire, take cover, and pull the mine from the hole. Safing involves checking the sides and bottom of the mine for anti-handling devices and disarming them if found;

replacing all pins, clips or other safety devices; turning the arming dial, if there is one, to 'Safe' or 'Unarmed'; and removing the fuse and, if possible, the detonator.

4   Neutralising

This means destroying the mine if safing is thought to be too risky, as in the case of improvized mines which will probably be unstable and dangerous. But do not detonate chemical mines: they will contaminate the area.

Anti-handling techniques

There are several devices for preventing someone disabling a mine. Enterprising engineers are apt to booby-trap their mines to make it difficult and dangerous to clear them. Anti-lift or anti-handling devices when attached to a mine, will detonate the mine or another charge nearby if the mine is lifted or pulled out of its hole. An anti-disturbance device sets off the explosion if the mine is disturbed or shaken. Shielded, twisted firing

ANTI-HANDLING DEVICES

Most anti-tank mines cannot be set off by a man's weight, so unless they are used in conjunction with 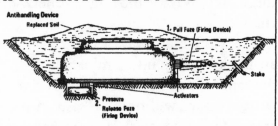 AP mines, infantry could lift them. For this reason, many mines will have anti-handling devices fitted to additional detonator wells.

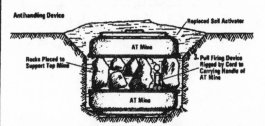 Slightly more sneaky is the use of a second mine to booby-trap the first using a pull-firing device. Most anti-tank mines are equipped with extra detonator wells, but the same effect can be achieved with quantities of explosive placed with the mine.

wire can be attached to command-detonated mines to defeat enemy ECM. Long pulse or multi-pulse fuses can defeat tank mine-clearing rollers and explosive mine-clearing charges.

Another way of dealing with mine-clearing rollers is to place an unfused anti-tank mine (or explosive charge) in the ground, connected with detonating cord to a pressure fuse of firing device about three metres away. The roller then rolls over the unfused mine and activates the fuse when the tank itself is over the mine or charge.

Avoiding Mines

The US Army manual on mine warfare says, 'train to prevent panic'. This is easy to say but rather harder to achieve. As you stand on a jungle trail with a screaming legless man in front of you, just what do you do? Rushing out of a live minefield is an obvious recipe for disaster, but staying put in combat will probably leave you in a killing ground under heavy fire. There is no guaranteed safe way out of a minefield, but if you know what different mines look like and understand how they work and the correct way of moving to safety, then you are in with a chance.

The only certain way of surviving the mined battlefield is to avoid blundering into a minefield in the first place. Although the famous skull and crossbones sign with '*Achtung Minen*' written above will only be seen in the cinema, well-trained armed forces do mark their minefields. Memorize the signs illustrated here and make sure you are fully briefed on marking used by an enemy. Nato minefields are signposted on the friendly side with triangular red markers; the side nearer the enemy is only shown by a single strand of wire about knee high. The Soviet markings shown are those used before the break up of the Soviet Union and the reunification of Germany, but are useful examples all the same.

NATO minefield marking

All minefields will be marked as in the diagram with the exception of 'nuisance clusters'. The area will be fenced with a strand at ankle and waist height with the 'Mines' inverted

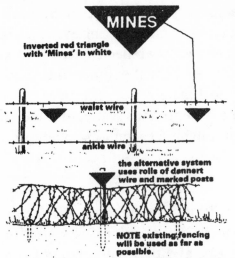

triangle every 20m. Minefield safe lanes will only be marked on the friendly side and maximum use will be made of existing fences so look at the signs, not at the type of fence

NATO minefield

SOVIET MINEFIELD MARKINGS

This sign indicates a Russian rectangular minefield. However, if the engineers were pressed for time your side of the field may only be marked by lines of sticks and stones. A German sign could say 'Minen' and a Polish one 'Miny'

The Soviet side of the minefield may have had a sign like this. The arrow points in the direction of the nearest safe lane through the field, not the minefield.

The minefield gap or safe lane was marked only on the Soviet side of the minefield, with a sign like this. Note that to the left the sign has the same word as the minefield sign as it points to the mines. The opposite direction leads to the passage, which was marked either with two rows of flags or semi-circular lane markers, camouflaged on the side facing the enemy. The safe lane is between the flags or semi circles

Marking safe lanes is a tedious and labour intensive job. The US Army uses the Hunting Lightweight Marking System, a set of steel-tipped plastic poles and yellow reflective tape. The kit is man-portable and the pins are robust enough to be hammered through tarmac. Unfortunately, not all armies are so diligent; witness the way the Argentinians scattered mines all over the Falkland Islands without even keeping a proper record of their position.

Air-dropped mines

The Soviets mined many guerilla infiltration routes in Afghanistan with air-dropped devices. Similar mines were used by the US Army in South East Asia and they will no doubt continue to be encountered in counter insurgency campaigns throughout the world. They are quick to lay and highly effective: Italian VS50 mines can be dropped by helicopter at a rate of 2,000 per pass. They are also the one type of minefield you can escape by rapid withdrawal from the area if you are unfortunate enough to have them dropped on your current position. Most air-dropped mines do not arm themselves for a couple of minutes, but you should make sure your identification is correct before hot-footing it away. Other characteristics of air-dropped mines are:

1   Fuses can be delay, pressure or magnetic.
2   Anti-tank and anti-personnel mines may be dropped together.
3   Most will self-destruct within a few days or even hours, but do not bank on them all self-destructing at the same time. Mines that self-destruct can be useful for security forces, which can then sweep the area in safety after the mines have done their damage.

Soviet liquid mines

One type of scatterable mine introduced by the Soviets in Afghanistan deserves a mention, although their use creates some interesting moral problems. They are small plastic cells filled with liquid explosives and are camouflaged or even shaped to look like transistor radios, dolls or other harmless items. They detonate when moved or compressed and are thought to contain an unstable explosive similar to nitroglycerine, which is safer when frozen. They are yet another good reason to be alert to the presence of booby traps. Stay switched on even when there is no obvious danger.

Soviet anti-personnel mines

Before you launch yourself onto the battlefield you must have a thorough knowledge of Soviet mines that have been exported worldwide in the last 30 years.

The PFM-1 AP mine/bomblet

Air delivered, plastic and filled with liquid explosive, this has a bulbous, irregularly-shaped body coloured green, sand or arctic white. Any distortion of the body will fire it; this includes light pressure while handling. It does not self-destruct and cannot be neutralized.

The PMD series

This wooden box has a hinged lid, overlapping the sides with a deep groove cut in it above the fuse assembly, and rests on the striker retaining pin. Some have a safety rod locking the lid. Pressure on the lid forces the winged retaining nut from the striker and fires the mine.

OZM-4

Pressure, command or tripwire detonated, this bounds 1.5-2.4 metres into the air and explodes showering fragments over a 50-m diameter.

POMZ-2M

A wooden stake with cast iron fragmentation body, activated by tripwire, this can be neutralized by securing the striker retaining pin and removing the wire. It is normally laid in clusters of three or four.

The PMN

The rubber-covered pressure plate on top of this small plastic mine is secured to the body by a thin metal bank. The mine has a side hole for the firing mechanism and primer charge, opposite which is an initiator adaptor. The mine is armed 15-20 minutes after removing the safety pin.

East European anti-tank mines
TM-62
This family of mines come in plastic, metal, wood or waterproof cardboard casings and are detonated by 175-600kg so a man's weight will not usually set them off. They have a two-second delay, so the tank is well over the mine when it explodes.

TM-46
The commonest mine in Soviet service, this has a metal body and can be laid by hand or machine. It is pressure-plate activated with an operating force of 210 kg.

TMN-46
Like the TM-46 this is activated by 210 kg pressure and can be fitted with a tilt rod fuse. The important difference is the extra fuse well in the bottom of the mine for booby trapping.

TMD-B
This is a wooden box mine dating from World War II. The top three slats are pressure boards, the middle one is hinged to allow the fuse to be inserted. When armed, the pressure board is held in place with a wooden locking bar.

TMA-3
A Yugoslavian plastic mine with no metallic parts found all over the world, this is blast and water resistant. It has three fuse wells and a fourth in the bottom for booby trapping. Operating weight is 180-350 kg.

MRUD anti-personnel mine
The Yugoslavian equivalent of the Claymore, this fires 650 steel balls over a 60-degree arc with a lethal radius of 50m. Activated by tripwire or remote control it will not damage tanks but will wreck soft-skin vehicles.

Mine injuries
One of the most widely encountered type of mine is the Soviet

PMD series of wooden and anti-personnel mines. Simple to lay and difficult to detect, they are used by guerilla forces all over the world. They are activated by pressure and were encountered by members of 22 SAS serving in Oman. It was observed that the local 'Firqha' – tribesmen fighting for the government and officered by SAS personnel – suffered less damage than the SAS if they stepped on a mine: treading on a PMD generally led to the tribesman losing his toes but SAS men in DMS or desert boots lost their whole foot at the ankle. British soldiers unfortunate enough to be wearing highneck boots like the US Cocorran jump boots often lost their leg up to the knee. Mines, like all explosives, will take the line of least resistance to cut.

Unfortunately it is not true to say that you can always minimize injury by swapping your combat boots for a pair of Ho Chi Minh sandals. In the Vietnam War, the tiny American 'gravel' anti-personnel mines contained only a very small charge. It was enough to cripple someone wearing light footwear, but a hefty pair of boots would actually reduce the damage. Moral of the tale; find out what mines you may be facing and act accordingly.

Where to expect mines

Mines are frequently positioned in specific locations rather than laid in rows in a field like potatoes. Favourite sites are roads and trails, especially junctions and bottlenecks. They may have been placed to block one route while troops observe another, ready to engage a target with direct fire. In jungle or thick forest the available tracks are screamingly obvious places to choke with mines, forcing the enemy to hack his way noisily through the undergrowth.

Detecting Mines

Mines vary in scale from anti-personnel weapons such as the US 'gravel' mine, shaped like and little bigger than a tea bag, to massive anti-tank mines designed to pierce armour plate and destroy a 60 ton armoured vehicle. The sheer diversity of modern mines rules out any single answer to them. All you can do is to employ as many techniques and procedures as possible. Each one provides a degree of safety; combined, they can significantly weaken a powerful weapon.

Military counter-mine operations consist of detection of individual mines; breaching and clearing minefields; sowing a cleared enemy minefield with your own mines; prevention of enemy mining; and detection of enemy mine-laying. In combat you must make full use of all intelligence-gathering resources to obtain enemy mine information. This will enable you to plan the use of sensors, aggressive countermining or other tactics as necessary to defeat his efforts. There are a number of basic rules to surviving the mined battlefield:

Denial of opportunity

Aggressive patrolling prevents the enemy laying his mines. The effects of patrols can be increased with night vision aids and sentry or scout dogs. In addition, sensors can be used on major routes and areas where enemy mining is heavy; sensors can alert quick reaction forces to move in on the threatened area, or can be used to bring fire on the enemy. However, US forces in Vietnam never really found an answer to local guerillas mining the roads – the infantry manpower needed for intensive patrolling was seldom available. South African forces were painfully aware how easy it is to mine isolated roads near their borders and have developed mine resistant vehicles designed to survive anti-tank mines.

Detection

The best way of detecting mines is by direct vision combined with a knowledge of minelaying methods. On the principle of setting a thief to catch a thief, if you understand how to plant mines properly you will have a much better grasp of mine detection. Sweep teams made up of trained observers, men with electronic detectors, and probers have proved highly effective, but security forces must be deployed to the flanks and rear of sweep teams to avoid ambush. Mine and tunnel dogs have been used with success to detect booby traps, trip wires, unexploded ordnance, punji pits and arms caches, as well as enemy troops.

These dogs should be used with other detection systems not as a single system.

Denial of material

The enemy may rely on captured material for this conduct of mine warfare. This is especially true in guerilla warfare; in Vietnam, many Viet Cong booby traps used captured American ordnance. VC sappers were also known to infiltrate American perimeters protected with Claymore mines and reverse them so that they exploded in the wrong direction. Strict measures must be taken to deny the enemy all materials which can be used for mine warfare.

Intelligence

There must be a complete system for reporting mine incidents. Analysis of reports may be combined with communication intelligence sources. The purpose is to reveal areas of heavy mining by the enemy as well as the types of mines and firing devices used.

Training

Proper training reduces casualties from mines and booby traps. Intensive unit-level training should be conducted on how the enemy emplaces and camouflages these weapons.

Protective measures

These measures may include the wearing of body armour and helmets by sweep teams, sandbagging the flooring of vehicles and requiring the occupants to keep their arms and legs inside. In the South African Army it was a chargeable offence not to be strapped into your harness when riding in a Buffel-type APC. Soldiers on foot must avoid bunching up at the site of a mine detonation; the enemy may have placed other mines to take advantage of this natural tendency.

Detection and search

Detection of mines is and action performed by soldiers in all phases of combat; search is a more deliberate action taken by single soldiers, teams or small units to locate mines or minefields. The following techniques are recommended for both.

1   Do not wear sunglasses; with them you are less able to detect tripwires and camouflage.

2   Be alert for tripwires in these places:
   • across trails
   • on the shoulders of roads at likely ambush sites
   • near known or suspected anti-tank or anti-vehicle mines
   • across the best route through dense plant growth
   • in villages and on roads or paths into them
   • in and around likely helicopter landing sites
   • in approaches to enemy positions
   • at bridges, fords and ditches
   • across rice paddy dikes

3   Check anything that might conceal a mine or its triggering device:
   • mud smears, grass, sticks, dirt
   • signs of road repair, for example new covering or paving, ditch and drainage work
   • tyremarks, skidmarks or ruts

4   Be alert for signs that might belong to mark or point to hidden mines:
   • signs on trees, posts or stakes, or signs painted on the road. Most are small and not easy to spot
   • marks other than signs, for instance sticks or stones placed in a line, clumps of grass placed at intervals. Look for patterns not present in nature.
   • wires leading away from the side of a road; they may be command firing wires
   • odd items in trees, branches or bushes; they may be explosive grenades, mortar rounds or artillery shells
   • odd features in the ground, for instance wilting plant camouflage

5   Watch the civilians. They may know where local mines are, so see where they don't go – for instance, one side of the road or certain buildings.

6   Be careful of any equipment left behind by, or belonging to the enemy; it may be booby trapped.

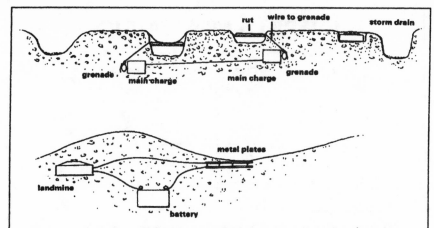

Old ruts in the road are dangerous; stay out of them. Here the pressure of a vehicle's tyres pulls the wire connected to the pins of the grenades. The grenades explode, setting off the main charges. Note the mine on the right by the side of the road, where troops are likely to try and take cover during an ambush.

Electrical detonation: the weight of a vehicle (or man, depending on how the mine is set) presses two metal plates together. This completes the electrical circuit, detonating the mine.

7   Listen for the sound of a delayed fuse device. If you think you hear one get down – fast.

8   Do not use any metal object as a probe; the metal can close the circuit between contacts. Use sharpened wooden sticks. When feeling for trip-wires, use a lightweight stick.

9   Use scout dog teams to detect booby traps.

10 Check all entrances (to buildings, caves, tunnels etc) for booby traps, and search the approaches and surrounding area for anti-personnel mines.

11 If you find an anti-tank mine, inspect by eye and probe for anti-handling devices.

12 Remember that the enemy can use command detonated mines. Search and clear road shoulders and surrounding areas before other mine-clearing work. Make sure you cover all potential firing positions and remove any wires and booby traps. Buried firing wires can be exposed and cut by

GUERILLA MINE TACTICS

If mines are laid in a group they will usually be in a logical pattern. This may be dictated by the ground, but will often follow a fixed formula. These three patterns of mine-laying were widely used during the Rhodesian war. They use the minimum number of their precious mines to give the best chance of hitting a vehicle.

Note the invariable habit of planting most of the mines in the ruts worn in the road. Despite all warnings it is very easy to follow the smoother route of old tracks and become another victim. Remember that when actually following another vehicle, the reverse is true and you are obviously safest by following the leading vehicle's exact route.

single-toothed rooters running along 10 to 50 metres from the road. Protect the clearing party with security forces

Probing

Probing is a way of detecting mines by piercing the earth with a sharp but non-metallic object e.g. a pointed stick. It is slow and hard work but is probably the most reliable way to find mines. When probing follow this procedure:

1 Move on your hands and knees or stay prone. Look and feel upward and forward for tripwires or pressure prongs. Keep your sleeves rolled up and remove watches and rings – your sense of touch must be at its keenest.

2 After looking and feeling the ground, probe every five centimetres across a one-metre frontage. Press the probe gently into the ground at an angle of less than 45 degrees from horizontal. Never push the probe straight down or you may detonate a pressure mine.

3 If the probe won't go in freely, the soil must be picked away with the tip of the probe and the loose earth or stones removed by hand.

4 If you touch a solid object, stop probing, remove the earth by hand and check it out.

5 If you find a mine, remove just enough of the surrounding soil to see what type it is. Then report it.

6 As you probe your way forward, the cleared lane must be marked for the following troops and mines you have located must be clearly signposted.

Caution: If you know or suspect the enemy is using magnetically influenced fuses, make sure no-one is carrying anything made of iron or steel in the vicinity of the mines. This means no steel helmets, bayonets, rifles etc.

NAVIGATION

As a special forces soldier, you will be expected to operate in the most remote an inaccessible regions of the world: this means being able to navigate with pinpoint accuracy under the most arduous circumstances. Although you are equipped with the most up to date satellite navigation and communication equipment, you must still be able to operate with the most basic navigational aids: a compass, map, altimeter and watch.

Forest navigation

Forest navigation is probably the most difficult, because your visibility is minimal and your path is obstructed. If you don't keep an accurate record of your precise location, you will soon get hopelessly lost, particularly in tropical rain forests. Under other navigational circumstances you are able to travel safely as long as you can recognize the prominent landmarks, but when you can only see trees and bushes it is all too easy to wander off course.

The Hollywood image of a forest navigation is of cutting a trail through the tangled undergrowth with a machete in one hand and a compass in the other. This had nothing to do with reality; the last thing any forest traveller wants to do is to 'cut a trail'.

Most forests are honeycombed with a complex network of unmapped tracks and trails. Although they may not seem to lead to your destination, using them will almost certainly make your journey far quicker and easier. If you have a choice of two trails to follow, and if you know precisely where you are, follow the path that points in what is the nearest to the right direction. By recording the bearings and distances between bends in the path, you will be able to plot its course on your map.

Continue this process until you are as near to your estimation as the trails will take you. You may now have to march on a direct bearing to your destination, cutting a trail. Better still, you could 'aim off' so that you intersect an easily recognisable land feature such as a road, railway or river that will lead directly to your target. If you are using a river, make sure you know which direction the river flows: it is not always obvious.

Surveying your path

Surveying a path is not difficult. You just need two pieces of information; direction and distance. Direction is obtained by using your compass to sight down the trail to the next bend adjusting your magnetic bearing to a grid bearing, and plotting a line from your known position. To work out distance, you now walk down the trail to the point at which you sighted counting your paces. When you reach your sighting, compare the pace totals of your team and take an average. This is called 'bracketing'. An experienced team will already know the relationship of their paces to distance, in varying terrain, having worked this out during training.

Another way of determining distance travelled is to estimate your speed of travel: speed = distance divided by time. By checking the time it takes you to pass between two identifiable land features and dividing this by the distance you have travelled (taken from the map), you will know your current speed. Update and revize this as often as possible, and make allow-

MAINTAINING DIRECTION IN THE JUNGLE

When bust cutting in secondary growth it is very difficult to keep walking exactly on a bearing. In really difficult country it may be necessary to use improvized survey poles.

With pole A in the ground a man is sent forward to the limit of visibility with pole B. Using the compass, the man with pole B is told to move left or right until he is on the bearing.

Pole A is then moved forward and either set in position using a forward bearing from pole B or a 'back' bearing taken from pole A to pole B.

ances for terrain changes. If, for example your speed is estimated at 4km/h and you have been walking at approximately that speed for 2 ^{1}/$_2$ hours, you will have travelled 10 km (distance = speed multiplied by time).

The most accurate way to establish your distance is to use both of the above methods. As commander, estimate your speed of travel while two of your team act as pace counters by notching a stick every 50 paces.

Trail cutting

Trail cutting means keeping a straight course. Accuracy is vitally important: if you are 4° off course, after three km you can be up to 250 metres off course – more than enough to miss your objective. By cutting two saplings and stripping the bark off them you can improvize two surveying poles. Use these to set your course by, and you should be able to navigate with pinpoint accuracy. Simply set the poles 20 metres apart in line with your intended direction of travel, so that they act as a visual guide for the trail you are cutting. As the trail progresses, leapfrog your rear pole forward, setting it in position by a back bearing to the remaining pole.

Navigating around obstacles

While walking on a bearing you may come across obstacles such as lakes, swamps, crevasses and ravines. To avoid these there are two techniques which will enable you to maintain your course.

1 Avoidance by landmark
   If there is an easily identifiable landmark within easy reach you can walk to it and take a fresh bearing from this point to your objective. If you are confident of your ability to judge distance you can avoid travelling all the way to the landmark.

2 Boxing
   Walking three sides of a box around the obstacle. By counting paces and walking a right-angled box you should be able to resume your correct course.

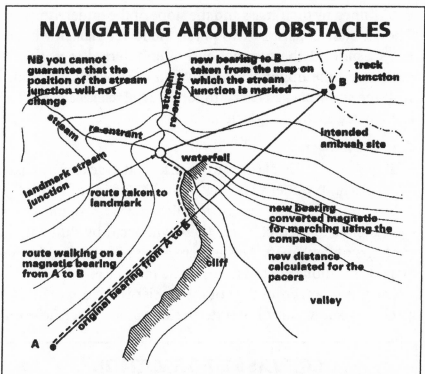

NAVIGATING AROUND OBSTACLES

NB you cannot guarantee that the position of the stream junction will not change

new bearing to B taken from the map on which the stream junction is marked

track junction

B

stream re-entrant

re-entrant

stream

intended ambush site

landmark stream junction

waterfall

route taken to landmark

new bearing converted magnetic for marching using the compass

new distance calculated for the pacers

route walking on a magnetic bearing from A to B

original bearing from A to B

cliff

valley

A

In tropical climax forest it is likely that you will come across obstacles not marked on the map that are impossible or very difficult to traverse. When you are walking on a compass bearing you cannot expect to walk around obstacles and maintain direction. Even at the end of a leg as short as 1000 metres, if you are only 30 mils out you will be at least 30 metres out at the other end – certainly enough to get you lost in close country. You have two choices; either box around the obstacles or pick a landmark from the map and plan a new route from that.

Alpine navigation

Another field of operations common to the special forces soldier is the mountain and Arctic environment. Navigation in these areas follows all the basic rules, but there are other considerations: probably the most hazardous is glacier navigation. Wherever possible, gain high ground before crossing glaciers so that you can scout a route through the ice falls.

Glaciers are basically huge rivers of ice. Their rate of flow is determined by their mass and the slope of the underlying rock. They usually consist of two parts; the lower glacier, which is free of snow in the summer and often referred to as the dry glacier and the upper glacier, covered in snow all year round with the snow packed down to form the glacier ice itself. This is often called the wet glacier.

Crevasse dangers

Although the ice is plastic at its surface, it cracks as it passes over rises in its underlying rock or at the outside of bends that it flows around. These cracks are called crevasses. In most cases it is possible to predict where these will occur by studying the contours of your map. 'Lurkers' crevasses which occur in predictable locations are caused by flows in the ice.

The most dangerous part of the glacier is the upper or 'wet' glacier as snow can obliterate the crevasses, often forming

CREVASSE FORMATION

Crevasses are formed wherever there is an irregularity in the underlying rock. In some areas you will be able to predict from your map where they will be, and the larger crevasses or crevasse zones may themselves be marked. But remember, the glacier is a system in motion, constantly changing, so you cannot rely on the mapped safe routes.

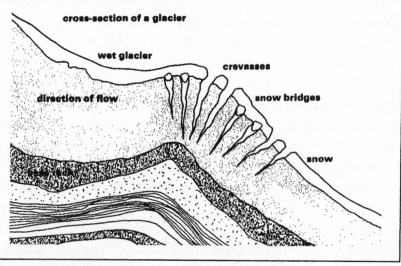

cross-section of a glacier

wet glacier

crevasses

direction of flow

snow bridges

snow

bridges across them. Whenever you cross 'wet' glaciers you should always be roped together.

Flowing water

As a general rule, where you can see water flowing across the surface of the glacier the danger of crevasses is minimal. This is because water will disappear down the first available crack or crevasse; so where you can see the water there can be few cracks.

Fixing your position

To gain an accurate fix on your position when crossing glaciers, you use a combination of information:

1 First measure the aspect of your position, by taking a bearing at 90° from your position to the direction in which the glacier is moving. By comparing this to the contour lines on your map you should be able to estimate your approximate location.

2 Secondly, take an altitude reading from your altimeter. This will enable you to gain a precise fix on your location. Remember to set your altimeter to the correct height each time you pass a spot height, as its reading will vary with the barometric changes of local weather conditions. If overnight you seem to gain height, it indicates a loss of pressure and therefore that bad weather is imminent. If, on the other hand, you lose height, the pressure indicates good weather imminent.

Navigation without instruments

As the truck brakes hard and your 'rookie' guard drops his cigarette, you take the chance to make a bid for freedom, vaulting the tailgate and running like a fox, looking for cover. After an hour you slump into the shade of a yew tree and look back. You can't see any sign of your pursuers, but they're there somewhere. You must put as much ground between them and you as possible.

   You were in the truck for about two hours, travelling at about 50 mph, so at the worst you're 100 miles behind the lines and probably much less. You could be back at HQ in a week. But your escape map and compass were taken when you were searched!

The mental map

No matter what your job is – running the field kitchen or leading the raiding party – make sure you know the geographical features of the location!

1　Where are the major rivers, and in which direction do they flow?
2　What are the local hills called and in which direction do they extend?
3　In which direction do the local railway lines run?
4　Where are your own lines and where are the enemy lines?
5　In which nearby towns or villages are there garrisons of enemy troops?

These are the beginnings of a detailed mental picture that you should build up and constantly update.

Your present situation

Using your mental map, you should be able to guess where you are and so decide what direction to head in. Remember that survival navigation is much less accurate than instrument navigation. Instead of a bearing you need a plan, such as 'trike NE to the southern hills, following them east to their end, then strike due north to the northern hills and follow them east until I reach a gap where the Blue river runs north west to our lines.' If you know where the areas of population are, plan your route to skirt round them.

To make even such a basic plan work, you must figure out your bearings. You need to know how the sun, stars, moon and planets act as indicators of direction and, you must practise using them.

The sun

This is your most obvious indicator of direction, so long as it is not covered by cloud. It rises in the east and sets in the west; this is always true, no matter what hemisphere you are in. Near

USING YOUR WATCH TO FIND NORTH

Northern temperate zone

1 Place a small stick in the ground so that it casts a definite shadow.
2 Put your watch on the ground so that the hour hand points along the shadow.
3 Find the point on the watch midway between the hour hand and 12 o'clock. A line from the centre of the face to this point indicates due south.

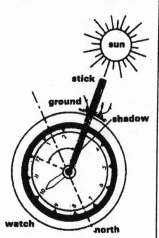

Southern temperate zone

1 Place the stick in the ground.
2 Put the watch on the ground so that 12 o'clock points along the shadow.
3 A line drawn from the centre of the watch to a point mid-way between the hour hand and 12 o'clock points north.

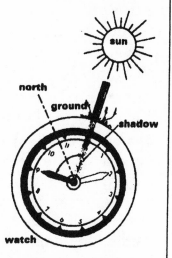

NOTE: If your watch is on British Summer Time (Daylight Saving Time) you must take the mid point of the hour hand and 1 o'clock. You can still use this method with a digital watch, simply draw out the clock face in the dirt with the hands representing the correct time GMT.

the Equator, the sun appears to be almost overhead; further north the sun will always be south of you, and further south it will be north of you.

Find out where true north is by measuring the shadow cast by a vertical stick. To do this, find a piece of level ground, preferably bare earth, and put a 30-cm straight stick vertically into the ground. Using a short marker stick, record the end of the shadow cast by the vertical stick. As the sun moves west the shadow will move east. Wait until the shadow has moved a few centimetres and mark its end again. By drawing a line between the two markers you will have a west to east line. If your need a north/south reference, simply draw a line that cuts the west/east line at a right angle.

The moon

If you're evading capture you will probably be travelling at night; to obtain your bearings you can use the moon and stars. In general, the moon can be seen more often than the stars.

Unlike the sun, the moon does not physically glow; it just reflects the light of the sun. A new moon occurs when the moon is between the Earth and the sun, with its dark side towards us, and a full moon is when the Earth is between the moon and the sun. Between the new and full moons, we see the moon partially illuminated on one side or the other.

USING THE MOON

The moon can be used to find direction in the following way in the northern hemisphere, imagine a line joining the tips of the crescent of the moon or bisecting the full moon and continuing to the horizon; this line is south. In the southern hemisphere use the same method to find north.

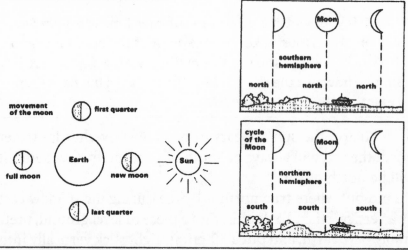

Like the sun, the moon moves in a regular and predictable manner. If the moon rises before the sun sets, the illuminated side is the west. If the moon rises at the same time as the sun sets, it will be a full moon and you will need to know the time to attain the direction. If the moon rises after the sun has set, the illuminated side is the east side.

When there is a crescent moon in the sky, you can gain an approximate cardinal point (south in the northern hemisphere, north in the southern hemisphere) by imagining a line joining the points of the crescent reaching to the horizon.

The stars

Gaining an approximate fix on north or south from the stars is an ancient and easy skill. The technique differs between the northern and southern hemispheres:

1   In the northern hemisphere, the star Polaris (the pole star) is your guide to true north. This is because it is never more than 1° from the North Celestial Pole. If you are facing the pole star, you are facing true north. To find Polaris, first

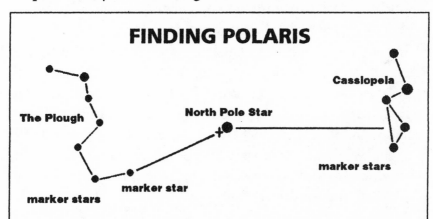

FINDING POLARIS

On a clear night in the northern hemisphere, the direction of north is indicated by the north star. This is not the brightest star in the sky and can be difficult to find. All other stars revolve around the north star. Or you can find the group of stars known as the 'Plough' or Ursa Major which is usually fairly prominent. A line joining the stars forming the blade of the plough points to the north star.

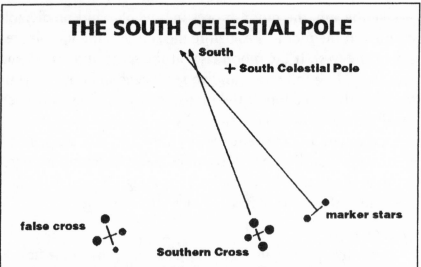

THE SOUTH CELESTIAL POLE

South

+ South Celestial Pole

marker stars

false cross

Southern Cross

In the southern hemisphere you can find the direction of true south by finding the south celestial pole. Unfortunately there are no convenient star markers and you have to work out the position from the southern cross and two adjacent bright stars.

find the easily recognized constellations 'The Plough' or 'Cassiopeia' which will guide you to Polaris.

2   In fact, the South Celestial Pole is so devoid of stars it is called the Coal Sack. If you are facing the South Celestial Pole you are facing true south. To find the pole, draw and imaginary line from the Southern Cross (do not confuse this with the 'false cross') and another imaginary line at 90° to the two bright stars east of the Southern Cross. The point at which these two lines intersect is a point approximately 5-6° off true south.

Cloudy nights

On cloudy nights you may not be able to see enough of the night sky to use these methods. If you can see some stars, choose a bright star that you will be able to observe, unobscured, for some minutes. If it falls, you are looking west; if it rises, you are looking east. If it arcs up to the right you are looking approximately south-east and if it arcs down to the right you are looking approximately north-west.

Natural landmarks

If you are on the move and in a hurry you will need quicker references. Because the landscape and vegetation is shaped by the local environmental conditions you can gain rough indications of direction by simple observation. However, you will find these indicators to be unreliable guides, and you should never rely upon one indicator alone.

1 – Wind

The generally prevailing wind in England is south-westerly (and in north-west Europe north-westerly).

Lone trees and isolated new plantations will lean away from the prevailing wind direction.

Make sure you are aware of the prevailing wind direction in any area in which you are operating.

Lone trees lean away from the wind, as do tussocks of grass and other forms of upright vegetation such as ferns. Small isolated woods, especially near the coast, have stunted trees on their windward sides.

In sandy areas, tails of sand form behind small bushes and plants, pointing directly away from the wind. Sand dunes and snow cornices are gently sloping on their windward side and steep on their lee (sheltered) side.

2 – Sun

The sun also greatly affects vegetation, in particular isolated trees, whose branches should be more numerous and foliated on the sunny side (south in the northern hemisphere and north in the southern hemisphere). Because of this you will also usually find that the decaying vegetation at the base of the trunk

NATURE'S SIGNPOSTS

Trees
Isolated trees have more branches with more leaves on the sunnier side of the tree: in the northern hemisphere this means south.

Isolated buildings
Barns in exposed position will be drier on the sunnier side with less moss and algae on that side, indicating south in the northern hemisphere.

Tree stumps
The growth rings of the stump will be more tightly packed on the sunnier side, indicating south in the northern

hemisphere. The leaf litter will also be drier at the base of the stump on that side.

is drier on the sunny side: a good night-time guide. The stumps of felled trees will show their growth rings more tightly packed on the sunny side.

Using natural landmarks
Remember that prevailing weather conditions vary from region to region and are especially unpredictably in hilly or heavily wooded areas. Success in navigation depends on your choice

of landmark; lone isolated trees in flat country are the ideal choice.

By comparing the results of several differing natural navigation aids for example, grass tufts, the way a star moves and the moisture of leaf litter at the base of a tree, you should be able to move over unfamiliar country in any direction you want.

RIVER CROSSING

If you are on the run or are operating in wild terrain, you are likely to encounter water obstacles that you may have to cross. They may be fast moving rivers or large marshy areas of clinging stinking and tiring mud. Each has its dangers, but also its drills for survival. Here we deal with rivers, using techniques from US Army Manual FM21-76.

Finding your crossing point

A river or stream may be narrow or wide, shallow or deep, slow-moving, or fast-moving. It may be rain-fed, snow-fed or ice-fed. Your first step is to find a place where the river is basically safe for crossing, so look for a high place from which you can get a good view and look out for the best crossing point. If there is not high place, climb a tree.

Check the river carefully for the following features:

1 A level stretch where it breaks into a number of channels. Two or three narrow channels are usually easier to cross than a wide river.

2 Obstacles on the opposite side of the river that might hinder your travel. Try to select the spot from which travel will be the safest and easiest.

3 A ledge of rocks that crosses the river. This often indicates dangerous rapids or canyons.

4 A deep or rapid waterfall or a deep channel. Never attempt to ford a stream directly above or even close to such spots.

5 Rocky places. Avoid these, you can be seriously injured if you fall on rocks. An occasional rock that breaks the current however, may assist you.

6 A shallow bank or sandbar. If possible, select a point upstream from such a feature so that the current will carry you to it if you lose your footing.

7 A course across the river that leads downstream, so that you can cross the current at about a 45} angle.

Avoid cold water

Be sure to check the water temperature before trying to cross a river or water obstacles. If the water is extremely cold and you are unable to find a shallow fording place, do not attempt to ford it. Devize other means for crossing; for instance, you might improvize a bridge by felling a tree over the river. Or you might build a raft large enough to carry both you and your equipment.

Crossing a fast river

If you are going to ford a swift, treacherous stream,remove your trousers and underpants so that the water will have less grip on your legs. Keep your shoes on to protect your feet and ankles from rocks and to give you firmer footing. Tie your trousers and important articles securely to the top of your pack; if you have to release it, everything will be easier to find.

Carry your pack well up on your shoulders so that you can release it quickly if you are swept off your feet. Being unable to get a pack off quickly enough can drag even the strongest of swimmers under. Don't worry about the weight of your pack, as this will help rather than hinder you in fording the stream.

Find a strong pole about 12 cm (5 in) in diameter and 2 to 2.5 metres (7 to 8 ft) long to help you ford the stream. Grasp the pole and plant it firmly on your upstream side to break the current. Plant your feet firmly with each step, and move the pole forwards, slightly downstream from its previous position, but still upstream from you. With your next step, place your foot below the pole. Keep the pole well slanted so that the force of the current keeps the pole firmly against you.

Crossing as a team

If there are other people with you, cross the stream together. Make sure that everyone has prepared their pack and clothing as above. The heaviest person should be on the downstream end of the pole and the lightest person on the upstream end. This way, the upstream person will break the current, and the people below can move with comparative ease in the eddy formed by him. If the upstream person is temporarily swept off his feet, the others can hold him steady while he regains his footing.

As in all fording, cross the stream so that you will cross the downstream current at a 45° angle. Currents too strong for one person to stand against can usually be crossed safely in this manner.

Do not rope your team together in fast-flowing water; the action of the current may hold any fallen member down.

Floating across

If the temperature of a body of water is warm enough for swimming but if you are unable to swim, make a flotation device to help you. Some things you can use are:

1   *Trousers*

Knot each leg at the bottom and button the fly. With both hands grasp the waistband at the sides and swing the trousers in the air to trap air in each leg. Quickly press the sides of the waistband together and hold it under water so that the air will not escape. You now have water wings to keep you afloat. These have to be re-inflated several times when crossing a wide stretch of water.

2 *Empty containers*

Lash together empty tins, petrol cans or boxes and use them as water wings. You should only use this type of flotation in a slow-moving river or stream.

3 *Plastic bags*

Air-fill two or more plastic bags and securely tie them together at the mouth.

4 *Poncho*

Roll green vegetation tightly inside your poncho so that you have a roll at least 45 cm (18 in) in diameter. Tie the ends of the roll securely. You can wear it around your waist or across one shoulder and under the opposite arm.

5 *Logs*

Use a stranded drift log if one is available, or find a log near the water's edge. Test it before starting to cross, however, as some tree logs, palm for example, will sink even when the wood is dead.

6 *Bulrushes*

Gather stalks of bulrushes and tie them in a bundle 25 cm or more in diameter. The many air cells in each stalk cause it to float until it rots. Test the bundle to make sure it will support your weight before attempting to cross.

Two-man rafts

If you are with a companion and each of you has a poncho, you can construct a brush or Australian poncho raft. With this type of raft you can safely float your equipment across a slow-moving stream or river.

Brush raft

The brush raft will support about 115 kg (250 lb) if properly constructed. Use ponchos, fresh green brush, two small saplings and a rope or vines.

1 Tightly tie off the neck of each poncho with the neck drawstring.

2 Attach ropes or vines at the corner and side grommets of

each poncho. Be sure they are long enough to cross to and tie with those at the opposite corner or side.

3   Spread one poncho on the ground with the tied-off hood upwards.

4   Pile fresh, green brush (no thick branches) on the poncho until the brush stack is about 45 cm (18 in) high.

5   Pull the poncho neck drawstring up through the centre of the brush stack.

6   Make an X-frame of two small saplings and place it on top of the brush stack.

7   Tie the X-frame securely in place with the poncho neck drawstring.

8   Pile another 45 cm of brush on top of the X-frame.

9   Compress the brush slightly.

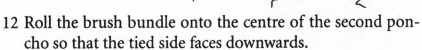

10 Pull the poncho sides up around the brush and, using the ropes or vines attached to the corner and side grommets, tie diagonally from corner to corner and from side to side.

11 Spread the second poncho, tied off hood upwards, next to the brush bundle.

12 Roll the brush bundle onto the centre of the second poncho so that the tied side faces downwards.

13 Tie the second poncho around the brush bundle in the same way as you tied the first poncho around the brush (10).

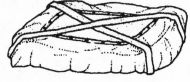

14 Tie one end of a rope to an empty canteen and the other end to the raft. This will help you to tow it.

Australian poncho raft

If you do not have time to gather brush for a brush raft, you can make an Australian poncho raft. Although more water-proof, this will only float about 25 kg (55 lb) of equipment. Use two ponchos, two 1-metre poles or branches, and ropes, vines, bootlaces or comparable material.

1 Tightly tie off the neck of each poncho with the neck drawstring.

2 Spread one poncho on the ground with the neck upwards.

3 Place and centre the two poles about 45 cm apart on the poncho.

4 Place the rucksacks, packs and other equipment between the poles, including items that you want to keep dry, such as boots and outer garments.

At this point you will need your companion's help to complete the raft.

1 Snap the poncho sides together.

2 Hold the snapped portion of the poncho in the air and roll it tightly down to the equipment

3 Twist each end of the roll to form pigtails in opposite direction.

4 Fold the pigtails over the bundle and tie them securely in place using ropes, vines or bootlaces.

5 Spread the second poncho on the ground with the tied-off hood upwards. If you need more buoyancy, place some fresh green brush on this poncho.

6 Place the equipment bundle, pigtail side down, on the centre of the second poncho.

7 Wrap the second poncho around the equipment bundle following the same procedure as you used for wrapping the equipment in the first poncho.

8 Tie ropes, vines or other binding material around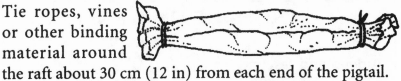
the raft about 30 cm (12 in) from each end of the pigtail.

9 Place and secure weapons on top of raft.

10 Tie one end of a rope to a canteen and the other end to the raft. This will help you in towing the raft.

When launching or landing either type of raft take care not to puncture or tear it by dragging it on the ground. Let the raft lie on the water for a few minutes to ensure that it floats before you start to cross the river or stream. If the river is too deep to ford, push the raft in front of you while swimming.

Log raft

This will carry both you and your equipment if you are unable to cross in any other way; if you have an axe and a knife you can build it without rope. A suitable raft for three men would be 3.5m (12 ft) long and (2m) 6 ft wide. You can use dry, dead standing trees for logs, but spruce trees that are found in polar and sub-polar regions make the best log rafts.

1 Build the raft on two skid logs placed so that they slope downwards to the bank. Smooth the logs with an axe so that the raft logs lie evenly on them.

2 Cut four off-set inverted notches, one in the top and bottom of both ends of each log. Make the notches broader at the base than at the outer edge of the log.

3 To bind the raft together, drive through each notch a three-sided wooden crosspiece about 30 cm longer than the width

CROSSING ON A RAFT

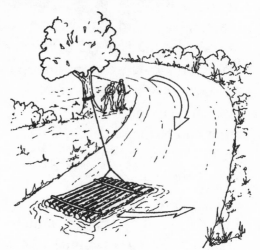

A deep and fast-moving river can be crossed several times using a pendulum action at a bend in the river; this is necessary when several men have to cross. However, remember the following.

1 The raft must be canted in the direction of the current.

2 The rope from the anchor point must be 7-8 times as long as the width of the river.

3 The attachment of the rope to the raft must be adjustable to change the cant of the raft so that it can return to the starting bank.

of the raft. Connect all the notches on one side of the raft before connecting those on the other.

4 Lash the overhanding ends of the two crosspieces together at each end of the raft to give it additional strength. When the raft enters the water, the crosspieces swell binding the logs together tightly.

5 If the crosspieces fit too loosely, wedge them with thin pieces of dried wood. These swell when wet, tightening and strengthening the crosspieces.

Flash floods

Beware of rapidly-increased water flows. Flash floods are a common feature in the tropics and can arrive suddenly many miles from any apparent storm. Try to cross steadily but quickly. Heat loss will be substantial and you could quickly become weak. Once out on the other bank, take your clothes off and wring out as much water as possible. Change into dry kit if you can. Otherwise, put your wet clothing back on – it will soon dry out as your body warms up.

Rapids

Crossing a deep, swift river or rapids is not as dangerous as it looks. If you are swimming across, swim with the current – never fight it – and try to keep your body horizontal to the water. This will reduce the danger of being pulled under.

In fast, shallow rapids, travel on your back, feet first; use your hands as fins alongside your hips to add buoyancy and to fend off submerged rocks. Keep your feet up to avoid getting them bruised or caught by rocks.

In deep rapids, travel on your front, head first; angle towards the shore whenever you can. Breathe between wave troughs. Be careful of backwater eddies and converging currents as they often contain dangerous swirls.

Other water obstacles

You may also face bogs, quagmire, muskeg or quicksand. DO NOT try to walk across; trying to lift your feet while standing upright will make you sink deeper. If you are unable to bypass them, you may be able to bridge them using logs, branches or foliage.

Another way to cross is to lie face downwards with your arms spread and swim or pull your way across. Be sure to keep your body horizontal.

In swamps, the areas that have vegetation are usually firm enough to support your weight and you should be able to crawl or pull your way through miles of swamp or bog. In open mud or water areas without vegetation, you can swim.

ROPEWORK

Whether you are rigging a camouflage net or tensioning a rope across a chasm, your success or failure – maybe your life – will at some stage depend upon your or a mate's ability to tie a secure knot. How many times have you seen a tangle of cordage, jammed knots, ropes unravelling at their ends? These are the signs of dangerous and sloppy rope-handling. Although you will not be in constant contact with ropes, an understanding of rope and knots is a fundamental requirement of the professional soldier.

Assuming you have no specialist equipment available, how do you learn to work efficiently and safely with rope?

Teaching yourself knots

There is no substitute for practice. You will find learning easier if you use two two-metre lengths of 5-mm climbing accessory cord, ideally of different colours. You haven't learned a knot until you can consistently tie it behind your back; in a combat situation you may have to tie a life-saving knot, quickly in the dark, and possibly under water, for example while crossing a river.

Basic rope terminology
Handling cordage
Nothing is more frustrating than having to constantly untangle rope or string when you need it in a hurry. Get into the habit of always coiling and hanking rope correctly.

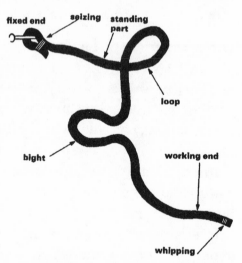

Hanking and coiling

Hanking is the term used to describe the correct method of gathering short lengths of small cordage such as paracord. Wind the cord around the thumb and little finger of one hand in a figure-of-eight fashion, leaving about a metre to spare. Take the coils off your hand and wrap them with the spare length, finishing off with half a hitch or two pulled tight.

Long lengths of small cordage should be coiled. Coiling is the correct method of gathering rope. Correctly coiled rope should not contain kinks. Before coiling, make sure the working end of the rope (i.e. the end not in your hand) is un-attached. As you take on the coils, twist the rope between your thumb and index finger so that perfect coils are formed, without twists or kinks. Once coiled, double back about a third of a metre of the fixed end, take off the last coil and wrap the coil tightly from the fixed end to the double-back. Pass the working end through the loop formed at the double-back, and pull on the fixed end to lock the whipping tight.

Types of rope

Choose your rope carefully. Each type of rope has its own characteristics and uses; the wrong choice of rope could easily prove fatal – for instance, you should never climb on hemp ropes. Wherever possible, familiarize yourself with the types and specification of the ropes available.

1   *Hawser-laid ropes*
    These are the traditional type of rope, normally constructed from three strands. The advantage is that the rope can be easily inspected for wear and tear, but the disadvantage is that it tends to wear more easily than braided ropes, and unless correctly handled tends to kink. More importantly, it does not stretch to absorb the energy of a fall in climbing.

2   *Braided ropes*
    Often referred to a Kernmantel, (Kern=Core; Mantel= Sheath), these ropes are almost totally made from man-made fibres. The core of the rope is the major load-bearing part, with the sheath acting as a protection from abrasion and other external hazards, and providing, in some cases, comfortable handling. The disadvantage is that it is impossible to detect progressive wear on the core of the rope. This type of rope has a limited safe lifespan if used for climbing: successive heavy falls will weaken it, so you must know a rope's history before you use it.

Materials

The material the rope is made from is more significant than its method of construction. Rope can be made from natural or man-made fibres; the latter is the most common nowadays.

1 Natural fibres

Hemp, sisal, cotton etc. are rapidly being replaced by the man-made fibres. The disadvantages of natural ropes are numerous; when wet they lose 30 per cent of their strength and are heavy and difficult to handle; they are prone to mildew and vermin, and are uncomfortable to handle.

They do, however, have one great advantage over man-made fibres; when hot they do not melt, which makes them the best choice in situations of high friction and fire emergencies. Sea-going vessels still have to have their ships' ladders made from natural ropes, in case of fire. The time gained by having ropes that smoulder rather than melt is a significant safety feature, even though the ropes need replacing more frequently.

The other advantage of a natural rope is its tendency to 'sing out' before it breaks – an audible warning that has so often saved Tarzan in the movies. Watch out: the acid from batteries will rot natural rope.

2 Man-made fibres

In most cases, these are stronger, more durable, lighter and cheaper than natural fibres. However, they are more slippery and require careful attention to knots. The cheapest man made fibres available are polythene and polypropylene ropes: these are the very smooth orange and blue ropes often seen on lifebelts and building sites. These ropes float (hence their use on lifebelts), but are weak compared with the other man-made fibres. They also tend to suffer more from ultra-violet decay, most noticeable as a lightening and opaque change in their colour, which greatly reduces their strength.

Polyester or terylene is much stronger than polypropylene and is often used by sailors. This is also the material from which modern abseiling and caving ropes are made. Although fine for these specific activities this type of rope should never be used for climbing with, because it is pre-stretched. A fall taken on such a rope would break the climber's back.

Nylon is the man-made fibre used for climbing ropes, due to its ability to absorb shock by stretching. If a climber falls, the force of the fall is taken gradually, thus cushioning the jolt.

Climbing ropes

Climbing ropes come in two main types; half ropes and single ropes. They are marked accordingly. Half ropes need to be used in pairs or doubled, whereas a single rope can be used on its own. Because climbing rope stretches it should not be used for towing or assault pioneering tasks.

Rope strength

To use the full strength of any rope, the load must be taken equally by all the fibres. This only happens when the rope is pulled in a straight line. When a rope is bent, for example over a cliff edge, the fibres on the inside, which severely weakens the strength of the rope. If an 11-mm climbing rope passes around a karabiner clip with a 5-mm diameter, the rope strength reduces to 70 per cent.

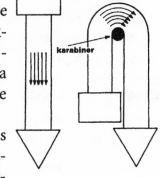

The strength of a rope depends on its weakest part. When you are constructing rope bridges, lifting weights or carrying out any other assault pioneering tasks, it makes sense to have a rough idea whether the system you have built is going to take the load.

The rule for the working strength of dry fibre ropes in hundredweights is given by its circumference in inches squared. So a safe working load for a new three-inch fibre rope is about 3 x 3 which is 9 hundredweight (500 kg).

Whenever a knot is tied in a rope, bends are introduced, causing weakness; some knots weaken rope more than others.

TRACKING

As a soldier, your knowledge of tracking will enhance your awareness, increase your ability to gather intelligence and sharpen your fieldcraft. If you are in command during extended border operation, a tracking capability will enable you to build an accurate map of the localized enemy movements without having to send out large numbers of patrols.

But for a survivor, tracking skill means food. If you're close to civilisation, man-made obstacles such as fences and irrigation channels force game to pass through bottlenecks, making trapping easy. But in remote sparsely populated areas it is not so simple. You must be able to recognize the trails of local game and be capable of following them from their resting areas to their feeding areas, where trapping is easier.

Good trackers are rare. When they are needed for military purposes, commanders usually employ hunters from the local indigenous population. But this does not mean that Westerners cannot track; some of them are among the world's best trackers. A tracker is a reader of 'sign'. He takes a few faint pieces of information and, but the process of deduction and comparison with previous experience, puts the puzzle together.

Obstacles to trackers

The more experience the tracker has, the better able he is to do the job. But he must still beware the following:

1 *Lack of confidence*

Even the best trackers use intuition, and a tracker must know when to trust a hunch. With lives at stake, lack of confidence can cloud your ability to think straight. Experience is the only solution.

2 *Bad weather*

'Sign' does not last for ever. Wind, rain and fresh snowfall will all obliterate it: many a trail has gone cold because the tracker has not paid enough attention to the weather forecast. With unfavourable weather imminent, short cuts may need to be taken to speed the ' follow up'.

3 *Non-track-conscious personnel*

By the time trackers are called in to follow the trail, the clues at the proposed start have usually been destroyed by clumsy feet. If you are fortunate enough to work with a team that can recognize 'sign' even though they cannot read it, you will have extra pairs of eyes to help you find the vital clues.

4 *Unsympathetic commander*

Tracking is a solitary business, requiring great concentration. A tracker must have the trust of the commander and must be able to trust his cover group. Tracking often seems to be painfully slow, but the tracker will be moving as fast as he can: never rush him. The more intelligence he has at his disposal the better, so tell him what is going on: your knowledge of enemy movement may make sense of an otherwise meaningless clue.

Try to allow the tracker time to impart a rudimentary knowledge of tracking to his cover group, and make sure the cover group are all patient men: the tracker has the challenge of the trail to hold his attention, but the cover and support group does not. If they make any noise it is the tracker who is at greatest risk.

Attributes of a tracker

Tracking is mainly a visual skill. Your eyesight, whether you wear glasses or not, must be 20/20. Short sighted people often seem to make good trackers once their eyesight is corrected.

A general ability to observe is not enough for tracking; you have to piece information together, like Sherlock Holmes. You must also be patient, persistent and constantly questioning your own theories, especially if you are 'solo tracking'.

Very often, you will trail your target to within touching distance. To reduce risks, self defence and close-quarter battle skills are vital.

Although modern equipment plays an important role in the task of tracking, remember that it does not replace your tracking ability; it just makes life easier.

Learning to track

Tracking is not a particularly difficult skill to learn, but it needs dedication and much practice. Once you have learned the basic principles and techniques you can practise in your own time. If you want to reach a high standard, it will help if you have a team mate who can lay trails for you. Make sure you keep a log: this must include the duration of the track, the time of the day, the ground conditions and the level of difficulty.

Teaching yourself is not easy. The biggest mistake you can

392 — TACTICS AND TECHNIQUES

make is to 'run before you can walk': for at least your first 50 hours, follow simple trails, concentrating on accurately interpreting the 'sign'. Then gradually increase the difficulty of the trails. When you have 100 hours under your belt, you should be following fairly difficult trails.

Your tracking kit

You should not need any special equipment, but the following will simplify your task.

1 *Notepad and pen*

This is a very important part of any track pack; a detailed drawing of the track you are following can easily be photocopied and distributed to other trackers. While learning to track, make frequent drawings. This will force you to notice the fine details in any footprint, such as wear patterns and sole damage, which will enable you to pick it out again later.

2 *Map and compass*

These not only show you where you are; they will often enable you to guide in a strike force or tracking team to cut the trail of the target and eventually intercept. Take your eyes off the trail frequently and study the map, to try and understand where your target might be heading. For example, if he is heading for a waterhole you may be able to insert a heliborne troop to ambush him.

3 *Watch*

An important tool. By acting out the target's trail for a given distance, you will be able to work out his speed of travel.

4 *Torch (Flashlight)*

This will enable you to control the light under difficult conditions and to track at night. The torch must be robust and ideally have a soft focus capability, which reduces the fatigue of 'eye strain' during extended night tracking.

5 *Tracking stick*

This is a unique tracking aid developed by the trackers of the US Border Patrol. It looks similar to a lightweight walking stick. On the stick are two adjustable markers, which are used to measure the step interval and track length. When you have difficulties finding the next track you should find the next sign at the point of the stick.

6   *Lolly (popsicle) sticks*
These are used to mark each track, enabling you to see at a glance the track pattern.

7   *Orange crepe paper*
This can be used to mark a trail, or a particularly interesting aspect. Again, this is favoured by the US Border Patrol. If a tracking team comes across a forgotten marked trail it is difficult to confuse with a fresh trail as crepe paper fades quickly.

8   *Mine tape*
This can be used to mark the start of the trail and sets of track of great importance. Always remove mine tape at the completion of the follow up.

9   *Magnifying glass*
A very useful aid to tracking although you would not use it as constantly as Sherlock Holmes might!

10 *Binoculars*
The use of binoculars is not always possible, but they can sometimes be used to read tracks at a distance as well as for making visual contact with the target.

Reading 'sign'
The first skill of tracking is the most important one you will learn, becoming sign-conscious. There is no quick way to achieve this. As you go about your everyday business, try to notice footprints, tracks, fingerprints, hairs and other signs. As you walk along a pavement, look out for the elastic bands discarded by postmen.

At first this will be a contrived activity, but with perseverance you will begin to notice these fine details in the overall pattern around you without thinking about it. When this happens, you are ready to start tracking.

You're unlikely ever to find a string of 'Man Friday' footprints. Instead you will have to follow a trail of scuffs, creased leaves, bruised grass stems, hairs and occasionally part of a footprint.

If you are lucky enough to find a clear print, study it carefully to glean as much information as possible about the target. Compare it with your own to determine the target's size, sex, age, weight, load or no load, speed of travel and whether he is fit or exhausted.

Marking up the track pattern

Once you have found a print, mark it up by drawing a circle round it in earth or sand, or with a piece of crepe paper held down with a stone. A second mark can be drawn: a semi circle with a tail on the right indicates a right foot, and a tail on the left of the semicircle is a left foot.

Mark each footprint and make a detailed sketch of the prints in your notebook. A better view of the pattern of the target's movement is obtained if you mark each print with crepe paper, lolly sticks or similar. This marking gives you an idea of where to look for the next print, if you are having problems. A Polaroid camera is a good idea for recording tracks, especially if you are using more than one team.

Using the tracking stick

The first mark to set on your stick, using the moveable rings, is the step interval. This is the distance from the tip of the toe to the heel of the opposite foot. Set the lowest ring to show the distance from the tip of the stick that represents the step interval. If you can't find the next print, you put the first marker over the toe and rotate, and the next heel print will be under the point.

The second mark you set on your stick is the foot length, measured heel to toe. This is set next up from the step interval mark. If you find a heel mark but can't see the toe, all you have to do is put the second marker over the heel and rotate the stick. The tip of the toe should be under the first mark.

Clothing and equipment

A tracking team must be totally self-sufficient and capable of operating as an independent unit. Communications equipment and plenty of supplies and ammunition must be carried.

Tracking can often be a slow process, so everyone must be warm, windproof and waterproof.

The tracker's load is normally carried by the support team, leaving him with only his belt kit. Make arrangements for his kit to be dropped where he can reach it at the first sign of trouble.

Animal signs

You must also be able to read animal signs, even when tracking people. For example, a human track with a badger print on top if it will show that the track was made before the badger was active at night. If you know the habits of the local wildlife, you will have gained a clue to the age of the track.

Animal tracks may also lead you to a rubbish or food cache, providing you with crucial information regarding the target's state of mental, moral and physical well-being.

Common tracks

dog   fox   cat   deer

How animals move

Each group of animals moves in a different way: they move different foot combinations, and to further complicate the issue they move in different patterns at different speeds. The numbers indicate which foot hits the ground first. The only way to learn more about these animals is through first-hand tracking experience and careful observation of the animal in its natural habitat.

Dog – walking

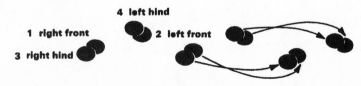

Fox – walking

The hind foot lands directly on top of the forefoot, obliterating the previous sign.

Badger

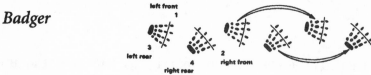

The hind foot almost covers the forefoot. Note that the toes point inwards.

Domestic cat

This is substantially the same as the fox pattern, but straighter.

Rabbit

The rear legs are usually placed down together in front of the forelegs. When eating the pattern changes.

Squirrel

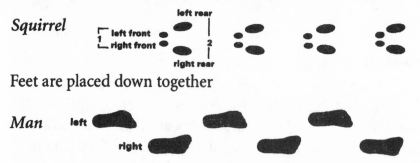

Feet are placed down together

Man

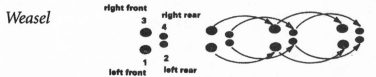

There are differences between men and women.

Weasel

This method of movement is known as the omega curve; the animal's body forms a curve in the shape of the letter as it bounds forward with the front legs and brings up its rear legs.

Animal tracking exercises

You need hundreds of hours of practice and regular tracking exercises. The following are designed to equip you with the basic skills. Practise them as often as you can, in as many different environments as possible. Try to spend three hours on each exercise each time and record your progress in your log.

1 Familiarize yourself with the track diagrams. Imprint their shape in your memory, paying particular attention to the details. Now try to find real examples of these tracks, draw them and measure them.

2 Having found the tracks of the animals represented, try to find out as much as you can about them by following the trail early on, this is a vital part of the learning process. Make a detailed drawing of the last two tracks you can find. When you've learned more, you may be able to decipher the clues to the next track.

3 Find out as much as you can from books about the animals represented. What do they eat? Where do they live? What noises do they make? What do their droppings look like?

4 With a teammate, compete to see who can find the most feathers lying on the ground. Now identify which birds they belong to. If you come across a heap of feathers indicating a kill, try to discover which predator was responsible.

5 Follow a well-worn trail and see how many hairs you can find.

Tracking: Using the light

Now that you have become more sign-conscious, you must learn to maximize your chances of seeing sign. To see the greatest detail in a clear print you need contrast: this means the light striking the ground at a low angle. Normally, this means that you are limited to tracking when the sun is low in the sky, during the morning hours and in late afternoon/early evening. Around midday the light is almost directly overhead and cast a flat light, which makes ground features disappear. However, time will usually be against you in most live tracking situations, forcing you to continue through the day and sometimes even into the night. In this case you will need to make use of techniques that have been devized to control the light conditions to your advantage.

Daylight tracking

When the sun is low in the sky, you can take advantage of the light just by positioning yourself correctly: make sure the track is between yourself and the light source by watching the shadows cast by your tracking stick. Probably the most common error of novice trackers is to align themselves incorrectly.

Once you are in the correct position, it is often an advantage to lower your line of sight, sometimes even right down to the ground. As you become more proficient you will do this mainly for seeing the finer details or when the light is bad. If you are not used to squatting on your haunches for long periods, include exercise for this in your fitness programme; novice trackers on their first extended follow-up often miss sign due to a reluctance to squat down.

When you are sign-cutting (searching for sign, normally aiming to cross the target at 90°), getting into the correct position relative to the sun is vital, but can pose problems. If the target is moving directly away from the sun, to 'follow up' you will have to look back over your shoulder. This must be practised, as it takes some getting used to.

If you have to follow up through the midday period, you will have to slow down and be more careful, which is more tiring. Ideally your commander will use several trackers and rotate them at point duty.

You may be able to gain some lighting advantage by using your torch. A torch is also the best answer when you are tracking in woodland where the light conditions can be very confusing, especially under dappled shadowing.

Night tracking

Night tracking is not always possible; it depends on the local ground conditions. Because you will be using artificial light you can precisely control the light angle. Wherever possible try to position your light source low and with the track between yourself and the light. A torch with a variable focus beam can be an advantage. If you are using vehicles on dirt roads fit them with tracking lights, set to point sideways creating constant lighting.

Night tracking should play an important part in your training programme as it helps to reinforce your use of light and enhances your ability to notice sign. Study clear prints as well as faint sign and experiment with the light angle and beam focus until you feel you have the correct combination.

At night your ability is severely handicapped by the change of colours to monochrome. In tactical situations follow-ups usually only continue at night when a life is at risk or if there is a high probability of changing weather conditions obliterating the available sign.

Tracking on a slope

Many novice trackers fail to notice that the ground conditions are changing from flat to slope because they are too wrapped up in the sign: even the very gentlest slope will dramatically affect the lighting conditions, sometimes favourably, sometimes not. There is little you can do except to be aware of the situation.

Moisture

Moisture can often make tracking easy. Dew that collects on surfaces, particularly plant foliage, will normally reflect light well. Places where a target has stepped will usually show as dark patches if he flattened down the vegetation before the dew settled, because the light will reflect off these patches at a different angle from the surrounding vegetation. However, if he passed by after the dew settled it will have been wiped off the vegetation.

On hard, flat surfaces such as rock, moisture can reveal the prints of the target as light patches. The dust on the surface will darken with moisture, but he will have removed dust by treading and so the moisture will not collect so easily.

Remember, don't just watch the ground. Sign can be left by any part of the body: for instance moisture missing on a shrub may give you accurate indication of the target's height.

Tracking by feel

You will usually be tracking by sight, but you may find yourself in situations when a track cannot be seen – although this does not mean that it can't be detected.

A track in short grass is an example. When a foot treads on grass, the grass is flattened and sometimes broken, bruised or torn. Greater damage is caused when the target is travelling at speed or under a load. If not too badly damaged, the grass slowly recovers to stand upright again. The time it takes for the grass to untangle itself and recover will depend on the local weather conditions and the variety of grass. It does not usually take long for the track to become invisible to the eye, but some blades of grass will remain depressed.

By very light and careful probing with the tips of your two little fingers you will be able to detect these blades of grass by a resistance to your probing. Compare this with the surrounding area. With care, you should be able to discern the overall shape.

Other signs

Do not make the mistake of looking only at the ground. Search also for other signs such as bruised vegetation, scuffed roots, broken cobwebs, pebbles turned to expose their darker, damp underside, and the smallest of details such as grains of sand deposited on large pebbles by the target's boot.

To become a successful tracker you must pay attention to all of these factors all of the time. These signs combine with the tracks to fill in the missing details in the mental picture you are building of your target. In a tactical situation, your life and those of your team may depend on you noticing a few grains of sand.

Improving your tracking skills

1 Find a piece of bare earth or sand, smooth it over and make a set of tracks inside it; do not make the tracks too obvious. By packing the ground hard you should be able to achieve a very fine impression. Make a careful study of the impression at different times of the day, mid-morning, mid-day,

mid-afternoon, dawn and dusk. Observe the track from the shadow side, the sun side, and with the sun to your side. Make drawings of the track under all of these circumstances, being careful to draw only what you can see.

2   With the same track impressions experiment with your torch. Draw what you can see with the torch between yourself and the track, with the track between you and the torch and with the torch illuminating from the side. Position the torch to point along the ground and also down onto the ground at about 30°. Finally, draw what can be seen with the torch directly above the track, with both hard and soft focus.

3   Armed with your tracking stick, tape measure, notebook and torch, follow the trail paying careful attention to the light. Ask a team mate to stop you randomly to check that you are correctly positioned in relationship to the light. In bad shadows or under a forest canopy, experiment in improving the light with your torch.

4   With a team mate, study a track; firstly while standing, secondly while squatting down and thirdly when on all fours and your head next to the ground. In each case, record the details you observe.

5   Follow an animal trail with your team mate. Try at first to find 10 tracks, then 20 and so on up to 100. When you are able to do this, repeat all these exercises in different conditions (remember, the more challenging the terrain, the more you will be learning).

Tracking involves more than just following a string of clues. You must constantly update and enhance your mental picture of the target until you can begin to predict his next move. This skill needs great concentration and attention to detail and comes only with many hundreds of hour's practice.

If you have been practising the techniques already shown you should now be following simple trails with some success. But there will still be questions: how old is the sign, how do I know the target wasn't walking backwards or with his shoes tied on back to front?

To answer any such questions when you are learning to track, you must return to ideal conditions. In your mind, build a picture of how the target you are following makes tracks under many varied circumstances. You can then adapt this to the more difficult conditions you face 90 per cent of the time. You will also need to experiment with the different soil and vegetation types in your locality to understand how they register the impression of a foot, and how they weather under different climatic conditions.

Reading a clear print

By now you know that clear prints are not the norm but occur sporadically along the trail, in places where the ground will accept a clear impression. These areas are know by trackers as 'tack traps', and can be either natural track traps such as puddles and cow pats or man-made track traps; deliberately prepared patches of ground where the target or enemy troops have to pass or are likely to pass. Such ideal spots often contain a wealth of information, so get into the habit of using them.

The following are major features that you will need to be aware of. To practise reading these signs set your self some problems under ideal conditions.

1   *Lines of force*
    These show as ripples or fracture lines within the track. They radiate from the major point of contact in exactly the opposite direction to the direction of movement. The faster the target is travelling, the more force produced, the greater the lines of force, and the further back they occur. When a target is moving very fast, sprinting for example, the whole track impression can be thrown backwards, very often breaking up. Pay careful attention to these lines for both speed and direction.

2   *Soil scatter*
    Soil is sometimes thrown out of tracks by being kicked or picked up by the foot. It is usually to be seen in front of the track, in line with the direction of travel. This is especially true of tracks in snow.

3   Risings

These are where the ground has risen outside the track in response to pressure generated within the track. They are caused by forces in a downward and horizontal direction – often sudden braking and acceleration.

4   Deep impressions

These indicate where the target has placed its whole weight within the track. Each represents a separate movement. By carrying out a comparison with your own tracks you will be able to determine whether or not the target is carrying a load. If so, and you are following the track for any length of time, you should expect to see the 'put down markers' of bergens or rifles.

There are many more signs to learn, such as twists and slides, but these are best learned by field practice. If the target decides to employ counter tacking procedures, it is your attention to fine details that will win the day. When a target tries something devious most trackers sense that something is wrong, and then test their hunch by studying the fine nuances in the track.

Make plaster casts

To develop this sense for detail make plaster casts of tracks: this will teach you to notice the finest sign. As an experiment ask a team mate to lay some clear tracks, imagining he has come to a path junction, and briefly cannot decide which path to take, before finally choosing one. Then carefully study the tracks. You should be able to detect the indecisions as a series of fine lines around walls of the relevant tracks.

Is he walking backwards?

One of the commonest problems a tracker faces is how to tell if the target is walking backwards or has tied his shoes on back to front. The simple answer here is that a tracker does not determine the direction of travel by the direction in which the tracks are pointing; instead he reads the sign within the track to determine the direction. *Regardless of which way the prints point,* the direction of travel must be directly opposite to the lines of force; and this is usually corroborated by a soil scatter.

Has he changed his shoes?

This is very difficult. Unless you find the signs of where the target changed his shoes, all you can do is to refer to your careful measurements of his stride and your appreciation of how he walks. If he tries to alter his gait, you may be able to detect this as an unnaturalness in the overall appearance of the trail, although this can be very difficult to determine.

If the target discovers that he is being trailed, he may take evasive action such as walking down roads, rock hopping or walking down the course of a stream. This should not pose too great a problem; cut for sign along both sides of the obstacle and beware of possible ambush.

Ageing

Determining the age of a set of tracks is a skill which is often neglected even by good trackers. With practice and dedication you should be able to determine the age of a fresh track to within 15 minutes.

Tracks can last for years under the right circumstances. There are parts of the world where dinosaur tracks can be seen, perfectly preserved by fossilisation. But in general terms, a track begins to deteriorate as soon as it has been formed. The wind and other climatic factors gradually cause the prominent features to collapse until no fine details remains; in fact, a track with very defined features, such as a heavily-soled boot will collapse and disappear faster than the track of a smooth-soled shoe.

Tracks with well defined features always appear to be fresher than smooth tracks. Make an impression with your thumb in the ground alongside the track so that you can see how the soil behaves.

Each soil type behaves in its own individual way, so you will need to experiment with the local soil before 'following up' a trail. Also some soils can give a false impression of the size of the track; for example tracks appear larger than life in sand and smaller than life in heavy clay.

Practice

Putting all this information together is actually much easier than it appears. The secret is constant practice; once you have used and learned a technique, you will never forget it.

The next stage in your training programme is to go back to the beginning and practise the skills we have shown you again, but paying much greater attention to detail and constantly estimating the tracks' age.

Successful tracking

It is not enough just to follow the clues left behind by the target. You must interpret those signs to gain an understanding of the target's movements so that you can predict his movements or his aim.

If the target is expecting to be tracked, he may be planning to ambush you of lay a booby trap. Only your tracking skill can help you here. Caution, careful interpretation and a steady tracking pace are your allies; tiredness, carelessly taking signs at face value and undue haste along the trail can be fatal enemies.

As you follow the trail, pay attention to all types of sign, not just the tracks. Stop to look around and listen every few paces; trackers are frequently shot because they spend too long looking at the ground! By looking up and studying the direction in which the target is moving you will gain a better appreciation of why the tracks are being made they way they are.

Try to pay equal attention to the ground on each side of the trail; you may detect sign that indicates the target is aware of your presence. Suspect everything. If you come across evidence such as dropped or discarded equipment, treat it as a probable booby trap.

Try to avoid destroying the 'sign' you have just followed, and never pass beyond a sign until you can see the next sign. If you cannot find the next track, pay careful attention to the last visible sign; the lines of force should indicate where a track lies. Use your tracking stick to help you, and make sure that the track has not been obliterated because of freak conditions. If you still cannot find the next sign check left or right of the trail. If that doesn't work, read the pattern of the last few tracks; do they indicate any change in pace or direction?

The last resort before 'cutting ahead' is to check near and far from the last sign. If you are using a tracking stick and are positioned to make the best use of available light, you will not often lose the trail. Remember the key to successful tracking is practice.

COMBAT TRACKING

The rotor blades clatter above imposing an unnatural silence on your team mates and giving you the chance for mental preparation. As tracker, the success or failure of the operation will be on your shoulders. You think through the devious ploys you have encountered and remember the many mistakes you made in training.

After what seems like an eternity the chopper banks. The side door slides back, revealing the perfect tracking light of dawn.

The 'point of last contact'

On arrival at the PLC you will be under pressure to begin the follow-up immediately. But without the correct preparation this can prove disastrous. If the track is 'very hot' (fresh), it may be feasible to follow up straight away; if there are several tracking teams: while one team follows up, the other teams can gather the relevant intelligence. But solo tracking without preparation is suicidal: do so only under what you judge to be exceptional circumstances.

Basic pre-follow up preparations

Time spent gathering information is never wasted. But remember that the weather will not wait for you; it is already smoothing away the 'sign'.

1   *Secure the vicinity of PLC*
    The greatest technical problem you are likely to face is finding the trail. Normally by the time you arrive, the area has been flattened by the feet of 'friendly forces'! As soon as you get there the PLC area and its surroundings should be made off-limits to all but the trackers and their cover groups.

2 *Set up an operational HQ*
Commanders using tracking teams should establish a forward support HQ near the area of operation to reduce transportation delays. Apart from normal military considerations the HQ must provide the following tracker support:
- Radio communications.
- Transportation, capable of inserting tracker teams, ahead of the target, ideally helicopters.
- Photocopiers or Polaroid cameras, to distribute photos or drawings of target tracks.

3 Gather intelligence
The usual difficulty is not in finding sign, but in distinguishing your target's sign from normal disturbances. Even in remote areas paths are used regularly by the local popula-

---

ASKING QUESTIONS

You can gain valuable information about your target from the locals and from your own troops. Here are some useful questions to help you build up a picture of the enemy.

1 Who were they?
2 What were they wearing?
3 What unit did they belong to?
4 How did they look?
5 Where they armed? If so what with?
6 What have the local weather conditions been like since they were seen?
7 What were they doing when you saw them?
8 Where might they have been going?
9 What was their average size?
10 What sex were they?
11 How tall were they?
12 How heavy were they?
13 What sort of build were they?
14 What was their hair colour/length/type?
15 Where were they last seen?

tion. The more you know about the target, the easier this task will be.

Develop close liaison with the Intelligence Officer. He will be able to give you valuable information, such as what the enemy ration wrappers look like, what footwear they use, and so on. When the operation is over you will hold a debrief to enhance the picture of the enemy.

The IO's information is invaluable, but more up to date information can be obtained by interviewing the troops or civilians who have had the most recent contact with the target(s).

Take care: if you ask a leading questions you run the risk of influencing the subject's reply. If you ask a village about jungle terrorists, for example, you should ask: 'What was their footwear?' You are likely to receive an accurate answer ranging from 'none' to 'jungle boots'. But if you ask 'What boots were they wearing?' you are influencing the answer, and if they cannot remember you may even fool yourself into believing they *are* wearing boots.

The fast 'follow up'

As soon as possible, organize a search for the trail. If you are the only tracker, you will have to follow the trail faster than it was made. Most teams begin by dividing the tasks: one or two teams may cut for sign in a circle around the PLC while others might cut along the edges of paths, roads or rivers in the area.

Once the trail has been found, the clock really begins to tick. With the general direction of the target's movement identified, the search teams can concentrate their effort in a narrow corridor. The team that has the trail 'tapes' their start point and begins following up.

Meanwhile, the other teams begin to cut across the search corridor some distance ahead of the follow-up team. If one of these teams discovers the trail they begin follow-up, and the first follow-up team leap-frogs past them to 'cut-ahead'. In this way the distance between trackers and target is reduced very rapidly.

Live tracking

As you round the bend in the track something catches your eye; there is some darkness around the base of a rock, perhaps showing that it has been moved. Carefully examining the surrounding area, you find the trail. There is no room for mistakes now. First of all, radio in your position and the details of the trail as you see it, number the targets, speed of travel, etc. HQ will be able to tell you whether your information corresponds to previous info. It may be that the enemy group has split up or joined a larger force.

Next mark the trail using coloured tape so that another tracker team will know the trail has been discovered, or so that you can easily resume tracking the next day.

Estimate the age of the trail and keep an eye on this factor; it will enable you to judge whether or not you are gaining ground. Your life may well hang on this thin thread of data.

From now on you must be alert to all that is going on around you. Make sure the cover group understand that they are your eyes and ears while you are concentrating on the trail. Be as silent as possible, use hand signals to communicate and at all costs keep the radio from bursting out or crackling. Tracking is tiring, so it's not a bad idea to take a rest every 10 minutes or better still, rotate point duty with another tracker.

As you close the distance, make sure to keep your cover group informed, otherwise they may not be alert, which will put all your lives at risk. Tracking is like reeling in a fish: you have to be careful not to move too fast. Gradually close in on the target until you establish visual contact (binoculars can be useful here), and radio in their exact location. It is here that your task will normally end, with the deployment of a fire force.

When the operation is over there will be a debrief. You may be able to shed some light on the enemy's SOP, and the tracking team will hopefully be allowed some rest. Expect no glory for tracking!

SURVIVAL

Shelter

Finding shelter from sun in the desert, or from the freezing cold of the Arctic, is even more important in such places than looking for food or water. Exposure to extremes of heat or cold can kill you in hours, and not just in exotic latitudes.

Even 'soft' climates like that of the south of England can be deadly on a bad winter's night. You'll discover in this section how to protect yourself from extreme conditions, and how to make yourself comfortable and secure in more friendly environments too.

Choosing a shelter site

You must start to look for somewhere to hide or spend the night at least two hours before it gets dark. This will give you time to find the spot, clear away enough undergrowth or rocks to make a sleeping area, and time to get the material together to make your shelter as well.

There's one more thing you may have to look for in a survival site: protection from enemy forces. Where this is important you have to consider these factors:

1 Concealment from the enemy
2 Camouflaged escape routes
3 Ability to signal to friendly forces

And don't forget ordinary things like protection from the elements, insects, rock falls, and wild animals.

A survivor will always look out for certain types of ground, and avoid them by instinct. Flash floods can be upon you in seconds as a result of heavy rain falling miles away. So you must avoid apparently dry gullies in and around the foothills of a mountain range. Avalanches and landslides don't give you a lot of warning, either, so if you're forced to sleep in country that might produce either one, make sure your shelter site will give you protection from anything that might come down from above.

Be wary of river banks, in case the water level rises suddenly. The same applies to the sea shore; make certain you're above the high water mark.

The season of the year has to be considered, too. In winter, you need protection from winds coming out of the north, and a source of fuel for your fire; in the summer, what you need most is a water supply and protection from biting, stinging insects. The ideal shelter in one season might be a completely different spot at another time of year.

Types of shelter

The type of shelter you'll build depends very much on the kind of material you have available. If you have a poncho, a ground-sheet or a parachute, or even a plain sheet of plastic, you're at a very big advantage.

In general, don't make shelters bigger than you need to. This is especially important in winter. A one-man parachute tent, for instance, can be kept just about bearable by the heat from a single candle. If you use it in a snow-fall, though, you'll have to keep the weight of snow off it constantly, so that it doesn't all cave in on top of you. The smaller your shelter, the easier this job will be.

The simplest form of shelter is a lean-to made from a poncho, a length of rope and two trees. First of all, make sure that the back of the lean-to will be into the wind. Tie support ropes to two corners of one of the long sides of the poncho. Tie off the neck opening. Secure the two support ropes to two trees at about waist height (lower if concealment is important), and peg out the free side with three short sticks. If there are no trees around, you'll have to cut poles to use instead.

'Bivvy' shelter

A poncho can be used to make a two-man shelter known to British soldiers as a 'bivvy'. In a wooded area, lay the poncho out on the ground to ensure that you have enough room, then clear the ground area of cones, roots, stones etc. Attach the poncho to four trees by its corners and make sure that it is stretched taut.

In a tactical situation it should be no more than 50 cm (20 in) above the ground. Tie the hood off and tie it to a branch to raise the centre of the poncho so that the rain can run off.

MAKING A PONCHO SHELTER

If you are in an unfamiliar environment, begin looking for your shelter site at least two hours before sunset. It is important to know how to construct a variety of different shelters so that you can use whatever is to hand.

Improvised lean-to

Making the maximum use of available cover, this lean-to is built against a wall on a simple framework of branches.

Poncho lean-to

A poncho tied between two trees makes a quick and easy shelter. Tie a short (10 cm) stick to each rope, about 1 cm from the poncho: this will stop rain water running down the rope into the shelter.

Poncho tent

This is lower than a lean-to and gives protection from the weather on both sides. On the other hand, it has less space and restricts your field of view.

Low silhouette shelter

Positioned no more than 50 cm above the ground, a poncho can make a good shelter. The diagram shows a one-man shelter made with a parachute and three logs.

In a desolate area where there are no trees, lay the poncho on the ground and, using it as a template, trace out its outline. De-turf the area 15 cm (6 in) or so inside the cut line, and build a low turf wall around the shape of the poncho, leaving one end open. This will be the entrance to the poncho/tent and should be posititoned facing the direction of any enemy threat.

Place one 60-cm (2 ft) tent pole at each end and peg down the corners and sides to make the poncho into a tent. The sides should overlap the layer of turfs and the poncho is again pulled taut and the hood tied off. Do not rest anything against the poncho or it will let in the rain.

If you have a parachute, you can make a very spacious teepee-type tent by lashing three poles – between three and four metres (10 to 12 ft) long – together into a tripod, and then spreading the material over this frame. Extra poles will give more support, but you can just lean these against the first three; there's no need to lash them.

You can tie the top of the parachute to the branch of a tree, and then keep the lower edge spread out with pegs. This type of tent doesn't work well if you need to conceal yourself – it's height and sharp lines make it very easy to see.

Even if you're on the move all the time, you can still use your parachute to make a rough and ready shelter. Fold the canopy into a triangle and run a line, something over head height, from a tree to the ground, five or six metres (17 ft) away. Drape the parachute over the line and peg out the sides.

If you have a little more time, cut a pole about five metres long and use that instead of rope to make the ridge. Cut two shorter poles and use these instead of pegs to keep the sides out. Tuck the canopy sides around the side poles until the fabric is taut, and then use the extra fabric as a groundsheet. Wedge another pole between the two lower ones to keep the mouth of the bivouac open.

The Basha

If you have no man-made materials, you can still make a very effective shelter, a basha, although it will take a great deal longer. Don't to too ambitious to start with. Just make a simple lean-to at first; you can always make another side to it later on, if you don't have to keep on the move.

Find two trees that are close together and face in the right direction – the line between them should be at right angles to the prevailing wind. Cut a straight pole, about $2^1/2$ cm (1 in) in diameter, and long enough for you to lash to the two trees, one or two metres off the ground. Cut six or eight three-metre poles and lean them against the first one. Weave saplings, vines and twigs through and around the sloping poles. Then cover these with leaves, grass, pine needles or anything else that's to hand, starting at the bottom and working up. Put more of this same material inside to make your bed. A similar basha can be built by supporting the end of the ridge-pole on an A frame, the other being driven into a bank or hillside.

One advantage of the lean-to made from local materials is that it blends in with its surroundings, and so is far more difficult to detect than one made from a poncho.

Shelter can mean more than just a roof over your head. In swampy or marshy country, for instance, it will be just as important to build a sleeping platform that is well off the ground, so that you can stay dry. Remember that a bed like this will have to bear all your weight. There's no point in trying to make one unless you have really substantial poles available.

Instead of building a platform, you can make a simple hammock out of a poncho, groundsheet or parachute canopy. Trees make better supports than poles that you have to drive into the ground.

Natural shelters

Often, you'll find it easier and more rewarding to spend time looking for a natural shelter rather than in building one of your own. Look for caves, crevices, rocks on the side of hills away from the wind, fallen trees and large trees with low-handging branches.

There are some places best avoided. Stay away from low ground if you can: these areas get cold and damp at night. Thick, undergrowth is often infested with insects; check for snakes, scorpions, spiders and other pests. And wherever you settle, make sure there's nothing loose about that could fall on you in a storm.

No matter where you find yourself, remember that the effect on your morale of having a place to 'come home to', even if it's only a lean-to made out of brush wood, could mean the difference between life and death. Your will to live is what will really keep you alive, and anything that strengthens it is in your favour.

Making Fire

Fire can be your best friend. It keeps you warm and dries your clothes; it cooks your food and purifies your water. But it can be your worst enemy, too. In enemy-held territory it can give away your position quicker than anything else. And a major burn is a dreadful wound, causing massive fluid loss and leaving you open to infection.

Fuel, heat and oxygen

You have to bring three things together to make fire – fuel, heat and oxygen. Take away any one of these, and the fire goes out. About a fifth of all the air around us is oxygen. All you have to do is make sure that there is free passage of air around – and especially up through – the fire.

Heat – the heat to start the fire – you have to provide. Friction in one form or another is the usual way, but you can use the rays of the sun, and perhaps even electricity, in its place.

Different forms of fuel

You have to provide fuel in three quite different forms – tinder, to catch the spark; kindling, to set the flame; and the fuel itself, to keep the fire going.

Most fuel will not burn when it's wet. The water surrounds it and cuts off the air supply. Non-porous fuels like coal will burn when they are wet, however, and liquid fuels like oil, kerosene and petrol are completely unaffected by water.

But in most parts of the world it's wood and vegetable matter that you'll be burning, and this you must keep dry. Gathering and storing fuel for the fire is a very good example of how forward thinking pays dividends. But there is always something you can do to make a fire, even if you're shivering to death in a freezing rainstorm and the matches are soaked through.

Look for:

1 A sheltered place to build a fire
2 Old, dead wood
3 Kindling
4 Tinder

Take these tasks one at a time. Look for a rock overhang on the lee side of a hill or outcrop; or a low fallen branch, or a fallen tree. At this stage you're looking for protection for the fire, not shelter for yourself.

Gathering fuel

Dead wood, as long as it's not actually lying in water, will usually have some dry material in it somewhere, but the best sources are dead timber that's still standing, and dead branches that are still attached to the tree. Look for the bark peeling off.

The main difference between kindling and proper fuel is its size. Remember, the kindling takes up the sparks and glowing embers from the tinder and turns it into flames that will ignite the fuel.

Small, bone-dry twigs are the best, but if necessary you can make 'fire-sticks' by shaving larger pieces of shallow cuts to feather them. This is a job much better done in advance.

Tinder must be dry. Absolutely, perfectly dry. You should have some already, packed up securely in a water-tight box next to your skin. If not, you'll have to find some.

Don't look too far to start with: you won't need very much. Try the lining of your pockets and the seams of your clothes. The lint that collects there makes good tinder, except for wool. Dry bark, shredded into tiny pieces; dread grass, fern and moss; dead pine needles; downy seedheads from thistles and smaller plants: all these make good tinder, as long as the material is dry.

The common factor is the size of the individual pieces or fibres. They must be tiny, so that as much of their substance as possible is exposed to the air and to the spark or flame.

The vital spark

If you don't have matches or a lighter that works, there are several alternative ways to start a fire. If you have direct sunlight and a magnifying lens, you can use the glass to focus the sun rays on to the tinder and start it burning that way. But this won't work at night in a rainstorm!

Alternatively, you could use the 'flint and steel' method.

If you have a so-called 'metal match' (a metal strip with tiny flint chips embedded in it), then use that, scraping your knife blade along it to produce a shower of sparks.

Or look for a piece of flint or other very hard stone. Then you can use your knife to strike sparks off it; use the back of the blade. If you have a piece of hacksaw blade, you should use that to save damaging your knife.

Alternative technology

There are two other ways of making fire. The bow and drill and the fire saw both rely on friction between two pieces of wood. You have to make a small part of one of those pieces hot enough to set the tinder going. It is possible – but you'll only need to try it once to become fanatical about carrying matches with you everywhere you go!

Fire Bow

Making a fire from the friction of wood upon wood really is a last-ditch alternative. The few aboriginal tribes that still make fire this way spend a very long time selecting exactly the right materials. Nevertheless, in the desert, where it's perfectly dry, it is possible to start a fire in this way.

You'll need:
1 A piece of green hardwood, about a metre (3 ft) long and $2^1/2$ cm (1 in) in diameter.
2 A piece of dry hardwood, 30 cm long and 1 cm in diameter.
3 A 5 cm hardwood cube, or a shell or a suitable stone.
4 A piece of dry softwood, $2^1/2$ cm thick.
5 A cord for the bow-string.

To make the fire bow:
1 Make the bow loosely using the cord and the long piece of hardwood.
2 Round off one end of the short piece of hardwood, and taper the other slightly.

3   Carve out the centre of the hardwood cube to fit the taper, or find a stone or shell of the right shape.

4   Make a depression in the softwood, close to one edge, and make a groove from it that leads to the edge.

5   Put some tinder next to the end of the groove.

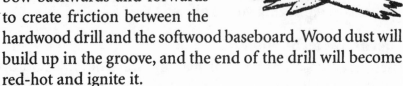

6   Loop the bow-string round the drill, maintain pressure on the top with the cap, and work the bow backwards and forwards to create friction between the hardwood drill and the softwood baseboard. Wood dust will build up in the groove, and the end of the drill will become red-hot and ignite it.

Fire Saw

You'll need:

1   A piece of bamboo, 5-8 cm in diameter and $\frac{1}{2}$ metre long.

2   A forked stick, to anchor it into the ground.

To make the fire saw:

1   Split the bamboo length ways.

2   Cut two notches in a straight line across the two exposed edges near to one end.

3   Brace the notched bamboo with the forked stick.

4   Fill the space between the notches with a handful of tinder.

5   Saw in the notches until the tinder ignites.

Fire Tongs

1   Make a thong (a strip or string of tough material) using rattan (a sort of tropical vine), leather or very tough cord.

2 Split a dry stick and hold the split open with a small wedge.

3 Run the thong through the split.

4 Place a small wad of tinder in the split.

5 Secure the stick with your foot and run the thong back and forth to create frictional heat. The tinder will eventually ignite.

Vehicle fuel

If you have a vehicle you have another option – use the battery. Rip out some wire and attach a piece to each terminal. Touch the bare ends together and you'll get a spark.

If the vehicle is petrol (gasoline) driven, you can use a tiny amount of the fuel to help the process along, but remember that petrol in its liquid form doesn't burn. You can only set fire to it as a vapour. So, use less than a teaspoonful, soak some rag and make it spark in the air just above the surface. Diesel fuel doesn't work in this way – you need a good size flame to set it alight at all.

Hints for the Firemaker

When you're making a fire under difficult conditions, you must start small and add to it very carefully. If you've been unable to find a site sheltered from the wind, then you must make a windbreak, although it may be simpler to dig a sloping trench and light the fire inside that.

If the ground is very wet, use stones as a base, but make sure that they're not porous. Wet, porous stones can explode: that will not only injure you, but also blow the fire all over the place.

Don't worry about making an elaborate fireplace at this stage. Get the fire alight first.

Make a nest of dry grass and the smallest twigs. If you can

Laying a fire

THE LOG CABIN PILE

This is a very good way of laying a fire. Plenty of air can circulate and it will not collapse until it's well away.

find a dry bird's or mouse's nest, so much the better. It will have down and fur mixed in with the grass, and probably some dry droppings too – all of them excellent tinder.

Put your tinder inside. Arrange dry kindling over it in the shape of a cone, or make a lean-to by pushing a green stick into the ground at an angle of about 30 degrees and build up the kindling along it to make a sort of tent.

Make sure that you've got all the materials you need to hand before attempting to light the fire – you may only get one chance, and at the beginning you'll have to work quickly, adding small amounts of kindling as the fire grows.

Keep the fire going

If you have a choice of different types of wood to use as fuel, use softwood – pine and spruce, for example – as the first load of fuel, but be careful of sparks. These woods contain resin and burn quickly. To keep the fire going, use hardwood such as oak or beech. They're much longer lasting.

You can use a mixture of green and dry wood to keep the fire going through the night, but don't just dump wood on it without thinking. Make sure that you keep a good stock of fuel close at hand, and arrange it so that the heat from the fire will help to dry the fuel out. Keep kindling at hand, too, so that you can revive the fire quickly if it looks like dying out.

Improving the fire

How you improve the fire site depends on what you're going to

The hobo stove

use it for. A fire that you use for smoking food, for instance, isn't much use for anything else. Its purpose is to produce lots of smoke inside an enclosure. You won't be able to cook on it, and it won't give out much warmth.

You can cook on an open fire, but it's not very efficient: it's better to construct a stove of some sort. The simplest stove needs something like a five-gallon oil drum. Punch poles in one end and in a ring all around the side at the same end. Cut out a panel about two inches above that ring of holes. Punch a large hole in one side of the drum near the other end, to let the smoke out. Place the stove on a ring of stones to allow the air to circulate from underneath.

Now you can transfer some of your fire into the stove, stoke it through the cut-out panel and cook on top. It'll give off enough heat to keep you warm, too, and has the very positive benefit of not showing sparks and flames like an open fire does.

The fire pit
You can achieve much the same effect by digging a circular pit, and then another smaller one, slantwise, that meets it at the

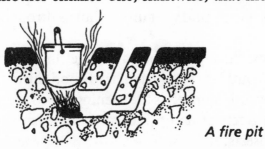

A fire pit

bottom. The slanting hole is for the air to circulate up through the fire, so dig it on the side of the prevailing wind.

If you dig it close to the trunk of a tree, the smoke will go up into the foliage and be dispersed, helping to disguise your position.

Reflectors and windbreaks

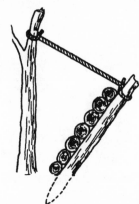

You can make a fire more effective as a source of warmth of building a firewall across one or two sides, to reflect the heat back towards you.

The simplest way is to drive four green-wood stakes into the ground in two pairs, three or four inches apart, with three or four feet between them. Fill up the space with trimmed branches and trunks, but don't bind them together. That way you get a firewall and a stack of dry wood all in one!

Poor conditions

You may have to build your fire in the wet – on snow, or in a swamp, for example. In the snow it's easiest to build a base out of layers of green wood. In swamp or marshland, raise that platform up on four legs.

Don't bother to chop or even break up long pieces of wood for an open fire. Start at one end and feed the log in as it burns, or lay it cross the fire and wait until it burns through, then turn the ends in.

Having gone through all the pain of getting your fire going, don't let it go out! Use well-dried hardwood during the day; it produces very little smoke. As the evening approaches, you may want to add green or damp fuel to produce smoke that will drive away insects.

A SIMPLE CRANE

Use a green-wood pole with a forked notch to hold a container over a fire. Beware of large, naked flames: a burning pole will wreck your meal.

Alternative fuels

If you have a vehicle, almost every part of it that isn't metal will burn. Mix oil, petrol or diesel with sand in a pit and set fire to it. Rip out the upholstery and the trim and use for fuel.

The tyres will burn if you get them hot enough, but stay up-wind of the smoke! Hydraulic fluid from the brake and clutch systems is highly flammable, and so is neat anti-freeze. All of this applies to aircraft as much as ground vehicles.

Animal droppings, if they are perfectly dry, are a very good source of fuel: easy to light, slow-burning and almost smoke-less.

After a while, looking after your fire will become second nature to you. You'll sense changes in its mood, and be able to change its character to do different jobs.

Water

Water is a basic human need. There is no adequate substitute, and without it you cannot live more than a few days. Within the human body water acts as a stabilizer; it helps to maintain warmth in cold environments, and is vital for staying cool in hot environments. It is also part of the body's mechanism for distributing food and removing waste. As soon as you are cut off from a source of fresh water, you begin to dehydrate.

The rate at which you dehydrate depends on a number of factors: the amount of water your body already contains, the clothing you are wearing, the local temperature, how hard you are working, whether you are in shade, or sunlight, whether you are smoking and whether you are calm or nervous.

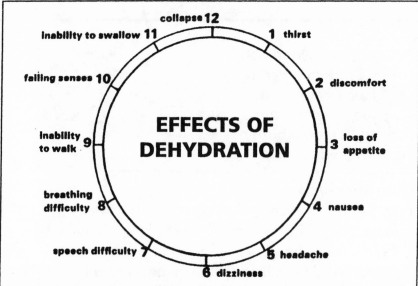

You will collapse after losing 12 per cent of your body weight; the diagram shows the progressive symptoms. Heat exhaustion is still a killer on exercises in the UK as well as abroad. You must be able to recognize the signs in your mates; it doesn't have to be a hot day to kill them. If all the danger signs are ignored, sweating will eventually stop and the victim will collapse.

If you allow dehydration to continue, there will come a point when you can no longer search for water. Your first priority is to minimize further dehydration and, having done this, you must find water. (If you are stranded in a desert with little chance of finding water, stay still to prevent further dehydration, and make efforts to signal for rescue.)

Points for survival

1 Avoid eating until you have secured a source of safe water.
2 Do not ration your water; drink as much as you can when you can.
3 Urine is a good indicator of dehydration. The darker its colour, the more dehydrated you are.
4 Bacteria multiples faster in warm water, so water gathered early in the morning, at its coolest, is safer.
5 To reduce dehydration:
   • Find shade

- Move slowly and do not smoke
- Cover exposed skin to prevent evaporation of sweat
- Suck a pebble (helps prevent exhalation of moisture through the mouth)

Finding water

You do not have to be in a desert to have difficulty finding water. Forests often offer such poor visibility that, although surrounding by water-loving trees, you cannot spot readily-available surface water. (In combat conditions, however, you may have to deliberately avoid obvious sources of water, for fear of ambush.)

So how do you go about finding water? The first thing you do is to remember the following points:

1 Water runs downhill, so make for lower country.

2 Where there is water, there is usually an abundance of lush vegetation. If possible, learn to recognize the moisture-loving plants in the area. If this vegetation is wilted or dead, it probably indicates chemical pollution.

3 Animals need water too. Observe the habits of the local wild-life; it may lead you to a source of water.

4 Grain- and seed-eating birds need water, so observe them too.

5 Listen for frogs croaking: they live in water.

6 Cliffs often have seepages of water at their base, so look care-fully.

Sources of water (assuming no equipment)

Familiarize yourself with the various sources of water and their relative merits.

1 Dew

Dew is one of the most reliable sources of water for the survivor. It can be collected soon after it has started to form until it evaporates in the morning sunlight. Improvize a mop from an absorbent article of clothing. Drag this through long grass or use it to wipe the condensed moisture from shrubs and rocks. If you do not have a convenient mop, finely teased, non-poisonous inner barks or grasses can be used. When the mop is saturated, wring out the water into a container. Although labour-intensive, this is a very effective way to collect water.

Dew itself is a pure source of water, but when you wipe it off vegetation and rocks you also wipe off bacteria and perhaps parasites. It is therefore best to boil this water before consumption.

2 Rain and snow

Rainwater is usually the safest source of water in the wilderness. If it rains, make sure you gather as much as you can. But remember the water is only as pure as your method of collection: if you are in doubt, boil it before consumption. Snow, if it is clean, is probably pure. The major problem with snow is melting it: a time-consuming and labour-intensive process, as you require eight to ten containers of snow to produce one container of water.

3 Ice

Ice is not pure and should always be boiled before consumption, but is far more economical as a source of water than snow. Icicles are often found hanging from trees and rocks, so may provide you with a ready source of water. Those hanging from trees may be slightly stained brown by the tannin in the bark, but unless they are very heavily stained they will be safe to drink after boiling.

4 Puddles and hidden water

Rain water is often trapped in depressions in rocks, called kettles, and in puddles. While it may smell foul and be stagnant, it only needs filtering and boiling to make it drinkable.

Rain water can also be found trapped in hollows in trees. Unfortunately, this is often so badly polluted with tannin that it is undrinkable. However, if you expect rain you can bale these hollows out and let them fill with fresh rain water; as long as you use the water before it too becomes tannin-stained, you have a handy water tank. Always boil this water before drinking it, and only use water found in non-poisonous trees.

5 Drinkable saps

For short-term relief of thirst, you may be able to tap the sap of certain trees. The sap of maple, birch and sycamore can be

INDIAN WELL

The Indian Well is an easily prepared and efficient method of collecting reasonably good water. Selection of the ground is all-important and the water produced requires filtering and boiling. Also, it takes some time to produce clear water, and quality is dependent on soil type. In practice, watch out for sources of contamination, boil very carefully, and add Steritabs.

1. Dig a hole about half a metre deep and half a metre wide. Water will begin to seep into the hole.
2. You can push a stick into the sides of the well to increase seepage of water into the well.
3. Bale out this water carefully so that you do not stir up the sediment at the bottom of the hole. Repeat this process until the seeping water is fairly clear.
4. After some time, the water at the top of the well will be clear enough to collect. Be careful not to disturb the muddy layer that usually lurks at the bottom.

tapped during the early spring (sycamore will produce sap from spring to autumn, depending on local conditions). Sap is thirst-quenching but it contains sugar, which if taken in sufficient quantity will hasten dehydration; in fact, the woodland Native American still boil maple and birch sap to produce sugar.

Only mature trees should be tapped, and the sap drunk while fresh, as it will ferment if stored. Some plants can also be used to provide water.

6 Springs and seepages

Springs are often regarded as fool-proof sources of drinking water, but unfortunately this is not true: spring water should always be boiled before drinking. Very often, springs are covered with soil and appear as patches of saturated ground supporting lush plant growth. To obtain water from these areas, dig an Indian Well.

7 Ponds

These are principally a feature of farmland, and are therefore a potential source of water for the evading soldier. Such water should always be considered suspect, as at the very least there will be fluke infestation. Keep contact with this water to a minimum, and if used as a source of drinking water, filter and thoroughly boil it before drinking.

8 Streams, rivers and lakes

Streams are often a tempting source of water, but care should be taken as they are very often polluted by decaying carcasses of animals that have drowned or become caught in boggy ground. In alpine regions, the clear ice-cold glacial meltwaters carry an invisible hazard: sediment – rock powder scoured from living rock by the awesome power of the glacier. If this is not filtered out, you may get digestive problems.

The further water travels from its source, the more pollutants it picks up. In an age where chemicals are an integral part of farming and land management, rivers and lakes should be avoided as sources of water.

Purifying Water

Now you've found a source of water. Is it safe to drink? The answer seems obvious – assume the water is dirty and purify it. but dehydration is causing you to be uncharacteristically impatient and irritable. You are tired, hungry, lonely and somewhat frightened. Your hands and shins are covered in the scratches you sustained searching what seemed like every patch of vegetation in the last 100 miles. And but for the incessant biting of the mosquitoes you would fall asleep.

You are faced with water that will need filtering and boiling before it is safe to drink, but you have no container and no fire. Surely one little sip won't hurt?

Without the support of modern medicine to fall back on, wilderness survival is all about maintaining good health. The human body is an amazing machine, but it is finely tuned: it only takes one drop of contaminated water to make you ill.

Of the many waterborne problems you may develop, the most common is diarrhoea. In a survival situation, diarrhoea may prove fatal. It causes dehydration and makes hygiene very difficult, increasing the risk of further unpleasant infections, and destroys the will to live.

To make your water safe, you will need three things:

1 Fire
2 A container
3 A filter

As a fire will also warm you, drive away the mosquitoes and boost your morale, it is usually best to start this first. Hopefully you will have practised your firelighting skill, as this is a bad time to learn!

Improvised water containers

Improvised water containers fall into three categories:

1 Kettles: containers that can be used directly over flames
2 Cauldrons: cannot be used directly over flames, but can be used for rock boiling
3 Storage: containers that should be solely used for carrying or storing safe water

Kettles

Kettles can be made from flammable materials because the water contained within them prevents their burning. The secret is not to allow the flames to reach beyond the water level.

1 Bamboo

In some tropical regions, bamboo can be found with stems large enough to be turned into kettles. Many other containers can also be improvised from bamboo, and sometimes fresh drinking water can be found trapped in the stems.

2 Birch or cherry bark

The woodland Native Americans routinely made kettles from birch bark while on their travels. Only the outer bark is used. It should be carefully removed from an unblemished section of

Cherry or birch
bark container

the trunk, and can be made pliable by either soaking or gentle warming by the fire. The brown inside of the bark is the most durable side, and is used to form the outside of containers, which are simply made by folding.

Cauldrons

Cauldrons are made from materials that will hold water but are not suitable for direct heating; put heated rocks into the water to boil it.

If your local soil is clay or clay-like enough to contain muddy water, a ground cauldron can be made. Dig a bowl-shaped depression in the ground and smooth the inside. Form a raised rim at the top, to help prevent humus falling into the cauldron.

Make the cauldron one third larger than the amount of water you intend to boil. This will allow for the water displaced by the heated rocks. To prevent sediment muddying your water, you will need to line the pit. For this you can use either some material (for example, a T-shirt) or large non-poisonous leaves such as dock or burdock. Take great care to ensure that the lining fits snugly.

The water purified in this type of cauldron will always be a little muddy, but if you leave it to settle you can skim clear water off of the top.

1 Rocks and trees

Water can often be found in depressions in rocks, and the hollows in trees, and these can be turned into ready-made cauldrons. Again, allow for the displacement of the heated rocks by choosing a depression large enough. If possible, it is best to scrape any slime out of these depressions prior to their use. This is especially important when using tree hollows. Remember, never rock boil in a poisonous tree.

2 Skin

If you are able to catch an animal of the size of a rabbit upwards, you will have secured meat as well as two containers good enough to stew it in: if you are careful with the skinning and gutting, both the skin and the stomach can be used as cauldrons.

To use the skin you can leave the fur on or take it off, as you please. To use the stomach it is best turned inside out. You have a choice when making your skin cauldron. You can line a pit with it, securing it around the rim by stakes, or you can suspend it from a tripod.

3 Wooden bowls

Bowls and containers can be carved out of wood. While not as quickly constructed as the previous methods, wooden bowls are well within the capabilities of a survivor. If carefully made, they are portable and very durable.

The best method of producing a wooden bowl is to 'burn and scrape'. To achieve this, make a small depression in the centre of your bowl-to-be and place a couple of glowing coals in this depression. By then blowing on the coals, ideally through a reed straw, you can use them to char the surrounding wood.

When you have charred a patch of wood, scrape it away using a sharp stone, and begin the process again. It does not take long to form a reasonable sized bowl.

Storage containers

The manufacture of storage containers is a long-term prospect. They can be made from the materials discussed above, and also from clay pottery and tightly-woven basketry.

Filtering

Having secured a container in which to boil your water, you now need a filter to remove the particles of dirt suspended in the water.

The simplest filter that can be improvised uses a pair of ordinary trousers. Simply turn them inside out, placing one leg inside the other, and tie the leg off at the bottom. Soak the material before use: this helps tighten the weave,

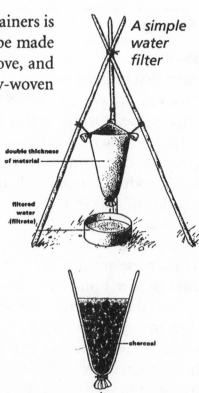

A simple water filter

double thickness of material

filtered water (filtrate)

charcoal

making the filter more efficient. Suspend the filter so that you can easily fill it, with the container positioned underneath to collect the clean water that drips out. Such filters can be improved by filling them with charcoal.

Rock boiling

Rock boiling is an easy and effective way to purify water. The rocks must be of a manageable size and weight, and thoroughly dry. (Rocks from stream beds and damp places contain moisture which, when heated, expands, causing the rock to explode. Also glass-like rocks such as flint and obsidian should be avoided.)

Heat the rocks in your fire, and when hot transfer them to your container with some improvised tongs. Tap off any ash before dropping them in the water.

Do not wait to use these skills until you have to. Practice is essential to success.

NB: When practising, only gather bark from dead trees.

Food

Plants

After two or three days without food, you will actually notice how you lack energy – and your morale will drop, your resistance to disease will diminish, and your hopes of making a quick getaway, if you have to, become mere wishful thinking. The old adage that an army marches on its stomach is especially true for a survivor. Having used up most of your body's stored energy in building your shelter and staying warm, finding food is the next priority.

You are probably thinking of hunting and trapping meat. While these are obviously important, few survivors are expert enough to rely on their hunting skills for at least the first three to four days. By that time you should be accustomed to the daily movements of the local wildlife. It is one thing to catch a rabbit on a survival exercise in Yorkshire, but quite another to trap a maned wolf in South America. Don't neglect the major source of food that can't run away from you – edible plants.

Meat or vegetarian?

For a survivor, the relative merits of meat or plant diets are academic. You can eat only what is available to you, and it is quiet likely that your diet will be severely imbalanced. But it will keep you alive.

In general, an all-plant diet will do you less harm than an all-meat diet, although in the Arctic you will need meat, and

SOME EDIBLE PLANTS

Hazel Catkins (Corylus Avellana)
The pollen has a high food value, as do the hazel nuts.

Wood Sorrel (Oxalis Acetosella)
The leaves taste of apple peel but should only be eaten in small quantities. It is useful for removing the taste of something nasty from your mouth.

Ramsons (Allium Ursinum)
The flowering stems are the survival spring onion or garlic seasoning. This plant is very widely distributed through Europe but rare in the north. It is found in damp woodlands, often occurring along stream banks.

Cattail (Typhus Latifolia)
This is an all-year-round survival feast. The pollen, green flower head and young stems are all edible. These are best boiled. the corm or bulb of the plant is high in food value and can be found in winter. The plant is distributed widely in Europe but not in Scotland.

Marjoram (Origanum Vulgare)
This aromatic herb is useful for flavouring meat. Marjoram is usually found in rough permanent grassland, hedge banks, scrub and roadsides in dry soils.

Spear Thistle (Cirsium Vulgare)
The green parts lose their prickles when boiled and make a tasty soup. The roots are also edible. This is common weed throughout Europe.

Wild Camomile (Chamomilla Recutita)
This makes a very smoothing tea. It is a frequent weed of arable crops and waste ground.

especially fat, to produce body heat. Ideally, you would combine a meat and plant diet, in much the same way as you would at home. The meat will provide protein to build muscle, while the plants provide carbohydrates and calories for energy, as well as useful starches and sugars.

If you are injured, you may not be able to hunt. So try to include nuts and seeds in your diet, so they will help to replace the protein lacking in a meat-free diet.

Many people think that subsisting on plants is like being reduced to an animal scrabbling around popping unmentionable berries and roots into your mouth. In fact, people have died because they were reluctant to eat plants.

You should try to live as normal a life as possible, gathering enough plants for a meal, and preparing them carefully. Many of the plants you are eating were once part of mankind's staple diet, the ancestors of the plants we presently cultivate.

Be adventurous, and experiment with your resources. A gourmet feast around the campfire is the greatest morale booster in the world!

Is the plant edible?

In answering this question, there is no substitute for knowing the plant. *Only eat a plant that you have positively identified as edible.*

Luckily you don't need a degree in botany to recognize edible plants. Many common 'weeds' are useful for food. This means that you need to be familiar with relatively few plants to get by.

Get a good naturalist's field guide to edible plants and carry it while on training exercises. You can enjoy the benefits of wild edibles at any time. Improve your compo ration diet by complementing it with fresh herbs, or try mixing fresh young hawthorn leaves into your compo minced beef for extra flavour.

Obtaining and preparing edible plants

It is equally important to know how to prepare the plants you find. Each part of a plant requires its own method of preparation.

MORE EDIBLE PLANTS

Rosebay willowherb (Chaemerion Augustifolium)
The young shoots and leaves are edible. It often forms dense stands in areas of felled woodland or waste ground.

Mallow (Malva Sylvestris)
The leaves and flowers make a tasty soup. It is usually found in dry, well-drained soil on roadsides, banks and waste ground.

Blackberry (Rubus Fruticosus)
All parts of this plant are edible, not just the berries. The dried leaves make an excellent tea.

Red clover (Trifolium Pratense)
The flower heads can be added to stews and tea can be made from the leaves. This is a common plant of pastures, meadows and rough grassland, roadside verges and cultivated ground.

White dead nettle (Lamium Album)
The dried leaves make a very refreshing tea and the fresh leaves can be added to soups. This is a plant of woodlands, fens, ditches and river and stream sides and is also associated with fire sites and abandoned buildings.

Acorn (Cuercus Petraea)
Acorns can be roasted and then ground into a passable coffee. However, you do need to spend time leaching them in water to remove some of the bitterness. They can also be ground and leached and used as a flour.

Underground parts: Edible roots, tubers and bulbs are vital to you, as they are extremely high in stored starch. They are usually best cooked. In winter the roots can often be discovered by searching for the withered stems of the plants.

Removing underground parts from the earth is not always easy. Plants such as first-year burdock have a particularly tenacious root, which requires major excavation before you can get it out. Use a stick to dig a crater around and under the root, and lever it out. If the ground is frozen, thaw it by lighting a fire or putting heated rocks above the root.

Roots can be cooked by steaming, pit baking or boiling. When learning to recognize edible roots make certain you examine them during the summer, when you can study them attached to identifiable stems. The roots and bulbs of poisonous plants are very often the most deadly parts.

Stems and leaves: The green parts of most edible plants are usually more bitter and fibrous than cultivated vegetables. For this reason you may find that you need to boil them in more than one change of water, but don't overcook them, or you'll destroy their nutrients. The best way to overcome this problem is to include them in a stew.

Try things out

Experiment with your local edible greens to discover which can be cooked like asparagus (the tender young shoots), those best used in stews, and those that make a good tea substitute.

Tea substitutes, such as dried bramble leaves, are very important as morale boosters. Try to build up a stock of them, so that in the dark evenings you can brew up. This will give you confidence in your ability to overcome your difficulties.

When picking edible leaves, choose the succulent young leaves just as you would in a market.

Bark: The inner bark of many trees can be used as a source of food – especially, in the high north country, birch, pine, aspen, willows and cottonwoods. The white inner bark is often fibrous, and the best way to prepare it is to dry it and then grind it into flour. In an emergency it becomes more palatable when toasted.

Pollen: Hazel catkins and bulrushes are two of the best sources of pollen. This can be cooked as a form of gruel or, better still, mixed in with other wild flours.

Flowers: The flowers of edible plants are often neglected as a source of food. They can be colourful as part of a wild salad. Many are full of flavour and can be used as seasoning for stews.

Fruits: Besides eating wild fruits raw, you can cook them into warm syrups and sweet fruit drinks. These too are tremendous morale boosters.

FROM FIELDS AND WOODS

Bracken (pteridium aquilinum)
The fern has coarse compound leaves about a metre long. The young leaves can be boiled and eaten as greens. Limit the amount of bracken you eat as it may contain substances that interfere with enzyme action in your body.

Foxtail grasses (Setaria species)
These are grasses recognized by their narrow cylindrical head containing long hairs. The dense heads of grain drop when ripe. The grains are edible raw, but become less bitter when boiled.

Juniper (Juniperus species)
Junipers or cedars are trees or shrubs with very small, scale-like leaves densely crowded around the branches. Each leaf is less than half an inch long. The berries and twigs are edible.

Mulberry (Morus species)
This tree has alternate simple, often lobed, leaves with rough edges. The fruits are blue or black and many-seeded, and can be eaten raw or cooked or dried for later use.

Nodding onion (Allium Cernum)
This is just one example of a great number of wild garlics and onions. The bulbs and young leaves are edible and if you eat enough they will give your body a smell that will repel insects.

Nutsedge (Cyperus esculentus)
This is a very common plant which has a triangular stem and grasslike leaves. It grows to a height of eight to 24 in (20 to 60 cm). Edible tubers of half to one inch (1 to 3 cm) in diameter grow at the end of the roots. They can be eaten raw, boiled or baked. They can also be ground into a coffee substitute.

Pines (Pinus species)
The seeds of all species of pine are edible, as are the young cones which appear in spring and should be boiled or baked. The bark of young twigs is edible, as is the inner bark of thin twigs. It is rich in sugar and vitamins especially when the sap is rising. Pine resin can be used to waterproof articles and made into glue by heating.

Grain and seed: Seeds and grain can be made into flour. While the process may seem laborious, the results are well worth the effort. First, thresh and winnow the seed to remove the chaff. After this it can be parched on hot stones, if you need to store it for long. Or you can grind it to produce flour. The easiest way to collect the seed in the first place is to beat it off the stem onto a spread tarpaulin or jacket.

Nuts

Nuts contain much protein and can even be used to produce cooking oil. Some nuts, particularly acorns, are too bitter to eat raw but can be leached (soaked in many changes of water) to remove their bitterness. Cook them into a gruel or dry them and use them for flour.

You can also roast nuts to use as a coffee substitute. One way to occupy your time is to blend different nut coffees to make the best approximation of real coffee.

Making the most of edible plants

Once you have learnt a bit about edible plants, you will be able to conjure up amazing meals. Make your menus as varied as possible, and always keep your eyes open for opportunities. Birds' eggs can be cooked into an omelette, or even scrambled. Wild birds' eggs have a strong flavour, so season the meal with herbs, such as wild marjoram, or even wild mushrooms such as the ink-cap or Jew's ear. Served with a side order of ramson stems (the survivor's spring onion) and boiled nettle leaves, this makes a survival meal of Cordon Bleu standard.

Presentation

Food is more important to you than you probably realize. In a survival situation food is crucial, for every meal you cook affects your level of morale. By making an effort in cooking and presenting your meal, you give your mind something to work on, helping you to retain your identity and self-esteem. It is also more likely that you will make full use of the nutrients in your food, and so remain fit and healthy.

During World War II many soldiers were stranded on islands in the Philippines. Daily diet became an all-absorbing part of their life, prompting the saying "You've got to have an appetite to survive."

Preparing plants and fungi

Rules for water

If you have plenty of water, drink more than your habitual amount every day. It'll keep you fit even when your food is in short supply.

If you are short of water but have plenty of food, remember that eating will make you thirsty. If you have to ration yourself to less than a quart of water a day, avoid meat, or dry, starchy foods, or those that are highly flavoured. Go for foods with a high carbohydrate content – hard sweets and fruit bars are ideal if you have them.

If both food and water are limited, keep work to a minimum. Hunting animals is hard work – another reason to learn how to survive on plants.

Preparing plant food

To improve the taste of plant foods you can soak, parboil, cook or leach them. To leach, crush the food, put it in a container, and pour boiling water through it.

Boil, bake or roast roots and tubers. Boiling gets rid of most harmful substances.

If the sap of the plant contains sugar, dehydrate it by boiling until the water has gone.

Bake or roast tough, heavy-skinned fruit. Juicy fruit can be eaten raw or boiled.

Cooking methods

You can boil, fry, parch, bake, steam, roast or broil food in the wild just as you would at home in your kitchen. But you'll probably have to make your own substitute pots and pans and cooker, as few plants take well to being cooked on a spit!

Boiling is one of the best methods, as it retains the plant's juices, which contain salts and vital nutrients.

Frying is something you can do on a hot, flat or concave

THE EDIBILITY TEST

1   Do not eat for eight hours before starting the test.

2   During the test period, take nothing by mouth except purified water and the plant part being tested.

3   Sniff the plant to test for strong or acid odours, but bear in mind that smell alone does not indicate that a plant is inedible.

4   Break the plant into its basic components – leaves, stems, roots, buds and flowers – and test only one part at a time.

5   Select a small portion of a single component and prepare it the way you plan to eat it.

6   During the eight hours before you try the plant, test for contact poisoning by placing a piece of the plant part you are testing on the inside of your elbow or wrist. Usually 15 minutes is enough time to allow for reaction.

7   Before putting the prepared plant in your mouth, touch a small portion (a pinch) to the outer surface of your lip to test for burning or itching.

8   If after three minutes there is no reaction on your lip, place the plant part on your tongue, holding it there for 15 minutes.

9   If there is no reaction, thoroughly chew a pinch and hold it in your mouth for 15 minutes. DO NOT SWALLOW.

10 If no burning, itching, numbness, stinging or other irritation occurs during the 15 minutes, swallow the food.

11 Wait eight hours. If you suffer any ill effects during this period, induce vomiting and drink a lot of water.

12 If no ill effects occur, eat half a cup of the same plant part, prepared in the same way. Wait another eight hours. If there are still no ill effects, the plant part as prepared is safe for eating.

CAUTION: Test all parts of the plant for edibility, as some plants have both edible and inedible parts. Don't assume that a part that was edible when cooked can also be eaten raw. If you want to eat it raw, test it raw.

rock if you don't have a frying pan. Use the rock just like an ordinary skillet.

Parching works well with nuts and grains. Put the food on a rock or in a container, and heat until it is scorched.

Baking calls for an oven and a steady, moderate heat, as does steaming. You can bake by using a closed container over a slow fire, or wrapping your food in leaves or clay. But both baking and steaming are best done in a pit when you're surviving in the wild.

To bake food, dig a pit and partly fill it with hot coals. Put your food – and some water – in a covered container, and put it in the pit. Cover it with a layer of coals and a thin layer of earth.

You can also line your pit with dry stones. Build a fire in the pit then, as it burns down scrape the coals back, put in your container of food, and continue as above.

Steaming works best with shellfish or other foods that need little cooking, such as plantains or green bananas. Wrap the food in large leaves or moss, and put one layer on the coals.

POISONOUS FUNGI

As well as the *Amanitas* and Inocybes, you must avoid:

- Cortinarius speciosissimus
- Gyromitra esculenta
- Entoloma sinuatum
- Pascillus involutus
- Agaricus incanthodermus
- Agaricus placomyces
- Ramaris formosa
- Clitocybe rivulosa
- Clitocyle dealbata
- Lepiota fuscovinacea
- Strepharia Homemannii
- Hebeloma crustuliniforme
- Boletus santanas
- Russula ementica
- Scieroderma aurantium

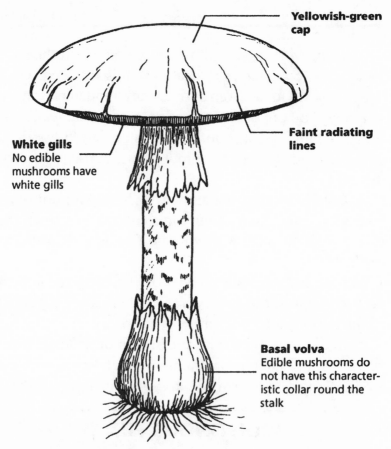

Yellowish-green cap

White gills
No edible mushrooms have white gills

Faint radiating lines

Basal volva
Edible mushrooms do not have this characteristic collar round the stalk

The Destroying Angel and the Death Cap belong to the genus Amanita and are the most deadly species of fungi. The Angel (Amanita virosa) is rare and is found on poor soils in mixed woodland, whereas the Death Cap (Amanita Phalloides) is relatively common under oak or beech. Fly Agaric (Amanita Muscaria) has a red cap with white spots and is found in pine or birch woodland.

Add another layer of moss or leaves, and then another of wrapped food, and so on. When your pit is almost full, push a stick right down through all the layers. Seal the pit with more leaves, or earth, and then remove the stick.

Poisonous fungi

Before beginning to learn about edible fungi, make sure you are familiar with the features common to the high poisonous *Amanita* family of fungi, with their bulbous base, 'volva' or skirt, and white gills. In fact you should avoid *any* fungus with white gills. *Amanita phalloides*, the death cap, is one of the most common deadly species of fungi, having all of the above features under a greenish yellow cap.

The toxin in this fungus destroys the liver and kidneys, but the symptoms may not appear for up to two days. The symptoms are vomiting, diarrhoea, fever and dehydration, followed by depression and, after apparent recovery, death. This takes place over a period of approximately a week – not a pleasant way to end.

Avoid all *Amanitas*, and all *Zinocybes*. Learn to recognize them – they are particularly dangerous families.

Edible fungi

There are a lot of myths about eating fungi, but if you are a survivor or evader, edible fungi give you a versatile, easily gathered and tasty source of nourishment.

Fungi are an unpredictable source of food. When you have a chance to gather edible fungi, take it. You can dry and store for future use what you don't eat immediately.

While the vast majority of fungi are harmless, the small proportion that are dangerous can cause serious poisoning, which may be irreversible. Never experiment with fungi you have not positively identified as edible. There are many old wives' tales about how to recognize edible fungi, but never follow such rules. If you do not know the fungi, leave them alone.

The field mushroom

Usually found in meadow or pasture, these are the mushrooms you usually buy in the shops. They can be dried for later use.

RECOGNISING EDIBLE FUNGI

The essential feature about fungus is that you must know exactly what you are eating. You cannot take short cuts; there is no general rule on what is and is not edible. Start by learning a few easily-recognized edible species such as those in the suggested list. Once you are confident you can identify these, you can add to your knowledge. Do not experiment: get expert help.

The parasol mushroom

A very tasty and large mushroom that grows in woods and pastures. In the early stages of development, before the cap spreads, it can look like a different species to the untrained eye. The parasol is excellent baked or sliced and added to stews. The delicate top is the best part and has a meaty flavour. Remember, some fungi are toxic if eaten raw. If in doubt, leave well alone.

The giant puffball

There are several species of puffball or edible boletus; all are more edible when young. They are white or grey when young, becoming yellow or brown with age.

The shaggy ink cap

The ink cap, which disintegrates progressively into an inky liquid mess, is edible before the rot has set in and is common in mixed woodland.

Dryad's saddle

This is a large fleshy fungus that, when cooked, has a similar flavour to meat and is very filing.

Sparassius crispa

This is an edible fungus that usually grows on rotting tree trunks and fallen branches. It is commonly associated with pine.

Jew's ear fungus

This is found in mixed woodland throughout the year. It is especially common in autumn and favours elder. It is one of the 'jelly' fungi and, although revolting to look at, tastes good.

Chicken of the woods

This fungus usually grows on the sides of trees, has a very tasty chicken flavour and can be eaten raw.

You can also eat:

Horn of Plenty (*Craterellus cornucopioides*)
Cep (*Boletus edulist*)
Morel (*Morchella esculenta*)
Oyster mushroom (*Plrurotus ostreatus*)
Chanterelle (*Chantharellus cibarius*)
Wood blewit (*Lepista nuda*)

Food value

The food value of fungi is high. They provide valuable fat, carbohydrate and protein in quantities between those of meat and green vegetables. More importantly, they are good stomach fillers, making you feel well fed. This is a big plus in psychological terms.

Seashore Food

The coastline offers the survivor a wide variety of food sources if you know what to look for. The major problem is a psychological one: you may have to eat some fairly unappetising items. The essential precaution is to learn as much as you can about the subject first by familiarising yourself with the food sources the seashore has to offer and trying some of the techniques described below. You will be able to overcome your initial reluctance. Then if you find yourself in a survival situation near the coast, you have already won half the battle.

Drinking water is always one of the survivor's top priorities. By digging a shallow well just above the high water level you will be able to collect fresh (if a little brackish) water. Don't dig too deep, or the sea will seep in. This is a good technique to practise next time you visit a beach. If you have a vessel to boil water in, boil sea water and collect the steam in a clean cotton

---

CONSERVATION

1. Never take excessive quantities of any of these wild foods.
2. Always cut seaweed rather than pull it up.
3. Do not take undersized molluscs or crustaceans.
4. Leave some roots of a plant for regrowth.
5. If a plant has gone to seed, scatter the seeds for next year's growth.
6. Do not kill birds or take their eggs: buy an unplucked chicken from the butcher and practise on that. Likewise, the fishmonger should be your source of most shellfish and fish.

cloth. Squeeze out the cloth and you have distilled, drinkable water. Now it is time to forage for food.

The coastline is abundant with food sources, but there are a few basic rules to remember to avoid food poisoning or contamination from all the waste man so thoughtfully dumps into the sea. The edible items discussed here are all standard European shore life; tropical beaches are more abundant but so are the dangers. The basic rules are:

1 Don't eat anything too brightly coloured red, yellow or green. It is a natural sign of poison being present.
2 Don't eat any items washed up or away from their natural environment.
3 Avoid anything with a very strong smell.
4 If in doubt, don't eat it.

Shellfish

Only eat shellfish you find alive; dead ones can be used as bait. Bivalve molluscs feed by filtering food particles out of the water. They also filter out and retain bacteria which, in warm weather, multiply and can cause food poisoning to humans. This is especially true of mussels and oysters, which filter large quantities of water daily and relish the warm, soupy conditions near sewage outlets.

Clam (Mya arenia)

Common in the middle and lower shore, clams look like large mussels and can be up to 10-13 cm (4 in) across. Wash thoroughly as for cockles and scald for 10 minutes. Remove the meat from the shell and cut syphons off. The remaining meat should then be fried or baked for 30 minutes or boiled until tender.

Cockle (Cardium edule)

Widely distributed along British coasts, they are normally found 25-75 mm ($^1/_4$-$^3/_4$ in) beneath the surface of the beach. Wash off the mud and sand and stand in clean water for at least six hours. Drop into a pan of boiling water and simmer for five minutes. Eat on their own or with soup.

Limpet (Patella vulgata)

Found on rocks below high water, limpets should be soaked

for about six hours then boiled for five minutes. They can be rather tough, but further boiling will tenderize them.

Mussels (Mytilus edulis)
Commonest of European shellfish, these are delicious but you must exercise considerable caution when collecting them. They are responsible for most cases of shellfish poisoning. Stand in at least two changes of fresh water and check carefully that each one is alive before cooking. They can be boiled, or baked in ashes.

Scallops or clams (Pecten maximus)
These are the classic shells we all recognize; found on the lower shore, they are only uncovered at very low tides. Like clams, they require a lot of cooking. Wash and scald, cut away the white and orange flesh and fry or boil until cooked.

Whelk (Buccinum undatum)
This is the largest of the gastropods (coiled shells). They are very meaty, but require a great deal of boiling otherwise you will still be chewing on the same whelk hours later. Like the smaller winkle, they can be found in rock pools and among seaweed.

Winkle (Littorina littoreal)
A small, spiral-shaped pointed shell, normally dark grey in colour, you will need a large number of them for a decent meal. Soak them in fresh water to clear them of sand, then plunge into boiling water for about 10 minutes. Extract the meat with the proverbial winkle pin.

Preparing shellfish
1 Test mussels by sideways pressure: if the animal is alive you will feel some resistance.
2 Other shellfish are tested by forcing the shell open a fraction of an inch. If alive and well it will shut again quickly once you release the pressure. If it is already open, opens wide with ease or fails to shut again, it is safer to assume the thing is dead and that you should not eat it.
3 Always wash seashore edibles in plenty of fresh water. Shellfish should be left to stand in clean water overnight if

possible. Check they are still alive when you come to cook them: a single dead one will contaminate the rest of your meal.

4 Always cook thoroughly to kill naturally present bacteria.

Seaweeds

Most seaweeds are edible raw or cooked, and they form a valuable addition to your diet providing your water supply is adequate, because they tend to make you thirsty. They are found in inshore waters and are found attached to rocks at low water. In addition to general rules, there are three specific rules concerning seaweed:

1 Only eat fresh, healthy specimens. Eat nothing with strong odours or flavour: they should be firm to the touch, not wilted, slimy nor fishy-smelling.

2 Do not eat threadlike or slender forms. Sea sorrels contain small amounts of sulphuric acid which can severely upset your stomach. They betray their presence by bleaching out other plants nearby. The test, if you are not sure what you've found, is to crush a little of it in your hand. The released acid will make the plant decay quickly and in 5-10 minutes it will give off an unpleasant odour.

3 Inspect seaweed carefully and shake out any small organisms, e.g. tiny crabs.

There are many types of seaweed. Those found in Europe include:

Bladder wrack: Fresh or dry fronds may be used, boiled in soups or stews. It can also be dried to make tea of a sort.

Carragheen (Irish moss): This is found on the rockier Atlantic shores. Though, feathery and many-branched, it is red/purple to purple/brown. Boil it and eat stewed with fish, meat or other vegetables.

Entomorphia intestinalis: A mouthful to say but a satisfactory mouthful to eat, this is widely distributed and can be eaten raw or dried and used in soups.

Laver: Found on the Atlantic, Pacific and Mediterranean coasts, this is plentiful around the UK and is eaten in Wales. A thin, leaf like transparent membrane with fine, wavy flat fronds, it is red, purple and brown in colour. Cut just above the base so that you don't kill the plant off. Wash it thoroughly to remove grit, and simmer slowly. It can be eaten like spinach or rolled into balls, dipped in bread crumbs and fried. If survival cuisine is beyond you, you can still eat it raw.

Sea lettuce: Found in the Atlantic and Pacific, this is lettuce-like in appearance and is coloured light to dark green. It may be eaten raw or used as a vegetable.

Shoreline plants

There are a few plants found along the shore which can provide the survivor with quite reasonable food.

Marsh samphire (Salicornia)

This thrives in salty marshlands along the foreshores of Europe and has been described as the next best thing to asparagus. Ready from the longest day in June to the last day of August, the young shoots can be eaten raw in salads or cooked in a little boiling water. Drain and add a little butter and pepper if you have any. Eat by stripping the soft flesh away from the hard, spiny stems with your teeth. Marsh samphire now appears on some restaurant menus as a delicacy.

Sea arrow grass (Triglochin maritima)

Found near north temperate coasts, salt marshes and grassy foreshore areas, this can be eaten raw but is best added to soups or boiled as a vegetable.

Sea Beet (Beta vulgaris)

Also known as wild spinach, this was the ancestor of our beetroot, sugar beet and spinach. The leaves may be picked from spring to autumn. They are full of natural minerals, especially iron and vitamins A and C. Wash the leaves well and remove the thicker stalks before boiling in a very little water. Better still, steam it for about 10 minutes.

Sea kale (Crambe maritima)

A cabbage-like plant growing in large clumps with huge, fleshy grey/green leaves, it is found in shingle, sand dunes and along cliffs on north temperate coasts and it was known to the

Romans, who preserved it in barrels for long sea journeys. Pick young leaves and white underground shoots from February to May. Boil briefly, chop and boil for a further 20 minutes in changed water. They can also be steamed or baked.

Crustaceans

These are a major food source but also a common cause of food poisoning, so proceed with caution. Never eat a raw crustacean. Cook them by covering with sand and earth and building a fire over the pile: they will cook in their own juices. A better way is to boil them in water.

Crabs, crayfish, lobsters, shrimps and prawns are found throughout the world and all are edible. They go off quickly, so eat them soon after catching them. Boil some water, insert crustacean, and eat 20-30 minutes later.

Fish

Fish can often be found in pools at low tide around the bases of rocks and under clumps of weed, and eels and small fish are often left behind by the tide. A great deal of fluid is stored in the flesh and the spine cavity of fish and, surprisingly, this is not salty. Hunting fish in pools is not easy: traps and spears will both work, but only if you have practised first. A maze trap works well for flatfish and others in coastal areas. It should be about 2-2.5 metres (6-8 ft) across with a mouth of 40-50 cm (2 ft). The outer walls of wood or stones should project 60 cm or so into the trap. Avoid small, spiny fish, which are likely to be poisonous.

Fish can be boiled, roasted in a fire, baked in clay or cooked on a spit. Prepare them by cutting off the heads, removing the guts and cleaning them out. A very sharp survival knife is an essential item here. Small fish can be eaten whole without cleaning. Never eat a fish with a suspiciously powerful odour, slimy skin, sunken eyes or flabby skin. If in doubt, prod it with your thumb: if it remains dented, do not eat it. Use it for bait instead.

The common octopus (Octopus vulgaris)

You may be able to spear octopus amongst the rocks, but the better method is to leave out large tin cans or sections of pipe with a few stones secured to the bottom just below the low tide mark. Octopi will adopt these containers as lairs when they move in at high tide: they will form the stones into a wall at the open end of the tin. The only real problem is getting the octopus out of the tin.

Birds

All sea birds are edible, either raw or cooked, although some may taste a little peculiar. Roasting and baking in clay are good ways of cooking, but boiling is most nutritious as you retain all the juices. Before cooking, a bird should be bled and drawn and the feathers removed, although a small bird can be rolled in clay and baked: the feathers and skin come away when cooked. The livers are particularly good, and the entrails make good bait for fishing. Do not attempt to kill or eat any bird unless you are in a genuine wartime survival situation.

Other food sources

Other possible food sources include sea urchins, sea cucumbers, starfish, razor shells and lug worms. And don't forget that the seashore will be inhabited by dune-swelling creatures such as mice, rabbits and lizards: all these can go in the survivor's pot. As in all survival situations, living on the seashore is all about making the maximum use of whatever is available.

Fish

If you are fortunate enough to be stranded in an area with a lake or river, you have a rich source of food waiting to be gathered. Fish are rich in protein, the brains and skin are rich in fat, and the meat can also be stored long term. The problem is how to remove the fish from his natural environment to yours.

As someone intent purely on survival, you cannot afford any sporting niceties. The fishing techniques you will need to use are usually outlawed. You must be able to catch your fish in quantity, and as easily as possible. Before you actually start fishing remind yourself of the danger of water, especially in your weakened physical state. Should you fall in, remember the tip of the old salmon fishermen – throw your arms out crucifix-fashion, and try to float down to a shallow pool where you can wade out. If you panic and throw your arms up in the air you will only sink faster. (In crocodile-infested waters try to stay as dry as possible!)

While fish may seem more easily trapped and hunted than other animals, you must bear in mind that you need to catch an awful lot of fish to provide the same volume of food as a medium-sized land animal. At the end of the day, your catch must be big enough to justify the time and effort. This will be largely dependent on how well stocked your river is.

Whether you decide to hunt or trap fish, the time-honoured hunting rules apply. Study the fish in your locality, see where the biggest fish prefer to swim as the position of the sun changes, get to know their habits – especially their feeding habits. Once you have caught a fish, study its stomach contents to find out what it was feeding on. The more you know, the easier your task will be.

Hunting fish

Although hunting fish usually produces a smaller catch than trapping them, it can be a quick way to a short-term meal, and is ideally suited to survivors on the move. The hunting tools are also simpler and more easily made than trapping gear.

Fish are able to detect unusual disturbances in the water, and can see movement above the water. To avoid alerting them to your presence, always try to minimize your movement and noise. Walk carefully – fish can feel heavy footfalls through the water.

1 Tickling

Some fish, particularly trout and salmon, will allow you to touch them while in the water. To catch fish like this you need to be actually in the water. The ideal type of stream is wide, and shallow and clear.

Approach your fish slowly and carefully, with your hands already in the water. Once you are close enough to touch the fish, pass your upturned hands under him very gently. You will probably fail the first time you do this, out of sheer astonishment, for the fish seem to nestle against your hands.

Once your hands are in position, grab the fish. Bend him in your hands and he won't slip away. In one smooth action, cast him on to the bank. While this technique does require the confidence that comes with practice, it does work, and can be a very effective way to catch fish in the right circumstances.

2 Torch and blade

At night, fish can be attracted to light. Wade into a shallow stream with a torch made of birch bark, and you should be able to catch the fish attracted by slashing at them with the blunt end of a machete or a thin blade carved of wood. Make certain you hold the torch high in front of you so as to avoid casting your shadow on the water.

If the river is too deep to wade into, you can use the same technique from the river bank, using a long spear to catch the fish.

3 Spear and lure

You can easily make fish spears from available wood, and they can be very effective. They fall into two basic categories – pin and snag. You use the simplest spears to pin the fish to the river bed. They are usually made of a single piece of wood, pronged or split at the point, and crudely barbed. They are very quickly made and very effective. The 'snag' or 'leister' spears are more complicated to make. They work by snagging the fish on barbs rather than pinning the fish to the bottom. For this reason they are better than pin spears in deep water. You can make these spears with detachable heads attached to the spear shaft by a length of strong cordage. In this way the fish can thrash around without any risk of breaking the spear head.

Spears are best used in conjunction with a suitable lure. Simply carve a small fish-shaped piece of wood, modelled on the local 'small fry', and attach it to a long length of cordage. By drawing this along in the water you should be able to attract the attention of a large predatory fish and 'lure' it within range of your spear. Because water refracts light you will need to aim slightly below where the target appears to be.

Trapping fish

Methods of trapping fish are more useful to you in the long run as they free you to work on your other important chores. However, the apparatus you need will take longer to make. If

FISH MAZE TRAP AND BASKET TRAP

The maze trap

The trap is made up of wooden staves hammered into the river bed with a supporting line connecting the tops of each stave. The trap takes some time to build, but is very effective. The collecting arm should cover the main flow of the river so that the majority of fish swimming upstream are directed into the trap. Each stave should be at least 2 cm thick.

The basket trap

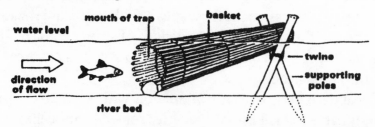

This fish trap is made up of wooden staves bound together to form a telescoping basket. In the faster-flowing parts of the river the fish swims into it but cannot turn round to get out, and finds itself beached at the end of the trap.

you are establishing your survival camp, setting fish traps should be one of your priorities. Your land traps will usually take less effort to set and can be more easily tuned to full effectiveness.

1 Maze traps

There are the simplest traps you can construct. They are simply holding pens, which fish can enter easily but cannot leave because of the design of the entrance. When you make this type of trap, make sure that the stakes are securely hammered into the stream bed with a stone maul. Lash the tops

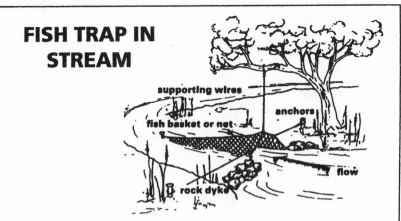

FISH TRAP IN STREAM

supporting wires

anchors

fish basket or net

flow

rock dyke

Fish traps can be used for freshwater and saltwater fish. They are very effective but take a good deal of effort to make and are difficult to carry if you decide to move on.

GILL NET IN STREAM

anchors

flow

suspension line

wood floats

gill net

stone anchors

supporting wires

The gill net is perhaps the best way to catch fish, but again it takes time to make it. Stones are used to anchor the bottom of the net and wood floats are set along the top. The net is set at an angle across the river from a suspension line between two suitable anchors.

of the stakes with cordage – your trap has the constant flow of the river to contend with.

2 Basket traps

Basket traps are slightly more complicated to make than maze traps, but have the advantage that you can carry them easily to wherever there are the most fish. Place the basket so that the river current flows into the basket entrance and raise the downstream end out of the water. Secure the basket with rock or slim willow branches. If you have time you can also construct a funnel of stakes to lead the fish into the basket.

3 Nets

Nets are the hardest fishing aids of all to make, requiring great lengths of cordage. Unless you have nylon cord to unravel for netting material or a gill net in your survival kit, this method of trapping is an unrealistic proposition.

If you do have a net, set it across a straight section of river. If the river is shallow, place the net at an angle in the water.

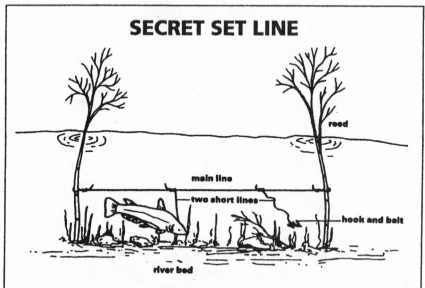

SECRET SET LINE

reed

main line

two short lines

hook and bait

river bed

You may not want to risk using a set line in an evasion situation, but you can use the above set line, known as a stakeout. This is a fishing device you can use secretly by setting a line in darkness between two reeds or similar with lines and hooks attached. Check the line at two-hour intervals until dawn, and then remove.

When you have one, a net is a first rate piece of fishing equipment.

Hook and line

If you have them, fish hooks and line can be used in an endless variety of ways. The easiest and most effective set-up is to set a fixed line across the river and suspend hooks from it at different depths. In this way you can fish several different levels of the river at the same time.

Always make absolutely certain that your hooks are tied on securely – your life may depend upon them.

Improvising hook and line

In the wild, on your own, you may not be lucky enough to have any hooks or line. But you can improvize them from natural materials.

The simplest improvised hook is the 'gorge' or 'toggle' hook. For this you will need a piece of bone or fire-hardened hardwood. Sharpen this at both ends and secure your line to its middle. When this is baited and taken by the fish it toggles inside the fish's throat, lodging tight. Thorns can also be turned into improvised hooks, and you might even carve a standing hook from a piece of bone.

Fishing line is far more difficult to improvise than a fish hook. The strongest line you are likely to be able to make is a very thin rawhide line. Although rawhide loses much of its strength when wet, it is still appreciably stronger than most of the plant fibres you will have available. Simply cut a piece of rawhide in a spiral until you have a long, thin fishing line. Soak the line before use and don't leave it submerged for more than a day or two.

Of the plant fibres you can use, nettle fibres are among the best. But, as with all plant cordage, you will need to gather a lot of nettles, and the process of turning them into cord is slow and laborious. Gather the longest nettles you can find and lay them out to dry in the sun. Once dry, they will have lost their sting and can be handled more easily. Take a mallet and split the stems, remove the pith until only the fibres remain. These can then be rolled on your thigh to produce strong cordage.

Meat, trapping

Meat is the most nourishing food for man, and is certainly the most satisfying for the fugitive who is surviving for any length of time in the wild. Collecting and eating grubs may be an easier option than trapping larger animals, but you have to get through a lot of worms and caterpillars to beat a decent rabbit or duck. Here we describe how to set about catching whatever you find.

The first thing to know is that all animals are edible (but not necessary the whole of the beast). The second thing is that they're nearly all very difficult to catch and you'll have to use all your skills to be successful; and that means understanding the animal's way of life.

Daily habits

They're usually fairly regular in their habits, using the same paths and trails, drinking at the same places on the river bank and from pools, sleeping in the same sheltered places. They also have a timetable, and stick to it; if an animal went to a certain place to drink at dawn this morning, there's a very good chance that it will do the same again tomorrow. Spend time looking for signs of animals.

If there's a lot of animal activity going on, find a hiding place and stay in it until you recognize the local wildlife patterns. It will make trapping or hunting them a great deal easier. All you've got going for you is your intelligence; they've lived there all their lives!

Unless you have an accurate weapon, such as a rifle, shotgun or cross-bow, hunting will be a lot less likely to provide you with dinner than trapping. In a hostile environment, where there are enemy forces or natives, hunting is almost certain to be impossible anyway, but let's look at some of the basic skills you'll need to hunt game in the wild.

Always assume that any small animals in the area will be wary and quick to run away. If they spot you, hear you or smell you (remember that their sense of smell may be a thousand times better than yours), they will either go to ground or disappear off into the distance. Seeing them before they become aware of you greatly increases your changes of catching them.

They often use the same pathways and drinking places, and make permanent homes. Look for their signs – tracks, paths in grass, faeces, dens, feeding places – and use that intelligence to help you set up a plan to catch them.

Camouflage and approach

Remember, the fieldcraft that makes you a good foot-soldier can also make you a good hunter. Always obey the rules of

DEADFALLS

The figure-four deadfall is simple to make and surprisingly sensitive. The props should be as thin as you can make them, the fall itself as heavy as possible. The one shown here is relatively small, but you can make larger ones too, to stun larger animals.

Cut two sticks of roughly equal length, and trim and notch them as shown. Sharpen one end of each stick, one to go into the ground and the other to take the bait.

Cut and notch a third, longer stick to form the third side of the triangle.

Pay careful attention to the notches. Cut them too shallow and they won't hold for very long.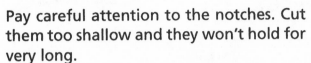

You may find it frustrating, trying to set the trap up. But remember, the harder it is to get it to stay together, the more sensitive it will be in use.

camouflage and approach. Never silhouette yourself against the skyline, even in woodland. Always move upwind or across wind. Approach streams, rivers and waterholes very carefully, especially around dawn and dusk. Find cover and get into it, and wait for the animals.

And stay still! Fidgeting may cost you a meal – and that may end up costing you your life.

Larger game, even if it sees you, may not take flight straight away. Stop and keep still until it loses interest, and then approach in a wide zigzag. In hills and mountains, always try to get above the animal you're stalking.

Best target areas

If you are shooting game, the best targets are the head, neck and the spine just behind the shoulder. Take your time, and make the first shot count – because you're not likely to get a second chance. If you hit and wound the animal and it runs off, follow the blood trail. A badly wounded creature won't have the strength to run far. Give it the chance to go to ground before following it up. Approach slowly and then make the

A POLE TO CATCH SQUIRRELS

Take a pole, fix some wire snares to it and lean it up against a tree where you've seen squirrels. It may seem too simple to be true, but these inquisitive creatures are quite likely to get caught up before too long.

kill. Don't waste ammunition if you can finish it off by clubbing it.

Hunting, however, should take second place to making and setting traps. Traps are much more likely to provide you with a lasting supply of meat. Simple ones are very easy to make and set: the simplest of all is a snare – a slip noose firmly pegged into the ground or anchored to a rock or tree. Make them from wire if it's available, or use plastic fishing line, string or even line made up from natural fibres.

These snares are especially effective when you set them at the entrance to burrows and dens. Set them in trees to catch squirrels, or make a 'squirrel pole': an eight to 12 ft (2.5 to 3.5m) pole with perhaps half-a-dozen snares around it, leaned up against a tree used by squirrels. It may sound too easy, but squirrels are inquisitive creatures and will often investigate something new just for the fun of it.

You're not likely to be able to kill anything larger than a rabbit or a small cat with a wire snare, though you may slow down larger animals so that you have a better chance of clubbing them to death.

Trapping, even more than hunting, depends on how well you can read the signs. There is no point in placing a trap just anywhere hoping that an animal will stumble into it by chance! Entrances to burrows and tunnels are the best place. Look for signs that they are occupied – fresh droppings, signs of feeding and movement in and out.

Unless you're using wire for the snare, which may stand up on its own, you will have to make a stand to hold the noose open. Two twigs, one each side of the mouth of the burrow or the path will do, with another one perhaps placed across the top to support the trap.

HANGING SNARES

Hanging snares are a more secure way of holding on to the animal that you've caught. They use the creature's own weight to keep it from wriggling out of the noose. Apart from the wire noose itself, to make a hanging snare you need a sapling close to the run you've chosen, and a forked stick, or one bent over into a hoop. The forked stick is used as part of the trigger, holding the wire noose down in the animal's way and presenting the bait. The example here uses a half-hoop, for increased sensitivity.

You can even scare off large animals this way – cats and bears, for instance. Building a fire when you've frightened them off will often make them stay away long enough for them to forget you've robbed them of their meal. But unless you're well armed, don't be too ready to take on these large predators yourself.

Human scent

Don't forget to cover your scent, both on the snare itself and on the surrounding ground: soaking the snare in a stream after you've made it and before setting it is one way. Or you can rub it with cold ashes, or disguise your own scent with something stronger – urine from the bladder of a dead animal, for example. Animals are usually attracted to urine from their own kind.

You can improve on the simple noose, and make it more

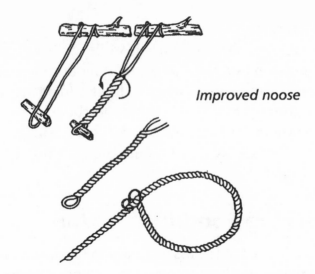

Improved noose

difficult for the animal to escape from the trap, by intertwining two lengths of wire. Use the two strands that are left at the end to make up a double running loop. These two loops will naturally catch in the twists of the wire that makes the body of the line and noose, and will make it much more difficult for the animal to wriggle out of the noose.

You can always let predators do your hunting for you. Watch until you can work out their pattern of activity, then wait for them to make a kill. If you rush them you'll often cause them to drop their prey.

SKINNING SMALL ANIMALS

1 Lay the animal down on its back, spread all four legs wide, and cut from the anus up to the breastbone, taking care not to rupture the intestine.

2 Cut the skin through around all four paws at the first joint. Remove the guts, starting from the throat and working downwards. Do not eat these innards.

3 Now you can peel the skin off. You may find it necessary to remove the tail first.

4 Take the skin off in one piece. A firm grip and a quick pull are all that is needed.

5 The last thing to do is to remove the head. Keep the skin for making clothing.

Obvious targets

Don't go around chasing squirrels while ignoring more obvious targets such as cows, sheep and other domestic animals – including cats and dogs. They're all food, and often they're just standing around waiting to become somebody's meal – it may as well be yours. Bats and mice make good eating, but do not eat any of their innards, and immediately discard their heads, skin, feet and tails.

Preserving Food in the Wild

To survive in the wilderness you have to become a predator – and that means you have to compete with other animal predators for the same prey. You can learn a lot about survival by watching the animals around you. Notice how the animal that makes the kill isn't always the one who enjoys the meal.

You can turn this to your advantage, but you also have to protect your kill from being stolen by other animals – not all of them friendly. You need to protect your food from the hordes of bugs and flies that want to eat your food and, worse, lay their eggs in it.

With care and the right techniques you should be able to keep your kill at least for long enough to let you eat all of it safely. With practice, you can even preserve your food indefinitely.

Preserving meat

First decide whether or not you intend to hunt large game. Preserving a large animal such as a deer will require considerably greater effort than will preserving a rabbit. The deciding factor is how long you expect to be stranded. If it's likely to be a long time, killing a large animal means less hunting and brings with it a large and useful skin. But it also involves hard work to preserve the meat. Until you become expert at preserving meat you will find it easier to rely on smaller game to stock your larder.

Because all wild meats can carry parasites harmful to man, they must be cooked thoroughly before consumption, regardless of how you preserve them. Efficient cooking destroys parasites and is therefore an essential part of field hygiene.

Drying

Drying or 'jerking' is the easiest way to preserve meat under survival conditions. First slice the meat into strips, approximately 2 in(5 cm) wide and ¼ in (0.5 cm) thick. Then string them on a thin stick or drape them over a bar on your drying rack. Make sure they are not touching each other.

Precautions against flies

Until the surface of the meat has dried you run the risk of flies

SMOKING MEAT

Smoke your meat over a wood fire using timber from a deciduous tree, ideally willow or birch. Do not use conifers like pine or fir trees because their smoke will impart a vile taste to the meat. You can hang meat high above a slow, smouldering fire, but a quicker method is to dig a hole about a metre (3 ft) deep and 50 cm wide. Get a fire going at the bottom and pile on green wood to create the smoke. Place the meat on an improvised grate over the hole. One night of heavy smoking will preserve meat for five to seven days; two nights and it will remain edible for two to four weeks. When properly smoked, the meat will look like a dark, curled stick. It is highly nutritious and, best of all, it tastes good.

laying their eggs in it. You can prevent this with two simple precautions. Either site your drying rack in a sunny and windy location or, the more effective method, lay a slow smouldering fire under the rack. This will speed up the drying process as well as keeping off insects. Make absolutely certain, however, that the fire is giving out only a low heat and not much smoke. Don't use green vegetation to produce the smoke, or you will taint the meat. If you need to increase the smoke, use some damp wood chips or bark from a non-poisonous tree.

The smoking can be stopped once the surface of the meat is dry. Allow the meat to hang in the sun or a dry place until it is brittle. It can then be stored, wrapped in dry grass and bark, until you need it. To use dried meat you can rehydrate it for broiling or steaming or, better still, just add it to a stew.

Pemmican

Once you have a store of dried meat, you can consider making pemmican, the survivors' home-made, high-energy, high-protein emergency ration. Pemmican is ideal for long hunting trips or if you intend to make a break from civilisation. Take your brittle dried meat and pound it between two rocks until it is a powder. You now have the equivalent of a survival stock cube. Next, mix the powdered meat with sun-dried berries and plenty of rendered fat. Form the resulting sticky mass into palm-sized pellets and place these in the cleaned large intestine of an animal. Seal the ends by tying and with fat. You now have a survival sausage which can be eaten as it is, or sliced and added to stews, or fried on a hot stone.

Freezing

In Arctic conditions you may be able to store your meat by letting it freeze. But remember – even when frozen, the scent of the meat will be detected by other hungry predators. Make certain it is out of their reach.

Be sure that you will be able to cope with the meat once it is frozen. The most common mistake made by survivors is to freeze large pieces of meat. Instead, butcher it into meal size portions – they don't take a week to defrost. Make quite sure the meat is thoroughly defrosted before cooking.

Preserving fish

Your fish can be preserved along with your meat. Treat fish in the same way as meat – dry it, or make it into pemmican. The only difference is that fish goes off far more quickly, so must be dried as fast as possible. In all but the sunniest weather, this will meal you have to use a smudge fire or a smoke house.

Smoking

You can also deliberately flavour fish by smoking it. To do this you will need to hang the fish in a smoke house. Score the flesh before hanging, so that the smoke permeates the flesh better. Smoking fish in a smoke house is a little different to operating a smudge fire. A slow trickle of woodsmoke does the trick. Once you have started smoking the fish, check it on a regular basis. There are two stages in smoking fish: half smoking and full smoking. Half-smoked fish is still soft and flavoured of wood, ready for eating. Fully smoked fish is dry and brittle. Treat it in the same way as dried meat.

Fish pemmican is certainly an acquired taste when eaten raw. But it is an excellent addition to soups and stews, and can be fried to make delicious fish cakes.

Preserving fungi

If you are lucky you may be stranded during a glut of edible fungi. To preserve them for future use, you can dry them.

First clean each individual fungus, cutting out any parts attacked by insects. Be particularly thorough with fungi that have gills or pores, as these are a favourite breeding ground for grubs. Then string the fungi together on a cord or stick, and hand them in your smoke house or shelter to dry. Some fungi such as the Horn of Plenty can be powdered to use as a stew flavouring, while others are best served whole as chewy stew ingredients.

Preserving plants

In general, plant foods are best used fresh. But at the onset of winter you must certainly consider stockpiling your supplies.

The easiest parts of plants to preserve are the young green leaves used for teas. Don't pick the leaves and store them in containers – simply dry the stalks of the plant itself. With plants such as nettles, use the fibres in the dried stem for cordage. Store bundles of useful herbs in your shelter or smoke house.

Dry and grind up roots to use as flour, or bury them in layers of dry sand. Cover this to keep it dry.

Nuts, fruits and seeds

Nuts are best stored either as a flour or in open containers, still in their shells. Keep them dry and stir them regularly to prevent mildew.

Dry fruits by laying them on warm stones in the sun, and store them in containers with lids. Above all keep them dry.

The best way to store seeds long-term is by parching them. Only make flour in small batches. Otherwise you risk losing your whole crop to weevils.

Storing food

Your food store must be safe from mammals, must be dry, and must have a constant temperature. A properly constructed smoke house will meet many of these criteria, but don't use it to store all your food. 'Never keep all your eggs in one basket' is the golden rule when storing your life-saving food.

The easiest larder to make is an underground cache. Try to find a dry sheltered piece of ground – for example, under an overhanging bush or log. Dig a hole about two feet deep, and line the pit with bark slabs. Birch or cherry bark is ideal for this. Further line the pit with dried and, if possible, smoked grass. Place your food packages into the pit, followed by more grass. Then add some dried aromatic herb (such as marjoram) to disguise any scent from the food. Finally, seal the pit with bark and the soil you originally removed.

Take care to note exactly where you have buried the food, or mark the location so that you can find it again even after a heavy snowfall.

Scavenged food

No animal will stop itself stealing your food out of a sense of fair play. In the same way, don't miss any opportunity to steal from a wild animal. You can turn even the rotting remains of a predator's meal into a life-saving stew if you are hungry enough.

Skin and gut the remains in the normal way, and then thoroughly boil the rancid meat for as long as possible. To eat the stew you will need to hold your nose, but it will keep you alive.

This emergency stew *cannot* be reheated. Discard what you don't eat. If you reheat it, a dangerous botulism results.

Medicinal Plants

On the run from enemy forces behind the lines or stranded in the middle of nowhere with no resources apart from your personal skills, you have little access to modern medicine. You must learn how to use whatever is available.

The first lesson of survival medicine is not to get sick or injured to start with. This is not as silly as it sounds. Soldiers have the advantage of being young and fit, inoculated against some diseases and trained in hygiene, but over-confidence can undo all this. A Para once got his jaw broken after prodding a 600-lb black bear with a stick, and another squaddie on exercise in the UK was bitten by an adder that was sunning itself on a rock. He thought he was quick enough to catch it behind the head with his finger and thumb: when he woke up in hospital four days later, he knew he wasn't!

Treat all animals with respect, particularly large, nasty ones and small venomous beasts. Generally speaking, if you don't bother them, they won't bother you. All animal bites are dangerous. They easily go septic, especially bites from carnivorous animals whose fangs cause deep, narrow wounds that soon close, leaving bacteria behind.

Sensible precautions

As a lone survivor you have to take good care of your feet. Keep your shoes on and improvise some footwear if you haven't got any. Your feet might be hardened against stones you tread on, but they won't protect you against snakes.

Don't paddle about in water with bare feet. Poisonous fish such as the lion fish lie motionless in the sand, with venomous spines waiting to be trodden on.

If you have to go barefoot through the shallows, shuffle along rather than taking proper steps, and prod the ground in front of you with a stick to clear anything nasty out of the way. This is not a problem confined to the tropics: on a recreational outing in Yorkshire, UK, someone stood on a weaver fish and within an hour was unable to walk. Imagine that in a survival situation.

Never wade, swim, or even walk through fresh water in the tropics. In much of Africa, South-East Asia and South America, the bilharzia worm is endemic. It burrows through your skin to lodge in your bladder, bowels, liver or intestines. If you have to drink water from such a source, boil it thoroughly, chlorinate it or leave it for 48 hours: any of these methods kills off the larvae.

It is wise to keep reasonably covered up to avoid inspect stings, even in a hot climate. The vile-smelling leaves of the elder tree rubbed on exposed parts will keep the worst of the insects at bay. Peppermint and bog myrtle are also fairly effective, as is a decoction of pine bark or, in the tropics, camphorwood. None are as effective as chemical bug juice.

These commonsense precautions may seem obvious and even tiresome, but remember: it is the man who has the self-discipline and character to observe the do's and don'ts, even when at the end of his tether, who is most likely to survive.

How to use herbs

To get the maximum value from herbs you have to know the processes used to extract the goodies, how to apply them, and whether they may be used internally or externally. Different herbs and treatments require different methods.

Internal preparations

Infusion: An infusion is made by pouring boiling or near-boiling water on the relevant plant or parts of a plant. Leave for 3-5 minutes; longer for tougher plants.

Decoction: Boil the plant for as long as needed to get the goodness from the herb. The tougher its tissues, the longer you have to boil. Decoctions are usually necessary for bark, stalks, roots and seeds. A cup of tea is an infusion; a pot of non-instant coffee is a decoction.

Maceration: Chop or crush the plant and leave for several hours in water. Use within 12 hours.

Powder: Dry the plant and then crush it. Be careful; powders are very concentrated.

Preparations for external use

Poultice: Chop or crush the plant into a mash, then heat it. Contrary to popular belief, it does not need to be very hot. Apply the poultice to the appropriate area and remove after five minutes, then re-heat and re-apply. Several short applications are better than one long application.

Compress: Soak a piece of cloth or a chunk of suitable moss in a strong decoction or infusion and hold it in place for about 10 minutes.

Dressing: Dressings are simply compresses made from weaker mixtures. Change the first few dressings on a wound or ulcer every two hours, then gradually increase the time between changes to a maximum of 12 hours.

Herbal remedies

Like most worthwhile skills, learning about herbs takes time and effort. Don't wait until you need them before you try to use them. The golden rule is: *do not swallow anything unless you have made a positive identification.* In the UK alone there are at least a score of plants that can kill you and many more that will make you very ill. The following are very safe, very effective and easily identifiable herbs which have preventive and curative properties.

Garlic

The onion family includes leeks, chives, shallots, garlic, garlic mustard ('Jack by the hedge') and ramsons ('bear's garlic'). Hedge garlic and ramsons are very common in temperate climates and the sub-tropics. They are safe to use: if it smells like garlic, it's a member of the garlic family. Garlic was so revered as a heating plant by the Egyptians that they worshipped it as a god. As a lone survivor, you may come to appreciate their point of view.

Garlic contains an antibiotic (allicine) and vitamins A, B and

B2. It is an intestinal disinfectant and helps protect you against food poisoning, amoebic dysentery, typhoid and other infectious diseases (which is why it was used by medieval grave robbers). It kills tapeworms and round worms if eaten in large quantities, relieves cramps, lowers blood pressure and fights fever. Garlic aids digestion and stimulates the appetite. It can also be used as a compress.

The most common garlic is garlic mustard, followed by ramsons. The latter is delicious: you will find it forming thick carpets in damp woods, ravines and riverbanks. The whole plant is edible and the seeds (which taste incredibly strong) can be kept for years.

Thyme (Thymus serpyllum)

Wild thyme is common throughout the temperate zone and sub-tropics. It contains thymol, a very strong antiseptic with few side-effects: it is retained in the gut and released into the bloodstream to counter infection throughout the body. Thyme helps kill worms and cures diarrhoea, although not quickly. For the evader it has another advantage: it reduces your body scent, which can give you a valuable edge against tracker dogs. Delicious when added to stews (the best way to take your medicine), it can also be used to make a tea. Sip it for coughs and gargle with it to ease sore throats.

Comfrey

Comfrey is the best herb to help mend broken bones. The plant contains starch and suger, particularly in the roots, and it is rich in mucilage (a gum-like substance) and tannin. The old country names for it are 'boneset' and 'knitbone', which describe one of its many uses. Its chemical action reduces swelling at the site of a fracture and fosters union of the bone, and the root can be used to help make a cast because it stiffens as it dries because of the mucilage, providing the vital rigidity.

The plant grows 3-5 ft (1-2 m) tall in ditches, by roadsides, on waste ground, beside riverbanks and in woods. It flowers blue, purple or white between June and October. The yellow tuberous comfrey flowers from March to June and lacks the thick root of the common comfrey.

Anaesthetics

Many plants in Europe can reduce the agnoising pain of bone setting and other injuries. The snag is that they can also produce unconsciousness or death. Their chemical composition, and therefore their effects, vary according to the soil, whether and time of year, so never experiment with any of the following: hemlock, dropwort, thorn-apple, henbane, deadly nightshade, wolfsbane or yew. Some of their poisons are used as homeopathic remedies, but a little learning is a dangerous thing: unless you are thoroughly trained, leave these plants alone.

Feverfew is your best herbal anaesthetic. It is chemically similar to aspirin, but takes some time to have an effect. It is sometimes prescribed as a cure for mirgaine: you can buy it in tablets which cost less than the price of a prescription for similar controlled drugs, or you can eat it in its natural form – one leaf a day is the dosage. Unfortunately it tastes disgusting: roll it into a 'pill' and knock it back quickly. Incidentally, don't neglect the humble aspirin tablet in your kit – it is a very useful and effective drug.

Treatments

Because you can't foresee the terrain where you will be injured, make yourself familiar with plants from many different habitats. The following cures are from 10 of the safest and commonest medicinal plants to be found in the temperate zone. Familiarize yourself with these before studying further.

Bleeding

A plant with haemostatic properties will help stop bleeding. You probably won't have such plants readily to hand when you first find yourself in survival conditions, so prepare and store these herbs in your survival medicine chest. The dried and powdered root of Bistort *(Polygonum bistorta)* can be applied direct to external wounds.

Use an infusion of the green stem of Horsetail *(Equisetum arvense)* to wash the wound. It will help stop the bleeding.

Antiseptic

To prevent wounds becoming infected they can be washed with an infusion made with these medicines:

1 Greater plantain *(Plantago major)* leaves and stem. In an emergency, chew the leaf of this plant to a plup and use it directly on the wound.

2 Selfheal *(Prunella vulgaris)* flowering stems. This plant too can be chewed, for a quickly prepared pulp.

3 Dried burdock *(Arctium lappa)* root, made into an infusion. this is ideal to prepare for long journeys. The leaves can also be infused but are less potent.

4 Birch *(Betula pendula)* leaves when infused make an all-purpose disinfectant.

Digestive disorders

An excellent cure for diarrhoea is charcoal and a herbal tea. Remember to keep your fluid intake high when suffering from diarrhoea.

THE HERBAL COMPRESS

1 Open wounds are vulnerable to infection, especially as your body's resistance will be low after a prolonged period in the field. A compress of an antiseptic plant like Greater Plantain is made by pulping the plant with a stone. Make sure you wash the stone beforehand.

2 Mop up the juice of the plant with the remaining flesh and gather it into a ball.

3 Apply the herbal pulp firmly into and around the wound. Do not attempt to stitch up wounds of a superficial nature as you may stitch in the infection, and pressure caused by the infection and the stitching may lead to restricted blood flow to the area and then perhaps to gangrene. Cuts left open that heal in this way do leave nasty scars, but in the absence of sterile conditions and antibiotics this is the safer course.

4 Keep the herbal pulp in place and maintain pressure on the wound with a wrapping of dock leaves held in place with strips of animal skin.

1 Dandelion *(Taraxacum officinale)* leaves, washed and eaten raw, or cooked like spinach, are an excellent aid to digestion. Try to include some in your survival diet as a preventative.

2 Dog rose *(Rose canina)* petals and/or hip are a very good stomach settler. Before eating any of the vitamin-C-rich hips, remove the hairy seeds inside them.

3 Water mint *(Mentha aquatica)* leaves and stems can be used as an infusion. This plant is also useful to flavour survival stews. Don't eat large quantities.

4 Horseradish *(Armoracia rusticana)* roots and leaves in your daily diet will add digestion and help prevent problems. The scrapings from the root make a strong flavouring for stews.

5 Selfheal flowering stems, infused, ease upsets. You can also prepare the leaves like spinach and include them in your diet.

For severe digestive disorders such as dysentery, use an infusion of powdered bistort root.

Insect bites and stings

Insects are always an irritation for a survivor. Besides the diseases, such as malaria, that they carry, their bites and stings can quickly become painful festering sores if scratched. Use infusions of horsetail, burdock, plantain or birch to soothe the inflammations. You will probably find that after a couple of days of eating wild herbs insects will pay less attention to you, particularly if you include a small amount of plantain in your daily diet.

Deal with stings from stinging nettles by rubbing them with a fresh burdock leaf or a dock leaf.

Bruises and headaches

You are certain to suffer some bruises and strains. To ease these, make compresses from bistort, horsetail or plantain.

Headaches are often encountered by survivors in the first few days of being stranded. Effective cures are soothing teas of mint or rose hips and/or petals.

Toothache

Minor cuts, bruises and bites are relatively easy to deal with under primitive conditions. But when it comes to survival dentistry there is very little you can do. Rose tea can ease pain, but the best answer is to care properly for your teeth. This means regular visits to the dentist, and especially before going on extended operations. When stranded, clean your teeth with ash or alder *(Alrus glutinosa)* bark.

Jellyfish

Jellyfish and other sea creatures can give you nasty wounds. Stingrays, weaver fish, lion fish and zebra fish venoms cause excruciating pain, swelling, vomiting, and diarrhoea, and can slow your heartbeat. Box jellyfish and Portuguese men o' war cause the same symptoms plus paralysis of your breathing muscles and fits.

Treatment for all these nautical disasters is the same. Apply a tight tourniquet between the wound and your heart. Remove tentacles or spines, but not with your bare hands. Any form of dilute acid, e.g. vinegar or lemon juice, prevents further releases of venom.

Fish venoms are destroyed by heat and the pain is eased greatly by the application of hot water. Also, the venom has a short-lived effect, so a casualty who is not breathing and has no pulse can be brought round by cardiac massage and mouth-to-mouth resuscitation.

Snake bite

An old farmer in Texas who reared rattlesnakes for their meat and skin was bitten by them four times. He nearly died the first time. Later, when living with Navajo Indians, he was bitten again. They applied a tourniquet between the bite and his heart, which is standard procedure. But then they cut an onion in half and pressed it against the bite; when it turned green, they threw it away and applied the other half.

The procedure was continued with more onions until no green showed. Although he continued to feel ill, the worst of the sickness passed in two days instead of the normal five or six. The moral of this is that with a knowledge of both modern and folk medicine, you can adapt to find the best possible course of action in circumstances where most people would give up and die.

Tips on preparing medicines

The secret of successful cures lies in how you choose and prepare your herbs. Try to collect only healthy plants, from areas of unpolluted ground. In wilderness areas, the best place to search for herbs are by water sources and where forest meets grassland. In escape and evasion situations, the edges of fields and along forestry rides are the places to search.

Having gathered your herbs, shake them clean of dust and insects. Most of the cures involve infusions, which basically means preparing the herb as a tea. Never boil your herb. Instead, allow it to brew in water just off the boil. This will retain all of the goodness in the plant.

Make paste for poultices by grinding up the herb between two rocks, with a little water. Apply this directly to the wound and wrap with cloth or large leaves.

You will have to judge the strength of your herbal cures by eye, as each plant has its own character, depending on the season or its location. If in doubt, always under-medicate.

Tools and equipment

Survival Knives

A civilian stranded after a disaster such as a shipwreck or a plane crash will not have chosen a survival knife. He will have to make do with whatever he's got with him – perhaps a piece of sharpened fuselage, or at best a Swiss Army Knife. But soldiers and adventurers operating in remote regions of the world

---

NOT A WEAPON

The survival knife is just that – for survival. The characteristics of a good survival knife are not those of a weapon. Besides, the law in many countries is strict and you may be committing a crime if you own one without good reason – and in some places if you own one at all. They are not for kids. When you buy one you also buy into a professional, adult level of responsibility in its use and security.

will almost certainly have a knife with them at all times, and they will have made a choice.

The wrong choice could be fatal, as a knife is literally a lifeline in the wilderness, upon which you must be able to rely completely. It's too late to find out your knife is not strong enough when you are trying to cut yourself free from a capsized white water raft heading for a waterfall!

Selecting the knife

When choosing your knife, find a reputable dealer with a large range of quality knives. Often the best shops stock custom knifemaker ranges.

Do not limit your choice of knife to those described as 'Survival Knives'; there are many hunting knives eminently suited to survival use. Try also to be practical. There are many beautiful knives for sale, well made and by top-class manufacturers; but they are not all practical for the specialized use you will be demanding.

You must always carry your knife with you; you never know when you'll need it. This means that your knife must be a convenient size to be carried without becoming a drag, and must also be capable of carrying out all those basic camp shores such as opening tins, hammering tent pegs, cutting string and so on. And if you become stranded or have to go to ground it will have to do the job of a small axe as well, so it must be strong. Generally speaking, a fixed blade is the better option as it is stronger and more rugged, but most professionals carry two knives: a large fixed blade and a small folding blade.

The metal

There are really only two basic choices: carbon steel or stainless steel. Carbon steel will rust (generally speaking) unless cared for, whereas stainless steel should not. It is widely recognized that carbon steel takes a keener edge than stainless, although in some modern aircraft and cutlery, stainless steels are challenging this traditional concept. Stainless steel should hold its edge longer than carbon steel, but is in many cases harder to sharpen.

In most cases, stainless steel would be the best choice. Take the advice of a reputable dealer, as there are many varieties in use, in many cases alloyed with other metals such as vanadium, molybdenum and chromium to change their qualities. In general, avoid divers' knives (unless made by a reputable manufacturer), as the steel is usually very poor.

When you are finding out about the type of steel used, try also to find out about the temper. If a knife is under-tempered it will be strong but will not take an edge; if it is over-tempered, it could shatter in use. There is a tendency for manufacturers to over-temper blades!

Size, weight and balance

The wise traveller tries to reduce the weight of his pack, but when travelling far off the beaten track don't try to economize on the weight of your knife. You need a knife with a weighty blade, as this reduces the force you need to apply and allows more control and efficiency. But if you choose a blade that is too heavy, it will cause fatigue in your fingers, wrist and arm, and this can lead to dangerous accidents.

The length and weight of your knife are critical factors, but no real formula exists to help you choose. In jungles, machetes and long, light knives are the norm, but for more general use these are really too long. As a rough guide, don't choose a knife that is more than two and a half times the length of your hand, and no less than one and a half times long.

Leverage principle

To illustrate the principle, imagine that you are striking a nail into a piece of wood with a one-metre steel bar. If you want to achieve the same result with a bar 50 centimetres long, you must either use a lot more force or a heavier bar. The shorter, heavier bar is more controllable as it exerts less leverage on the wrist, and can be used in more confined space. The same is true of knife lengths.

Once you have chosen the length and weight of your blade, try to decide where the point of balance lies. Ideally it should be just in front of the guard. This means that the knife is slightly blade-heavy, yet easily controlled by adjusting your grip.

If the point of balance is too far forward it will cause muscle

THE PARTS OF A SURVIVAL KNIFE

In war, there is no room for the amateur. You must have the right knife for the job and be skilled in its use: you won't have time to start thinking about it if you're on the brink of a war zone.

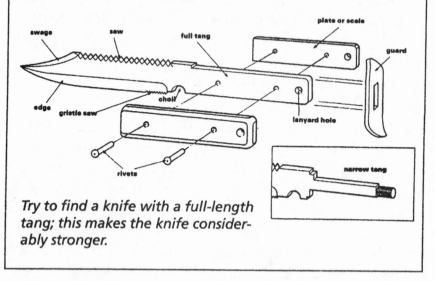

Try to find a knife with a full-length tang; this makes the knife considerably stronger.

strain, which makes the knife slip from your grasp. The more common fault is that the knife is too handle-heavy. Excess weight in the grip is a burden, as it does not contribute to the blade's cutting ability.

Features and fittings

The most important fitting to your knife is the grip; probably the commonest fault in most survival knives is the way by which the grip is attached. The part of the blade that goes to make up the handle is called the 'tang'.

In many knives, this narrows at the join of the guard and grip. This is an inherent weakness, at the point of greatest strain. The ideal attachment is what is called 'full tang', where the blade remains the width of the grip throughout.

Hollow handles often mean that the tang not only narrows but shortens as well. While not all hollow handles are weak, take great care in your choice.

The guard is an important feature of any survival knife. Its purpose is to prevent your fingers slipping forward onto the sharp edge while using the knife. Remember: even the smallest cut can fester and prove fatal under survival conditions.

The point of your knife is another important feature. It needs to be sharp, and strong enough to pry with. It is an advantage if it falls below the horizontal mid-line of your knife: this is a 'true drop point', and prevents the point snagging the flesh of an animal's stomach wall during skinning and gutting.

Saws and hollow handles

Saws are a regular feature of survival knives. Do not expect them to saw through wood. They will, however, cut grooves in wood and cut ropes, making them a useful additional feature although not essential.

Gristle saws are sometimes found in front of the guard. These again are a useful additional feature that will find many uses.

Hollow handles are designed to accommodate useful survival tools such as fishing lines or firelighting aids, and as long as they do not weaken the grip are an excellent addition.

Sheaths

Sheaths are an important feature of any knife. As well as protecting the knife, they must be strong enough to protect you from injury if you fall on the encased blade. Good-quality leather sheaths are almost as good as the very strong scabbards being made from modern plastics, but beware of cheap leather. If you find a good knife that has a poor sheath you may be able to have a better sheath made for it.

The method of carrying the sheath is entirely up to you, and you may want to make some modifications. You may also consider taping additional survival gear to the outside of your scabbard, as long as you don't end up looking like a Christmas tree.

Having carefully selected your knife, work it in, personalize it, practise using it and, above all, look after it. Your life may one day depend on it.

Personalising your knife

Your choice of survival knife speaks of your knowledge of survival; the state it is in and the way in which you use it speak of your experience. To a survivor, a knife is the most versatile life-saving aid. To a survival expert it is a craftsman's tool, treated with the same care and attention as a master carpenter's chisels. It is not toyed with: it remains in its sheath until it is needed, and is then used with great dexterity and ease for a multitude of tasks before being returned to its resting place.

The grip

The grip is the best place to begin your personalisation. It is an essential feature of your knife, and must allow for exact and secure control of the blade in many differing uses and environments.

1 If a grip is too large you will not be able to hold onto it for heavy cutting.

2 If a grip is too small you will have to clench it tightly for heavy cutting; this is very tiring and dangerous. Blisters and severe hand cramps can result.

3 If a grip is too long it may pull out from your hand.

4 If a grip is too short you will not be able to hold onto the knife correctly, which may be dangerous.

As a general rule, it is better to have a grip that is slightly too big, as it is less tiring to use than a too-small grip – and when your hand tires you will have accidents. A large grip is easier to hold when wearing gloves. Your grip should be easy to hold in

GRIP CROSS-SECTIONS

Altering the grip may seem a drastic thing to do, but once the knife fits your hand, there will be a vast improvement in its effectiveness as it will take less effort to use.

The best shape for the grip

Too square: this will need reducing.

Too round: this will need to be built up.

Antler handles are not suitable: substitute a better-shaped grip.

a variety of different ways, with no sharp edges or protuberances that will impede its use. It should be the correct shape in cross section, which is a blunt oval shape.

Improving the shape

1 If your grip is too round you may be able to build it up using Gaffa tape or nylon webbing and a strong resin. Very often round grips are all-metal: these are best covered, as metal is a 'non-friendly' material, hot in the desert, dangerously freezing in the Arctic and always hard. Remember that whatever you use as a grip covering must be resilient to a variety of temperatures and environmental conditions.

2 If your grip is too square you may (if the grip material is soft or man-made) be able to file or sand it to the correct shape. This is preferable to covering because the performance of the grip will not be impaired by changing climates.

3 If your grip is of bone it may feel as though it is more comfortable when gripped as for hammering. In this case there is usually little that can be done other than replacing the grip entirely.

The blade

Having set up the grip, give your knife a 'road test': there should be an immediate and definite improvement in its performance. But the blade is where the major transformation will occur. You will have to alter the angle of the edge to improve its cutting ability, which in most cases means a long session of filing. Avoid using a high-speed grinding wheel, unless you are very expert in its use, and back-street knife sharpeners, as the risk of the blade overheating and losing its temper is high.

To help you, some of the better established knife manufacturers will supply a knife with a 'professional edge', but only on request. Once the edge has been altered you should never have to regrind the edge, because you will now 'parallel sharpen'.

Sharpening

To sharpen your knife you will need a stone. The best type of stone is still a natural stone such as a Washita or Soft Arkansas stone, although there is much to be said for the strength of a diamond whetstone for field use.

PARALLEL SHARPENING

Once you have a professional edge, make sure you do not destroy it while honing. A common failing is to tilt the edge too sharply; this gradually blunts the knife. These cross-sections of the blade show the right and wrong methods, and the results of each.

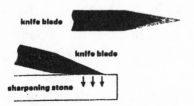
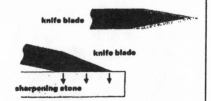

WRONG: Pressure is greatest near the edge.
Sharpening with too much pressure on the edge of the blade progressively changes the cutting angle, blunting the knife. The only remedy is to have the whole edge reground: an expensive business. In the field, the knife will become blunter and more difficult to sharpen.

RIGHT: Pressure is exerted at a shallower angle.
Maintaining the pressure in the correct way retains the cutting edge. Patience is the essential ingredient: remember that a blunt knife is not just an inefficient tool, but is also dangerous.

At home base you should have a large stone. This makes sharpening an easy task, using six long strokes on the left of the blade, six on the right, and six alternately.

In the field you will need a small pocket stone, or failing this a suitable local stone or large pebble. Hold the knife steady and move the stone: the opposite to home sharpening.

Whenever you sharpen your blade, maintain an even pressure across the full width of the edge. If you place to much pressure on the edge itself you will not be sharpening parallel to the edge angle you originally laboured to achieve, but will be gradually blunting the knife.

Honing

Having sharpened your knife, a really razor-like edge can be

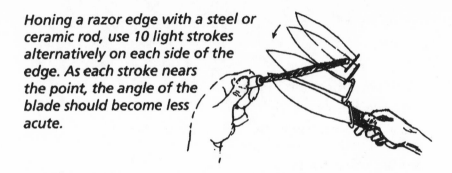

Honing a razor edge with a steel or ceramic rod, use 10 light strokes alternatively on each side of the edge. As each stroke nears the point, the angle of the blade should become less acute.

achieved by lightly honing with a ceramic rod. Use this before all major cutting to help maintain the edge.

Common uses for your knife

Slashing: Grip the knife as far back as possible. Use long, sweeping motions with a straight arm.

Chopping: Grip the knife further forward, with your cutting action more from the elbow than the shoulder.

Stake pointing: Hold the grip even further forward and, using mainly wrist action, cut away from you.

Hammering: Use the flat of the blade, keeping the edge aimed away from your body.

Draw knife: Fit a makeshift split stick-handle to the point end of your knife to create a second handle.

Sawing: Sawing is not designed to cut through wood but is mainly for grooving wood and cutting ropes. Cut on the draw stroke.

Rasping: If your knife has a saw back, you can set it into a log and work bone on it.

Whittling: Control is the name of the game. If you can lever with the thumb of your free hand, on the back of the blade, do so. Otherwise take your time with many small, shallow cuts.

Splitting: This is an important operation. Strike the blade through the work piece with a wooden baton (not stone or metal).

Professional use

In the hands of a professional a survival knife takes on jobs that seem impossible. This is because he has learned to use the correct cutting techniques and angles. Experience and practice will be your best guide here, although the most basic principles are:

1 Safety first.
2 Cut with the grain in your favour.
3 Always follow through.
4 Use smooth, steady cuts, the fewer the better.

Making other tools

A professional's knife is a tool to make other tools. Wherever possible he avoids any use of the knife which may result in its damage or loss. If a root needs to be dug up, make a digging stick; if a spear point is needed, whittle one.

Safety first

1 When you carry your knife, carry a first aid kit.
2 Plan every cut before you make it.
3 Keep all limbs away from the arc of your cut.
4 *Always* cut away from the body.
5 Be aware of what is going on around you.
6 Replace the knife as its scabbard immediately after use.
7 Never lend your knife; you may never see it again.

IMPORTANT: *The privilege of owning a survival knife is one that all survival students must uphold and defend. Be professional in your approach and your use of your knife, and be seen to be professional.*

Bows

IMPORTANT SAFETY NOTE

Bows can kill! Treat them like a firearm. Never point your bow and arrow at something you do not intend to shoot. When practising, check your backdrop: if you can't see that it is safe to shoot, don't. Never shoot at anything on the skyline.

One surprising omission from most survival training and survival literature (including Special Forces) is a weapon that has been used by millions of men and women, and all young boys, from the stone age to the present — the bow and arrow. This may be because the skills of bow-maker, arrowsmith, fletcher and archer are not perfected overnight, and you don't learn them best in a survival situation.

The bow and arrow have been ignored in survival training because some knowledge of tree types is necessary, and professional bow-makers insist that wood *must* be seasoned for three years to make a bow.

Neither of these notions will hold water. A soldier should be knowledgeable about nature, especially if he is trained in survival techniques. But, yes, a longbow *must* be seasoned for three years – if you want one that will last for years and can drive an arrow-head through the breastplate of a knight at 400 metres. But that's rather unlikely on the modern battlefield.

Most survivors or evaders, if offered a weapon that would get their dinner and kill an enemy at a range of up to 150 metres, would say, 'That'll do nicely, thank you.' That weapon can be made in as little as four hours, and not more than a couple of days depending on materials available, and the power required.

Bows and the Law

Game hunting with bows is illegal almost everywhere so don't do it. Target shooting can teach you the basics of archery but it cannot prepare you for survival archery. The nearest you can get is to try the sport of Field Archery in which you shoot different shaped targets at unknown ranges deployed in woods and fields. This enables you to practice instinctive shooting without getting jailed for poaching.

Shooting tips

A strong upper body is both necessary for, and developed by, archery. You need this strength to draw the bow and to hold your aim. In a survival situation your strength may be reduced, perhaps greatly, by hunger, fatigue, illness or injury.

If so, do not try ambitious shots. Use a shorter 'draw length' – the distance the arrow is drawn – and engage your target from as close a range as possible. A quick, instinctive shot is less likely to be wrong because of fatigue. In fact, this is often the best way to shoot in any case. Field archery is mostly snap shots, perhaps at moving targets, and target archery bears as much resemblance to it as shooting on the range does to field-firing or combat shooting. Some archers are always more accurate with an instinctive shot than an aimed shot. Use the style that suits you best.

What to wear

Note the dress of the bowman. Do not wear headgear with a peak – a fatigue cap. for example – even when shooting into the sun, as it will foul your draw.

Gloves are one of the most under-emphasized survival items. After a few days of using fires, building or collecting and using sharp or toxic materials, your hands will get rather painful. For the archer, gloves prevent your holding arm being painfully bruised by the string. Pressure on the fingers on your drawing hand can be very painful without gloves, and is distracting in the aim. But you can make a 'shooting tab' and a bracer from hide.

If the skirt of your jacket is hanging, or if the sleeves are bulky, remove the jacket, or it will foul the string when you release it, causing loss of speed, range and accuracy.

Wood for the bow

The first step on the road to equipping yourself with a bow and some arrows is to find the materials from which you'll make them – which means knowing how to recognize the right wood where it's growing. You may already be familiar with the species of tree and shrub mentioned in this article, of course. If not, the best ways to find out about them are to ask someone who's country-wise to show them to you, or to go to a botanical garden.

If the idea of visiting a botanical garden seems weird, bear in mind that paragraph 87 of the old Air Ministry publication on jungle survival recommends unit visits for aircrew. Servicemen in survival-oriented units should ask their CO to arrange a day visit, which most parks and gardens anywhere in the world will be happy to set up.

A day's visit will give you all the knowledge you need about trees to find the material for a bow. On top of that, you'll learn to recognize a huge variety of edible, medicinal and otherwise useful plants. If you think it's a waste of a day's training, just think about it – it beats the hell out of square-bashing, or humping a loaded Bergen over 50 kilometres.

PARTS OF THE BOW

Bows are described by their shape when they are unstrung, not braced. Note the reflexed bow and the re-curved bow are curved away from the belly. Three quarters of the handle is below the centre of the bow and the bow string corresponds to this, so that if the bow string is braced the wrong way round the nocking point for the nock of the arrow will not correspond to the centreline of the bow. Cheap practice bows are available in nylon and fibreglass.

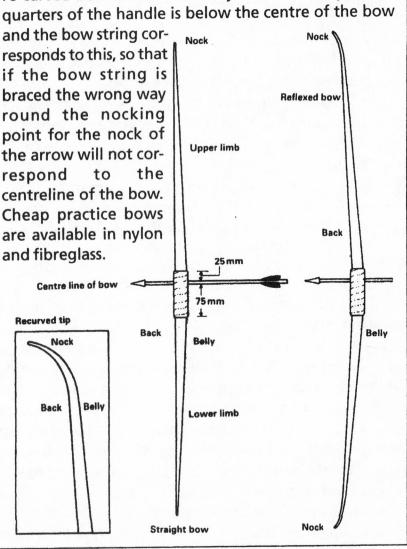

Let's assume you've now armed yourself with a fair knowledge of the local flora. So what do you look for?

Hard, well-seasoned, springy woods are best for making a bow. Don't even think about making one from softwoods such as pine, fir, new elder shoots, larch, spruce, and so on. You'll only be wasting valuable time and energy.

Look for hardwoods like wych elm, elm, oak, ash, rowan, birch, greenheart, wild rose, hornbeam, dagame, lemonwood, osage orange, juniper and ironwood. Some of these will make a good bow, and some will make a passable one. None will make a bow equal to the king of bow woods, the yew.

Poisonous yew

Yew grows in most of Asia, the Americas and throughout Europe. It's very common in southern England, and you'll see it in churchyards, estates, parks and gardens.

Be careful with the yew. The leaves, berry arils (an extra covering over the fruit) and sap contain a deadly nerve poison, taxine. Celtic warriors dipped their arrows in the yew sap, just to make sure!

So don't use the leftovers from your bowmaking as skewers or spoons or whatever. You won't come to any harm from handling yew, though, as long as you wash the sap off your hands.

A quick one

You can make an excellent bow very quickly – seasoning the wood in a day, over a fire – from rowan. (This is sometimes called mountain ash in England).

Ideally, you should take the wood from a slim sapling growing in dense wood. This is because trees growing close together have to "shoot for the sun", and so grow slim and straight with few branches low on the trunk: just what you need for a bow. You don't harm the environment by taking a few of these saplings, since you help the other trees to spread. And if you cover or dirty the stump, you won't leave any sign of your presence to be spotted from the air.

Rowan bows are 'sweet' to use, giving no jar or kick. But they do creak ominously when you're shooting them in. It takes fine judgment and a steely nerve to find out how far you can draw them – but then a good bow properly drawn is seven-eighths broken!

The correct size of a bow

A bow 1.47 m (4ft 10 in) long, is quite handy for someone of the author's height (1.75 m/5 ft 9 in). A long bow for someone this height would be 1.85 m (6 ft) long. When deciding what length to make your bow, consider the following:

1   The longer the bow is, the better it will resist a given pull.

2   If you change your mind and shorten an existing bow it will shoot further for the same draw but will be harder to pull and is more likely to break.

3   Experiment to find your ideal draw length and try to make your bow to suit, but any bow drawing between 60 and 90 cms (2 to 3 ft) will be sufficient for most 'survival archery'. A bow should not bend in the middle – the central foot or so should be rigid. To determine the position of the handgrip, find the centre of the bow, then mark 75 mm (3 in) below and 25 mm (1 in) above. This section will be the handle. The arrow is shot from the bow centre while you grip beneath it. The upper part of the bow should be cut slightly more than the lower in order to compensate for the handle. Trim your bow to its finished size, then cut the nocks at either end.

Tools

Once you've selected your bow stave, you'll need some tools to carve the actual bow from it. Professional bowmakers first use a hammer and steel wedges to split logs into workable dimensions. Then a small hand-axe trims the stave to the rough shape and size of the bow. A spokeshave brings it down to the exact size, with final minute shavings removed with shards of glass.

In the middle of nowhere and on the run you're not too likely to have any of these. But an issue-type machete or a heavy survival knife will do the job, given some skill and elbow grease.

It's always worth having at least Stanley knife blades in your survival kit. You can use them on their own as scalpels for fine work, and you can use one to cut its own wooden handle. You can use the Stanley to make your bow from scratch, but it's invaluable for making arrows.

If you haven't got any of these, tough titty. It's back to basic stone-age survival technology.

Season the wood

Now to making the bow. Look for a branch or trunk of the right wood that's as straight as possible. It should be at least 6ft 6in (2m) long, although you can go as short as 4ft (1.25m). If you can get a piece of seasoned – that is, properly dried-out – wood, terrific. Look for uprooted trees, cuttings and trimmings, at rail- and roadsides, and near farms and houses.

In conventional bowmaking the entire log is seasoned, sometimes for years, and then thinned down to a bow. Survivors have to reverse the process, and cut out the rough bow and then dry it. This is a lot faster, though it may cause some warping. Trim the stave to the approximate size of the bow, leaving a good quarter inch surplus in both thickness and breadth.

Drying out

At this point, decide how quickly you need your bow. Some woods you can use straight off, but *all* of them improve enormously with drying out. In a very hot climate a day or two makes a huge difference, and the bow keeps improving as you use it. In cold or temperate climates you will have to dry it over or near the fire. Yew and rowan make the best quick-dried bows.

While you have the bow near the fire, you may as well make sure that the stave is straight when viewed from the back or belly.

If you heat – or, preferably, steam – the staff where it's bent, you can put it permanently into shape by applying pressure in the right direction. This doesn't set up any stresses in the wood.

You can also re-curve or reflex the bow by the same method. But if the stave you've chosen is naturally reflexed, or re-curved at one end or the other, don't straighten it. If it ain't broke, don't fix it!

Making the string

The English longbowmen of the Middle Ages used bow strings able to take a weight of 140 lbs (60 kg), and these were made from the stalks of the common stinging nettle. Unfortunately this takes a long time to master, so the average survivor must improvise. Silk is ideal for a bow string because it stretches very little, but it is not available in every survival situation. Nylon paracord is a more feasible material. Although it does stretch a little, this can be taken up when bracing the bow and paracord has the bonus of being near rot-proof and very strong.

Bracing a bow

Putting the string on a bow is called bracing, and it is very important to get this right. Place your hand 'thumbs up' on the back of the bow: the string should touch your thumb when correctly braced. You need not be too slavish to this rule with a survival bow, but the nearer the better. Use a timber hitch to tie the bottom end of the string permanently in place and use a simple loop to attach it at the top. When you need the bow, brace it and slip on the top loop. Always unstring the bow when not in use or it will lose strength and never leave it standing on end.

Arrows

The arrow is at once both beautifully simple and extremely sophisticated. It is a *missile*, developed by human ingenuity over thousands of years. Many of the lessons learnt in the manufacture of *millions* of these missiles, with hundreds of variations, were forgotten after the Middle Ages, only to be painstakingly relearnt by twentieth-century missile scientists.

For survival purposes, you will not have to make an arrow anywhere near as good as those used at Agincourt, which had heavy armour-piercing warheads and had to withstand 120 lb of thrust from the string.

The first thing to learn about arrows is that the missile (the arrow) must match its launcher (the bow). At this stage, an explanation of what's known as the Archer's Paradox is helpful. Due to the impact of the string, the inertia in the arrow, and the fact that the arrow is set at an angle to the string (which is in line with the centreline of the bow), and the edge of the bow, the arrow actually bends over the bow when you release it. You will not see this with the naked eye, but it does happen. When it leaves the bow, the arrow springs the other way and, after a few more bucks, straightens out and flies off to your target.

If the arrow is too weak for the bow, it will wobble in flight and lose power. It may also break, usually about six inches from the nock, usually with jagged edges, and usually getting stopped by the inside of your wrist, which is damned painful. If the arrow is too strong, it will go off a little to your left (if you are right handed).

For survival purposes, you don't have to match bow and arrow exactly. Instead, learn how each of your arrows flies. It is better in every way to err on the side of the strong arrow.

Woods to use

So now we have the theory, let's make some arrows before we starve to death! Good woods are birch, ash, hornbeam, alder, willow, bamboo, ramin, pine, fir, oak, elm, beech, elder, dog rose, bramble and some reeds. As a survivor you will do best by not confining yourself to the rules, but to use your common sense.

The simplest, quickest and most versatile wood is bamboo, which is *not* confined to the jungle but is common worldwide. Bamboo breaks always have many dead canes amongst the green: these can be used instantly – dry the green ones near the fire, or leave them for a few says after cutting. Don't forget that you can eat the young shoots, raw or cooked, after you remove the poisonous hairs along the edges of the leaves! Next (for ease, not quality) come strong reeds, followed by willow. Surprisingly, thick bramble and wild rose can provide good arrows. The thorns are easily removed with your front teeth, leaving a nice round shaft.

The shaft

The arrow should be as straight as you can make it, as bends and kinks cause inaccuracy and wind resistance. Use steam, or bend it over a warm stone, to straighten it, as you did making your bow. Some woods you can straighten cold, either by bending and holding for a minute, or by tying the bow with thread or string and leaving it for an hour or so.

It is easier than you think to cut an arrow from a billet of wood, especially the softwoods such as pine, using your knife or, better still, your Stanley blade from your survival tin, suitably mounted.

If you have the time, it is back to stone-age technology for a sanding block, to give perfect roundness. Make this from two pieces of sandstone, about $2^1/2$ by $^1/2$ by 1 inch. Chip out a semi-circular groove along the length of each one. When you put one on top of the other, they should make a circular groove that's the same diameter as you want your arrows to be. Draw the arrow through these blocks until it's smooth. A far better device, if you can make one, is a small steel plate $^1/8$ inch thick with a 'V' cut in it. This cuts better, *and* allows you to vary the diameter of the arrow.

The flights

By far the easiest way to fit the flights is to use plastic – not quite as good as feathers, but requiring much less skill, time and effort. Sadly, there is no shortage of plastic litter anywhere. Near houses, where farmers, climbers and forestry workers are, along any roadside, beach – in fact, just about anywhere – you will find a profusion of plastic drink bottles, oil cartons, milk cartons, etc.

Cut them into strips with your Stanley blade or knife. If nec-

POSITIONING THE FLIGHTS

The flights should be positioned at 120 degree intervals. Plastic flights will need a little moulding to give them a slight curve, and if you are using bird feathers do not mix the feathers from either wing: this will make the arrow wobble and reduce its velocity.

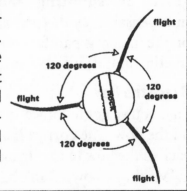

essary, put them momentarily in boiling water or near heat for a few seconds to soften them, then smooth them flat. Fix them by cutting one slot through the arrow for a pair of flights and a groove at right angles for the third flight.

If you use feathers, those of geese or large gliding birds are best – for example the eagle, buzzard, hawk, flamingo, pelican, crow, seagull or turkey. A good place to find them are farmers' or game keepers' gibbets: rows of dead crows hanging upside down on fences to scare other crows away. Use the large flight feathers from the wing. Do not mix feathers from right and left wings, if you can help it – it causes wobbling and loss of power, as they set up opposing wind currents.

Arrowheads and nocks

You can make your arrowheads out of steel, slate, stone, bone, flint, horn, glass, or just sharpened wood. You can even use staples from a fence post.

For the nock, it's simplest just to groove the wood. Put a whipping above the nock to prevent it splitting, if necessary.

Shooting the Bow

Although you can shoot without them, it is far better to have a pair of gloves, or a shooting tab and a bracer, to stop the inside of your bow arm being bruised by the string. You can easily make a bracer out of rabbit skin or hide, and a shooting tab too. If you have a jacket with close-fitting sleeves, you can do without the bracer. But a glove or shooting tab is virtually indispensable, as the pressure of the string on the fingers is painful and can be very distracting in the aim.

target

Correct standing position

Brace the bow

First you've got to 'brace' or put the string on the bow. The correct height from the back of the bow to the string was covered in 'Making a bow'. Don't be a slave to this

shooting line

dimension for a survival bow, especially when you first use it. Use a timber hitch for the bottom end, permanently in place, and a simple fixed loop for the top. When you need to use the bow, just brace it by slipping on the top loop.

Shooting

Archery can be broken down into five component skills: standing, nocking, drawing, aiming and loosing. The principles outlined below hold good in target and field shooting, although it is not always possible to stand correctly in field shooting. Here are the ideals in the five disciplines.

Standing

Put your feet in the 'stand at ease' position, at right angles to the target. Leave only about 8 inches between your heels. Keep your knees straight, body upright and turned towards the target, so that if a line were drawn through your shoulders it would run to the target.

Nocking

Hold the bow with your left hand (right hand for left-handed people). Without touching the flights, engage the nock in the whipping on the string (if fitted). The nock should be in the exact centre of the string, with the arrow resting on the midpoint of the bow, on the left-hand edge of the bow (right-hand side for left-handed people). You can make a mark in the middle of the bow to ensure quick, accurate nocking.

Drawing

Place the fingers with index finger above and next two fingers below the arrow. You will probably prefer the three-finger draw, but the two-finger draw did not harm mediaeval Englishmen! If the terrain permits, your weight should be evenly distributed on both feet. Bring your bow across your body at waist level, and slightly incline the head. This helps the chest muscles to assist the draw.

Both arms should be bent at this point, and your body relaxed. Begin to straighten your arms and bring the bow up as you continue the draw smoothly and continuously to the full draw position.

AIMING YOUR BOW

Modern target bows have adjustable peep sights which can be zeroed in once your draw length is consistent and you are using the same type of arrows. The bows you make yourself can also be marked up with aiming marks with different ranges. It is best to start at 20 yd/18m and find the correct point of aim to hit the centre of the target, and then paint on an aiming mark which you can use as a point of reference when you move back to 50 yd/45m and 100 yd/90m.

aiming point

At 20 yards your sight picture should look like this, and your mean point of impact of five arrows should be the centre of the target. At closer ranges with very rigid arrows you may have problems with the Archer's Paradox and arrows going out to the right. You must compensate by aiming off.

For target archery, *exactly* the same draw length is taken for every shot. This is not always possible (due to illness or fatigue), or desirable, in survival archery. And you are not very likely to have produced such perfectly matched arrows; it is far better to know how each arrow flies.

Aiming

Make a straight mark, or marks for different ranges, on the outside of the bow. If your arrow lengths and draw lengths are uniform, line up the arrowhead on the point of aim. Remember that the target and the point of aim may not be the same, due to windage or range.

The trick is to get the line of sight between your eye, sight marks or arrowhead, and the aiming point to coincide with the trajectory of the arrow. In field archery it is usually far better to make a quick draw, aim and shoot.

Remember the Archer's Paradox? This can effect your aim at

very close range (up to 10 yards/9m), and if the arrow is too rigid it will tend to go to the right, at any range. Compensate for these problems by aiming off.

Loosing

Letting go of the string, or loosing, is one of the most important aspects of archery.

It is a lot easier to achieve a correct loose than it is to describe it accurately, a fact agreed upon by all writers on the subject! The loose should be both sharp and smooth, with the bow arm kept rigidly in place.

This is important, as the sudden release of the load on the muscles of the bow arm tends to make you push the bow to your inside before the arrow has cleared the bow, or to pull hard the other way in anticipation. Something similar happens when a rifleman or machine-gunner tenses in expectation of the recoil after squeezing the trigger, and pulls or pushes his weapon off the aim.

Stay in the aim

It is best to 'follow through', that is, stay in the aim, eyes on the aiming mark, until the fall of shot, just as you do with a firearm – unless, of course, your target can do you some damage, or is likely to escape!

In all the above aspects of archery, strange as it may seem, your posture and movements should be smooth, graceful and pleasing to the eye of the beholder. This has been accepted by *all* writers and instructors of archery through the centuries. It is not just for aesthetic appeal; for various reasons, if it is not done gracefully and smoothly, missed targets and pulled muscles are the result!

The quarry

This may be fish, fowl, four-legged and furry – or your enemy. It is important to have the right bow and the right arrow for your particular prey. A heavy bow, shooting steel broadheads, will kill anything including an elephant – if it hits it. English fifteenth-century war bows and arrows would kill a man at 300 metres – even through chain mail and steel plate. But this is ridiculous overkill for fish and birds: a heavy bow is difficult to aim, tiring and unnecessary. Ordinary arrows are alright.

On larger game, you achieve the kill by penetrating a vital organ, or by causing a haemorrhage. Tests indicate that flint has better flesh-penetrating properties than steel. American archer Bob Swinhart boasted of shooting buffalo and rhino with a 90 lb bow and steel broadheads, leopards with a 70 lb bow, and a five ton bull elephant from 15 yards using a 100 lb bow and *five* arrows. But he did have a back-up rifleman beside him, and it would have been some sort of world record to have missed an elephant at 15 yards!

Barbed arrows are only for holding fish; on birds and game they are cruel and unnecessary. For an evader they can be positively fatal – to you. If you shoot game with an *un*barbed arrow, it either kills it, or falls out in a very short time. If you do not retrieve it, there is not much chance of it being found by anyone. But a barbed arrow will stay in, and, if you don't find your prey, it will probably fester. A dead animal surrounded by scavengers will surely be spotted, and *you* have left your calling card struck in it!

Spears

On your foraging excursions, you have spotted signs of large mammals. If you can catch one you will provide yourself with a large amount of meat that can be preserved and stored, as well as useful skin and bone. But how do you catch the animal? Of the many hunting techniques at your disposal, the age-old method of spear hunting is a practical answer. Spears are easy to make, easy to learn how to use, and allow you to hunt while on the move.

In fact, spears are so effective that early man, hunting in bands, was able to catch animals as big as mammoths. In areas where there are large carnivores that pose a serious threat to your survival (obviously best avoided), a spear is about the most effective deterrent you can carry with you, as these predators will almost certainly have encountered horns and antlers and have therefore learned to respect long, sharp points. There are even native American tales of grizzly bears backing away from spears, but don't count on it!

Simple spears

The quickest and simplest spear you can make is the 'self spear'. In its crudest form, this is simply a straight piece of hard, natured wood with a sharpened point. You can vastly improve it by fire hardening the point and fashioning it into a leaf-shaped blade. But the self spear is a primitive and brutal weapon and a skilled survivor should make every effort to kill as cleanly as possible, reducing the suffering of his prey to the minimum.

An effective spear must have a sharp cutting edge that is wide enough to cause maximum bleeding, but not so wide that it prevents the spear penetrating to the vital organs. So the most important part of a spear is the point. As a survivor, you can never be certain of precisely what raw materials you will have to hand, so the broader your knowledge of spear design the better.

Basically, spears fall into one or both of two categories: thrusting spears and throwing spears. As the name suggests, thrusting spears are used at very close range so the spear point can be broad, as the impact force is guaranteed to be great. Throwing spears, on the other hand, are used at a distance: they need to be light so that they can fly fast, and the point needs to allow penetration as the impact force of a throwing spear can vary greatly. Throwing spear points are also often barbed.

The design you choose should be tailored to meet your circumstances, and with a specific prey in mind. Obviously you will be limited in raw materials. If you have difficulty finding a suitable spear shaft, consider using a lighter material – reed bamboo or elder – with a short, hardwood foreshaft.

The length of the spear is also important. Where dangerous animals are concerned, you will obviously need a long spear, but if you are in an area of scrub bush you may find a long spear too unwieldy. Try to achieve the right balance of factors. Lastly, make sure you are happy with its feel and heft.

Hunting with spears

To hunt with spears you need to be as close to your prey as possible. You can do this only by careful stalking and attention to camouflage and descenting.

1 Hunting with thrusting spears

These are used from 'Lying up positions' beside frequently-used animal runs. As the animal passes by, you thrust the spear into it. The best hiding place is in a tree above the run, as large game rarely looks up. An added bonus in such a hiding place is that you can drop on your prey, imparting the full force of your body weight to your spear. The disadvantage of this hunting method is that it is static; you may spend many fruitless hours waiting to pounce with no luck.

2 Hunting with throwing spears

Success comes more from stalking than from throwing, and a good stalker should be able to get within touching distance of most prey. If necessary, though, a throwing spear can be used over some distance.

Throwing a spear is not like throwing a javelin. Having stalked to within a few metres of your prey, you cannot risk a 'run up' or a large movement of your throwing arm, 'pulling back' before the throw. You should launch the spear before your prey detects any movement at all. Try at all times to remain hidden; if your first shot misses, you may be allowed a second chance.

Having stalked close to your quarry, very slowly draw your throwing arm back like a coiled spring. Do not draw it back beyond your shoulder; to do so means that you will have to turn your body. Instead use the resistance of your shoulder as the buffer from which all your throwing force is generated. If you feel it will help, raise your free hand as an aiming aid.

When you are ready, cast the spear like a dart in one explosive movement. Follow the movement through and be still. Do not chase after the wounded animal but remain hidden, until the prey is lying down, then swiftly put the injured animal to sleep. This is the theory, but even for experts things do not always go so smoothly; whatever happens, remain calm.

INDEX